The thirteen chapters in this volume are written by philosophers at the forefront of feminist scholarship, and are designed to provide an accessible and stimulating guide through a philosophical literature that has seen massive expansion in recent years. Ranging from history of philosophy through metaphysics to philosophy of science, they encompass all the core subject areas commonly taught in anglophone undergraduate and graduate philosophy courses, offering both an overview of and a contribution to the relevant debates. Together they testify to the intellectual value of feminism as a radicalizing energy internal to philosophical inquiry. This volume will be essential reading for any student or teacher of philosophy who is curious about the place of feminism in their subject.

THE CAMBRIDGE
COMPANION TO
FEMINISM IN PHILOSOPHY

OTHER VOLUMES IN THE SERIES OF
CAMBRIDGE COMPANIONS

THE CAMBRIDGE
COMPANION TO
FEMINISM
IN
PHILOSOPHY

EDITED BY
MIRANDA FRICKER
Heythrop College, University of London

AND
JENNIFER HORNSBY
Birkbeck College, University of London

CAMBRIDGE
UNIVERSITY PRESS

CAMBRIDGE UNIVERSITY PRESS
Cambridge, New York, Melbourne, Madrid, Cape Town, Singapore, São Paulo

Cambridge University Press
The Edinburgh Building, Cambridge CB2 8RU, UK

Published in the United States of America by Cambridge University Press, New York

www.cambridge.org
Information on this title: www.cambridge.org/9780521624510

First published 2000
Reprinted 2004

A catalogue record for this publication is available from the British Library

Library of Congress Cataloguing in Publication data

The Cambridge companion to feminism in philosophy / edited by
Miranda Fricker and Jennifer Hornsby.
p. cm.
ISBN 0 521 62451 7 (hardback). – ISBN 0 521 62469 X (paperback)
1. Feminism – Philosophy. I. Fricker, Miranda. II. Hornsby, Jennifer.
HQ1154.C25 2000
305.42'01–dc21 99–21117 CIP

ISBN 978-0-521-62451-0 hardback
ISBN 978-0-521-62469-5 paperback

Transferred to digital printing 2008

CONTENTS

Contents

CONTRIBUTORS

DIEMUT BUBECK is Lecturer in Political Theory at the London School of
Economics. She has worked on feminist political theory and ethics,
particularly on the ethic of care debate, and is the author of *Care,
Gender, and Justice* (1995). She also has research interests in Nietzsche
and in virtue ethics, and is currently working on a project entitled
'Women: Victims or Agents?'

MIRANDA FRICKER is Lecturer in Philosophy and British Academy
Postdoctoral Fellow at Heythrop College, University of London. She
contributed to *Knowing the Difference*, ed. Lennon and Whitford
(1994), and has published articles in epistemology and social philosophy.
Her current work focuses on the idea of an ethics of epistemic practice,
and her book *Epistemic Injustice* is forthcoming with Oxford University
Press.

MARILYN FRIEDMAN teaches philosophy at Washington University in St
Louis. She has published articles in ethics, social philosophy and feminist
theory. She is the author of *What Are Friends For? Feminist Perspectives
on Personal Relationships and Moral Theory* (1993) and co-author with
Jan Narveson of *Political Correctness: For and Against* (1995). She co-
edited *Feminism and Community* (with Penny Weiss, 1995) and *Mind
and Morals: Essays on Ethics and Cognitive Science* (with Larry May
and Andy Clark, 1995).

SALLY HASLANGER is Associate Professor of Philosophy at Massachusetts
Institute of Technology. She has published on topics in metaphysics,
epistemology, ancient philosophy (on Aristotle's metaphysics) and
feminist theory, with a recent emphasis on feminist epistemology,
critiques of objectivity and theories of social construction (especially
the social construction of race and gender). She was guest editor for a

Philosophical Topics issue on 'Feminist Perspectives on Language, Knowledge, and Reality' (Fall 1995).

JENNIFER HORNSBY is Professor of Philosophy at Birkbeck College, University of London. She is author of *Actions* (1980) and of *Simple-Mindedness: A Defence of Naïve Naturalism in Philosophy of Mind* (1996) and editor, with Elizabeth Frazer and Sabina Lovibond, of *Ethics: A Feminist Reader* (1992). Her published articles and current work are in philosophy of mind, philosophy of language, metaphysics and in those areas of political and social philosophy that have been informed by feminist thinking.

ALISON JAGGAR is Professor of Philosophy and Women's Studies at the University of Colorado at Boulder. Her books include *Feminist Politics and Human Nature* (1983), *Morality and Social Justice*, co-authored with James P. Sterba et al. (1994) and *Living with Contradictions: Controversies in Feminist Social Ethics* (1994). She is currently working on a project entitled 'Sex, Truth and Power: A Feminist Theory of Moral Reason'.

SUSAN JAMES is Reader in Philosophy at Birkbeck College, University of London. She is the author of *The Content of Social Explanation* (1984) and *Passion and Action: The Emotions in Early Modern Philosophy* (1998) and editor, with Gisela Bock, of *Beyond Equality and Difference* (1992). She is also a General Editor of Oxford Readings in Feminism.

RAE LANGTON is Professor of Moral Philosophy at the University of Edinburgh. She has published articles in the history of philosophy, and in moral and political philosophy, where she has drawn attention to feminist arguments about pornography and objectification. She has also published in metaphysics and epistemology, and is author of *Kantian Humility: Our Ignorance of Things in Themselves* (1998).

GENEVIEVE LLOYD is Professor of Philosophy at the University of New South Wales, Sydney, Australia, and a fellow of the Australian Academy of the Humanities. She is the author of *The Man of Reason: 'Male' and 'Female' in Western Philosophy* (1984, 1993), *Being in Time: Selves and Narrators in Philosophy and Literature* (1993), *Part of Nature: Self-Knowledge in Spinoza's Ethics* (1994) and *Spinoza and the Ethics* (1996). She has published articles on seventeenth- and eighteenth-century philosophy, on philosophy and literature, and on feminist philosophy.

SABINA LOVIBOND is Fellow and Tutor in Philosophy at Worcester College, Oxford. Her published work includes *Realism and Imagination in Ethics* (1983), *Ethics: A Feminist Reader* (1992), edited with Elizabeth Frazer and Jennifer Hornsby, and *Essays for David Wiggins: Identity, Truth and Value* (1996), edited with S. G. Williams. Her main philosophical interests are in ethics, feminist theory, practical rationality and the idea of a postmodern 'critique of reason'.

SARAH RICHMOND is Lecturer in Philosophy at University College London. Her published work has been in the area of continental philosophy, focusing in particular on the relationship between recent continental and analytical philosophy. Her current research is in the areas of ethics and psychoanalysis, with a special concern to explore the insights into moral psychology that psychoanalytical thought can provide.

NAOMI SCHEMAN is Professor of Philosophy and Women's Studies at the University of Minnesota. She is the editor of *Feminist Interpretations of Wittgenstein* in the Re-reading the Canon series (2000) and the author of *Engenderings: Constructions of Knowledge, Authority, and Privilege* (1993). The essays in that book and her subsequent published work and current research focus on understanding the distinctive problems and methods of philosophy in relation to historically specific constructions of identity, with particular attention to especially unstable or 'impossible' identities, such as transsexual or secular Jew.

ALISON WYLIE is Professor of Philosophy at Washington University in St Louis. She writes on philosophical issues raised by archaeology and on the implications of feminist critiques of science. She is co-editor of *Critical Traditions in Contemporary Archaeology* (1989) and has contributed articles on feminist research in archaeology to special issues of *Osiris* (1997) and *Philosophical Topics* (1995), and to collections such as *Women in Human Evolution*, ed. Hager (1997), *The Disunity of Science*, ed. Galison and Stump (1996), and *Changing Methods*, ed. Burt and Code (1995).

PREFACE

Our authors were presented with an especially demanding task, being asked to introduce the reader to feminist debate in a whole area of philosophy as well as to make a contribution of their own. We thank them all, for their essays, for their flexibility, and for their enthusiasm and encouragement along the way. We are grateful to our editor at Cambridge University Press, Hilary Gaskin, for her help with the project, and to our colleague Chris Janaway for suggesting the Gabriele Münter painting for our cover picture.

There are more influences on this book than are apparent from all its footnotes and the many works cited in the lists of Further Reading. When women first began to make distinctively feminist contributions to philosophy, their work was not supported by the usual institutional structures and it was often not recorded on the printed page. Feminist philosophy forced its way into the academy through the political and practical commitment of women whose intellectual courage and professional daring made books like this one possible. The international profile of the contributions here may hide a particular, more local influence on the two of us. We should like to record a debt to the UK Society for Women in Philosophy, and to its dedicated core members, past and present.

M.F. J.H.

MIRANDA FRICKER AND JENNIFER HORNSBY

Introduction

This *Companion* represents a departure from the previously published volumes in its series. Each of those dealt with a single philosopher and with a male one in every case, whereas this one brings women in and treats a theme rather than an authority. So far as the departure allows, this book's principal aim is in line with that of other *Companions*: it consists of new papers by an international team of philosophers at the forefront of feminist scholarship; and these have been written with non-specialists in mind, so that the collection can serve as an introduction to the area. We have tried to design it to be helpful to any student or teacher of philosophy who is curious about feminism's place in their subject.

The present *Companion* has a further aim. It is intended to foster appreciation of the potentially far-reaching impact of feminist thinking in philosophy. As departments of women's studies and gender studies have grown up in the last twenty years, there has come to be more and more published work falling under the head of feminist philosophy. In our experience as members of philosophy departments, students and teachers of philosophy find it difficult to relate much of this work to their own projects. It needs to be made clearer that – and how – feminist concerns can be brought to bear on philosophy. Then 'pure' philosophers may feel less disconnected from work that they are now perhaps inclined to ignore, and genuine interdisciplinary links may be made between philosophy and other subjects on which feminism has had an impact.

In this Introduction, we address at a general level the question of how feminism can impinge upon philosophy, and we say some more about the book's organization and rationale. We hope to illuminate our view of the role of feminism *in* philosophy, by explaining why we wish neither to advocate an understanding of feminist philosophy as a separate and distinctive branch of philosophy, nor to argue for the ability of feminist philosophy to replace philosophy. We also attempt to situate the work it presents in the context both of the political movement that has inspired it and of the discourse of philosophy that it seeks to engender.

One might ask whether it has made a difference to philosophy that it should have been the creation largely of men and not women. Feminists are bound to ask this question. So long as philosophy is an object of their critical reflection, they will insist on viewing its authors as socially situated beings with a specific location in history. But the question makes perfectly good sense even for someone who usually abstains from the historicizing perspective of a feminist.

The publication twenty years ago of Genevieve Lloyd's *The Man of Reason*[1] incubated an influential line of argument. Lloyd's central claim was that philosophers' conceptions of reason have tended to be aligned with cultural conceptions of masculinity, reason being conceived as contrasted with and superior to intuition and emotion which the cultural imagination has associated with femininity. When one sees the bearing of gender on the understanding of such faculties as reason – which is taken often enough to be the faculty distinctive of human kind – one comes to be concerned also with gender's bearing on the philosophical conception of individual human subjects, whether in the role of thinker, of agent, of speaker, or of inquirer. It may be agreed that the great subjects of philosophy ought to be concerned with us in the sense of 'us' in which we are all human. But when the association of 'man' and 'reason' is acknowledged, it is possible to think that the male philosophers who have addressed these questions have actually not always subsumed everyone with their 'we's and their 'our's. Although philosophers' accounts of what 'we' know, or of how 'we' relate to 'our' bodies, purport to have universal application, one can question whether their authors' generic conception really is the socially and historically neutral one that their universal claims would require. In doing so, one takes issue with traditional philosophy on its own, 'neutralist' terms. One arrives, from a starting point within philosophy, at a place at which questions about male bias arise.

Feminism's own starting point tends not to be this neutralist one. By starting from the idea that human subjects are socially concrete and socially diverse beings, feminists encourage suspicion of any given universal claim. Of course feminists are not alone in their commitment to the social specificity of the subject. Other politicizing theoretical perspectives can equally place emphasis on the socially concrete character of any human being. If a feminist perspective is unique, then it is probably unique only in its insistence on the importance of gender. But we can see how a feminist perspective tends to take one more quickly to a point at which philosophy itself may arrive unaided so long as it allows that its texts are written by real people. Given philosophy's reflexive character – given that philosophy is concerned with 'ourselves and our place in the world', so that its authors belong among its objects of study – a questioning of philosophers' self-image cannot be simply external to philosophy.

When the gender-ideological aspects of a piece of philosophical theory are unveiled, the theory is exposed as masculist. The theory might be less sophisticated or less complete than it had purported to be, or it might simply be in error – as when an account records only male experience while putting forward claims about the whole of humanity. But an account may also be charged with masculism in a different sense, when its generalizations are taken to exclude the *symbolically* feminine. This sort of charge might be made as a psychoanalytic claim – in which, for instance, some tendency in philosophical thought is diagnosed in terms of male philosophers' unconsciously living out an exclusively masculine psychology (see Susan James's chapter here). Or, again, such a charge might be made as a historical claim – in which a tendency is diagnosed by reference to the operation of a 'philosophical imaginary'[2] that arises from distinctively masculine social experience. There are feminist writers who think that all of philosophy excludes or subordinates the symbolically feminine, so that they take the whole philosophical enterprise to be irredeemably masculist. Theirs is a radical view, in which the task of feminism is to find a surrogate for philosophy – philosophy in the feminine.[3]

Evidently, the radical view is not our own view. (There is no space for the project of this book on the radical view.) But we share with the radical view a belief that a feminist perspective can bring enlightenment by introducing insights gained from lived experience. Philosophical reflection has always been conditioned by background intuitions and assumptions about how people generally behave or what they would think, say, want, intend, in particular circumstances. To the extent that it may have been conditioned by a consensus among its (*de facto*) white, male, middle-class practitioners, there are likely to be new debates as other sorts of people find their way in.[4] Feminism will impinge upon philosophy wherever feminist insights challenge prevailing intuitions and assumptions. We agree with Sabina Lovibond, in the first chapter here, that 'the relation of feminist thought to its discursive environment' can be grasped in terms of Neurath's boat, 'which cannot find a haven safe from error but has to be repaired while out at sea'. Feminism is then one among the critical impetuses for the ongoing repair work that determines philosophy's historical development and its sense of its own history.

As our title signals, the idea of feminism *in* philosophy guided us in commissioning chapters. We think that the work presented here is testimony to the intellectual value of taking feminism to be a radicalizing energy internal to philosophical inquiry. We resisted using the more generic 'feminist philosophy' in the title, partly because our own enterprise is more circumscribed than that would suggest, and partly because that label can be misunderstood. People sometimes suppose that 'feminist philosophy' must either name a subject area – as, say, 'political philosophy' does – or else stand for something that is meant to supplant philosophy. But at least as we understand 'feminist philosophy', it stands for philosophy informed by feminism; and feminism has different sorts of relevance as it impinges on different philosophical subject areas.

Feminism *in* philosophy is the product of a single understanding of how feminism may relate to philosophy. But it is not the product of any monolithic conception of feminism. A feminist may be hostile or sympathetic to essentialist styles of thought, for instance; she may take feminist politics to have social androgyny as its goal or think that it should aim at creating cultural and intellectual spaces for sexual difference. On matters such as these, no party line is toed here. Indeed we hope this collection exhibits pluralism within feminism. What unifies the present work is our conception of philosophy and of feminism's relationship to it.

There are other conceptions of feminism's relationship to philosophy than our own. That ours is not the only fruitful one is evident from the enormous and disparate body of work published under the heading 'feminist philosophy' which is informed by different conceptions. There is, for instance, the 'radical' view already mentioned, which sees feminism's philosophical task as finding a truly feminine counterpart to an irredeemably masculist tradition. There is also the postmodernist view which sees feminism's task as bringing philosophy *per se* to an end, so as to make way for some preferred, perhaps more literary, discourse. Although work deriving from these views is not represented here, several of the chapters are in dialogue with it. Perhaps this dialogue is possible because of a common purpose – the exploration of the philosophical implications of gender and sexual difference. But however that may be, the important thing, which we hope to have achieved, is to encourage continuing debate across different conceptions of feminism's relation to philosophy while producing a volume whose content and organization promotes a particular one.

Our idea of feminism *in* philosophy is also born of the ambition that feminist contributions should take their place in the philosophical mainstream. This will require feminist work to be included in philosophy courses – whether these are courses in particular branches of philosophy, or courses specifically devoted to feminist themes. The pedagogical rationale has determined this *Companion*'s overall organization. The divisions between chapters correspond to divisions between traditional philosophical areas – history of philosophy, metaphysics, ethics, etc. Wanting to aid and abet the entry of feminist work into philosophy teaching, we asked each of our authors to set the stage in her area – to provide material suited to show how the claims of her chapter fit into a broader context of feminist debate. Most of the chapters have an early section or sections which play the stage-setting role. (In a few cases, where a chapter as a whole has the character of a survey, such a section would have been redundant.)

A casual run through the book will reveal a lack of uniformity between subject areas in the quantity of existing material referred to while setting the stage, and in the length of their Further Reading lists (collected at the end of the volume). This is no accident, and reflects the unevenness of the development of feminist work in the different areas. This unevenness may be thought to be explained in its turn by differences in subject matter, with some areas naturally lending themselves more readily to feminist intervention. We see no need to judge: these are still early days for feminism in philosophy. We hope that this *Companion*'s existence will encourage more feminist-informed work in the areas where it is scarce, and, in the areas where it is plentiful, assist in its incorporation into the mainstream.

The goal, then, has been to produce a collection that encompasses at least all of the core subject areas commonly taught in anglophone undergraduate philosophy courses. One difficult decision that has resulted has been to omit work that is usually categorized (though this may be a misnomer) as continental philosophy – work with roots in post-structuralism, or in critical theory, for instance. To many people such philosophy has seemed more immediately hospitable to feminist perspectives than its analytic counterpart. Indeed there is now so much innovative feminist continental work, both existing and ongoing, that we have considered it part of our task to help redress the balance by providing a space for analytic work. Students specializing in feminist continental philosophy who encounter no special difficulty in obtaining guidance to the literature in their area often find that they are stuck for want of bibliographies when they set out to discover what is happening under the analytic head. The absence of an essay on feminism in continental philosophy, then, results from the nature of our editorial task, given the volume's pedagogical ambition.

The only departure from our normal principle of inclusion comes with 'Feminism and Psychoanalysis'. Despite the fact that psychoanalysis is seldom on the philosophy syllabus, we felt that the volume would be incomplete without an essay in this area. It belongs here because of the enormous impetus which psychoanalysis has given to feminist work, including work of the 'feminism in philosophy' sort. Given that psychoanalysis can be a resource for feminists and for philosophers, it becomes an important question which of the various psychoanalytic theories we make use of. Sarah Richmond's chapter provides a corrective to the recent tendency among feminists to draw exclusively on Lacanian psychoanalytical theory. She presents the work of a female analyst, Melanie Klein, as a springboard for fresh feminist philosophical reflection.

Psychoanalysis draws our attention to sexual difference – something that is relevant to all feminist thought. But the work collected here should also be read in relation to a concern with 'difference' of another kind. As a watchword of feminism, 'difference' refers to social differences *between* women – differences of ethnicity, or of sexual orientation, or of class, for instance. In feminist theory, 'difference' has come to signify all of the complexities thrown up by the sociological observation that women are not possessed of a uniform social identity.

Here as elsewhere, feminist philosophical thinking reveals its roots in the women's movement. An articulated commitment to acknowledge difference sprang from a problem that second wave feminism, which emerged as a political force in the 1960s, found itself confronting a decade or so on. Perception of an exclusionary white, middle-class bias in the movement led to a split.[5] At the level of practice, issues of difference drew attention to the need for a feminist politics which could furnish political solidarity among women yet do full justice to the intricacies of social identity. There is a continuing need for a transformative gender-politics that is suitably sensitive to relations of oppression besides gender. Diemut Bubeck argues for the possibility of such a transformative politics in her chapter here. She develops a dialogical, as opposed to antagonistic, model of communication across difference.

It has come to be a central feminist philosophical project to respect difference by treating the subject (or self) so that she is represented as socially situated in many dimensions of power and identity besides gender. Some work in mainstream philosophy has also come to make room for social differences between human beings. Sally Haslanger refers to such work under the heading 'natural and social kinds', in the course of discussing how feminism might contribute to the more abstract issues in metaphysics. In some quarters, at least, mainstream philosophy has arrived at accounts that can acknowledge the fully social character of any human subject. Such accounts resist individualism of a sort which assumes that people must be conceived atomistically in the first instance, so that social relations between them are conceived as secondary. Not that it has been the aim of any mainstream account to accommodate social difference as such: the aim may be simply to ensure that the space of reasons is a socially articulated space,[6] so that all conceptual activity is understood as activity within a setting in which people adopt attitudes towards one another.

Although the 'socialized' conception of the human subject that results is itself too abstract to include ideas about any socially specific subject, it is a merit of this conception (in our view) that when the accounts which embody it purport to record *a priori* truths about any 'knower' or 'agent', they speak of something ineluctably related to other such subjects. It is then a question for philosophers whether the pluralism that results from taking account of the socially specific characters of *diverse* human subjects leads inevitably to the kind of relativism that postmodernists endorse. This question is answered negatively in Miranda Fricker's chapter on epistemology.

Epistemology provides a good example of an area reshaped by the socialized conception of people. When the knowing subject is treated as a social being, testimony assumes its place as a fundamental mode of knowledge acquisition, attention is given to epistemic practices, and relations between knowers are brought to the fore. Epistemology then contains resources for exposing the political aspects of quotidian epistemic practices. Such practices are now seen as instantiations of what the epistemologist theorizes about; and we know that equality between the people who are parties to these practices, in respect, for instance, of whether one takes another as reasonable, or as trustworthy, cannot be assumed. Social difference then makes for epistemic difference. In the chapter by Rae Langton, the question of epistemic difference is discussed in relation to how women may be excluded and even harmed by certain conceptions of knowledge.

The socialized conception of the subject contrasts with the individualistic conception which has thrown up so much of modern philosophy's distinctive problematic. The individualistically conceived subject is the self-sufficient individual, represented in the figure of the philosopher when he finds himself on one side of a gulf – whether a gulf between himself and his body, himself and others, or himself and the world outside him. (Thus we encounter the 'mind–body' problem, the problem of 'other minds', and the problem of the 'external world'.) In one way or another, many of the chapters here inveigh against this picture of the subject: most directly, perhaps, Susan James's, Naomi Scheman's and Jennifer Hornsby's, in connection with personal identity, mentality and language use respectively. Alison Wylie's chapter addresses the socialization of the subject in the context of feminist philosophy of science which adopts a sceptical attitude towards the traditional ideal of value-neutrality in scientific enquiry. Marilyn Friedman's and Alison Jaggar's chapters reveal how feminist thinking, whether about autonomy or about moral justification, aims to reconcile the social interconnectedness of individual moral subjects with the differences in their social experience. And in the concluding essay, Genevieve Lloyd advances a conception of feminist history of philosophy as focused on the interface between philosophical texts and the cultural context of the present. Here, as in the collection generally, that cultural context is to be understood not in terms of gender relations alone, but in terms of the myriad categories of social identity.

Feminists are not alone in wanting to get past the compulsory 'neutralism' of traditional philosophy. And they are not isolated in their manner of intervention. Most notably, perhaps, an historicizing perspective entered philosophy of science with the work of Thomas Kuhn, who treated science as an institution, under historical pressures, rather than as, at any particular time, a body of theory simply.[7] But the importance as it seems to us of the idea that humans' mode of being is being alive in some social setting appears to be dawning in analytic philosophy more generally.[8] Insofar as feminist work cannot be viewed as continuous with the mainstream, we take this to be explained by the fact (as we put it above) of feminists' having a different starting point from the philosopher who has to be brought to acknowledge the historical and cultural locatedness of the subject.

Analytic philosophy creates an intellectual climate in which it is especially problematic to acknowledge locatedness. This is surely an important part of the explanation why continental philosophy can seem more hospitable to feminist projects. Feminists, who believe that the personal is political (to use the terms of a familiar slogan), are bound to be concerned not only with macro structures of power but also with human relations' permeation by power at the micro level. So the imperative of social criticism will ensure that feminist philosophy of any kind is likely to share an affinity with work in the continental tradition (most obviously, perhaps, with the work of Foucault and of Habermas). We believe it is philosophically valuable that work written in the anglo-american paradigm can produce a genuine engagement with questions typically raised in the continental tradition. What we put on display, in assembling this volume, is the possibility of an intellectual breadth in philosophy that is, as yet, largely foreign to the mainstream.

NOTES

1   *The Man of Reason: 'Male' and 'Female' in Western Philosophy* (London: Methuen, 1984).

2   For a germinal account, see Michèle Le Dœuff, *The Philosophical Imaginary*, trans. Colin Gordon (Oxford: Blackwell, 1989).

3   We borrow this concept from Margaret Whitford's *Luce Irigaray: Philosophy in the Feminine* (London: Routledge, 1991).

4   Several special issues (or issues containing special clusters) of *Hypatia: A Journal of Feminist Philosophy* are devoted to new critical thinking of this kind. See vol. 7, no. 4 (Fall 1992), vol. 9, no.1 (Winter 1994), vol. 12, no. 4 (Fall 1997) and vol. 13, nos. 2 and 3 (Spring and Summer 1998), on, respectively, lesbian philosophy, Spanish and Latin-American feminist philosophy, citizenship in feminism and multicultural and postcolonial feminist challenges to philosophy. See also relevant sections in *A Companion to Feminist Philosophy*, ed. Alison Jaggar and Iris Marion Young (Oxford: Blackwell, 1998).

5   No doubt there were other factors contributing to the split. In Britain, at least, a political climate of virulent conservatism was in place by the early 1980s, discouraging and demoralizing radical movements for social change. See Lynne Segal, 'Generations of Feminism', *Radical Philosophy* 83 (1997), which we heard as a talk at 'Torn Halves', Radical Philosophy Conference, London, 9 Nov., 1996.

6   As Robert Brandom puts it in 'Knowledge and the Social Articulation of the Space of Reasons', *Philosophy and Phenomenological Research* 65 (1995), 895–908. See also his *Making it Explicit: Reasoning, Representing, and Discursive Commitment* (Cambridge, MA: Harvard University Press, 1994).

7   *The Structure of Scientific Revolutions* (Chicago: Chicago University Press, 1962).

8   Such an idea is at work, for instance, in Bernard Williams when he stresses the importance for ethics of the cultural and historical embeddedness that shapes a human life (*Ethics and the Limits of Philosophy* (London: Fontana/Collins Press, 1985)), and in John McDowell when he introduces the Aristotelian concept of 'second nature' into his account of thought's bearing on the world (*Mind and World* (Cambridge, MA and London: Harvard University Press, 1994).

I

SABINA LOVIBOND

Feminism in ancient philosophy
The feminist stake in Greek rationalism

Introduction

Despite the internal diversity of extant 'ancient philosophy', it has generally been agreed that the main intellectual legacy of classical Greece and Rome to the modern world is the idea of the value of truth and the capacity of human reason to discover it. This idea, powerfully expressed in the dialogues of Plato and in the more systematic teaching of Aristotle, has provided an implicit point of reference – usually, though not invariably, positive – for all subsequent 'philosophy' in the western world, and feminist thought has been no exception to the rule. What remains unresolved, however, is the proper ratio of positive to negative in the attitude of feminism to 'reason'. Since the eighteenth century at least, there has been an effort to rethink the rationalist ethical and political tradition for the benefit of women, and to detach its characteristic themes (legitimate social order; mutual recognition among citizens; co-operative pursuit of a common good) from the ideology of male supremacy. But the sexual egalitarianism which we inherit from the age of Enlightenment is complicated, today, by a rival impulse of *solidarity* with what the rationalist tradition symbolically excludes – that is, with reason's supposedly feminine 'other' or complement. It is this tension that sets the scene for our discussion.

Probably the burden of argument can be said to rest at present on those who still wish to speak of continuity, rather than of discontinuity or rupture, between feminism and its philosophical past. There is at any rate no doubt that the overall effect of feminist scholarship since the 1970s has been to jolt the traditionally educated classical student into a less respectful attitude. Although it has been cheering to learn of a number of individual women who practised philosophy in the Greek world (even if their access to this activity may have been principally through their male kin or sexual protectors),[1] the most influential theme during this period has been that of the masculinism of ancient thought – its assumption, explicit or otherwise, of the centrality and superiority of the male point of view. Of course it is no secret that Greece and Rome were patriarchal societies,[2] and one can hardly expect their theoretical products to be unmarked by this fact. Rather, what has produced a *frisson* has been the cumulative revelation of something intellectually embarrassing or scandalous in our classical heritage. In particular, where liberal modernity has prided itself on a supposedly universal respect for 'rational nature', feminist criticism has enabled us to see in the dominant philosophical culture the enduring effects of a different and more sinister tradition – one that teaches the individual thinking subject to understand himself as essentially *not* a bearer of the attributes associated with his sexual, social or ethnic inferiors. Such criticism suggests that the other side of the rationalist coin may be a defensive, or 'paranoid', attitude to these putative boundaries.[3]

In the face of growing resistance to any idea of a 'canon' of western literature, it would be pointless to deny that there is a kind of conservatism involved in choosing to study certain ultra-canonical texts which stand at the origin of 'our' tradition. If nothing else, the choice implies a willingness to believe that these texts possess the interest and importance claimed for them. Yet to contribute to the work of handing on a tradition does not imply an attitude of simple deference towards it: here as elsewhere, historical insight is at least as valuable to emancipatory causes as it is to the forces opposing them. Nor can we tell, except by experiment, what materials from the corpus of European philosophy may be of continuing use – in Europe or anywhere else in the world – to people with the ambition to think politically. This chapter aims to describe, and to participate in, one phase of the experiment.

An account of the feminist reception of ancient philosophy should perhaps begin by looking at the way in which the concept of reason took shape. When ancient Greek culture is described as having a 'rationalist' bent, some or all of the following points are likely to be intended:

(i) By the fifth century BC a high value had come to be placed on the fact of culture itself – on social stability, the rule of law, speech, intelligence. This is a recurrent theme, in particular, in the literature of classical Athens, where it is memorably set forth by writers as diverse as Sophocles, Thucydides and Plato.[4] 'Reason' is opposed, in the first instance, to instinct and brute strength; extant Greek literature shows a vivid consciousness of how far humanity had advanced in this respect, and of pride in the achievement, however incomplete.

(ii) By extension from this, value is attached to speech in its more particular capacity of representing or expressing 'what is', i.e. reality. This is arguably still an aspect of the ethical value of culture, since (truthful) communication is a co-operative act – the information communicated is a potentially useful gift to the recipient; hence the power of human intelligence to make contact, through language, with realities elsewhere in space or time is a resource naturally suited to the furtherance of common aims (though not, of course, guaranteed to be so used by any particular person). In any event, speech (*logos*) and thought ('the mind's dialogue with itself', Plato, *Theaetetus* 189e–190a; *Sophist* 263e) are seen as outstandingly precious human attributes.

(iii) Next, the value attached to the capacity for representation in general suggests the idea of the value of *theory*: the ability to represent features of reality which are apt to be hidden from view, and perhaps even to grasp the underlying constitution of reality as a whole. This leads to the elaboration, on one hand, of materialist theories of nature (the Ionian tradition, which asks what the world is *made of*), and on the other hand, of formalist theories (the Eleatic tradition, which sees mathematical structure as the ultimate reality, taking precedence over the matter organized by it). The latter, formalist, approach (inaugurated by Pythagoras and exemplified above all by Plato) gives rise to what will subsequently be known as 'rationalism' in a more technical sense – the kind of philosophy based on mathematical or other *a priori* methods of enquiry, and contrasted with 'empiricism'. The former achieves its most lasting influence through its contribution to a system – that of Aristotle – which has many points of continuity with Platonism, but which develops that philosophy along a path determined not so much by mathematics as by Aristotle's extensive researches in biology.

The Aristotelian approach to sexual matters offers a relatively obvious target to feminist criticism. Aristotle (384–322 BC) holds that the essence of a thing is to be identified with its *function*, or with what it is 'for' from the point of view of some organic whole to which it belongs (*Politics* 1253a20–25; cf. *de Anima* 412b18–20). This identification rests on the assumption that 'Nature does nothing in vain' (*Pol.* 1256b21), and hence that in order to understand a thing we must first come to see the point or purpose of it. Moreover, 'nature' for Aristotle is hierarchical: here, as in the realm of human goal-directed activity, 'the lower always exists for the sake of the higher',[5] and indeed every kind of natural thing contributes in its own way to a single ultimate good (e.g. by being available for human beings to eat: *Pol.* 1256b15–20). The natural world is like a household in which some have greater responsibilities than others, and consequently greater authority;[6] relations of 'ruling-and-being-ruled' occur spontaneously and ubiquitously within it.[7] This doctrine is applied most notoriously to the moral justification of slavery (some men 'differ from others as much as the body from the soul or as an animal from a man', *Pol.* 1254b16–17), but another clear instance of natural dominance and subordination, in Aristotle's view, is the relation of men to women – 'a union of the naturally ruling element with the naturally ruled, for the preservation of both'.[8]

Aristotle can appeal to his postulate of a purposive nature to explain why there are two sexes in the first place. In his work *On the Generation of Animals*, which maintains that in sexual reproduction 'body' comes from the female and 'soul' from the male,[9] he says that 'As the proximate motive cause, to which belong the *logos* and the form, is better and more divine in its nature than the matter, it is better also that the superior one should be separate from the inferior one. That is why wherever possible and so far as possible the male is separate from the female . . . The male, however, comes together with the female and mingles with it for the business of generation, because this is something that concerns both of them' (732a3 ff.). In this way Aristotle equips himself at a stroke not just with a 'scientific' explanation (in terms of final causality) of the existence of two differently sexed kinds of animal body, but also with a rationale for the accepted way of organizing social space (as for example in the Greek household, where women typically had their own separate quarters).

Probably the most important result of the study of Aristotle by feminists has been the transformation into objects of historical – and hence critical – study of some of the central themes of male supremacism. We have just encountered one of these in the shape of the idea that women as such have a natural 'place' which is fixed by their role in reproduction. Another has been the idea of femaleness *per se* as a disability. When Aristotle opines that 'we should look upon the female state as being as it were a deformity, though one which occurs in the ordinary course of nature',[10] he lends his authority to what has proved a remarkably durable conception of the female animal, *qua* female, as defective. And this supposed defectiveness is as much psychological as physical, for we read in *Politics* I (1260a10 ff.) that 'All these persons [freeman and slave, male and female, adult and child] possess in common the different parts of the soul [namely, the rational/ruling and the irrational/ruled elements]; but they possess them in different ways. The slave is entirely without the faculty of deliberation; the female indeed possesses it, but in a form which remains inconclusive [*akuron*, lacking in authority]; and if children also possess it, it is only in an immature form.'

The idea that human rational capacities are realized to an unequal degree in different classes of person leads Aristotle to reject the view advanced by Socrates in Plato's *Meno* (73ac) that virtue must have a common structure wherever it is found, and to assign to men and women respectively distinct grades of virtue corresponding to their distinct social functions. 'The ruler', he argues, 'must possess moral goodness in its full and perfect form [i.e. the form based on rational deliberation] . . . but all other persons need only possess [it] to the extent required of them [by their particular position] . . . [So] temperance – and similarly fortitude and justice – are not, as Socrates held, the same in a woman as they are in a man. Fortitude in the one, for example, is shown in connection with ruling; in the other, it is shown in connection with serving; and similarly with the rest of the virtues' (*Pol.* 1260a17–24).

Aristotle is on the lookout for the 'full and perfect form' of moral goodness because he holds that the function (and hence the nature) of any given type of thing is to be discovered by looking at an example that represents the norm for that type: 'We must fix our attention, in order to discover what nature intends, not on those which are in a corrupt, but on those which are in a natural condition.'[11] This principle, when conjoined with the assumption of superior perfection in the male (not just biologically, which would follow from the considerations about sexual difference noted earlier, but in respect of the functions of thought and deliberation that define our humanity),[12] is of interest to modern feminism because it underwrites the tradition whereby 'man' denotes – by a non-accidental semantic slippage – both humanity in general *and* the male sex as its 'natural' representative. It is only since the nineteenth century that there has been an effective challenge to the brute social facts rationalized by this tradition, namely the denial of full legal and political personality to women; and much more recently that attention has come to be paid to related symbolic phenomena such as the 'inclusive' use of the masculine pronoun.

The evidence introduced so far has had a purely negative significance for our topic.[13] Turning now to the somewhat different tradition represented by Socrates (c. 470–399 BC) and Plato (c. 429–347 BC), we will find that the picture becomes more complex. On one hand, it is not surprising that the extreme intellectualism of these philosophers should have been seen as hospitable to the idea of sexual equality, especially since one of the most influential Platonic texts contains a ground-breaking argument – however limited and flawed in detail – for that very idea. This is the famous passage (*Republic* V, 455de and context) where Socrates is made to point out that in a rational political order (sexual) anatomy – at least for some women – would not be destiny, since it is irrelevant to the ability to perform social functions other than that of producing children. Despite the solemn concession that on average men as a sex are better at everything than women as a sex, this passage leaves us with the all-important insight (454de) that while biological sexual difference assigns different 'natural roles' to women and men *within* the sphere of sexual reproduction, it does not determine a 'natural' way for each of the sexes to contribute to the wider social order, so that there is no reason why women (for example) should not take part in the traditionally masculine activities of law-enforcement and defence. In a comment celebrated for its amusement value,[14] Aristotle complains that Plato's vision is flawed by his failure to notice that human beings, unlike other animals, live in households and consequently have sexually differentiated functions. This criticism, of course, misses the point that there is nothing in their reproductive biology to prevent human beings from replacing the traditional household with some alternative system of meeting their day-to-day material needs; but it is no more questionable on that score than the present-day habit of worrying about the welfare of children whose *mothers* (as opposed to 'parents') go out to work, and even in the twentieth century there have been those for whom Plato's disregard for orthodox sexual psychology has retained a certain power to disturb.[15]

Against this passage, however, must be weighed the evidence amassed by recent scholarship that Plato's 'feminism' is no more than superficial. This evidence ranges from the frequent occurrence in his writings of common-place psychological sexism,[16] through the unselfconscious application of conventional notions of gender to more speculative metaphysical or cosmological questions (as at *Timaeus* 50c7 ff.), to the kind of motif which – most disturbingly for those who would like to see Plato as rising above the biologism of Aristotle – convicts his thought of a refusal, at the 'imaginary'[17] level, of the fact of sexual difference. Under the last heading fall those elements which can be read as symptoms of an *unconscious* impulse to equate femininity with the darkness of unenlightened nature (the womb-like Cave of *Republic* VII),[18] to diminish women's powers of physical reproduction by treating them as a mere symbol of the genuine (spiritual) reproduction accomplished by men through the power of *logos*,[19] and in general to suppress the emotionally unacceptable theme of natural transience or 'becoming' through a variant of the philosophy of 'being' derived from the Presocratic philosopher Parmenides.[20]

This negative evidence looks more powerful than any grounds for optimism provided by the fleeting appearance in a Platonic dialogue of the idea that 'nature's' intentions for women may not be exhausted by family life. It also possesses the kind of prestige accruing to a 'suspicious' reading

– one that claims the authority to go beyond a mere reconstruction of what the text was *meant* to convey. I think that in the case now before us this authority is incontrovertible and that whatever else we may find in Plato's writings, we can hardly recover our innocence with regard to the fantasy enacted there of a woman-free regime of procreation and eternal life. The disclosure of this barely suppressed gender theme at the origin of western philosophy has produced a kind of epistemological break in feminist theory, and has largely overturned the older view that the Socratic school – by virtue of its insistence on the *psyche* ('soul' or 'mind') rather than the embodied creature as the real person – could be credited with a 'well-reasoned and deliberate attempt . . . to improve the position of women in Greece'.[21]

However, rather than dwell on the unconscious provocation offered by Platonism to the (woman-identified) woman reader, I would like to turn the tables and discuss an unacknowledged *debt* which that reader may owe to the philosophy responsible for her symbolic annihilation. The debt I have in mind relates to the concept of *form* or *limit*, and to the organizing role of this concept in Pythagorean–Platonic philosophy. Limit (*peras*) is contrasted with the *apeiron* (the indeterminate or formless – a character attributed, in this way of thinking, to matter), and together the two make up one of ten pairs of opposed terms which Aristotle (*Metaphysics* 986a22 ff.) says were recognized by the Pythagoreans as ontological or cosmological 'first principles'.[22] The pairs (which in fact include 'good' and 'bad') each comprise a 'good' and a 'bad' term, though in some cases the values attaching to them are derived from a highly specific philosophy of mathematics; 'limit' falls on the 'good' side of the table, prefiguring the role of 'forms' or universals as ideal paradigms in middle-period Platonism. For us, though, the important point is the appearance of 'male' and 'female' in the list. What this has suggested to feminist readers, especially to those influenced by 'deconstructionist' modes of reading, is that Platonism – and by extension all 'rationalist' philosophy, in the technical sense introduced earlier – possesses a *gendered* conceptual structure. For example, in addition to portraying form or determinacy *per se* as good and indeterminacy as bad, there seems to be a fair amount of textual evidence that Plato pictures their distinctive goodness or badness in a way that is shaped by images of sexual difference.[23]

Now to note the existence of such a structure is not yet to work out how we can best negotiate the hazard it may present to our thinking; and on this question I have nothing of a general methodological nature to offer. Instead, what I want to pursue in the rest of this chapter is the more concrete suggestion that however integral the hierarchically ordered 'male–

female' pair may be to Greek rationalism, feminist students of the tradition have at least one powerful incentive not to treat that fact as decisive for their own 'theoretical practice'. There is, of course, something uncomfortable in the prospect of continuing to acquiesce in a cognitive order within which the attribute of femaleness has, historically, borne a negative value.[24] Yet it would be hard to deny that the consciousness of this metaphysical misogyny – a consciousness which the 'feminism of difference'[25] has done so much to enforce – has to co-exist in our minds with much else that we have learned about what is to count as *enquiry* or as (ordered, purposive) *thought*. In particular – and as if we still heard an echo of the Platonic proposition that 'the source of all fine things is found in a mixture of the unlimited with that which has limit' (*Philebus* 26b) – the quest for a satisfying accommodation between 'form' and 'matter' continues to pre-occupy us. This holds good both in the theoretical sphere (we see it as a merit in a theory that it should organize its subject-matter into a unified whole, but without doing too much violence to observational or intuitive data), and also in the practical (we aspire to a political order that would extend legal rights and duties to all citizens, but without denying their individuality). We may not know exactly what would constitute the concrete fulfilment of either of these ideals, but this does not prevent us from using them for purposes of orientation. All attempts to pass beyond a purely abstract or 'minimalist' account of truth (or beyond a dogmatic 'intuitionism' about questions of value), and to specify under what conditions we feel we are making theoretical or practical progress, seem to owe something to the Platonic schema.

Feminists who acknowledge the persistent (if not unquestioningly accepted) presence of rationalist values in their own thinking have found it natural to explain this phenomenon in a spirit of 'critical realism'. That is, they point out that if there is to be any possibility of the kind of active response to female subordination that consists in *understanding* it, there must first be the possibility of *understanding* anything at all, i.e. of successfully bringing thought to bear on it. Our criteria of success here, if they are to command the kind of recognition that will mediate agreement, cannot be conjured out of thin air by each individual thinker for her own use but must owe something to a common background of intellectual experience – even if, as is inevitable, this background incorporates the common *social* experience of subordination on which feminism tries to reflect. So despite the strictures of those theorists who see any project of truth-orientated enquiry as structurally incapable of accommodating the fact of sexual difference, it is plausible to represent the relation of feminist thought to its discursive environment in terms of 'Neurath's boat', which cannot find a haven safe from error but has to be repaired while out at sea.[26] This is in effect the position of all those who look with scepticism on the idea of a *radical*, or absolute, break with existing habits of thought.[27]

The reasoning just sketched takes the form of a 'dialectical' argument, where our partners in dialogue would be the proponents of an absolute break with epistemic tradition. It assumes that feminists, as such, will think of themselves as a body of people characterized not just by certain behavioural *symptoms*, but by a project of collective *action*, i.e. of behaviour which is purposive (and hence – so far as any human behaviour merits this description – intentionally controlled). And it is ready to build on this assumption by arguing that if we think of the feminist project as defined by certain controlling purposes or values, these must be capable of being discursively recommended to people not already persuaded of their practical claim upon us; otherwise they would not be *values* but merely arbitrary objects of pursuit.

This first dialectical argument appeals to what we might expect feminists to acknowledge as the logical consequences of adherence to anything recognizable as a politics. However, it may be possible to construct a further, less familiar dialectical argument to the same conclusion – namely, the impossibility of a complete severance of feminism from its rationalist antecedents – on the basis of the substantive political views we can expect feminists to hold. These views have to do with the defence of women's generic interests, in so far as these can be identified in a given context, against any unjust precedence enjoyed by the generic interests of men.[28] So our second dialectical argument will be addressed to feminists, no longer simply as 'political' beings in the abstract, but now as adherents to a *specific* politics.

It will start from the suggestion that we can discern within modern normative thinking two main themes, each with its distinct 'genealogy'. This suggestion has no claim to originality, but derives from the nineteenth-century paradigm of modern culture as a zone of contention between the rival forces of 'Hebraism' and 'Hellenism'. Our terminology here, which gained currency in English from Matthew Arnold's essay *Culture and Anarchy* (1869),[29] obviously belongs to the synthetic or imaginative genre of historical thought rather than to exact philology. Still, it may be that this contrast between the Judaeo-Christian and the classical elements in western culture can be of service in rendering the perception of our Greek inheritance more determinate, and so in clarifying the sense in which feminist thinking may need to reconcile itself to the presence of 'Hellenic' elements within it.

In *Culture and Anarchy* Arnold explains 'Hebraism' and 'Hellenism' as two distinct spiritual disciplines with a common goal – 'man's perfection or salvation' (p. 121). Both are 'profound and admirable manifestations of man's life, tendencies and powers' (p. 125), but they diverge dramatically in content. For Hellenism the key to salvation is to think truly or 'see things as they really are', whereas for Hebraism it is 'conduct and obedience' (p. 123). Again, while the leading idea of Hebraism is that of *strictness of conscience*, that of Hellenism is *spontaneity of consciousness*: 'to follow, with flexible activity, the whole play of the universal order, to be apprehensive of missing any part of it, of sacrificing one part to another, to slip away from resting in this or that intimation of it, however capital' (p. 124). The materials already assembled in this discussion suggest another way of putting Arnold's point: what he understands as the 'Hellenic' ideal consists in the capture of all the content, or matter, of reality within our thinking, which must therefore be organized in such a way as to accommodate it, assigning every element to a place from which it will not be dislodged. So it consists in giving thought a form that will do justice to the seemingly anarchic plurality of what there is for us to think. And this looks like a natural point of application for the duality of 'limit' and 'unlimited' which we have seen to be central to the Pythagorean–Platonic tradition.

We know that within that tradition the principle of 'limit', for example, is *dominant* with respect to that of the 'unlimited'. But by now, with the feminist critique of 'reason' before us, we may be disposed to look around for alternatives to this way of thinking. And, in fact, a number of resources for questioning it can be discovered *within* Greek culture. Hegel and Nietzsche have drawn attention to some of them: the contrast between 'written' and 'unwritten' law explored in Sophocles' *Antigone* calls into question the Platonic value-hierarchy (while preserving its gendered character);[30] the contrast between the 'Apollonian' and 'Dionysian' principles sees in the artistic achievement of Greek tragedy a distinctively aesthetic solution to the problem of existence – a device which works by affirming, and converting into a ground of triumph over personal suffering, the merely superficial character of separate individual existence.[31] And it is worth recalling that even for Plato the principles of form and formlessness do not stand in a relation of unmitigated opposition, but need to be correctly combined with one another in order to produce objects of value within the domain of experience – just as the principle of 'difference', along with that of 'sameness', eventually has to be understood as part of the structure of 'what is'.[32]

However, what may be of more significance for our second dialectical argument is a mode of thought in which positive value is associated with the limitless *as such*. It is at this point that we encounter the 'Hebraic' element in our moral tradition – that concerned with *obedience*.[33] Nietzsche writes in *Beyond Good and Evil*:

> What Europe owes to the Jews? – Many things, good and bad, and above all one thing that is at once of the best and the worst: the grand style in morality, the dreadfulness and majesty of infinite demands.[34]

Infinite demands – as exemplified by the Old Testament story of God's incomprehensible order to Abraham to sacrifice Isaac, the story which prompts Kierkegaard's famous reflections on the inadequacy of an ethics grounded in social or 'universal' rationality.[35] Greek rationalism offers us the ideal of a moral order characterized by perfect integration or *harmony* – the condition in which every element in a complex whole has been stabilized, setting the whole at peace with itself (Plato, *Rep.* 443c9–444a2); or where the actions that give expression to an individual personality are as perfectly judged as a work of art in which one 'wouldn't change a thing' (Aristotle, *Nicomachean Ethics* 1106b8–16).[36] 'Limit' is of the essence here because if we think of a moral entity – be it a social unit comprising a number of persons, or a human life comprising a variety of particular actions – as a complex object capable of displaying a greater or lesser degree of formal perfection, then clearly that perfection will be compromised by the exaggerated development of any one component part or tendency, or by any local feature that detracts from the overall 'balance' of the object. This moral ideal is shaped by a sensibility that is apt to condemn any such feature as absurd, barbarous, 'offensive to reason'. By contrast, a morality centred upon the value of *obedience to God's will* (whatever blend of the literal and the metaphorical we may bring to our understanding of this phrase) will never see an object of moral appraisal as disfigured, but on the contrary as fulfilled or perfected, by the ever more extreme realization of this disposition; its demands will thus take on the 'sublime' aspect associated with immeasurable depth or height.

What is the bearing of each of these traditions on modern moral or political thought? Suppose we 'begin with what is known *to us*', as Aristotle says, and consider a contrast that has become very familiar to feminist students of philosophy since the 1980s: that between the 'ethics of justice' and the 'ethics of care'.[37]

At first glance there is no apparent connection between this contrast and that of 'Hellenism versus Hebraism' which we have just been considering. Yet it seems to me that on closer inspection an interesting congruence emerges between the nineteenth-century schema and the contemporary one, and that this finding can be used to shed light on the significance of each for feminism. Of course such a procedure makes sense only in so far as we credit feminism with some determinate belief-content by virtue of which feminists have reason to react in a particular way to this or that phenomenon: this was why I noted that the argument now under construction, like our earlier 'Neurath's boat' considerations, could be regarded as dialectical in form.

The standard way of introducing the contrast between an 'ethics of justice' and an 'ethics of care' is by reference to the different degrees of authority they give to abstract principle relative to the claims arising out of concrete involvement with others. An ethics of justice represents the thinking of a morally competent person as centred on the search for universal rules; though prompted by the moral difficulties of daily life, it passes beyond them in so far as it works towards a stable view of what should happen in *any* situation 'relevantly similar to this one'. An ethics of care on the other hand sees moral intelligence as consisting primarily, if not exclusively, in (suitably informed) sensitivity to the needs of others – 'sensitivity' here retaining its connotation of emotional responsiveness, capacity for vicarious distress, etc., as opposed to the theoretical awareness of life's evils which exists more or less inertly in most of us. We might say that for the former approach the characteristically ethical question is: 'Has everyone got what is due to them in this situation?',[38] while for the latter it is: 'Has everyone got what they need here?' (Or, more ambitiously: 'Is everyone *happy*?)' These questions, or perhaps the 'carer's question' in particular, encapsulate states of mind whose gendered nature should be obvious; their importance for feminism stems from the conviction that the care-centred component of moral rationality has been systematically (though not of course inexplicably) underemphasized at the level of theory.

I think it is plausible to represent the contrast between these two approaches – or if they are seen as jointly realized to some extent in the moral consciousness of every individual, between these two components of morality – in terms of the Platonic principles of 'limit' and the absence of limit. And if this is accepted, then we can see the opposition of 'justice' and 'care' – understood as they have been within recent feminist writing – as a reworking of that between 'Hellenism' (with its ideal of order and balance) and 'Hebraism' (with its ideal of submission).[39]

Nietzsche's vision of the 'dreadfulness and majesty of infinite demands' may seem far removed from the range of activities celebrated by feminist exponents of the ethics of care, much of which is accounted for by the daily round of women's physical service to others, especially to young children. But the theme of limitlessness within the ethics of care emerges once we attend, precisely, to the cyclical and interminable nature of such service: 'a woman's work is never done', or as Simone de Beauvoir observes, it is such as to condemn the worker to 'immanence'[40] because of the continual need to repeat actions such as feeding and cleaning. The demands acknowledged by someone adhering to an ethics of care can be described as infinite, to begin with, in this mundane sense. But there is another, less literal sense in which they can be so described: because the adherent of such an ethics accepts, even if only by default, the role of *one whom others count on* to meet their needs, she cannot think of her obligations as ending anywhere short of the point where those needs have been ('well enough',[41] if not perfectly) met – and the location of that point depends on contingencies not fully predictable or controllable by her. We may recall here Emmanuel Levinas's reflections on the *'empirical* event of obligation to another', a responsibility to which he says it is 'impossible to fix limits', so that 'to be one's brother's keeper is to be his hostage'.[42]

The aptness of picturing the traditionally feminine side of ethics as 'unlimited' in character is reinforced by Kant's contrast between 'narrow' and 'wide' obligation.[43] A narrow obligation is such that failure to comply with it is automatically culpable, as when we encroach on another person's rights; whereas failure to comply on any given occasion with a 'wide' obligation (like that of helping others or cultivating one's own talents), provided it does not express any vicious principle, is merely a 'deficiency in moral worth'.[44] Now this implies that in the case of wide obligations, just as there is no definite point of transition from permissible to transgressive behaviour, so there is also no definite point at which one can say one has done *enough*. 'No rational principle prescribes specifically how far one should go'[45] in such an effort, yet the effort itself is mandatory: without it, one does not qualify as a conscientious person. In this way we arrive at a classification of duties which seems to align itself with the structures we have just been exploring: narrow obligations are those associated with the realm of law, or at any rate of some authority which can determine what is due to or from any given person; wide obligations belong, rather, to the realm of upbringing, i.e. to the scene of a continuing effort – not however mediated in any direct way by the exercise of formal authority – to establish certain dispositions of character. Again, a gendered contrast: women can recognize themselves as the *de facto* custodians of the domestic or 'indefinite' part of ethics, men as the custodians of the juridical or 'definite' part.

The tendency of our second dialectical argument will therefore be to suggest that even in the face of all the disrespect, whether literal or symbolic, offered to women by the Greek rationalist tradition, feminism cannot afford to regard the condition of indebtedness to that tradition as an intolerable contamination. For it is within this part of our inherited corpus of 'morality' that we have the best prospects of finding a counter-weight to the Judaeo-Christian theme of *unconditional obedience*, which, for all its grandeur, is (in 'worldly' terms) full of danger for women. No doubt the 'justice versus care' theme in recent feminist theory represents a legitimate protest against the excessive prominence of the 'Hellenic', or form-related, contribution to ethics. But the fact remains that 'care' is, or must at some point be expressed in, *work* (the *practical* love of one's neighbour, as Kant would put it), and if we fail to question the social distribution of the burdens and benefits of such work, we effectively acquiesce in the systematic injustice towards women that exists in this domain.[46] Worse, if we seek to reclaim as a source of female pride the particular form of moral consciousness that makes one 'hostage' to the needs (or demands) of others, we are liable to provide further proof of the principle that any attempt to promote feminism by affirming the 'feminine' leaves one 'wallowing in the mire of ideology'.[47] So our present line of thought can be summed up by saying that feminism needs to grasp historically, and to resist politically, the imaginary link between femininity and the indeterminate or infinite;[48] not to accept this particular cultural product as a source of insight into 'moral reality', but on the contrary to *bring* 'limit' into female ethical experience where it is currently lacking – especially where that experience reflects the power historically enjoyed by men to limit their own exposure to ethical claims, and to transfer any unwanted surplus to women.

To concede that we can learn this much from Greek philosophy is not to argue that 'caring' values should be assigned a subordinate place within ethics, still less that they should be banished from it. Rather, it is to suggest that there is a sense in which feminists can endorse the search for a 'correct mixture' of the relevant principles of limit and non-limit. Justice, under-stood as the manifestation of a will to impose limit (or form) on human relations, would be superfluous if it were not for the *vulnerability* of human beings – their susceptibility, not just in infancy but potentially at any moment in life, to conditions which prevent them from asserting themselves successfully and which make them dependent on the readiness of others to fill the gap by appeal to a common understanding of rights and duties. It arises, however flickeringly and erratically, from an awareness of this shared vulnerability, which is in effect a continuing shared dependence on the power of 'care' to motivate others to help us. However, because of the practical demands imposed by the caring attitude, the systematically skewed *de facto* distribution of these demands between women and men is itself a moral problem which calls for redress. For us, if not for the ancient world, it constitutes a situation of precisely the kind to which the concept of justice applies: one in which a vulnerable group (here, women as family members, exposed to exploitation by the stubborn survival of the idea that the business of 'care' falls particularly to them) must look for protection to a certain moral (or political) consensus. I think it is fair to say that that consensus does not yet exist, but is something that feminism aspires to create, at least in so far as it declines to be drawn into a romantic celebration of the state of exposure to 'infinite demands'. And in attempting, more soberly, to spell out what *is* demanded of each of us in the name of social and generational solidarity, perhaps we can after all think of ourselves as engaged in something akin to the classical endeavour to apply reason to human life. For however different the prospective solution, the problem – as ever – is that of how best to organize our collective existence, given the kind of natural species that we are.[49]

NOTES

1   See M. E. Waithe, ed., *A History of Women Philosophers*, vol. 1 *Ancient Women Philosophers 600 BC–500 AD* (Dordrecht: Kluwer, 1987); R. Hawley, 'The Problem of Women Philosophers in Ancient Greece', in L. Archer, S. Fischler and M. Wyke, eds., *Women in Ancient Societies: An Illusion of the Night* (Basingstoke: Macmillan Press, 1994); S. Hornblower and A. Spawforth, eds., *The Oxford Classical Dictionary*, 3rd edition (Oxford: Oxford University Press, 1996) under 'Women in Philosophy'.

2   For a wide-ranging collection of literary and epigraphical evidence, see M. Lefkowitz and M. Fant, *Women's Life in Greece and Rome* (London: Duckworth,1982).

3   On the 'logic of paranoia', see N. Scheman, *Engenderings: Constructions of Knowledge, Authority and Privilege* (London: Routledge, 1993), esp. p. 77; on ethnicity and the Athenian civic ideal, see E. Hall, *Inventing the Barbarian: Greek Self-Definition through Tragedy* (Oxford: Oxford University Press, 1989).

4   Sophocles, *Antigone*, lines 332 ff. ('Many things are wonderful and none more wonderful than man'); Thucydides II, 35–46 (the funeral oration of Pericles); Plato, *Protagoras* 320c–328d (Protagoras' account of the historical development of justice).

5   *Politics* 1333a20–21. (Translations from the *Politics* are based on E. Barker, *The Politics of Aristotle* (Oxford: Clarendon Press, 1946).) For the meaning of 'lower' and 'higher' compare *de Anima* 414a29–b19: plants have the nutritive faculty only, animals also have sense-perception and locomotion, while 'human beings and anything else that is similar or superior to them' add the faculties of thought and intellect.

6   *Metaphysics* 1075a16–25.

7   *Pol.* 1254a24–33.

8   *Pol.* 1252a30–31.

9   *De Generatione Animalium* 738b26 ff.; cf. 716a20ff. (the male is that which has the power to generate in another, the female is that out of which the generated offspring comes into being); 734b35 (the generating parent is *actually*

what the material from which the offspring is formed is *potentially*); 729b12 ff. (the offspring comes from its male and female parents respectively in the sense in which a bedstead comes from the carpenter and the wood). (Translations from this text are based on that of A. L. Peck in the Loeb Classical Library edition (1942).)

10 *De Gen. An.* 775a15. See also 728a17 ff. ('A woman is as it were an infertile male'); 766a31 (maleness as a capacity, femaleness as an incapacity); and for further references and discussion, S. M. Okin, *Women in Western Political Thought* (Princeton: Princeton University Press, 1979), ch. 4.

11 *Pol.* 1254a36–7 (a biological application of the more abstract thought in Plato, *Republic* 504c2–3, 'Nothing imperfect is the measure of anything').

12 See *Nicomachean Ethics* 1166a16–17; 1168b31–69a3; 1177b31–78a3.

13 I do not wish to suggest that this represents the last word on 'Aristotle and feminism', however. For more optimistic approaches see M. C. Nussbaum, 'Non-Relative Virtues: An Aristotelian Approach', in M.C. Nussbaum and A. Sen, eds., *The Quality of Life* (Oxford: Clarendon Press, 1993) and 'Human Capabilities, Female Human Beings', in M. C. Nussbaum and J. Glover, eds., *Women, Culture and Development* (Oxford: Clarendon Press, 1995); also C. A. Freeland, ed., *Feminist Interpretations of Aristotle* (University Park, PA: Pennsylvania State University Press, 1998).

14 *Pol.* 1264b4–6: 'It is odd to base on an analogy with animals, who have no domestic duties, the claim that women ought to engage in the same occupations as men.'

15 Thus E. Barker, *Greek Political Theory*, 5th edition (London: Methuen, 1960), p. 261 objects to the egalitarianism of *Rep.* V that 'the fact of her sex is not one isolated thing in a woman's nature, in which, and in which alone, she differs from man: it colours her whole being . . . She has by nature a specific function of her own, which she will always refuse to delegate to a crèche; and the long period of growth and the need of nurture of her children . . . will always make the discharge of this function the work of a lifetime.'

16 See L. Irigaray, *Speculum of the Other Woman*, trans. G. Gill (Ithaca: Cornell University Press, 1985), pp. 152–60; J. Annas, 'Plato's *Republic* and Feminism', in J. K. Ward, ed., *Feminism and Ancient Philosophy* (London: Routledge, 1996).

17 'Imaginary' is used here in a sense deriving from the psychoanalytic writings of Jacques Lacan. 'The Imaginary order . . . is the domain of transference relations' – that is, of behaviour manifesting 'affective conflicts which remain unresolved from childhood' – and is 'governed by jealousy, competition and aggressivity, mediated through idealization, love and the rationalizations which Lacan calls misrecognition' (E. Ragland-Sullivan, 'The Imaginary', in E. Wright, ed., *Feminism and Psychoanalysis: A Critical Dictionary* (Oxford: Blackwell, 1992), p. 174).

18 See Irigaray, *Speculum*, pp. 243 ff.

19 *Theaetetus* 149b–151d, Socrates as a midwife of the intellect; *Symposium* 206b–212c, the object of love is 'procreation in the beautiful': for some men this process involves physical intercourse (with women), for some intellectual intercourse (with other men). See also P. duBois, *Sowing the Body: Psychoanalysis and Ancient Representations of Women* (Chicago: University of Chicago Press, 1988), ch. 8.

20 See A. Cavarero, *In Spite of Plato: A Feminist Rewriting of Ancient Philosophy*, trans. S. Anderlini-D'Onofrio and Á. O'Healy (Cambridge: Polity Press, 1995), ch. 2.

21 J. Adam, *The Republic of Plato*, vol. 1 (Cambridge: Cambridge University Press, 1905), p. 280 (on *Republic* 451c ff.). (But it may be that the pendulum has begun to swing the other way on this point: see S. Levin, 'Women's Nature and Role in the Ideal *Polis*: *Republic* v Revisited', in Ward, ed., *Feminism in Ancient Philosophy*, esp. at pp. 26–7.)

22 Pythagoreanism had its first flowering at Croton, a Greek community in southern Italy, around 500 BC. Aristotle (*Metaphysics* 987a30) describes Plato as 'in most respects a follower' of this school; hence the term 'Pythagorean–Platonic' in the text above.

23 I discuss some of this evidence in 'An Ancient Theory of Gender: Plato and the Pythagorean Table', in Archer, Fischler and Wyke, eds., *Women in Ancient Societies*. Of related interest are the essays by Judith Genova and Cynthia Hampton in B. Bar On, ed., *Engendering Origins: Critical Feminist Readings in Plato and Aristotle* (Albany: SUNY Press, 1994).

24 'Uncomfortable' fails to do justice to the gravity of the situation, some feminists would argue. I explore this position in 'Feminism and the 'Crisis of Rationality'', *New Left Review* 207 (Sept./Oct. 1994), 72–86.

25 Works representing, or inspired by, what I would call the feminism of difference include those of Irigaray, duBois and Cavarero cited in notes 18–20 above. For explicit advocacy of what the author describes as a 'radical feminism of sexual difference', see R. Braidotti, *Patterns of Dissonance* (Cambridge: Polity Press, 1991). A valuable account of this style of feminist theory is to be found in M. Whitford, *Luce Irigaray: Philosophy in the Feminine* (London: Routledge, 1991).

26 The image is named after its originator, the 'Vienna Circle' anti-foundationalist philosopher Otto Neurath.

27 A classic statement of this position can be found in G. Lloyd, *The Man of Reason: 'Male' and 'Female' in Western Philosophy* (London: Methuen, 1984) (see esp. 'Concluding Remarks').

28 Some feminist writers, such as Judith Butler, would now condemn the uncritical acceptance of the dualistic categories 'woman' and 'man' as a residue of conventional (and oppressive) modes of construction of gendered identity. However, since it is admitted that this view does not debar us from 'speaking as and for women' for strategic (political) purposes (see Butler in S. Benhabib et al., *Feminist Contentions* (London: Routledge, 1995), p. 49), I will not pursue it here.

29 See M. Arnold, *Culture and Anarchy* (London: Macmillan,1938), ch. 4; and compare F. Nietzsche, *On the Genealogy of Morality*, trans. C. Diethe, ed. K. Ansell-Pearson (Cambridge: Cambridge University Press, 1994), esp. Essay I. The same theme figures in Wittgenstein, who is reported as saying – for related reasons – that his own thoughts are 'one hundred per cent Hebraic' (R. Rhees, ed., *Recollections of Wittgenstein* (Oxford: Oxford University Press, 1981), p. 161; and cf. L. Wittgenstein et al., 'Wittgenstein's Lecture on Ethics', *Philosophical Review* (1965), 13, 15).

30 See G. W. F. Hegel, *The Phenomenology of Spirit*, trans. A. V. Miller (Oxford: Oxford University Press, 1977), §§446–76.

31 See F. Nietzsche, *The Birth of Tragedy*, trans. Walter Kaufmann (New York: Random House, 1967). Nietzsche argues here that Apollo, the sun-god, is associated with clarity of outline and hence with determinate form; Dionysus, the wine-god, with an ecstatic loss of identity.

32 Plato, *Sophist*, esp. at 258ab and context.

33 It may be worth stressing once again that for present purposes, 'Hebraic' means Judaeo-*Christian* in contrast to Graeco-Roman.

34 F. Nietzsche, *Beyond Good and Evil*, trans. R. J. Hollingdale (Harmondsworth: Penguin, 1973), §250. Arnold likewise describes Christianity as a matter of '*boundless* devotion to that inspiring and affecting pattern of self-conquest offered by Jesus Christ' (*Culture and Anarchy*, pp. 124–5, emph. added).

35 S. Kierkegaard, *Fear and Trembling*, trans. A. Hannay (Harmondsworth: Penguin, 1985).

36 More precisely, the reference is to works which do not admit of anything being added or subtracted, 'since excess and defect are destructive of goodness'.

37 This contrast owes most of its importance in recent ethical theory to the impact of Carol Gilligan, *In A Different Voice: Psychological Theory and Women's Development* (Cambridge, MA: Harvard University Press, 1982).

38 This terminology raises the question of how to give substance to the idea of what is 'due' to people – a question beyond the scope of this discussion, though the choice of a form of words vague enough to embrace both retributive and distributive justice is deliberate.

39 To imply that the Old Testament is unconcerned with justice would, however, be a misrepresentation. See B. M. Metzger and M. D. Coogan, eds., *The Oxford Companion to the Bible* (Oxford: Oxford University Press, 1993) under 'Righteousness'.

40 S. de Beauvoir, *The Second Sex*, trans. H. Parshley (Harmondsworth: Penguin, 1972), pp. 94–5. 'Immanence' as opposed to 'transcendence': the implicit picture of masculine work, however stylized, conforms to the familiar Aristotelian example of a 'process' (see e.g. *Nicomachean Ethics* 1174a19–27) – the building of a temple which, on completion of the process of making it, continues to exist as a monument to the maker's work. This achievement figuratively lifts the maker above the flux of events, whereas a 'product' that promptly deteriorates or disappears drags its maker down with it.

41 Compare S. Ruddick, *Maternal Thinking* (London: The Women's Press, 1990), p. 161.

42 E. Levinas, 'God and Philosophy', in S. Hand, ed., *The Levinas Reader* (Oxford: Blackwell, 1989), pp. 180, 181 (emphasis added). (But for evidence that Levinas too wishes to see cross-fertilization between 'Athens' and 'Jerusalem', see S. Critchley, *The Ethics of Deconstruction: Derrida and Levinas* (Oxford: Blackwell, 1992), esp. p. 239.)

43 See I. Kant, *The Metaphysics of Morals*, trans. and ed. M. Gregor (Cambridge: Cambridge University Press, 1996), pp. 153–7.

44 Ibid., p. 153.

45 Ibid., pp. 154–5.

46 See D. Bubeck, *Care, Gender and Justice* (Oxford: Clarendon Press, 1995), Parts II–III.

47 Compare M. Le Dœuff, *Hipparchia's Choice*, trans. Trista Selous (Oxford:

Blackwell, 1991), p. 103. My own reservations about the 'feel-good' genre of feminist writing on motherhood (and 'caring' relationships generally) are stated in 'Maternalist Ethics: A Feminist Assessment', *South Atlantic Quarterly* 93:4 (Fall 1994; Toril Moi and Janice Radway, eds.: special issue on materialist feminism), 779–802.

48 Space is lacking here to pursue the distinction between the Presocratic 'un-limited' or 'indefinite' and the more precise notion of the infinite which evolved from it in later Greek (and subsequent) philosophy. For more on this see M. Inwood, *A Hegel Dictionary* (Oxford: Blackwell, 1992) under 'Infinity'; or at greater length, A. W. Moore, *The Infinite* (London: Routledge, 1990).

49 I am grateful for comments on earlier drafts of this chapter to seminar audiences at the Universities of Oxford and Edinburgh, and (especially) to the editors of this book.

2

SUSAN JAMES

Feminism in philosophy of mind
The question of personal identity

1 Introduction

A great deal of recent feminist work on philosophy of mind has been grounded on a central claim: that the key oppositions between body and mind, and between emotion and reason, are gendered. While the mind and its capacity to reason are associated with masculinity, the body, together with our emotional sensibilities, are associated with the feminine. Evidence for this view comes from at least two sources. First, overtly sexist philosophers have in the past claimed that women are by nature less capable reasoners than men and are more prone to ground their judgements on their emotional responses. These authors have been repeatedly opposed by defenders of women, whether male or female. Secondly, feminists have explored ways in which gendered oppositions are at work even in the writings of philosophers who do not explicitly differentiate the mental capacities of men and women or connect women with the bodily work of reproduction and domestic labour. By studying the metaphorical structures of philosophical texts, looking at what may appear to be digressions from the main line of argument, and paying attention to examples, they have identified persistent patterns of association running through the history of philosophy. These patterns can fluctuate from century to century, from author to author, from work to work, and even from paragraph to paragraph, but they keep cropping up. They indicate that the terms associated with the feminine are persistently marginalized by comparison with those associated with masculinity, as when the rational powers of human beings are habitually regarded as more valuable than their emotional skills.[1]

In the light of this analysis, many feminists have worked to develop philosophical positions which do not devalue the symbolically feminine. They have done so by unsettling the hierarchical relations between mind and body, and between reason and emotion, approaching their task in

29

various overlapping ways. Sometimes they have criticized existing, influential theories of body and mind; sometimes they have reconceptualized particular topics within the philosophy of mind; and sometimes they have drawn on the work of authors who have written 'against the grain'.

A prominent example of the first approach has been the engagement of feminist philosophers with the phenomenological tradition, and particularly with the work of Merleau-Ponty.[2] However, by far the most striking case of this type of constructive criticism is to be found in the troubled relationship between feminism and psychoanalysis. In the anglophone world, this originated in a sequence of critical readings of Freud,[3] and subsequently developed into a debate which both takes issue with the psychoanalytic tradition, and deploys its resources. Diverse contributors to the discussion have drawn not only on the ideas of Freud himself, but also on those of Klein, Winnicott and Lacan to explain aspects of sexual difference and to reconsider the oppositions mentioned above.[4] Interest in Lacan, and indeed in other strands of psychoanalytic thought, has been stimulated by the work of some extremely influential French authors, notably Luce Irigaray and Julia Kristeva.[5]

Turning to the second approach, feminist writers have directly addressed the opposition between body and mind, in an effort to reveal how the body is tacitly marginalized in philosophy and to find ways of reinstating it. Much of this work aims to question the distinction between the mental and the physical by showing how mind and body interrelate, and how the body contributes to, and is implicated in, thought.[6] A number of influential contributors to this project have focused on the distinction between sex and gender. Originally coined to mark a division between the biological and social characteristics differentiating men and women, this distinction has been repeatedly questioned, to the point where there is now widespread doubt as to whether it is fruitful to try to keep these two groups of properties apart. Querying the idea of the purely bodily casts doubt on the existence of a clear division between the mental and the physical, while emphasizing the social challenges the sufficiency of an opposition between body and mind.[7]

Directing their attention to the relation between reason and emotion, feminist philosophers have argued that emotion is integral to reasoning, and have brought out some of the ways in which emotion traverses the divide between mind and body.[8] In addition, they have taken a step which characterizes a good deal of feminist work in philosophy of mind, and is one of its claims to originality. By charting the ways in which particular emotions are held to be appropriate in men and inappropriate in women, or appropriate in women and inappropriate in men, they have linked together issues which have generally been held apart, and shown how political philosophy and philosophy of mind are connected.[9]

2 Personal identity

Several of these themes can be traced in contemporary feminist writing about personal identity, which has tended to draw on the insights of psychoanalysis and postmodernism to explore the ways in which selves are embodied, discontinuous, malleable and socially constructed.[10] At the same time, anglophone theorists of personal identity have continued to develop a conception of the self which revolves around a distinction between the psychological and the bodily, and a related notion of psychological continuity.[11] It is tempting to suppose that these two groups are addressing different questions: that feminists are for the most part interested in the variety of ways in which identity can be moulded, lived, or transformed; and that theorists of personal identity are concerned with the prior question of what it is to have an identity at all. But this suggested division of labour is too simple. Feminist explorations of the self are, among other things, attempts to depart from the symbolically masculine character of much of philosophy, and their concern with embodiment, discontinuity and social construction is driven by a desire to avoid reiterating the hierarchical oppositions outlined in the preceding section. By embodying the self, they aim to undo the deeply rooted association between the self and the masculine mind; by emphasizing discontinuity, they aim to put pressure on the cultural alliance between unity and masculinity. From a feminist perspective, therefore, the continued dependence of personal identity theorists on various oppositions that feminist philosophy aims to dismantle is at least suspicious. In this chapter I shall explore some of the grounds for this suspicion, and suggest ways in which it is well-founded.

Within the analytic tradition, discussion of persons focuses largely on the question: what criteria have to be satisfied in order for it to be true that a person at t1 survives at t2? Or: what criteria have to be met for a person at t1 to be the same person at t2?[12] Until recently, these were generally taken to be questions about personal identity, and it was widely assumed that any relation specifying continuing personhood would have to share some key features of the identity relation, such as transitivity and being one–one. Feminists who have argued that philosophy places too much emphasis on identity, and uses it to maintain the system of binary oppositions which exclude the feminine, might have found this objectionable. But in any case, Derek Parfit's work has prompted a reconsideration of this claim. What matters, he has suggested, is survival.[13] And if persons can survive without being identical, the way is open to allow that survival may be a matter of degree. We reach the possibility of a more flexible conception of selfhood which is consonant with at least some feminist arguments.

At the same time, contributors to the debate have found it helpful to distinguish two criteria for continuing personal identity – bodily continuity and psychological continuity – and in this way to separate body and mind. Among feminists, this sort of approach is widely regarded as worthy of scrutiny, as it is sometimes the prelude to an attempt to marginalize the body, and with it the symbolically feminine. In this particular case it is undoubtedly the prelude to a manoeuvre which reinforces the mind/body divide, namely the construction of thought experiments which press these two apart. In the last few years, a good deal of weight has been placed on imaginary examples which suggest that psychological as opposed to bodily continuity is what constitutes a person's survival. One kind of example, in particular, has been crucial in securing this view: the much-cited cases in which, by some means or other, one person's character and memories are transplanted into a second person's body.[14] Although other scenarios such as fission and fusion are also appealed to,[15] transplant cases are a crucial resource on which theorists of various persuasions rely, and are used to create a framework within which different accounts of survival can be discussed.

To make a case for the view that the debate about personal identity marginalizes the feminine, and is one of the ways in which philosophy privileges the symbolically masculine over its feminine counterpart, I shall concentrate on these examples. I shall not discuss the relative merits of psychological and bodily continuity as conditions of survival, nor shall I consider the relation between survival and identity. Instead, I shall try to show how imaginary examples of character transplant are used to sustain a symbolically masculine conception of personhood. I shall take up four points: one about the delineation of character; a narrower one about memory; a third about the role of the social world in sustaining identity; and a fourth about identity and male sexual power.

3 Delineation of character

Imaginary cases in which one person's character is transplanted into another person's body generally assume that character has to be lodged in a material body of some sort. It may be a whole human body, a brain, or half a brain. The body in question may be inorganic, as when an imaginary machine stores the information from one brain and prints it off in another.[16] But in all these versions the body is thought of as a container or receptacle for character. The brain figures as a container in which a person's psychological states can be preserved, and the body figures as a more elaborate receptacle for the brain. Equally, a machine which copies the information from one brain and prints it into another is a receptacle for storing psychological states.

Several contributors to the literature on personal identity acknowledge that thinking of the body as a receptacle may be an excessive oversimplification, but brush this thought aside. In 'The Self and the Future', for example, Bernard Williams notes that body swapping between people of different sexes may be hard to imagine, but comments 'Let us forget this',[17] so turning his back on a point he makes elsewhere, that it may be impossible for an emperor to express his personality when his body is that of a peasant.[18] Other writers, such as Noonan, note the problem, but bypass it by specifying that the bodies in question are either only numerically distinct, or extremely similar.[19] Any characteristics that might enable the body to disrupt the psychological continuity of the character transplanted into it are removed, with the result that bodies are regarded, for the purposes of the experiment, as uniform. They do of course differ in various ways, but these differences are held to be irrelevant.

Making the body anonymous in this way simultaneously affirms a particular view of what character is. The things that really matter about a person's character, the traits which constitute their psychological continuity, do not depend on their having a particular body, or a body with any particular properties. Anthony Quinton makes this point explicitly. 'As things are', he writes, 'characters can survive large and even emotionally disastrous alterations to the physical type of a person's body . . . Courage, for example, can perfectly well persist even though the bodily conditions for its obvious manifestation do not.'[20] Courage, perhaps, but what about dexterity? Patience, perhaps, but what about delight in one's sexuality? (It would be interesting to consider whether all the traditional virtues can be construed as independent of the body in this way.) Quinton's argument exemplifies a tendency which runs through imagined cases of character transplant – a tendency to rely on a conception of character or psychological continuity which serves to emphasize, and even create, a division between the psychological and the bodily. Properties which do not fit neatly into the category of the psychological are held to be marginal or irrelevant to character. Then, if continuity of character is taken to be what matters in survival, merely bodily states become irrelevant to survival.

4 Memory

Partly because the states that contribute to psychological continuity are specified as states that are not bodily, theorists of personal identity are able to be both non-committal and inclusive about what exactly they are. Lewis, for example, regards this as a question of detail,[21] and Noonan claims that 'in general *any* causal links between past factors and present psychological traits can be subsumed under the notion of psychological connectedness'.[22] However, a central role is often given to memories as states which give us access to our pasts, and secure our sense of temporal continuity. How must memory be conceived if it is to fulfil this function, while leaving intact the division between body and character?

At least, I suggest, as a storehouse of recollections able to survive bodily vicissitudes. Take the case of Adam. Whatever happens to him – even if he has one of his ribs removed, even if his body changes beyond recognition, even if God refuses to recognize him – he will still be able to think of a sequence of things he did and things that happened to him as *his* actions and experiences. More particularly, changes in his body will not interfere with this capacity. For example, even when he is weak and wasted he remembers that he took the apple from Eve as a strong young man. Why, then, should this capacity not endure in the imaginary case where Adam's character is transplanted into a different body?

There are some obvious exceptions to the view that memory is unaffected by bodily vicissitudes. For instance, brain damage may make Adam amnesiac, and if his character is transplanted into a body with a damaged brain, it is not obvious that his memories will survive. A more interesting example is provided by cases of physical violation such as rape, other forms of torture, or malicious attack, which often have a profound impact on memory. In an illuminating paper, Susan Brison makes the point that experiences like these do not simply add to the victim's stock of memories, as a camera operator might shoot another few feet of film, nor are they safely lodged in the mind, as the camera operator might store the exposed film in a tin.[23] First, memories of trauma are in many cases closely tied to the body, indeed are *in* the body, and manifest themselves in physical states as much as in psychic ones. Here any neat separation between bodily states and memory as the bearer of psychological continuity seems to break down. To press a tasteless question, would a trauma victim retain her memories if her character were transplanted into a different body? Secondly, trauma destroys or alters existing memories, so that people who have been subjected to extended torture or deprivation lose conscious memories of their own pasts, and lose, too, the easy sense of continuity that memory is here supposed to provide. Their time scale may shrink so that their memories of their own experiences become mainly short-term ones. And the continuity of memory may be punctured and jumbled by uncontrollable, nightmarish recollections.

Writers on personal identity usually try to take account of the loops, breaks and fade-outs in our memories by emphasizing that psychological continuity does not require a single sequence of memories, but only a sequence of overlapping sequences. Furthermore, it is not constituted by memory alone. Where memory breaks down, other continuities such as those in a person's desires, intentions, or hopes can take over. The fact that trauma victims lose memories therefore need not imply that they lose psychological continuity. However, Brison's discussion identifies one of the limitations of such an approach. This way of thinking about continuity suggests that, when memory fails, other psychological states remain un-changed and serve as the guarantors of personhood. But trauma victims do not just lose their memories of past events or actions. They lose the pattern of memory in which their expectations, emotions, skills, desires, and so on are rooted, so that loss of memory is, in these cases, part of a broader destruction of character. The ability to enjoy dancing, for instance, is grounded on remembered physical skills (how to tango), expectations derived from past experience (that one will be safe), emotional dispositions (taking pleasure in music), the confidence that one can keep one's own memory under control, and so on. When all these are gone, enjoying dancing will be gone also. And so for other character traits.

If, as much discussion of personal identity assumes, memory is to be one of the guarantors of psychological continuity, and if psychological con-tinuity is to be separable from bodily continuity, memory must be inter-preted in a particular and selective way. Memories in the body have to be set aside in favour of those which appear to have no bodily aspects; and it has to be assumed that the impact of memory loss on other character traits is sufficiently limited for psychological continuity to survive. It is arguable that these are not very contentious assumptions. But they nevertheless help us to see that the division between body and character, around which imaginary transplant cases are organized, can only be sustained if the traits constituting character are laundered, and all traces of the body washed away. The purified conception of 'the psychological' which emerges then appears as an unsullied self for which the body is simply a convenient receptacle.

5 Social circumstances

The two steps we have examined – the expelling of everything bodily from the mind, and the simultaneous devaluation of the bodily – are familiar to feminists, many of whom have read them as an attempt to demarcate the masculine from the feminine and exclude the latter from philosophy. We can find further traces of this way of proceeding in discussions of personal identity if we focus on another curious feature of the persons around whom debate rages – their complete lack of any history or social context. As we have seen, the key question that concerns philosophers is what it takes for x at t1 to survive at t2. This assumes that we start out with a fully-fledged person, which is why I've called him Adam. And it assumes that in ordinary circumstances (if he doesn't die) he will survive until t2. Philosophers who regard psychological continuity as what matters in survival thus assume that psychological continuity is a property of normal human beings.

To take it for granted that Adam at his creation is a person is to suppose that at that point he has both a body and a character – a suitably integrated set of memories, emotions, desires and so on. The expectation that in normal circumstances he will survive to be expelled from Paradise has built into it the expectation that he possesses the means to maintain his character in some body or other, to satisfy the demands of psychological continuity. These are large assumptions which exclude a good deal. The first excludes the fact that character, in the sense of the ability to understand oneself as the subject of diverse psychological states, is not a birthright, but the fruit of a child's relations with the people who care for him or her. Theorists of personal identity appear to take a Lockean view of the genesis of character: once Adam is created, or once a baby reaches a certain stage, memory starts to roll and an integrated character develops. In doing so they exclude from consideration some of the ways in which the self is dependent on others, particularly on its mother figure. At the same time they make it unnecessary to consider whether features of the process by which the self is constituted may effect its subsequent continuity. The second assumption has complementary consequences: it brackets the question of whether the maintenance of psychological continuity also depends on social relations.

From Freud onwards, writers in the psychoanalytic tradition have elaborated the view that a child's experiences are not initially integrated or continuous, and are not initially the experiences of an individuated self. Coming to understand itself as separate from its mother figure, and becoming able to claim its experiences as its own, is for a child a process in the course of which it becomes able to locate its experiences in its own body. As a number of feminists have stressed, both Freud and Lacan describe the ego as a psychical mapping of the libidinal intensities of the body, a mental projection not of the actual body, but of the body as a kind of emotional map.[24] Freud's ideas are elaborated in Lacan's argument that, during the mirror stage, the child forms an image of its own body as it is represented for it by the images of others, and by its own reflection in a mirror. This image, which is of the body as a whole, forms a sort of provisional identity. It is itself a precondition of the more stable symbolic identity the child acquires as the result of the resolution of the Oedipus complex. And it survives the Oedipus complex as the ego ideal, a model of bodily integrity. Work on body images suggests that they make an important contribution to psychological continuity. During the mirror stage the child embarks on the process of coming to understand itself as situated in the space occupied by its body; or, to put the point differently, embarks on the process of acquiring a stable emotional investment in its body. Only once it has a body image can it understand its body as 'mine', and only then can it possess a perspective on the world.[25]

The self for whom psychological continuity is a possibility therefore has to be created through a series of interactions between the child, people around it, and the broader culture in which it lives.[26] Equally, psychological continuity has to be sustained, and social circumstances can either foster or damage it. To return to Susan Brison's argument, trauma victims who describe the selves they were as dead, or beyond recognition, provide searing evidence of the ways that continuity can be shattered. As well as losing the memories and character traits which defined them, they may have lost the ability to inhabit fully the lives they are now living. Brison quotes a poem by Charlotte Delbo about her return from Auschwitz to Paris:

> life was returned to me
> and here I am in front of life
> as though facing a dress
> I cannot wear.[27]

To recover the sense of subjectivity that personal identity theorists so often take for granted, such people need to recover the ability to care about themselves and the world, to feel emotions that, as Brison puts it, are more than counterfactual.[28] Others can play a crucial part in this process. By listening to, and recognizing, the victims of trauma, others seem to be able to help them piece together their memories into narratives with which they can identify, and master the troubling bodily manifestations of memory which further disrupt the self. Extreme cases like these suggest that psychological continuity has a social dimension insofar as it depends on recognition by others. When recognition is withdrawn, the emotional investment in our memories and characters that holds the self together may be weakened, so that, to varying degrees, we suffer a kind of depersonalization – an inability to feel that our experiences are our own, and a subsequent inability to integrate and order them.

The view that psychological continuity has to be created and sustained has some impact on the personal identity theorists' assumption that bodily and psychological continuity are conceptually separable. The arguments I have just sketched help us to elaborate an account of what is left out in the imaginary cases where it is assumed that psychological continuity would survive body transplant. Suppose we assume that psychological continuity does depend on the possession of a body image, and on an emotional investment in it. Is it now so obvious that the features of the body into which a character is transplanted are irrelevant to its survival? To dramatize the issue in a manner typical of this philosophical literature, what about a female fashion model whose character is transplanted into the body of a male garage mechanic? Might she not find it impossible to reconcile her body image with the body that had become hers, and suffer such a level of dislocation that she became unable to locate her experiences in that body? At the limit, might she not experience the depersonalization suffered by some psychotics, who lose interest in the whole body and do not invest any narcissistic libido in the body image? Their self-observations seem viewed from the perspective of the outsider and they display no interest in their own bodies.[29] Suppose, by contrast, we imagine a character whose body is transplanted into that of her identical twin. The point is that she remains psychologically continuous (if she does) because the body that is now hers has properties which make it possible for her to live in it as her own. Psychological continuity is not independent of the body. It is a feature of embodied selves.

If recognition makes a difference, the degree of a person's psychological continuity may also depend on social circumstances. To return to the case of the model, will her friends and lovers continue to recognize and affirm her? Will she be able to find anyone able to believe her story and hear her out? Anthony Quinton touches optimistically on the first point. 'In our general relations with other human beings their bodies are for the most part intrinsically unimportant. We use them as convenient recognition devices enabling us to locate the persisting characters and memory complexes . . . which we love or like. It would be upsetting if a complex with which we were emotionally involved came to have a monstrous or repulsive physical appearance . . . But that our concern and affection would follow the character and memory complex . . . is surely clear.'[30] Quinton is aware that this may not quite settle the argument, and addresses the looming objection that some personal relations, such as those 'of a rather unmitigatedly sexual type', might not survive a change of body. But here, too, he resolves the problem confidently. 'It can easily be shown that these objections are without substance. In the first place, even the most tired of entrepreneurs is going to take some note of the character and memories of the companion of his later nights at work. He will want her to be docile and quiet, perhaps, and to remember that he takes two parts of water to one of scotch, and no ice . . . As a body she is simply an instrument of a particular type . . .'[31] This solution to the problem employs the strategy we have already examined: it resolutely divides psychological properties from bodily ones and insists that the former are what matter in recognition. The wish to be loved for oneself alone and not for one's golden hair is simply granted. What this solution does not countenance, however, is the possibility that a person's ability to sustain psychological continuity may depend on other people recognizing and affirming the properties and potentialities of their embodied selves, and that where this possibility is removed, their psychological continuity may be damaged.

6 Marginalizing the symbolically feminine

We can now see more clearly that when personal identity theorists specify that characters are transplanted into bodies identical with the ones they had before, they are not introducing innocent simplifications. Instead, they are covering up and discounting ways in which psychological continuity is woven into the histories of our embodied selves. However, this is not the end of the matter. A theorist of personal identity may concede that psychological continuity has to be created, and that in extreme cases such as psychosis it can be destroyed. But he or she may nevertheless maintain that, in all ordinary cases, once psychological continuity is created, it survives. We see this, for example, in the testimony of the victims of extreme and extended trauma. While they may not remember much about their earlier lives, and may now lack well-defined characters, they identify with their past selves and speak about them in the first person (albeit sometimes rather oddly as when they say things like 'I died there' or 'I shall always miss myself as I was then'). We see it, too, in cases of physical mutilation where, although the body image usually takes some time to adjust, people do not lose all sense of who they are.[32] Only in pathological conditions such as psychosis and multiple personality does the self really fragment. So, putting these last cases aside, are we not right to posit a sense of psychological continuity which is independent of both bodily and social vicissitudes, or to imagine that this sense of continuity could survive if a character were transplanted from one body into another?

The arguments I have offered aim to show that, once we strip this imaginary situation of features which function to make it appear unproblematic, the kind of continuity that can be relied on is comparatively attenuated. All we are able to assume is that the transplanted character is able to locate its experiences in its new body, and that it remains sufficiently integrated to claim some memories as its own. We need not assume that it has much emotional investment in its memories. Nor need we assume much continuity of other character traits. Psychological continuity features here as a slender lifeline which enables the transplanted person to say to themselves 'I know that such and such happened to me and that I am so and so' and just about to believe it.

The personal identity theorist must be prepared to argue that this minimal level of continuity is sufficient to sustain the claim that we can fruitfully explore the question of what is involved in survival by playing off bodily and psychological continuity against one another. It seems to me, however, that the attractions of psychological continuity as a separable component of survival have been considerably reduced. Let me labour this point. Before, we were imagining that, transplanted into a new body, I would feel pretty much the same as I do now, would be able to continue the projects I have now, would be no less committed to my future than I am now, would have the memories and characteristics I now possess, and would retain the relations with other people that, so it seems to me, make life worth living. Now we imagine a situation in which it is much less clear what transplant will be like, and in which it may give rise to psychic and physical pain comparable, perhaps, to the pain of torture which looms so large in one of the problem cases constructed by Williams.[33] I may lose many memories and character traits, so that my hold on my own past is tenuous and emotionally numbed, and my grasp of who I now am is fractured and confused. I may lose the affection and even recognition of the people who matter to me, and also the capacity to form new relationships. I may be unable to pursue my projects or embark on new ones, and may have very little emotional investment in the life I am living.

Some theorists of personal identity would, I suspect, insist that as long as there remains a thread of continuity between the pre- and post-transplant selves, we have a case for the conclusion that they are the same person. The barest 'I' is enough to hold the self together and to underwrite an approach to the problem that separates psychological and bodily continuity. But in the light of the sorts of difficulties I have discussed it seems reasonable to ask: Why cling to this doctrine? Why deploy such resources of imagination to prise the bodily and the psychological apart? And why go to such lengths to protect psychological continuity from the effects of the body and the rest of the world?

At this point a reader might object that these questions misrepresent the current debate. Contemporary theorists of personal identity, it might be claimed, are by no means agreed that psychological continuity is essential, or even important, to personhood, and many of their accounts emphasize the centrality of the body. This is undoubtedly true. However, the approach I have been discussing is extremely influential, and continues to shape our understanding of what the problem of personal identity consists in.[34] As long as this much is conceded, the questions I have posed remain pertinent.

Feminists who have addressed these questions have frequently drawn on a conception of the self which is set over against, though not completely irreconcilable with, the view of personal identity we have been examining, insofar as it holds that there is an important aspect of the psyche, the unconscious, which this view neglects. To accept that the unconscious is at work when we philosophize is to accept that the psychological discontinuities so evident in pathological cases are present to some degree in all of us. Some aspects of the self are simply not picked up by accounts which emphasize psychological continuity, and the decision to discount these may itself have unconscious motivations. Taking the unconscious into account, then, feminist philosophers have explained the prominence of views which regard the body as unimportant to identity in various ways. Some have argued for the view that, in European culture, the mind is associated with masculinity and the body with femininity. One term can stand in for, or symbolize, the other. Philosophers (most of them men) have employed these associations. They have assumed (often unconsciously) that personal identity is male identity, and have developed accounts in which the symbolically masculine mind is given priority over the body.[35] Other writers have provided psychological explanations for this downgrading of the symbolically feminine. When male personal identity theorists construct imaginary examples which separate the bodily from the psychological, they resolve in fantasy the always-unresolved conflicts of the Oedipus complex – the separation of a male child from his mother figure, and his subsequent identification with his father. In establishing and maintaining a firm boundary between the maternal body and the paternal mind, they deny their own unconscious desire to be reunited with the mother figure. And in fixing on psychological continuity as the mark of identity, they construct a picture in which masculinity and selfhood coincide.[36] A further aspect of the transplant fantasy also serves to exclude the feminine. By positing fully-fledged persons whose history is irrelevant to the problem at hand, male philosophers imagine for themselves a condition of self-sufficiency, from which their indebtedness to a mother figure, or indeed to anyone else, is excluded.

These two types of explanation (one cultural, the other psychological) have a good deal in common. Both rest on the claim that philosophers (male and female) are themselves psychologically discontinuous, in the commonplace sense that their unconscious fears and desires play a part in determining the way they formulate and argue about problems, and the sorts of arguments they find persuasive, although this is not an aspect of their philosophizing over which they have conscious control. Moreover, both assume that particular associations at work in our culture continue to play a significant part in shaping our philosophical beliefs. According to the first kind of view, symbolic associations help to explain the fact that we privilege some terms over others. According to the second, these symbolic associations are themselves embedded in the psychological processes that form sexual identity.

Over the last two decades, feminist philosophers have amassed a range of evidence for both the explanatory hypotheses I have sketched. However, it remains to ask what internal support we can find for the view that theorists who equate personal identity with psychological continuity are upholding (however unconsciously) a masculine conception of identity. I have assumed, uncontentiously I hope, that we sometimes find clues to the unconscious in questions that hover round the margins of a text, so that when Williams or Noonan allow that transplant from one body into a very different one might be difficult, and then immediately put the problem aside, it is probably worth looking further.[37] I have also assumed – and Williams and Quinton make this explicit – that what they are putting aside here is the issue of sexual identity.[38] To return to the fantasy of character transplant, there are in principle a variety of ways of thinking about the case of a male character transplanted into a female body. Maybe it would be the ideal sex-change operation. Maybe it would condemn the resulting person to the unhappy condition of someone who desperately wants a sex-change operation. Maybe it would produce psychological breakdown. As we have seen, most writers block off exploration of lines of thought like these, which require us to think of the people concerned as embodied, in their investigations of personal identity. Why? Perhaps because they take it that the identity of a person is the identity of a male. Perhaps because an unconscious fear of jeopardizing their sexual identity prevents them from doing so, and helps to direct them towards an approach which brackets the body and concentrates on the mind.

It may be helpful to consider what kinds of criticism I have offered of the view that personal identity consists in psychological continuity. In the preceding sections of this essay I have voiced some objections to this analysis which *can* be assessed independently of any claims about gender as arguments to the effect that authors who appeal to a particular kind of thought experiment rely on an inadequate conception of the self. The limitations of the conception they employ undermine not only the particular conclusions they draw from their thought experiments, but their very approach, which works with an oversimplified conception of memory, neglects the social construction of the self, and is insensitive to the ways in which selves are embodied. At the same time, however, I have claimed that the issue of gender is woven into arguments which rely on fantasies of brain transplant, and to bring this out I have asked what is going on when philosophers advance them. What is being said, explicitly and implicitly, and why? One of the things going on, so I have suggested, is that a symbolically masculine account of identity is being unselfconsciously articulated. A sceptically inclined reader may still wish to ask whether this diagnosis amounts to a criticism beyond those set out in the first part of the chapter. What is wrong with the symbolically masculine account, other than the fact that it suffers from the deficiencies just summarized?

To answer this question, it is helpful to distinguish the type of criticism which pinpoints a particular flaw in a position from the type which indicates the shortcomings of an approach. The diagnosis I have offered is of the latter kind. Its critical force rests on the assumptions that we are in search of philosophical interpretations that answer to our experience and acknowledge the complexity of our lives, and that, in the case of personal identity, part of this complexity lies in sexual identity. Theories which neglect or disavow sexual difference therefore cut themselves off from an important set of issues, and in doing so render themselves philosophically impoverished. To show how this occurs is not, of course, to specify what a feminist analysis of personal identity would be like, or to explore how a focus on sexual difference alters our understanding of the relation between personhood and embodiment, though many of the works cited throughout the chapter undertake these very tasks. My aim has been to articulate some of the features of an analytical approach to personal identity which leave feminist philosophers dissatisfied, and which explain the fact that their work has developed in different directions.

7 Identity and social power

The symbolic gendering of the opposition between body and mind, on which I have so far concentrated, has provided an exceptionally fruitful focus for feminist research. Nevertheless, it is important not to assume too readily that the body always figures as feminine and the mind as masculine,[39] or to take it for granted that gender is exclusively associated with these terms. Some theorists, I have been arguing, locate personal identity in a mind which they interpret as masculine; but there is also evidence that a man's continuing identity is sometimes implicitly understood to depend on his ability to control a woman. Here the issue is not how the 'components' of a person are gendered, but how the relations between people of different sexes bear on the problem of identity. If social relations can secure or destroy continuing identity, as I suggested earlier on, they will provide another area in which identity and gender intertwine.

This motif is central to some works of literature. For example, in Janet Lewis's novella, *The Wife of Martin Guerre*,[40] Martin Guerre leaves his village and family and does not come back. Eight years later he returns – or rather, an impostor arrives, who slips into Guerre's place and takes up the life he had left behind. Some time goes by before Guerre's wife, tortured by the belief that the impostor is not her husband, and that she is an adulteress, confesses her suspicions, and the impostor is brought to trial. Just as judgement is about to be announced, the original Martin Guerre walks into the court room, and the impostor is punished with death. In this narrative, it becomes important to establish the impostor's identity because he is usurping Guerre's sexual rights over his wife, or to put it another way, because Guerre has lost control over her. She is out of his control, and her independence of him is part of what threatens to obliterate Guerre's social identity, insofar as it is one of the conditions that allow the impostor to 'become' him. The trial restores both Guerre's identity and sexual order.

We find the same link between identity and male sexual power in Balzac's story about Colonel Chabert[41] who, when the tale begins, has been listed among the casualties of Napoleon's Russian Campaign. His name has appeared on the list of valiant heroes who sacrificed their lives for France, his wife has remarried, and his house has been sold. But in fact the Colonel has survived, and after several years returns to Paris, determined to reclaim his wife. Once again, loss of identity is linked to loss of control over a woman, and his desire to have his wife back is what drives the Colonel to explain his plight to a young lawyer, who takes up his case and tries to negotiate a settlement. In the course of the negotiations the Colonel comes to see that his wife is a ruthless and avaricious woman who will never return to him, and has never loved him anyway, and renounces his desire to reclaim her. But the recognition that he cannot possess her destroys him, and in the final scene the lawyer comes across him, unkempt and listless, sitting on a log beside the road staring vacantly into space. Here, loss of power over a woman is associated not just with loss of social identity but with psychological discontinuity. To be sure, Colonel Chabert is deprived of his social identity; but he loses more than this, and although the man sitting on the log may know who he is, his discontinuity with his past self prevents him from functioning.

8 Conclusion

When theorists of personal identity focus on psychological continuity as the stronghold of the self, and construe psychological continuity as independent of bodily continuity, they secure only a self which would in other circumstances be regarded as pathologically disturbed. This is, to be sure, a self of sorts, and one consonant with the problem 'What is it to survive?' which already carries connotations of minimal continuity, of enduring against the odds and in the face of obstacles. Perhaps the question we should be addressing, then, is why the analytical philosophical tradition has been so concerned to explore and defend this minimal notion of survival, and hence personhood. Part of the explanation, I have suggested, lies in cultural constructions of masculinity and femininity which are at work in the unconscious, and consequently in philosophy. At the heart of identity lies the issue of sexual identity, and with it the desire of a male-dominated tradition to secure the masculinity of the subject and the subordination of women. This commonplace drama is played out in various philosophical arenas, but is worked through with particular intensity in the problem of identity itself.[42]

NOTES

1   Carolyn Merchant, *The Death of Nature: Women, Ecology and the Scientific Revolution* (San Francisco: Harper & Row; London: Wildwood House, 1980); Elizabeth Spelman, 'Woman as Body: Ancient and Contemporary Views', *Feminist Studies* 8:1 (1982), 109–31; Genevieve Lloyd, *The Man of Reason: 'Male' and 'Female' in Western Philosophy* (London: Methuen, 1984), and 'Maleness, Metaphor and the "Crisis" of Reason', in Louise M. Antony and Charlotte Witt, eds., *A Mind of One's Own. Feminist Essays on Reason and Objectivity* (Boulder, CO: Westview Press, 1993), pp. 69–83; Evelyn Fox Keller, *Reflections on Gender and Science* (New Haven: Yale University Press, 1985); Luce Irigaray, *An Ethics of Sexual Difference*, trans. Carolyn Burke and Gillian C. Gill (Ithaca: Cornell University Press, 1985); Michèle Le Dœuff, *The Philosophical Imaginary* (London: Athlone, 1980); Tina Chanter, *Ethics of Eros: Irigaray's Rewriting of the Philosophers* (London: Routledge, 1995); Penelope Deutscher, *Yielding Gender: Feminism, Deconstruction and the History of Philosophy* (London: Routledge, 1997).
2   Sharon Sullivan, 'Domination and Dialogue in Merleau-Ponty's *Phenomenology of Perception*', *Hypatia* 12:1 (1997), 1–19; Judith Butler, 'Sexual Ideology and Phenomenological Description: A Feminist Critique of Merleau-Ponty's Phenomenology of Perception', in Jeffner Allen and Iris Marion Young, eds., *The Thinking Muse: Feminism and Modern French Philosophy* (Bloomington: Indiana University Press, 1989), pp. 85–100; Iris Marion Young, 'Throwing Like a Girl: A Phenomenology of Feminine Body Comportment, Motility, and Spatiality', in *Throwing Like a Girl and Other Essays in Feminist*

Philosophy and Social Theory (Bloomington: Indiana University Press, 1990), pp. 141–59.

3 Juliet Mitchell, *Psychoanalysis and Feminism* (Harmondsworth: Penguin, 1974); Jane Gallop, *Feminism and Psychoanalysis* (London: Macmillan, 1982).

4 Nancy Chodorow, *The Reproduction of Mothering* (Berkeley: University of California Press, 1978); Dorothy Dinnerstein, *The Mermaid and the Minotaur* (New York: Harper and Row), published in the UK under the title *The Rocking of the Cradle and the Ruling of the World* (London: Souvenir Press, 1978); Teresa Brennan, ed., *Between Feminism and Psychoanalysis* (London: Routledge, 1989) and *The Interpretation of the Flesh. Freud and Femininity* (Routledge: London, 1992); Jessica Benjamin, *The Bonds of Love: Psychoanalysis, Feminism and the Problem of Domination* (London: Virago, 1990); Elizabeth Grosz, *Jacques Lacan: A Feminist Introduction* (London: Routledge, 1990). There is a list of Further Reading in Feminism and Psychoanalysis at p. 266.

5 Luce Irigaray, *Speculum of the Other Woman*, trans. Gillian C. Gill (Ithaca: Cornell University Press, 1974); Margaret Whitford, *Luce Irigaray. Philosophy in the Feminine* (London: Routledge, 1991); Julia Kristeva, *Black Sun. Depression and Melancholia*, trans. Leon S. Roudiez (New York: Columbia University Press, 1989); Kelly Oliver, ed., *The Portable Kristeva* (New York: Columbia University Press, 1997).

6 Rosi Braidotti, *Patterns of Dissonance* (Cambridge: Polity Press, 1991); Elizabeth Grosz, *Volatile Bodies* (Bloomington: Indiana University Press, 1994); Moira Gatens, *Imaginary Bodies* (London: Routledge, 1996); Christine Battersby, *The Phenomenal Woman* (Cambridge: Polity Press, 1998).

7 Simone de Beauvoir, *The Second Sex*, trans. and ed. H. M. Parshley (Harmondsworth: Penguin, 1972); Toril Moi, *Simone de Beauvoir: The Making of an Intellectual Woman* (Oxford: Blackwell, 1994); Ann Oakley, *Sex, Gender and Society* (London: Temple Smith, 1972); Judith Butler, *Gender Trouble: Feminism and Subversion of Identity* (London: Routledge, 1990) and *Bodies that Matter: On the Discursive Limits of Sex* (London: Routledge, 1993); Gatens, *Imaginary Bodies*; Evelyn Fox Keller, 'Gender and Science: An Update', in *Secrets of Life, Secrets of Death: Essays on Language, Gender and Science* (New Haven: Yale University Press, 1985).

8 Alison Jaggar, 'Love and Knowledge: Emotion in Feminist Epistemology', in A. Garry and M. Pearsall, eds., *Women, Knowledge and Reality: Exploration in Feminist Philosophy*, 2nd edition (London: Routledge, 1996), pp. 166–90.

9 Sandra Lee Bartky, 'Shame and Gender', in *Feminity and Domination: Studies in the Phenomenology of Oppression* (London: Routledge, 1990), pp. 83–98; Naomi Scheman, 'Anger and the Politics of Naming', in *Engenderings: Constructions of Knowledge, Authority and Privilege* (London and New York: Routledge, 1993), pp. 22–35; Elizabeth Spelman, 'Anger and Subordination', in Garry and Pearsall, eds., *Women, Knowledge and Reality* 1st edition, pp. 263–73; Sue Campbell, *Interpreting the Personal: Expression and the Formation of Feelings* (Ithaca: Cornell University Press, 1997).

10 See for example Rosi Braidotti, *Nomadic Subjects* (New York: Columbia University Press, 1994); Butler, *Gender Trouble*; Gatens, *Imaginary Bodies*; Grosz, *Volatile Bodies*; Young, *Throwing like a Girl*.

11 See for example S. Shoemaker, 'Personal Identity, A Materialist View', in S. Shoemaker and R. Swinburne, *Personal Identity* (Oxford: Blackwell, 1984); Bernard Williams, 'The Self and the Future', *Philosophical Review* 79 (1970), 161–80, reprinted in *Problems of the Self* (Cambridge: Cambridge University Press, 1973), pp. 46–63; Derek Parfit, *Reasons and Persons* (Oxford: Clarendon Press, 1984); David Lewis, 'Survival and Identity', in *Philosophical Papers* vol. 1 (Oxford: Oxford University Press, 1983).

12 For a recent work which aims to recast this framework, see Marya Schechtman, *The Constitution of Selves* (Ithaca: Cornell University Press, 1996).

13 Parfit, 'Personal Identity', *Philosophical Review* 80 (1971), pp. 3–27; see also his *Reasons and Persons* (Oxford: Clarendon Press, 1984).

14 See for example S. Shoemaker, *Self-Knowledge and Self-Identity* (Ithaca: Cornell University Press, 1963); Williams, 'The Self and the Future'. For further discussion, see the articles collected in H. Noonan ed., *Personal Identity*, International Research Library of Philosophy (Aldershot: Dartmouth Publishing Company, 1993).

15 See for example David Wiggins, 'Locke, Butler and the Stream of Consciousness: and Men as a Natural Kind', *Philosophy* 51 (1976), 131–58; Parfit, *Reasons and Persons*.

16 See for example Shoemaker's example in Shoemaker and Swinburne, *Personal Identity*, pp. 108–11.

17 Williams, 'The Self and the Future', p. 46.

18 B. Williams, 'Personal Identity and Individuation', in *Problems of the Self*, pp. 11–12.

19 Harold Noonan, *Personal Identity* (London: Routledge, 1989), p. 4.

20 A. Quinton, 'The Soul', in J. Perry, ed., *Personal Identity* (Berkeley: University of California Press, 1975), p. 60.

21 Lewis, 'Survival and Identity', p. 56.

22 Noonan, *Personal Identity*, p. 13. See also Parfit, *Reasons and Persons*, p. 205.

23 Susan J. Brison, 'Outliving Oneself: Trauma, Memory and Personal Identity', in D. Tietjens Meyers, ed., *Feminists Rethink the Self* (Boulder, CO: Westview Press, 1997), pp. 12–39. Sections 4 and 5 of this chapter are deeply indebted to this article. For discussion of some closely related issues, see Sue Campbell, 'Women, "False Memory" and Personal Identity', *Hypatia* 12.2 (1997), pp. 51–62.

24 See for example Moira Gatens, 'Woman and Her Double(s)', in *Imaginary Bodies*, pp. 29–45; Grosz, *Volatile Bodies*, pp. 62–85. For a useful discussion of ways in which the notion of a body image is used, see Brian O'Shaughnessy, 'Proprioception and the Body Image', in J. L. Bermudez, N. Eilan and A. Marcel, eds., *The Body and the Self* (Cambridge, MA: MIT Press, 1995).

25 Jacques Lacan, *Ecrits* (London: Tavistock, 1977); Grosz, *Jacques Lacan: A Feminist Introduction*; Bice Benvenuto and Roger Kennedy, *The Works of Jacques Lacan: An Introduction* (London: Free Association Books, 1986).

26 For a non-psychoanalytic treatment of this theme, see Annette Baier, 'Mixing Memory and Desire', in *Postures of the Mind* (London: Methuen, 1985).

27 Charlotte Delbo, *Days and Memory*, trans. Rosette C. Lamont (New Haven: Yale University Press, 1985). Quoted by Brison, 'Outliving Oneself', p. 19.

28 Ibid., p. 21.

29 Elizabeth Grosz, *Volatile Bodies*, pp. 76–7.
30 Quinton, 'The Soul', p. 64.
31 Ibid., pp. 65–6.
32 See, for example, the discussion of phantom limbs in Paul Schilder, *The Image and Appearance of the Human Body* (New York: International Universities Press, 1978), p. 64.
33 Williams, 'The Self and the Future', pp. 48ff.
34 With some exceptions – see for example the animalist views defended in Eric Olson, *The Human Animal: Personal Identity without Psychology* (Oxford: Oxford University Press, 1997) and Paul Snowdon, 'Persons, Animals and Bodies', in J. L. Bermudez, N. Eilan and A. Marcel, eds., *The Body and the Self* (Cambridge, MA: MIT Press, 1995) – even philosophers who do not regard psychological continuity as essential to personal identity continue to treat the body as a container for the mind.
35 See for example Lloyd, *The Man of Reason*; Spelman, 'Woman as Body'.
36 There are several variants of this view. For discussion of Freud, see Juliet Mitchell, *Psychoanalysis and Feminism* and Jane Gallop, *Feminism and Psychoanalysis*; on object relations theory, see Benjamin, *The Bonds of Love*; and for the view that these patterns of development are to be explained by child-rearing practices, see Chodorow, *The Reproduction of Mothering*.
37 For discussion of this view, see Le Dœuff, *The Philosophical Imaginary*; Deutscher, *Yielding Gender*.
38 At the same time, they are implicitly putting aside other dimensions of identity, for instance racial identity, which may be intimately connected to the body.
39 For a particularly helpful discussion of these instabilities, see Deutscher, *Yielding Gender*.
40 Janet Lewis, *The Wife of Martin Guerre* (Harmondsworth: Penguin, 1977). Originally published 1941.
41 Honoré de Balzac, *Le Colonel Chabert*, ed. M. Didier (Paris: Société des textes français modernes, 1961).
42 Many helpful comments were made on an earlier draft of this essay. I am grateful to the contributors to a conference on Feminism and the Philosophy of Mind held at the University of London; to the Philosophy Department seminars at University College Dublin and at the University of York; and to John Dupré, Miranda Fricker, Jennifer Hornsby, Moira Gatens, Kathleen Lennon, Quentin Skinner and Catherine Wilson.

3

NAOMI SCHEMAN

Feminism in philosophy of mind
Against physicalism

We talk of processes and states and leave their nature undecided. Sometime perhaps we shall know more about them we think. But that is just what commits us to a particular way of looking at the matter. For we have a definite concept of what it means to learn to know a process better. (The decisive movement in the conjuring trick has been made, and it was the very one we thought quite innocent.) – And now the analogy which was to make us understand our thoughts falls to pieces. So we have to deny the yet uncomprehended process in the yet unexplored medium. And now it looks as if we had denied mental processes. And naturally we don't want to deny them.

> Ludwig Wittgenstein, *Philosophical Investigations* 308

When I do not see plurality stressed in the very structure of a theory, I know that I will have to do lots of acrobatics – like a contortionist or tight-rope walker – to have this theory speak to me without allowing the theory to distort me in my complexity.

> María Lugones, 'On the Logic of Pluralist Feminism'

Introduction

For most contemporary analytic philosophers, the physical sciences are the lodestone both for epistemology and for ontology; other ways of knowing and other ways of saying what there is have somehow to be squared with what physics might come to say. In the philosophy of mind, central problems arise from the difficulties in accounting for the phenomena of consciousness (in Thomas Nagel's terms 'what it's like to be' a subject of experience), and from the apparent intractability (compared, say, to chemistry or even biology) of psychological explanations. This sense that – both ontologically and epistemologically – something distinctively mental would be unaccounted for, after physics had accounted for everything it could, has often been taken to motivate dualism: the mental is left over after the physical is accounted for just as (though, of course, not nearly so unproblematically) the forks are left over after the spoons are accounted for.

Feminists have been critical of dualism in part for its implicit if not explicit privileging of the mind over the body and for the misunderstanding of each that results from their being prised apart. Such criticisms remain apt, as Susan James argues in her chapter here, even in relation to accounts that, while metaphysically non-dualist, nonetheless continue to prise the mental apart from the physical, by abstracting such phenomena as memory from their attachment to (better: their realization in) specific, socially embedded bodies. But if dualism has been unappealing to feminists, its usual alternative – physicalism – has seemed to many an unpalatable alternative, in large measure because the sort of attention to bodies that, for example, James encourages is not the attention of the scientist to an object of study, but the attention of a subject to her or his own experience, as well as the attention of diversely engaged others.[1]

Feminists' work on topics such as the emotions, the nature of the self and of personal identity, and the relations between minds and bodies can seem irrelevant to the issues that concern physicalists: the starting points, the puzzles and perplexities that call for theorizing, seem quite different. I want to argue that the appearance of irrelevance is misleading: while it is true that feminist theorists are asking different questions and thereby avoiding direct answers to the questions posed in the literature around physicalism, the reorientation of attention characteristic of the feminist questions usefully reframes the problems that vex that literature – problems of accounting for ourselves as physical beings in the world. In particular, what comes to be crucial in accounting for psychological explanation are the ways in which such explanations are irreducibly *social*, a 'problem' to which dualism is an entirely irrelevant response. Understanding our emotions, beliefs, attitudes, desires, intentions and the like (including how it is that they can cause and be caused by happenings in the physical world) is akin to understanding families, universities, wars, elections, economies and religious schisms: positing some special sort of substance out of which such things are made would hardly help, nor does it seem metaphysically spooky that there is no way, even in principle, of specifying, on the level of physics, just what they *are* made of. (The university buildings count, but what about the dirt on their floors? If we count the faculty, do we count the food in their stomachs?)

Consider the performance of a piece of music. There is nothing going on *in addition to* the physical movements of the bodies of the members of the orchestra, but there is no way, appealing just to physics, to specify which of those movements are parts of the complex event that is the performance and which are not. What is and is not part of the event has to do with what sort of thing a performance is, what norms and expectations determine what its parts are. For example, the first violinist's coughing is not typically part of the performance, but it certainly can be – if, for example, it's written into the score. When it comes to identifying the performance as a cause, there are two very different possibilities. To say, for example, that the performance caused a crack in the ceiling is to say that there are physical events more or less loosely associated with the performance that caused the cracking, but the performance *per se* is not among them (that certain sounds are part of the performance is irrelevant to whether they contributed to causing the crack). If, by contrast, as with the premiere in Paris of Stravinsky's *Le Sacre du printemps*, the performance caused a riot, its being a musical performance (something about which the audience had certain expectations) is crucial: in this case the performance *per se* was the cause, but not as a physical event, since it is not one. To say that a performance is not a physical event is not to embrace some odd form of dualism; it is to acknowledge that, from the perspective of physics, the performance is not a particular complex event – one whose (physical) cause and effects we can inquire into – but rather an inchoate jumble of events. Performances are 'socially constructed', meaning that their integrity as particulars is dependent on sets of social practices that make them meaningful wholes.

It is not, of course, at all clear how to relate social explanations to physical ones: the relationships between the social and physical sciences are deeply vexed. But the problems are importantly different from those that have engaged the philosophy of mind, less likely to provoke the a prioristic metaphysical demands that characterize the discussions of physicalism, however empirical those discussions are meant to be. What I want to suggest is this: in explaining ourselves to ourselves and to each other we allude to such things as beliefs, intentions, emotions, desires and attitudes. Physicalism consists in the claim (specified and argued for in a wide range of very different ways) that, insofar as these explanations are true, the events, states, and processes to which they refer must be identical with or somehow dependent upon or determined by events, states and processes in or of the body of the person to whom they are attributed. Such a claim is neither required for nor supported by empirical research that shows how it is that, for example, emotional responses are related to changes in brain chemistry. Surely how we act and feel has enormously to do with what goes on in our bodies, but recognizing that fact no more supports the claims of physicalists than recognizing the importance of physiology to the carrying out of the actions that constitute a performance or a riot would support the claim that physiology explains why the premiere of *Le Sacre du printemps* caused a riot. The performance as such does not survive abstraction from social context, and neither do its causal powers: its 'realness' and its causal efficacy are dependent in part on its being the socially meaningful type of thing that it is. Similarly, I will argue, beliefs, desires, emotions and other phenomena of our mental lives are the particulars that they are because they are socially meaningful, and when they figure as those particulars in causal accounts, neither those accounts nor the phenomena that figure in them survive abstraction from social context.

Most of those working in the philosophy of mind today subscribe to one or another of the dizzyingly many varieties of physicalism. They share a demand for the mental to be composed of, or determined by, the physical – however differently they work out the details – in some way that attributes to mental phenomena not only continuity with the physical but also the sort of reality that the physical is presumed to have, including independence from our practices of noticing and naming. The failure of such independence, the possibility that much of what we talk about when we talk about our mental lives – our beliefs, emotions, desires, attitudes, intentions and such – do not exist as determinate physical 'somethings', is thought to undermine the possibility of taking such talk seriously, of taking it to be part of a true account of what there is in the world. It is here that feminist discussions both in the philosophy of mind and in seemingly remote areas can shed light, since they lead us to see the importance and the possibility of holding on *both* to the idea that our mental lives are constituted in part by the ways we collectively talk and think about them, *and* to the idea that such talking and thinking are not arbitrary and that the realm of the mental is no less real for being in this sense 'made up'.

Disputes among feminist theorists frequently take the following form: theorists of type A argue against the appeal to absolute standards of truth or rightness that exist in abstraction from our lives and practices, on the grounds that such appeals reflect a suspicion of plurality and diversity and a disdain for that which is local, particular, contextual, contingent, embedded and embodied; while theorists of type B argue for the importance of standards of truth or rightness that are independent of what people happen to do or say, on the grounds that what most people happen to do and say – expert discourses and common sense alike – is prone to sexist and other forms of bias, and that we need a more compelling response than simply that we don't like it. Thus arise the debates between universalists and particularists in ethics, essentialists and social constructionists in gender and sexuality theory, empiricists and postmodernists in philosophy of science, objectivists and relativists in epistemology. The tendentious nature of all those labels reflects the divisiveness of the disputes, a divisiveness that obscures the fact that for many of us the disputes are internal to any position we might occupy. They are, I want to suggest, better thought of as necessary tensions, as reminders of the theoretical and political importance *both* of attention to diversity and particularity *and* of non-arbitrary, rationally defensible justification.[2]

One way of characterizing the disputes is as between the suspicion of and the demand for some special kind of thing, which answers to our needs precisely by being independent of them, by being what it is – Reality or the Good, the essence of something or the measure of an argument – no matter what we might think or do. Such disputes are not, of course, peculiar to feminist theory: they are arguably at the heart of the problems of modern philosophy, where, however, they tend to be treated as purely intellectual puzzles. In their feminist articulations, they reanimate the very practical urgency that gave birth to them – in the turmoil of early modernity, out of the need to ground the claims to truth and rightness being made by upstart rebels against the prevailing standards of a theocratic and aristocratic social order. As part of those struggles it was necessary to articulate new conceptions of the nature of persons and their states, the subject matter of the philosophy of mind. Feminist perspectives at this late stage of modernity throw into relief the historical specificity of those projects of articulation – for example, the field-defining epic struggle between the self as subject of inner experience, abstracted from the surrounding world (even, supposedly, from its own body) and the body as object of scientific scrutiny.

Feminist perspectives shift attention to understanding persons as both bodily and social, and knowledge as interpersonal and interactive. Physicalism then appears not so much false as empty: ontologically, it puzzles over how to establish a relationship – whether of identity or of some form of supervenience (see discussion below) – between what ought not to have been analytically distinguished in the first place; and epistemologically, it concedes to (a philosopher's fantasy of) physics a dominating role even over explanatory schemes explicitly being argued to be non-reducible to it. To reject physicalism is not, as Wittgenstein says, to deny anything – not anything, that is, by way of actual investigation into or explanation of how our experienced lives are shaped by our being the bodies that we are. What is denied is the demand that such explanations have either to underwrite or to supplant the accounts of those lives that rest on appeal to the social practices and norms that make us the persons that we are.

The demands of physicalism

Jennifer Hornsby, in a series of articles going back to 1980 and collected in her book, *Simple Mindedness*, argues against the ontological foundations of physicalist theses. One of the central targets of these arguments is what she identifies as 'mereological conceptions' of the objects in an ontology, according to which relatively big objects can be identified with the unique 'fusion' of the smaller objects – their parts – which make them up. [3] John Dupré similarly identifies mereological conceptions as at the heart of what he finds problematic about physicalism (or any requirement of a unified account of diverse phenomena).[4] Both these authors see themselves as blocking at some very early stage a frequently unvoiced argumentative move that not only licenses a range of diverse positions but frames the arguments between them. Such a move, if noticed at all, can seem obvious, unavoidable: avoiding it can seem like being committed to something like a soul, a mysterious addition to the physical stuff that constitutes the goings on in and of our bodies.[5]

Supervenience theses most explicitly mobilize this picture, since, unlike other physicalist theses, they typically are mute about actual explanation and insistent on what are taken to be the requirements on the possibility of any explanations at all. Consider the following:

> We think of the world around us not as a mere assemblage of objects, events, and facts, but as constituting a system, something that shows structure, and whose constituents are connected with one another in significant ways . . . Central to this idea of interconnectedness of things is a notion of dependence (or its converse, determination): things are connected with one another in that whether something exists, or what properties it has, is dependent on, or determined by, what other things exist and what kinds of things they are . . . Activities like explanation, prediction, and control would make little sense for a world devoid of such connections. The idea that 'real connections' exist and the idea that the world is intelligible and controllable are arguably an equivalent idea.[6]

This paragraph is the start of an essay in which Jaegwon Kim lays out a range of supervenience theses.[7] He goes on to argue for the strongest among them, on the grounds that only it can meet the demands he lays out here. The demands themselves, however, are widely accepted among physicalists, including those who believe they can be met by some form of non-reductive supervenience, much weaker than the reductionism Kim promotes. The paragraph perfectly accomplishes the slide from saying something quite ordinary to being in the grip of a picture, one that leads us to lay down requirements on what the world, or our accounts of the world, *must* be like.[8] The argument is a transcendental one: given that explanation is possible, what *must* be the case? The appeal is to (what is taken to be) explanation *per se*, not to the details of particular explanations or explanatory practices. Later in the same essay, in fact, Kim explicitly argues for the importance of separating metaphysical from epistemological considerations: the mental can be said to be determined by the physical whether or not we ever could be in a position to provide the explanations that determinacy underwrites.[9] The picture (and on this point there is wide agreement with Kim) is that physicalism provides the ontological grounds for the possibility of mental explanations, however autonomous or irreducible such explanations might be argued to be.

A linchpin of Kim's arguments to the conclusion that attempts at non-reductive supervenience are doomed is what he calls the principle of 'causal closure': 'If we trace the causal ancestry of a physical event, we need never go outside the physical domain.'[10] Davidson and Fodor, among many others, explicitly commit themselves to essentially this principle (though they disagree with Kim as to its consequences), and it is one Hornsby and Dupré, among others, have challenged. I am persuaded by those challenges, but want, for the purpose of this chapter, largely to bracket that issue and focus instead on the question of ontology. In the passage quoted from Kim, he refers repeatedly to 'things', as in 'things that happen', and at the start of the passage he refers to 'objects, events, and facts'. For his argument to work, such 'things' need to be related in ways that exhibit structure, they depend on and determine each other, their 'real connections' are what make the world intelligible.[11] One of my central arguments is that taking commonsense psychology seriously is to be committed *not* to a theoretically vexing ontology of objects (mental events, states and processes), but rather to practices, explanation among them, and to the nuances of our lives as shaped and made intelligible through those practices.

For Kim, as for some others, notably Davidson, the 'things' in question are pre-eminently events, and there are long arguments between them and others as to what it is that events are. Beyond those arguments lies an even murkier ontological swamp – the 'states and processes' that usually get appended to the list of mental phenomena.[12] Any physicalist theory is going to have to say something about the ontology of swamp-dwellers – something that provides a way, in theory at least, of individuating the contents of the swamp independently of the norm-laden, interpretive social practices that characterize commonsense psychology. Those 'things' have to be individuated in ways that suit their role in the properly physical causal accounts in which they are thought to have to figure if common sense is to be scientifically vindicated. Issues about individuation often slip by, as 'the initial move in the conjuring trick', the assumption that mental events, states, and processes are particulars whose nature can be investigated: we can ask what *they* are, whether *they* are identical with or constituted by physical events, states, and processes, and how *they* enter into causal relationships.

When Robert Wilson, in a careful and detailed account of individualism in the philosophy of mind, says that anti-individualist arguments have concerned taxonomic rather than instantial individuation, he is, I think, right. Wilson suggests that one cannot ask whether A is the same as B (a question of instantial individuation) without asking what sorts of things A and B are taken to be (a taxonomic question).[13] Davidson's anomalous monism exploits the idea that the framework of space-time can provide for material objects, and the framework of causation can provide for events, a way of individuating that doesn't depend on any *finer* taxonomizing. That solution is, however, ultimately question-begging, in its assumption that, in particular in the case of events, the presumptively closed and complete system of physical causation individuates all the events that there are.[14] As my example of the performance was meant to suggest, this assumption is deeply problematic, amounting to what Davidson and other non-reductive physicalists are committed to denying – that the explanatory system within which the performance exists as a particular complex event (in terms of which we can make sense of what's part of it and what isn't) can ultimately be reduced to (or otherwise explicated in terms of) physics. If it can't be – if, in general, the discourses with respect to which we understand performances, or our mental lives, can't be systematically connected to physics – then the objects that are constituted in its terms will not be *any* sorts of physical objects, since, with respect to physics, they will have the status not of complex objects but of incoherent jumbles or heaps – certainly not the sorts of things to enter as particulars into nomological causal relationships.

The useful vacuity of global supervenience

Nothing happens in the world, not the flutter of an eyelid, not the flicker of a thought, without some redistribution of microphysical states.
W.V. Quine, *Theories and Things*

. . . a thesis of such blinding epistemological vacuity as to add nothing to the thesis of the nonexistence of the immaterial
John Dupré, 'Metaphysical Disorder and Scientific Disunity'

Global supervenience, which is frequently criticized as both excessively permissive and explanatorily opaque, has a role for theorists like Dupré and Hornsby in making the point that the denial of the existence of immaterial stuff does not commit one to physicalism.[15] As such it is proffered not as a positive thesis but as a way of granting the falsehood of dualism and of articulating the minimal truth of physicalism (so minimal as not to count as physicalism on the terms of most physicalists). Thus Dupré says: 'if one removed from the universe all the physical entities . . . there would be nothing left.'[16] Global supervenience has been formalized by John Haugeland, though that is not his term for it. (He calls it 'weak supervenience', which for most authors in this terminologically confusing literature refers to something quite else, involving a different parameter of variation among theses from the one that concerns me here.) Haugeland's formulation (replacing his use of 'weakly' with 'globally') is: 'K *globally supervenes on L* (relative to W) just in case any two worlds in W discernible with K are discernible with L.' (K and L are languages, W is a set of possible worlds. For present purposes let L be the language of microphysics and K be the language of commonsense psychology.)[17]

Global supervenience captures the idea that if anything happens at all, something has to happen on the level of microphysics. If everywhere and for all of time all the microparticles (or whatever microphysics turns out to be about) were exactly as they in fact are, then nothing *else* could be any different. What is important to note is just how weak this thesis is. It does not imply token identities. (Haugeland in fact proposes it explicitly as an alternative to token identities, which, he argues, fail for cases far less complex than the mental.)[18] Nor does it imply that supervening (e.g., mental) events are 'determined by' or 'dependent upon' physical events – an implication that is crucial for what most theorists want out of a supervenience principle and partly definitive of what is meant by 'physicalism'.[19]

The point of calling global supervenience 'global' is to stress (what 'serious' supervenience theorists find problematic) that there need be no spatial or temporal contiguity between a difference on the supervening level and a difference in the supervenience base. A difference in my mental state need not be correlated with a difference in my body or in anything near or causally connected to my body,[20] nor must there be a physically describable difference simultaneous with or prior to the mental difference. All that matters is that there be some difference, even if far away and long ago or even yet to come. Such laxity is frequently expressed as a (supposed) reductio: Post calls it ARFL, the 'argument from licentiousness'.[21] But whether such laxness counts for or against global supervenience ought to depend on what sorts of connections one thinks there actually are. It is a feature, for example, of many of our ordinary psychological terms that whether they truly apply can be a genuinely open question with respect to everything, known or unknown, in the present or the past, but become retroactively settled by something in the future.

It is, of course, precisely features of commonsense psychology such as this that many psychologists and philosophers of psychology will want to 'clean up', in part by imposing constraints on what can belong in the supervenience base. But such constraints have nothing to do with avoiding substance dualism and ought to reflect, rather than dictate, ordinary judgements of explanatory adequacy. One may, for example, believe that the best (most explanatory, most nearly true) accounts of love include this feature: that ascriptions of it remain, up to a certain point (as Aristotle argued for happiness) hostage to the future. Up to that point it can be indeterminate, to be settled by how things go on, whether or not one's feelings are really love.[22] And if one thinks that, then one will, for reasons having to do with explanatory adequacy, reject a restriction of the supervenience base to the present and past. A common move at this point is to posit some state that, it is claimed, does supervene on the person's current physical state – as, for example, the notion of narrow content was developed to try to deal with arguments about the non-individualist nature of propositional attitudes. But if, as I will argue below, our beliefs, attitudes, desires, and so on are explanatory – e.g., have the causes and effects that they do – in virtue of their being socially meaningful, then such posits will lose their point, which is precisely their supposed explanatory role.

Thus, the 'licentiousness' that physicalists deplore in global supervenience – the fact that it licenses neither token identities nor theses of determination or dependency – is part of its appeal – not because anything goes, but because the question of what goes and what doesn't cannot, and should not, be settled *a priori*. Kim charges adherents to global supervenience with accepting it as 'a mere article of faith seriously lacking in motivation both evidentially and explanatorily';[23] but as I am appealing to it, it no more requires either evidence or explanatory usefulness than does my non-belief in imperceptible and causally inert fairies. The work that appears to be done by physicalist theses – including reductionism, eliminativism, functionalism, and token identity theses – is actually done by complex and diverse explanations, including explanations that may be locally reductive. We may in particular areas have well-founded expectations for one or another sort of explanation, but those expectations do not rest on, nor are the successes explained by or evidence for, any metaphysical theses such as physicalism in any of its forms. The unmotivated act of faith is, thus, on the part of the physicalists, who not only have boundless and groundless faith in the explanatory powers of some unimaginably remote

Future Physics, but who are willing to sacrifice common sense (as well as real science) on its altar, placing ontological requirements on the objects of explanation in advance of working out what those explanations are.

Taking explanation seriously

> How could human behaviour be described? Surely only by sketching the actions of a variety of humans, as they are all mixed up together. What determines our judgement, our concepts and reactions, is not what one is doing now, an individual action, but the whole hurly-burly of human actions, the background against which we see any action.
>
> Wittgenstein, *Zettel* 167

If we actually look at psychological explanations – in particular, if we attend to the aspects of those explanations that lead functionalists and Davidsonian anomalous monists, among others, to reject the reductionism of type-identity theories – we find that the phenomena that give such explanations their explanatory force cannot be identified with, or be determined by, particular physical phenomena, for two general, related sorts of reasons. First, the anomalousness of psychological explanations entails that the phenomena that figure in them cannot be presumed to satisfy the constraints on being a physical particular, and will, in fact, typically fairly obviously *fail* to satisfy such constraints, however loosely conceived. And second, in many cases in which psychological explanations *can* be seen to rest in some sense on physical goings-on, such 'supervenience' is on happenings that are sufficiently scattered and remote in space and time as to defeat any general, substantive claim of determining supervenience. The irreducibility of psychological explanation is inherited by psychological ontology: we have no grip on what the phenomena of psychology are other than whatever they have to be for psychological explanations to be true.[24] In general, our ordinary explanations of human action, thought, and feeling appeal to social practices and norms; and there is no reason to require, and much reason to deny, that our *best* explanations will be compatible with an ontology whose objects' individuation is independent of the social and the normative.

I want to urge an understanding of socially constructed phenomena that has close connections with understandings, such as those of John Dupré, Ian Hacking and Michael Root, of socially constructed kinds.[25] Such kinds can figure in explanation, even causal explanation. Consider:

1. Q: Why didn't Alex get a heart attack when she was younger?
    A: Because she's a woman.

2. Q: Why didn't Alex become CEO of the corporation?
   A: Because she's a woman.
3. Q: Why does Alex use the toilet marked with a stick figure with a triangle in its middle?
   A: Because she's a woman.

In the first exchange, referring to Alex's being a woman points in the direction of some physiological property that accounts for her having been less at risk of a heart attack. 'Woman' need not be a biologically real kind; gender can be (as many feminist theorists have argued) socially constructed, perhaps to be distinguished from sex, which some have argued *is* biologically real. The explanation works by gesturing toward something both causally related to the risk of heart attacks and typically true of those in the social category 'woman', though by no means true of all women (like, for example, the currently suspected property in question, namely, the presence of relatively high levels of oestrogen). The answer in the second exchange is explanatory, by contrast, because of the social significance of the category 'woman'; thus, it might function as a cautionary admonition to a biological male contemplating sex change. Not only does this explanation give us no reason to attribute biological reality to the category 'woman', but any biological category that might be proposed would inevitably lead to a 'cleaning up' around the edges that would hurt rather than help explanations such as this one (whereas explanations like the first, while useful as they stand, would be helped by replacing the social category with the relevant biological one, if any). The third exchange is explanatory in a rather different sense. It notes a connection between gender and segregated public toilets, and what exactly is being explained is a matter of what the questioner can be presumed not to know or to understand: it might, for example, explicate the meaning of the international sign for 'women's toilet', or it might be a reply, albeit a somewhat impatient one, to someone who finds Alex's womanhood questionable, perhaps because, unlike the stick figure, Alex does not wear skirts.

Mental phenomena can be real in the same sort of way. Through our social practices we interpret as meaningful bits of experience that may well be related in significant, non-social ways (as people who share a race or a gender will typically be similar or otherwise related in many non-social ways). But those relationships are not such as to constitute particular entities of any sort. That constitution is done by our finding and acting on patterns of salience, interpreting ourselves and each other, and having and acting on expectations formed in the light of those interpretations. As feminists have argued, for example, not just anyone can be angry at any time, since part of what constitutes the pattern that counts as anger has to do with who you are and whom you might be thought to be angry at, about what, and so on.[26] It was easier not to notice this fact when theorizing was in the hands of those who were less likely to run up against the limits of intelligibility and who, when they did, had little reason to see their failure to make sense as anything other than an idiosyncratic glitch. (Similarly, noticing the social constructedness of gender was greatly helped by the experiences of those, such as transsexuals, whose identities were, according to the biologically naturalized view of gender, literally impossible.)

Consider the following explanations:

1a. Q: Why did her blood pressure shoot up?
     A: It must have been because she got angry.
2a. Q: Why did he fire her?
     A: It must have been because she got angry.
3a. Q: Why do they think she hates men?
     A: It must be because she got angry.

The first and second examples offer causal explanations and would seem to call for an account of her getting angry that indicates how it can cause something in her body, or some piece of his behaviour. By analogy with the first set of examples, however, neither 1a nor 2a supports the idea that her getting angry is (or supervenes on or is determined by) some particular physical event(s). In 1a we can adequately account for the explanatoriness of A while taking anger to be a socially salient pattern of behaviour, thoughts and bodily feelings – once we note that the feelings typical of getting angry are correlated with sorts of bodily tension that can cause a rise in blood pressure. Particular emotions are more or less closely associated with bodily feeling (anger more closely than happiness, less closely than rage), and the nature of such associations is one of the ways in which cultures differ in their emotional repertoires, explanations and styles.[27] What is important to note – just as with explaining the ceiling crack by blaming the performance or explaining Alex's lesser vulnerability to heart attack by her being a woman – is that as we move toward the more physically explanatory, getting angry *per se* drops out; what matters is the tension, not what the tension means.

In 2a, by contrast, her getting angry (that it's angry that she got) does not drop out of the explanation – any more than the performance drops out of the explanation of the riot or Alex's being a woman drops out of the explanation of her not being promoted. He fired her because of what he took anger to mean and because of his views about its (in)appropriateness for a woman. In Davidsonian terms, we can put the point by saying that the anomalousness of psychological explanation is inherited by psychological ontology. The normative, interpretive element in psychological explanation enters into the construction of psychological phenomena. No more physicalistically respectable phenomenon could play the causal role getting angry plays in this explanation (as getting tense plays such a role in 1a), since abstracting from the social constructedness means abstracting from the context-specific, normatively laden nature of (her) anger, and hence from precisely what makes an appeal to it explanatory.

The third example would not usually be regarded as offering a causal explanation: rather, getting angry (at something like that) is taken by A to be part of what it is to be a feminist. Furthermore, we can argue over whether to count whatever she said and did as anger, as well as whether to count her anger as marking her as a feminist. The patterns we note as salient and what we take them to signify are matters for real dispute, as real and as resolvable as are disputes over causal explanations; and we need an account of emotions and other psychological phenomena that makes such disputes intelligible.

One might ask at this point whether we, the serious participants in the discursive practices of commonsense psychology, are ontologically committed to such things as beliefs, desires, attitudes, intentions and emotions? Yes and no. No – if by 'ontological commitment' you mean, as Quine meant, that the phenomena in question need to be in the domain over which range the bound variables of a well-regimented theory that we regard as (approximately) true. There is no particular reason to believe (and some good reason to doubt) that the explanatory practices of commonsense psychology will (or should) ever be so regimented. Nor is there reason to think that anything is to be gained by insisting on the role of specifically nominalized explanations: on 'her anger' rather than 'she was angry', on 'his belief' rather than 'he believes', on 'her arrogance' rather than 'she's talking arrogantly'. But yes – if what's at stake (and I do think this is what matters more) is the possibility of objective, true accounts of ourselves and each other, accounts that we can intelligibly challenge and revise, justify and rebut, accounts that actually explain. That sort of commitment requires not theoretical regimentation but seriousness about our roles and stakes in the practices that construct the phenomena to which we are committed.

Thus, far from urging with respect to commonsense psychology something analogous to Moore's 'Defence of Common Sense' with respect to physical objects, I am arguing that attention to our practices is needed precisely because what we are presumed to have in common, what 'we' do or say is, from a feminist perspective, far from unproblematic. 'The common woman', the poet Judy Grahn told us in the 1970s, 'is as common as the best of bread / and will rise . . . I swear it to you on my common / woman's / head'.[28] Feminist writers, artists, and theorists have often valorized common women's lives, including the knowledge that emerges from hands-on engagement with the messiness of daily life, in contrast to the idealizations of science. When we want to urge experts to take us and our concerns seriously, common sense is what is 'ours', not 'theirs'. But appeal to what 'we' are supposed have in common, to what 'everyone' knows or values, can prove notoriously uncongenial to feminists and our allies. Many of us stand condemned by common sense: our lives are variously immoral, foolish, obscene, misguided, or impossible. Expert discourses of various sorts can offer real or imagined refuge from those condemnations: we may feel on firmer ground casting our lot with 'them' than with an 'us' that places us on the margins or beyond the pale. We may, for example, be confident that science will reveal the unnaturalness of heterosexist construals of sexuality or the ungroundedness of presumptions of male superiority.

When, however, María Lugones writes about the tyranny of common sense, as the expression of what the comfortable can presume to be obvious, in contrast to the improvisations of those she calls 'streetwalkers', she is articulating a perspective from which science and common sense are, as they are for many philosophers, continuous, one the disciplined extension of the other, both grounded in what we all are presumed to have and to know in common and which, she argues, actually excludes many from the realm of sense-making.[29] Such are the ambiguous resonances of the word that one could even say that being 'common' (not, as some would say, 'our kind of person') is one way of being excluded from the commons, the space of commonality. The exclusion Lugones describes – from the easy truths of common sense, what all 'right-thinking' people know – is the epistemic analogue of the ejection of homeless people from the public library.

Once we acknowledge the ways in which, in Lugones's terms, we 'make each other up', set the terms in which we will be intelligible, mark out the patterns of salience that construct the phenomena of mentality, we can ask about who 'we' are, how and why we do what we do, who reaps the benefits and bears the burdens of the practices that give our lives the shapes they have, and who has what sort of power when it comes to issues such as these. These are questions that redirect our attention, away from what is presumed to lie under and to underwrite the truths of common sense, and toward the practices through which such truths are constructed.[30]

NOTES

1 On feminist accounts of the social nature of the self, see, for example, among philosophers in the analytic tradition, A. Baier, *Postures of the Mind* (London: Methuen, 1985); M. Friedman, 'The Social Self and the Partiality Debates', in C. Card, ed., *Feminist Ethics* (Lawrence: University of Kansas Press, 1991); and M. Lugones, 'Playfulness, "World"-Travelling, and Loving Perception', *Hypatia* 2 (1987), 3–19 and 'On the Logic of Pluralist Feminism', in Card, ed., *Feminist Ethics*.

2 On the recasting of the central schisms between feminists as fruitful tensions, see Ann Snitow, 'Pages from a Gender Diary: Basic Divisions in Feminism', *Dissent* 36 (1989), 205–24.

3 J. Hornsby, *Simple Mindedness: In Defense of Naive Naturalism in the Philosophy of Mind* (Cambridge, MA: Harvard University Press, 1997), pp. 48–9.

4 J. Dupré, *The Disorder of Things: Metaphysical Foundations of the Disunity of Science* (Cambridge, MA: Harvard University Press, 1993), pp. 91–4.

5 See ibid., p. 90; Hornsby, *Simple Mindedness*, p. 12. For an account of and argument for an anti-dualist anti-physicalism, which draws on Dennett's distinction between the personal and the sub-personal, see J. Hornsby, 'Personal and Sub-Personal: A Defense of Dennett's Original Distinction', in J. Bermudez and M. Elton, eds., *Personal and Sub-Personal: New Essays in Psychological Explanation* (London and New York: Routledge, forthcoming).

6 J. Kim, 'Concepts of Supervenience', in *Supervenience and Mind: Selected Philosophical Essays* (Cambridge: Cambridge University Press, 1993), p. 53; reprinted from *Philosophy and Phenomenological Research* 45 (1984), 153–76, emphases in the original.

7 Kim actually argues in this essay that the positions he calls 'strong' and 'global' supervenience are equivalent, and to be contrasted with (and preferred to) what he calls 'weak' supervenience. He was later persuaded that this equivalence doesn't hold and that global supervenience is, in fact, too weak a principle to be intelligibly defended. See J. Kim, '"Strong" and "Global" Supervenience Revisited', in *Supervenience and Mind*, pp. 82–6; reprinted from *Philosophy and Phenomenological Research* 48 (1987), 315–26. I will discuss global supervenience below.

8 On the laying down of requirements, see C. Diamond, 'Introduction II: Wittgenstein and Metaphysics', in *The Realistic Spirit: Wittgenstein, Philosophy, and the Mind* (Cambridge, MA: MIT Press, 1991). On the slide into the problematically philosophical, see W. D. Goldfarb, 'I Want You to Bring Me a Slab: Remarks on the Opening Sections of the *Philosophical Investigations*', *Synthèse* 56 (1983), 265–82.

9 Kim, 'Concepts of Supervenience', pp. 175–6.

10 J. Kim, 'The Myth of Nonreductive Materialism', in *Supervenience and Mind*, p. 280, reprinted from *Proceedings and Addresses of the American Philosophical Association* 63 (1989), 31–47.

11 Here I don't take exception to Kim's use of 'things' *per se*. I myself use 'phenomena' in a way that won't stand up to heavy ontological scrutiny. For the use of 'phenomena' as an ontologically neutral umbrella term, see G. Rey,

Contemporary Philosophy of Mind (Oxford: Blackwell, 1997), fn. 4, p. 13. My own use is even more neutral than his, since he claims neutrality only with respect to the *sort* of phenomenon in question (event, state, process etc.), whereas I intend to be neutral on the prior question of ontological commitment.

12 H. Steward in *The Ontology of Mind: Events, Processes, and States* (Oxford: Clarendon Press, 1997) argues for shifting the question of mental causation from that of causal relations between such an array of entities (she argues for reserving that relation to events) and toward an account of causal relevance, which holds among facts and which does not raise the sort of problems, such as over-determination, which have both driven and plagued the philosophy of mind.

13 R. A. Wilson, *Cartesian Psychology and Physical Minds: Individualism and the Sciences of the Mind* (Cambridge: Cambridge University Press, 1995), pp. 21–5; quotation, p. 23.

14 For Davidson's argument that this is the case, see 'The Individuation of Events', in *Actions and Events* (Oxford: Oxford University Press, 1980), p. 180. For a similar argument to mine against the idea that token identities can survive the demise of any theory connecting types, see Hilary Putnam, 'Reflections on Goodman's *Ways of Worldmaking*', *Journal of Philosophy* 76 (1979), 603–18. Putnam recognized, as Davidson has not, that views about the holistic, normative nature of psychological explanation are incompatible with taking such explanations to be *about* things whose existence as particulars is independent of the practices that ground the explanations. The claim for such independence is often made by separating what Quine referred to as 'ideology' from 'ontology', a move that proceeds as though in general an ontology – a range of particulars – survives abstraction from a specific way of characterizing what those particulars are, including how those that are complex are constituted. (See the discussion in Rey, *Contemporary Philosophy of Mind*, pp. 179–80.) The ideology/ontology distinction is, I think, one way of accomplishing the 'initial move in the conjuring trick'.

15 Hornsby never explicitly endorses any form of supervenience, but I have no reason to think that she would find global supervenience, as I am understanding it, problematic. She is certainly not committed to Cartesian, or substance, dualism; her argument is that it is a mistake to think that dualism and physicalism (all events/objects are physical events/objects) exhaust the ontological options.

16 Dupré, *Disorder of Things*, p. 91.

17 J. Haugeland, 'Weak Supervenience', *American Philosophical Quarterly* 19 (1982), 97.

18 His example is of 'wave hits' caused by waves from two directions converging on a bobbing cork. Ibid., pp. 100–1.

19 It is not clear to me how much of what I say Haugeland would agree with. His argument is meant to show that physicalism does not require token identities, but it is not clear to me what Haugeland means by physicalism, in particular, whether he appreciates and accepts just how very weak what he calls weak supervenience is and whether he would argue against any stronger thesis.

20 Thus, the insights of Tyler Burge, Hilary Putnam and others about the social nature of the content of propositional attitudes goes much deeper than is usually presumed and cannot, for example, be met by appeals to narrow content.

21 J. F. Post, '"Global" Supervenient Determination: Too Permissive?', in E. E. Savellos and Ü. D. Yalçin, eds., *Supervenience: New Essays* (Cambridge: Cambridge University Press, 1995), p. 76.

22 For a fuller discussion of this example, see N. Scheman, 'Feeling Our Way toward Moral Objectivity', in A. Clark, M. Friedman and L. May, *Mind and Morals* (Cambridge, MA: MIT Press, 1995). See also Wittgenstein, *Zettel* (Oxford: Blackwell, 1967), §504: 'Love is not a feeling. Love is put to the test, pain not. One does not say: "That was not true pain, or it would not have gone off so quickly."'

23 J. Kim, 'Supervenience as a Philosophical Concept', in *Supervenience and Mind*, p. 159; reprinted from *Metaphilosophy* 21 (1990), 1–27.

24 The parallel to Quine's famous dictum 'To be is to be the value of a variable' is, of course, intentional. I would argue, however, that psychological explanation cannot be sufficiently regimented to meet Quinean standards for ontological commitment, and that, in fact, there is no good reason to commit ourselves to any particular *ontology* for the mental at all, which is not to say that we don't have good grounds for committing ourselves to the possibility of objectively true psychological explanations.

25 See Dupré, *Disorder of Things*; I. Hacking, 'World-Making by Kind-Making: Child Abuse for Example', in M. Douglas and D. Hull, eds., *How Classification Works: Nelson Goodman and the Social Sciences* (Edinburgh: Edinburgh University Press, 1992) and 'Making Up People', in T. C. Heller, M. Sosna and D. E. Wellbery, eds., *Reconstructing Individualism* (Palo Alto: Stanford University Press, 1986); and M. D. Root, *Philosophy of Social Science: The Methods, Ideals, and Politics of Social Inquiry* (Oxford: Blackwell, 1993), pp. 149–72 and *Dividing the World*, forthcoming. Root is developing an account of what he calls 'real social kinds', whose realness consists in the ways in which systematic social practices make all those things (typically, people) that fall within the kind interchangeable. He argues that social kinds are relative to times and places, reflecting the variability of the relevant social practices: if, for example, race or gender is real here and now, it is because we make it so.

26 M. Frye, 'A Note on Anger', in *Politics of Reality* (Trumansburg, NY: The Crossing Press, 1983); and Scheman, 'Anger and the Politics of Naming', in *Engenderings: Constructions of Knowledge, Authority, and Privilege* (London and New York: Routledge, 1993).

27 Bodily goings-on are taken to be differently significant, to form a more or less central part of patterns that are emotions, in different cultures. See for example R. Rosaldo, 'Grief and a Headhunter's Rage', in *Culture and Truth: The Remaking of Social Analysis* (Boston: Beacon Press, 1989), pp. 1–21.

28 J. Grahn, 'The Common Woman Poems', Stanza VII, in L. Chester and S. Barba, eds., *Rising Tides: Twentieth Century American Women Poets* (New York: Pocket Books, 1973).

29 M. Lugones, 'Strategies of the Street-walker/Estrategias de la Callejera', unpublished manuscript.

30 This chapter was meant to be a revision of a paper I wrote in 1983, which has been haphazardly circulating under the title 'Types, Tokens, and Conjuring Tricks'. It contains arguments (valid, I still believe, and not all since made by others), mostly via counterexamples, that the anti-reductionist arguments that

motivate anomalous monism, functionalism and substantive supervenience theses in general tell equally against those proposed alternatives. For various reasons I had put that paper aside to pursue what I thought were rather distant interests in interdisciplinary feminist theory. The invitation to contribute to this volume seemed the perfect occasion for finally revising it and for making explicit the connections that were coming to seem more and more obvious to me, especially when I belatedly discovered Jennifer Hornsby's and John Dupré's work. As subsequent drafts worked their way through my computer, however, the relationship of the present chapter to its ancestor became sufficiently attenuated as to strain any plausible criterion of identity. I would, nonetheless, like to thank David Golumbia and Lisa Banks for first encouraging me to re-enter the philosophy of mind fray; Ernie Lepore for his criticisms of the 1983 paper and for (only partially heeded) advice on updating it; and Louise Antony, Richard Boyd and especially Georges Rey for pushing me to explain why I professed to believe things that sounded completely crazy. I have presented versions of the present chapter at the University of Toronto, University of London (where John Dupré was my commentator) and Gothenburg and Umea Universities, and was greatly helped by the discussions, as I was by Michael Root's and Georges Rey's careful critical readings of an earlier draft (though Rey, in particular, may wish to dispute any influence on the current version) and by long conversations with Hornsby, Dupré and Miranda Fricker. Thanks to the Department of Feminist Studies at Gothenburg for providing a congenial setting for writing this chapter.

4

SARAH RICHMOND

Feminism and psychoanalysis
Using Melanie Klein

The relationship between feminism and psychoanalytical theory has been stormy. Feminists of all stripes have criticized Freud and his followers for many different aspects of psychoanalytical thought and practice. While some of these criticisms are relatively local in scope, concerning features of psychoanalysis that can be regarded as inessential or transient, others are directed against more central theoretical commitments. The first category includes examples such as the sexist expectations manifested by Freud in his analyses of female patients: the case history documenting Freud's treatment of 'Dora', for example, has been discussed at length by feminist critics.[1] More theoretical criticisms include the charges of false universalism, ahistoricism (in particular the reification of the nuclear family), heterosexism, biologism and phallocentrism. The aim, also, of psychoanalytical therapy has been criticized as reactionary, insofar as it is thought to divert patients from a political understanding of their discontents to the 'individualist' solution of personal adjustment to the status quo.

Some feminists, on the other hand, have believed that psychoanalytical theory has much of value to offer and that its alleged flaws rest on misunderstanding, or are unimportant, or eliminable, or remediable. From a feminist perspective, three distinctive emphases of psychoanalytical thought recommend it: first, human embodiment; second, human development from infancy to adulthood; and third, the irrational side of the human mind that forms the backcloth to our rationality. The centrality accorded to these themes provides a striking corrective to the tendency that has dominated much western philosophical thought about human beings, in which they are conceived of as contingently embodied rational minds, and as if the intellectual capacities that characterize adulthood did not need to develop. This distorted conception of human beings has been inimical to women in a number of ways. By overlooking facts about human embodiment and infancy, philosophers have neglected the reproductive and maternal labour carried out by women. And, where philosophers *have* recognized the salience of embodiment and the non-rational features of our mental lives, they have regarded them as essentially female characteristics, and maintained a conception of rationality that was essentially masculine.[2]

Of course this distorted conception of human beings can be challenged, simply by reflection upon its omissions, without needing to invoke psychoanalytical theory. A large quantity of thought, much of it feminist (and, in consequence, informed by the experience of women, who are less prone to overlook the implications of embodiment or the demands made by children), has developed this challenge. Political philosophers have had to take account, within their theories of justice, of arrangements made within the so-called 'private sphere', such as domestic labour and childcare;[3] phenomenology has been supplemented by accounts of the experience of female embodiment;[4] moral philosophy has considered the possibility that moral reflection might be gendered, in the light of evidence that women employ a more 'care'-oriented style of moral reasoning than men;[5] 'abstract individualist' accounts of the self, deployed within various areas of philosophy, have been challenged by 'relational' conceptions, in which membership of a community is held to play a constitutive role in self-identity.[6] And these examples do not exhaust the field of feminist interventions and influence within philosophy.

The advantages offered by psychoanalytical theory go beyond its mere inclusion of aspects of humanity that have often been neglected. What it has seemed to offer feminist thinkers is an *explanatory* framework within which, for example, phenomena such as the formation of gender identity may be understood.[7] Moreover, its theory of unconscious motivation has provided feminists with a critical, diagnostic resource that can be used to reveal unacknowledged male psychological interests involved in the treatment and representation of women in patriarchal culture.[8] Feminists concerned with types of psychological distress suffered predominantly by women (such as eating disorders and postnatal depression) have also put psychoanalytical theory to the clinical use for which it originally developed. While maintaining the need for a political analysis of such disorders that relates them to the oppressive social conditions suffered by women, some feminists have argued that, for a complete explanation, psychoanalysis is also required. A psychoanalytical understanding can illuminate the 'emotional underpinnings' that make some women more psychologically vulnerable to these conditions than others, and may also help these women become more resistant.[9] A further feminist therapeutic use of psychoanalytical ideas has been in women's 'consciousness raising' group endeavours. Here women have sought to understand, among other things, unconscious forces that lead them to collude with their own subordination.[10]

A great deal of recent feminist theory that has drawn on psychoanalytical thought has been shaped by the hugely influential work of the French psychiatrist and psychoanalyst Jacques Lacan. Lacan's writings, produced between 1926 and 1980, propose a radical reinterpretation of Freud's texts, in which language is given a far more prominent place in the constitution of the psyche and the unconscious than followers of Freud had hitherto allowed. Lacan, like many other French intellectuals of his time, believed that the model of language provided by Saussure's structuralist linguistics could be extended to illuminate phenomena beyond the linguistic behaviour theorized by Saussure. Lacan's rendering of Freud's thought is couched therefore in terms that derive from Saussure's linguistic theory: Lacan attributes to 'desire', for example, the structure of endless substitutivity that governs the Saussurean linguistic signifier, and characterizes the phallus as 'the privileged signifier'. Freud had hypothesized that a 'splitting of the ego' could take place: in Lacan's theory it is language that imposes that split, and insuperable self-alienation, by dividing the self who utters 'I' from the self to whom the pronoun refers.

Lacan's ideas have stimulated much interesting reflection, including the critical reactions of the French feminists Luce Irigaray and Julia Kristeva. The linguistic basis of Lacan's theory, and in particular his alignment of the domain of language, the 'Symbolic Order', with masculinity, have encouraged those feminists who have been influenced by him to conceive of their task primarily in terms of developing strategies of speaking, writing or reading that might subvert phallocentrism.[11] If one accepts Lacan's account, that may be the consequence. However, Lacan does not provide much in the way of clinical evidence to support it, and his claim to be faithful to Freud's thought (which claim, if true, would earn Lacan whatever support is lent by Freud's clinical data) is, at the least, controversial.

French 'post-structuralist' psychoanalysis may have appealed to feminist theorists because of its distance from 'essentialism', a much-used term, which we can understand as the idea that there are innate psychological differences between men and women. Perhaps because unsupported assumptions about women's nature have so often been used to try to legitimize the restriction of women's rights, freedom and opportunities, many feminists have been unwilling to allow that there might exist innate sexual differences. Indeed post-structuralist and postmodernist thought has sought to problematize the idea of 'nature' – human or otherwise – altogether. Thus deconstructionists have argued that the nature/culture opposition, along with the other binary oppositions fundamental to western philosophy, can be made to collapse under scrutiny; and Lacan in particular vehemently rejects 'biologism' in psychoanalytical thought. In line with this suspicion of the concepts of 'nature' and 'biology', the recent wave of feminist writing about the body has emphasized the extent to which it is a sociocultural phenomenon, or a site of cultural 'inscription', and denied the applicability of the distrusted concepts.[12]

Perhaps this consensus explains the relative neglect on the part of feminists of the work of Melanie Klein.[13] For Klein, who published her contributions to psychoanalytical theory between 1921 and 1960, believed there was such a thing as human nature, and that the task accomplished (more or less successfully) in psychic development was the organization and integration of our innate instinctual endowment. The fact of our embodiment, which plays a central role in Klein's theory, is understood in *biological* terms, not only sociocultural ones.

This chapter aims to go some way towards remedying the feminist neglect of Klein. I believe that Klein's development of classical psycho-analysis, antedating the Lacanian 'linguistic turn' taken by feminist psycho-analytical theory, provides a more productive body of thought for feminist theorists to mine. In rejecting the idea of human nature, feminist theory has deprived itself both of some valuable insights about human beings, and of an understanding that can inform proposals for change. Klein's delineation of our innate, biologically based mental dispositions, and her sophisticated account of their interaction, in forming the personality, with the social environment, offer valuable suggestions about the parameters that may constrain possibilities of transformation, and ought to constrain the feminist imagination.[14]

Klein considered herself to be a disciple of Freud, extending his thought rather than revising it; whatever the truth on this matter, many of her departures from Freud's theory serve to correct (some of) its androcentric aspects (criticized by many feminists), and surely reflect her perspective as a woman and a mother. Thus (as I will illustrate), Klein's theory places much greater emphasis on the infant's relationship with his mother, and demotes penis envy from the primary role that it plays in Freud's thought.

The areas of experience theorized by Klein exhibit a striking overlap with the concerns of feminist theory: many of the themes motivating the feminist interventions in philosophy mentioned above are further illumi-nated by Klein's work. Her 'object relations' theory, in which one or more internalized interpersonal relationships come to constitute the core of the self, offers one way in which a 'relational' account of personal identity can be substantiated.[15] Her account of the mother's role in the infant's psychological development provides a valuable resource for the feminist projects of understanding what mothers do, seeking recognition for their labour, and arguing for its redistribution.[16] And Klein's hypotheses about the foundation of our moral sense advance an account of its genesis, within the context of familial relationships, that may usefully contribute to feminist thinking about morality.

Klein's particular interest was in infancy, and her contribution to psychoanalytical thought lies both in her development of the 'play-technique' that allowed her to amass clinical evidence about the infantile mind, and in the theoretical hypotheses to which this evidence led her. Klein, along with other post-Freudian thinkers, extends Freud's thought by studying the period of psychic development preceding the Oedipus complex that, Freud argued, occurred in the fourth year of life. However, although these thinkers are often characterized as theorists of the 'pre-oedipal' stage, the term is misleading in Klein's case: her claim was that oedipal anxieties were experienced much earlier than Freud had thought, and she attributed such anxieties to infants in the first year of life.

The investigation of early psychic development required, of necessity, an understanding of the infant's relationship with his earliest caregiver whom Klein invariably equates (not without justification) with his mother.[17] For Klein, this relationship is crucial in the infant's psychological development; the mother's care influences not only the degree of psychic integration he achieves, but also his moral sense.

To understand this maternal contribution, we need to chart the transition the infant makes (more or less successfully) in the first year of life, from his initial mental organization, called by Klein the 'paranoid-schizoid position', to the 'depressive position'. In this transition, the infant's relationship to his mother alters, and the alteration mirrors a change in the phantasies that represent her: she ceases to figure as a part-object, and comes to be recognized, more realistically, as a whole object.

The term 'part-object' is used to characterize the infant's earliest object relations. The prefix, 'part-', is applicable for more than one reason: first, because in part-object relations the infant only minimally distinguishes the object from himself; second, the part-object is often a body-part; third, the part-object includes only one aspect, or part, of qualities that in reality are co-instantiated. Part-objects are the items, located inside or outside his body, that the infant conceives of, in phantasy, as the causes of his sensations. The infant relates to these part-objects as if they had intentions, corresponding to the type of sensations they are thought to cause: thus part-objects thought to cause pleasant experiences are regarded as being benevolently disposed towards the infant, while those at the source of unpleasant experiences are thought of as malevolent. These 'personal' attitudes are entertained by the infant whether or not the part-object concerned is, in reality (a part of) another person. An example of a part-object that *is* part of another person in reality is the mother's breast, the infant's most significant early part-object, to which his feeding experiences are referred; an example of one that is not is the attacking creature that he phantasizes as being inside his stomach, causing the pangs that assail him when he is hungry. Relations to part-objects are highly changeable, becoming established or dissolving in accordance with current sensations, and they are charged with either good or bad feeling (but never both), according to the goodness or badness attributed to the object.

The Manichean split between the unmixed goodness and badness of part-objects reflects the split between the two conflicting instincts that, according to Klein, dominate the early, highly unintegrated ego: libido and aggression, or love and hate. Klein, following Freud, believed in the existence of the death instinct: an innate impulse for aggression and (self-)destruction that causes terror in the infant, who fears 'being destroyed from within'.[18] The infant responds to this fear by deflecting his aggression, both to discharge it and to give it an external target. He directs it against his mother's breast, understood in the mode of an evil part-object, the 'bad breast' that frustrates him when it is not available to relieve his hunger; his libidinal impulses are reserved for such good part-objects as the 'good breast' that produces the pleasant sensations of feeding. By virtue of this twofold 'splitting' – of objects and of instincts (which, by taking different targets, are kept firmly apart from each other) – the infant is defended against his own destructiveness.

In an attempt to lessen the psychological chaos in which he finds himself at birth, unpredictably assailed by good and bad sensations, impulses and objects, the infant employs two fundamental mechanisms of phantasy: introjection and projection. In the phantasy of introjection, he installs an object within his body; by projection, he expels it outside. These phantasy operations are modelled on the infant's real corporeal experience: introjection corresponds to eating, and projection to urinating, defecating and vomiting. In general his goal is to take possession of good objects by installing them inside him and to get rid of bad ones by expelling them.[19]

We may pause here to note that, on this account of infantile experience, the idea that the mind and mental operations are only contingently embodied appears grossly implausible. For Kleinians, bodily experiences are not only the first *concern* of the instinctual beings that we are, they also supply the *models* on which the earliest mental operations are based, and in terms of which those operations are understood.[20] The earliest phantasies of introjection and projection are of a highly concrete character, in which the infant, as when he eats and defecates, feels himself to be relocating items with respect to his body boundaries.[21]

It is not surprising that Klein, believing the subject's experience of embodiment to be the central concern of early mental life, should also believe, with Freud, that the 'anatomical distinction between the sexes' has 'psychical consequences'.[22] However Klein departs from Freud's views on sexual difference in several respects. Possession of the penis and female envy of it play a less important role in her theory: as an object of envy, the penis is secondary in relation to the envied mother's breast (I return to this topic later). Also, Klein pays greater attention to the distinctive experiences and anxieties of girls that are rooted in their own bodies (as opposed to the reactive anxiety that stems from their realization that, unlike boys, they lack a penis). Thus she records numerous phantasies demonstrating the anxieties about their 'insides' that arise from girls' experience of their embodiment, and their rivalry with their mothers.[23] Further, Klein differs from Freud in claiming that girls know, through genital sensations, of the existence of the vagina from infancy. Indeed, she claims that infants of both sexes know of both the penis and the vagina, as the sensations experienced in owning either of these 'imply' the existence of the other.[24] It is hard to resist the conclusion that these departures from Freudian doctrine reflect the fact that Klein's 'anatomy' was female.

What is phantasy? Kleinians define it in a number of (compatible) ways. Susan Isaacs' definition (formulated in 1943 to present and defend Kleinian theory to its more orthodox Freudian opponents in the so-called 'Controversial Discussions' held in London at that time) is commonly cited. Isaacs defines phantasy as '(in the first instance) the mental corollary, the psychic representative, of instinct'.[25] As we have seen, instinct is represented, within the paranoid-schizoid position, by means of 'animistic' phantasies of active good and bad part-objects.[26] Phantasy has the additional function, beyond that of registering instinct, of defending against it, as displayed in the phantasy of the 'bad breast' which provides a target for the infant's aggression. Equally, it often plays a wish-fulfilling role, for example when the infant introjects the good breast to take possession of it. An important point about these uses of infantile phantasy is that, to some degree, they vindicate the infant's attitude of 'omnipotence' with respect to reality. By representing reality otherwise than it is the infant succeeds, at least temporarily, in altering his experience of it. Take the example (used by Isaacs) of an infant sucking his thumb, and thereby stimulating the phantasy of feeding at the breast. The thumb = breast equation is effective for a while: the infant's experience is hallucinatory, such that his sensation of sucking feels like that of feeding. But as hunger increases, reality reasserts itself and the wish-fulfilling phantasy breaks down. The infant's hunger pangs force themselves upon his attention, to be registered in a more unpleasant phantasy.

The phantasied 'solutions' to the pains of the paranoid-schizoid position just described are highly unrealistic and we can list at least three disadvantageous consequences. First, as we have seen, phantasy is effective, if at all, only in the short term. When it collapses, the infant is left as helpless in relation to external circumstances as he was before he initiated it. Second, within the logic of the phantasy, the infant's 'actions' may have costs. For example, the infant's aggressive attacks on his 'bad' objects cause him intense persecutory anxiety, as he now fears retaliation from his victims. Perceiving them as even more threatening than before, he attacks them again, thereby establishing a vicious circle of mounting aggression and terror. (This is the 'paranoid' aspect of the paranoid-schizoid position.) Third, the defences used in the paranoid-schizoid position, by redistributing fragments of psychic reality, militate against its integration. (Hence, 'schizoid'.) Projection and splitting, by dissociating the infant from his bad objects and impulses, impede him from recognizing them as 'his'. This is particularly true of the mechanism of projective identification which, only briefly discussed by Klein (in connection with the paranoid-schizoid position), has been at the centre of Kleinian theoretical and clinical developments since her death. In this phantasy the subject projects outwards, often into another person, a part of his self with which he is identified. The aim might be to get rid of it, or perhaps to invade and control the person in whom it gets lodged.[27] Because it is through phantasy that a subject represents his mind to himself, he only has access to that which is represented as 'his': thus, the effect of projective identification is to deplete his ego of the projected state or impulse. While this may procure the desired relief from anxiety that motivated the projection, the consequent fragmentation of the self leaves the subject with a confused or deluded sense of ego-boundaries (characteristic of psychosis), in which he may imagine that he inhabits the body of another. Thus, ironically, the omnipotent solution resorted to in phantasy leaves him in reality with less control over the parts of his mind than he had before.

All three of these disadvantages are lessened in the depressive position which, in normal development, supersedes the paranoid-schizoid position. The depressive position, it should be noted, is an achievement *in phantasy*, characterized by Klein as the secure internalization, resulting from its introjection, of the good object.[28] Phantasy, therefore, has a further role, in addition to those discussed: it is a vehicle of psychic development. Repeated instances of introjection and projection alter the subject's sense of what he 'contains' and extend his psychic capacities. In this development, in which the subject's internal reality modifies his perception of external reality, and vice versa, the mother's care is crucial.

To illustrate this, we can consider how the hungry infant's phantasy about his mother's breast, narrated earlier, might develop.[29] We said that eventually, under the pressure of hunger, the phantasy of the introjected good breast would collapse, leaving the infant at the mercy of bad, attacking internal objects. At this point he may '[turn] in distress to the outer world, seeking a "good" breast there'.[30] Simplifying the range of possible outcomes, we can say there are two: one good, one bad. If a 'good' breast – in the form of food – is provided, the infant is rescued. Feeding dissipates his hunger (and, at the same time, the bad internal objects that represent it) and increases his confidence in the external world, teaching him that 'bad things go and good things come'.[31] Moreover, the fresh encounter with a good breast allows him to re-introject it, thereby renewing a good internal object. Through repeated experiences of this kind, the infant becomes less terrified of his bad internal objects and of his aggression, as he sees that real good objects remain, undestroyed. This 'reality testing', to which phantasy is subject from the outset, teaches the infant the difference between internal and external reality, and to modify his expectations accordingly. But if the infant's need is not met, and he is left in distress, no contrast between inner and outer can be drawn: his destructive phantasies will seem to be confirmed, and he may imagine that he has destroyed everything good. If this experience is repeated, the result may be someone who is continually overwhelmed by his own aggression and the associated persecutory anxiety.

The infant's establishment of the whole good object within his ego depends in large part (but not entirely; I will return to this qualification) on the care that he receives. The experience of being loved and cared for fortifies his confidence in his own loving feelings and reduces his fear of his hateful ones; he comes to believe, in phantasy, that the loved object may be kept safely inside him. Moreover, as his internal world comes to seem less dangerous, he has less need to resort to projection and projective identification. Thus, as he finds his own aggression more tolerable, and acknowledges his 'psychic reality' more completely, he becomes better integrated. This, in turn, renders his perception of external reality more accurate, as it is less distorted by projective phantasies.

Most significantly of all, the infant comes to recognize, in the depressive position, that the 'good' and 'bad' breasts are one and the same, a 'whole' object, at the source of his satisfaction and his frustration alike. The internalized object is no longer unmitigatedly 'good', unlike the earlier, utterly good, part-object; instead, it is a *basically* good, imperfect object. Indeed, as the introjected content approximates to the care received by the infant, the 'goodness' of his internal good object approximates to that of his mother. Hanna Segal suggests that the baby's cognitive achievement, when he learns to recognize his mother, corresponds to the transition to a whole-object relation.[32] The object is 'whole', therefore, in two ways: it encompasses multiple qualities (not just one), and the entirety of a person's body (not just a part). A feature of the infant's improved grasp of reality, then, is that even his phantasy becomes more realistic.

The recognition of the object as a multifaceted whole has far-reaching psychological consequences. It forces the infant to acknowledge his mother's separateness and independence as he realizes that the person who is present when his needs are met, and the one who sometimes is missing, are one and the same. And this obliges him, painfully, to give up his earlier attitude of omnipotence vis-à-vis the world, and to acknowledge his dependence on his mother. The introjection of the whole object, therefore, is less concrete, and more symbolic, than the earlier introjections of parts; the mother's *care* and understanding are internalized, along with a sense of her separateness. The 'internal mother' becomes established within the infant's internal world as a figure whom he can turn to, and identify himself with, at moments of psychological need throughout his life.

The recognition of the whole object also occasions intense anxiety of a new kind. This arises as the infant realizes that his fiercely destructive attacks have in fact been launched against the object he loves; in consequence, he experiences guilt for the first time, as well as anxiety about the damage he may have done to his object. Moreover, since his attitude to the whole object necessarily remains ambivalent (insofar as, being a 'mixed', imperfect object, it denies him the unlimited possession and gratification he would like), his anger against it does not disappear.[33] If the infant's aggressive impulses are too strong, he will be overwhelmed by the weight of depressive guilt and anxiety they occasion; in this situation, unable to sustain the depressive position, he may revert to the paranoid-schizoid position (in which the attacked object is represented as unmixedly bad). Where the infant can face his feelings of guilt, he may respond with an attempt to restore his damaged object; in Klein's view, the reparative impulse plays a major role within the psyche, and is the unconscious desire that many creative achievements, symbolically, fulfil.

In Klein's view, we grapple with the difficult constellation of unconscious phantasy and feeling that constitutes the depressive position throughout our lives. Our engagement with the external world is driven by the state of our internal relationships, which it symbolically expresses and modifies; at the same time, these relationships, projected outwards, colour our perception of the world. Sanity does not require the absence of phantasy (which is impossible), but the possession of an *enabling* internal world, in which the helpful figures from our infancy are represented without too much distortion, so that their demands can be fluently translated into symbolic form.[34]

I said earlier that the mother's contribution to the infant's transition to the depressive position needed to be qualified. The complicating factor, documented by Klein late in her career, is envy.[35] Klein argued that envy is a further, irreducible influence on the infant's object relations. Envy is a destructive impulse, manifesting the death instinct. The form it takes, however, differs from the aggression directed against 'bad' objects discussed earlier: the objects of envious attack are perceived to be good. Envy's primary object is the 'good' maternal breast, attacked because the infant can not tolerate the existence of goodness outside and separate from himself. This intolerance exemplifies the narcissistic character of envy, in which all goodness has to be regarded as an attribute of the self, and interferes with the establishment of the depressive position (which requires, precisely, the capacity to acknowledge one's dependence on a 'good' object separate from oneself).

Envy, in classical psychoanalytical thought, is primarily attached to the penis: Freud argued that girls' envious response to the discovery that they lacked a penis was a fundamental component of feminine gender identity (generating, for example, a desire for items that might compensate for this lack, such as a husband's penis or a baby). By maintaining that envy is directed, in the first instance, against the mother's breast (and only secondarily against the penis), Klein makes envy an important factor in the development of *all* individuals. In her view, the tendency to feel envy is innate, varying in strength between individuals. Thus, although early experience may foster or diminish envy (Klein suggests that weaning sometimes intensifies it), no style of childcare can wholly eradicate it. Indeed, out of the innate instinctual repertoire, envy is especially refractory to the mother's influence, insofar as it works precisely to deny what she has to offer.

Envy's baneful influence notwithstanding, the mother's contribution to her child's mental development is, on Klein's account, hugely important (and of greater scope than the maternal influence explored in most feminist accounts).[36] The mother's influence is vital in enabling the infant to overcome his earliest anxieties; with the transition to the depressive position, it is her care that the infant internalizes. In these two stages (if development is 'normal'), the mother can almost be said to create her child's self, and in two distinct ways: by providing the infant with the experiences required for the integration of his ego, she makes it the case that there is a relatively unified self at all; by providing him with a whole object relation to introject, she becomes the model (albeit distorted by affect) for the internal figure at the core of his personality. In addition, the lifelong motivating role that Klein accords to the emotions of the depressive position ('love, guilt and reparation' as one of her essays was called) means that our lives continue to express our (internalized) relationships with our mothers when we are adults and even after they are dead.

In demonstrating the importance of the care of young children, Klein's work provides powerful arguments, in addition to those of justice, for ensuring that those who undertake it are properly rewarded. If, as Klein thinks, the central transaction of childcare is emotional, it follows that the psychological resources of the carer are a determining factor in its success.[37] The interests of the next generation are hostage to the happiness of their (currently mostly female) carers and ought to be taken into account. Further, where the unhappiness of female carers is a result of social factors such as their enforced financial dependence on men, and the (related) sense of unworthiness about their role, we can expect this experience of sexual inequality to influence the children's care. Thus some feminists have, ironically, seen the mother–daughter relationship as a site for the 'reproduction' of female subordination: mothers, expected to renounce their own needs in favour of those of the rest of the family, 'prepare' their daughters for this role by subjecting them to greater deprivation than their brothers. An initially 'external' social condition is perpetuated by becoming part of the psychological constitution of girls.[38]

*

The mother–child relationship has often been idealized (Mary's relationship with Jesus being an early, rather extreme, instance). While some feminists (seeking, for example, to draw attention to the oppressive aspects of motherhood) have opposed this, others have colluded in it. Recent feminist theory that has focused on the mother–child dyad has argued for its importance in a number of ways. Carol Gilligan's psychological research has led her, and others, to claim that the relationship involves a particular style of moral reflection – an ethic of 'care', as opposed to 'justice'; in the same vein, Sara Ruddick has hypothesized a distinctive, pacifistic, style of 'maternal thinking'.[39] These theories, concentrating on valuable aspects of the mother–child relationship, have tended to underplay its less congenial ones.

Klein's work contrasts with this trend. Her view of the mother–infant relationship, in which envy, frustration and aggression figure alongside more agreeable qualities, is far from idealizing. Interestingly, Klein also draws a connection between that relationship and the moral sense ('conscience', as she calls it); she focuses, however, on the *acquisition* of this sense, rather than its employment, and thereby offers an account of its psychological grounding.

Klein's account is complex. Distinguishing more sharply between two strands of her description than she did, we can see her grounding the moral sense in two different ways: in paranoid-schizoid thinking, where a great deal of violent and fearful phantasy features; and in depressive thinking, where the source of moral feeling is more benign. Klein's work convinced her that authoritarian 'superego' figures entered children's internal worlds much earlier in life than Freud had thought. Moreover, these figures were of an extremely harsh, punitive and threatening character – far more, it seemed, than the actual parents had been. Klein concluded that the terror these figures induced reflected the scale of the infant's aggressive impulses, often bound up with early oedipal ambitions, against his parents: their capacity to terrorize him derived both from the aggression he projected onto them, and from his fear of retaliation. And because, as we have seen, some of the infant's most violent impulses were directed against the mother's body, the terrifying retaliatory figure of his phantasy was often maternal. Thus, in her analysis of two-year-old Rita, Klein uncovered a hostile wish to rob her mother's body of her babies and a 'corresponding anxiety that her mother would attack her and rob her of her imaginary babies'.[40] We have here an explanation of self-restraint in terms of the fear of revenge.

Klein's account of the origin of the early superego departs strikingly from Freud's (although for many years she tried to play this difference down). Freud believed the superego is only established with the resolution of the Oedipus complex in the fifth year of life, and marks the child's capitulation, in renouncing his oedipal ambitions, to the authority of his parents. For Freud, as for Klein, the power of the superego derives from the fear it inspires, but in his theory there is a pronounced sexual asymmetry: for boys, the fear of castration provides a powerful motive for surrendering to their father; girls, lacking a penis from the outset, also lack this motive. In girls, Freud thought, 'the formation of the super-ego must suffer; it cannot attain the strength and independence which give it its cultural significance, and feminists are not pleased when we point out to them the effects of this factor upon the average feminine character'.[41] Although Klein acknowledges that boys experience castration anxiety, it is not the key factor in the generation of the superego (which often arises, as we have seen, out of fear of retaliatory *maternal* attack). Her account, then, does not entail sexual asymmetry in the strength of the superego.

The early 'persecutory' superego, mirroring the infant's overwhelming aggression, is extremely violent; in Klein's view, the level of anxiety it generates can make it *antithetical* to a moral outlook. 'Thus, we must assume that it is the excessive severity . . . and cruelty of the super-ego, not the weakness or want of it, as is usually supposed, which is responsible for the behaviour of asocial and criminal persons.'[42] As, with development, the infant's object relations become less extreme, the superego becomes a less harsh, and more benign, influence.

The theory of the depressive position accounts for a second, quite different motivation for moral behaviour that approximates more closely to altruism. The motivation here is concern for the internal good object rather than for oneself, and involves depressive guilt (in relation to one's harmful impulses) rather than persecutory fear. This second source of moral motivation is more self-knowing than the first, and allows for greater recognition of personal responsibility.[43]

Klein's account of the way in which the moral sense emerges within our internal world is not incompatible with the claim that, through some sort of socialization, males and females develop different, gendered, styles of moral reasoning. It does, however, challenge the *tabula rasa* conception of the mind that many 'socialization' claims seem to presuppose. Klein's view is that the moral 'education' that we receive in society acts upon a range of moral emotions and dispositions that we have brought to it.

Klein's discussion of the mother–infant relationship seems to depict two points of view. Seen objectively, the mother is the agent who transforms the infant's internal world into a tolerable mental environment; seen subjectively (as the infant represents her in phantasy), she is a figure who incites envy, paranoid fear and aggression, and who, to various degrees, may also inspire guilt, concern and reparative impulses. It might seem, then, that Klein's work, by focusing only on infantile phantasies about the mother, is of no relevance to understanding *mothers'* experience. But this would be to overlook the role that the internal world established in infancy plays throughout our lives. Women who become mothers cannot avoid an unconscious identification with their own internal maternal figures: and are thereby placed at the receiving end of their own feelings towards their mothers. Thus one's relationship with one's 'internal mother' affects one's ability to take on the maternal role. Rita, who was unwilling to adopt the role of mother in her games, exemplifies this: 'When Rita could not play at being her doll's mother, this inhibition derived from her feelings of guilt as well as from her fear of a cruel mother figure, infinitely more severe than her actual mother had ever been.'[44] For Kleinians, the residue of these hostilities is a factor, additional to and independent of their current circumstances, in many women's fraught experience of motherhood.

*

Klein's depiction of the mother–child relationship, and in particular of the envy and hostility that characterize infantile dependence, seems to add further weight to the arguments in favour of redistributing the task of 'mothering' so that men do more of it.[45] The hoped-for result would be that the psychological meaning of the maternal figure would become equally associated with men, and child-rearing practice would thereby cease to provide psychological fuel for cultural misogyny. While Klein's thought does not rule this possibility out, it generates two reservations about it. These arise from the idea that psychological response may be grounded in biological particularity.

The first reservation is that envy might not be so easily diverted. If its target is women's capacity to breast-feed (rather than, say, the person who actually feeds the infant), then a mother who refrains from breast-feeding can still be envied. Klein, in fact, claims that the newborn does unconsciously *know* 'that an object of unique goodness exists, from which a maximal gratification can be obtained and that . . . [it] is the mother's breast'.[46] The question is left open whether bottle-feeding permits an equally good introjection of a (metaphorical) 'breast' or whether it may leave the infant feeling he has missed out on the 'maximal gratification'. In any case, her discussion reminds us that the capacities to breast-feed and bear children remain (at present) female, and casts doubt on the idea that misogyny based on these capacities would be eliminated if women used them less. The second reservation also raises the question of whether a substitute for a biologically based relationship can take on the significance of the original: but here the concern is about the infant's welfare rather than his envy. Some psychoanalysts believe that a psychological mother–infant relationship first establishes itself in the womb. If so, the disruption or loss of this relationship may be psychologically harmful for the infant.

The implications of this last point are not necessarily conservative. Even if it turned out that the infant's interests were adversely served by some proposed alteration in childcare arrangements, the advantages for the mother might still recommend it. Further, developments in technology have already made it possible to perform functions (such as conception) without the participation of women's bodies that was formerly required, and there is no reason to think their range may not be extended. (The functions under discussion here, however, may be particularly difficult to replicate because they are psychological and not merely physical.) Some feminists, such as

Shulamith Firestone, convinced that a precondition of women's emancipation is their emanicipation from biology, have pursued this line of thought.[47] It is also important to remember that the oppressive nature of contemporary mothering stems (at least in large part) from the conditions in which women are obliged to care for their children, rather than from the children themselves: isolation, for example, financial dependence, exclusion from other activities and sacrifice of employment opportunities.

Feminists have been suspicious of theories that emphasize the importance of the maternal role, and with reason: such theories have often served the ideological function of disguising social imperatives as natural ones.[48] But it is a mistake, in my view, to translate this suspicion into an *a priori* rejection of the idea, explored so interestingly by Melanie Klein, that some aspects of our mental lives are grounded in states and relationships that are biological.[49]

NOTES

References to Klein's works are to *The Writings of Melanie Klein*, ed. R. Money-Kyrle (London: Hogarth Press, 1975), vols. 1–4 (abbreviated as *WMK* 1, 2, etc.).

1   See for example C. Bernheimer and C. Kahane, eds., *In Dora's Case* (London: Virago Press, 1985).

2   For a study of this tendency, see G. Lloyd, *The Man of Reason: 'Male' and 'Female' in Western Philosophy* (London: Methuen, 1984).

3   See for example S. Okin, *Justice, Gender and the Family* (New York: Basic Books, 1989).

4   See I. Young, *Throwing Like A Girl and Other Essays in Feminist Philosophy and Social Theory* (Bloomington: Indiana University Press, 1990).

5   See C. Gilligan, *In A Different Voice: Psychological Theory and Women's Development* (Cambridge, MA: Harvard University Press, 1982). E. Kittay and D. Meyers, eds., *Women and Moral Theory* (Totowa, NJ: Rowman & Littlefield, 1987) is a useful collection for this debate.

6   For an example of a feminist anti-individualistic argument in the philosophy of mind, see Naomi Scheman's 'Individualism and the Objects of Psychology', in S. Harding and M. Hintikka, eds., *Discovering Reality: Feminist Perspectives on Epistemology, Metaphysics, Methodology, and the Philosophy of Science* (Dordrecht: D. Reidel, 1983), pp. 225–44, and her chapter in this volume; and in political philosophy, Seyla Benhabib's 'The Generalized and the Concrete Other', in Kittay and Meyers, eds., *Women and Moral Theory*, pp. 154–77.

7   Nancy Chodorow sets out to do just this in *The Reproduction of Mothering* (Berkeley: University of California Press, 1978).

8   Dorothy Dinnerstein's *The Mermaid and the Minotaur* (New York: Harper and Row, 1976) postulates that misogyny expresses residual hostility from the infant's dependent relationship on his mother. Similarly, Jane Flax ('Political Philosophy and the Patriarchal Unconscious: A Psychoanalytical Perspective on Epistemology and Metaphysics', in Harding and Hintikka, eds., *Discovering*

Reality, pp. 245–81), traces many philosophers' dualisms to the 'repression of early infantile experience'.

9 S. Orbach, *Hunger Strike* (London: Faber, 1986).

10 Susie Orbach's *Fat is a Feminist Issue* (London: Hamlyn, 1978) describes how women's groups in the 1970s developed a feminist understanding of the experiences of being fat.

11 See for example Jane Gallop's *Feminism and Psychoanalysis. The Daughter's Seduction* (London: Macmillan, 1982). Although Kristeva and Irigaray reject many aspects of Lacan's thought, much of their work is concerned with overcoming structural difficulties in the representation of femininity.

12 See for example E. Grosz, *Space, Time and Perversion* (London: Routledge, 1995); M. Gatens, *Imaginary Bodies* (London: Routledge, 1996).

13 Relative, but not total, neglect. Dorothy Dinnerstein, Juliet Mitchell and Janet Sayers have related Klein's work to feminist concerns.

14 See N. Holmstrom, 'Human Nature', in A. Jaggar and I. Young, eds., *A Companion to Feminist Philosophy* (Oxford: Blackwell, 1998), pp. 280–8 (pp. 285–6)for an excellent critique of feminists' rejection of the concept of biology.

15 Although Klein theorizes 'object relations', the term has come to be used, confusingly, to refer to a group of thinkers (including Balint and Winnicott) from which she is excluded. Klein's thought, and that of her followers is referred to, simply, as 'Kleinian'.

16 See Sabina Lovibond's chapter in this volume for discussion of the idea that justice demands such a redistribution.

17 I return to the question of the equation between 'mother' and 'main carer' later. The equation is justified to the extent that the overwhelming majority of young children are cared for, at least for a period, mainly by their mothers. As one cannot assume that the psychic development Klein describes would be unaltered by different social arrangements, I retain the term 'mother' in my account of her work. For the sake of clarity, I refer to the infant as 'he'.

18 Melanie Klein, 'Notes on Some Schizoid Mechanisms', *WMK* 2, pp. 1–24, (p. 5) (hereafter 'Notes'). The belief in innate destructiveness and envy marks Kleinians out among object-relations thinkers, and leads to their reputation for holding a pessimistic view of human nature.

19 However, as Hanna Segal points out (*Introduction to the Work of Melanie Klein* (London: Hogarth Press, 1973), p. 26), there are other possible uses of these mechanisms. 'Bad' objects might be introjected in an attempt to control them, or 'good' ones expelled to protect them from perceived dangers 'inside' the subject.

20 See Richard Wollheim, 'The Bodily Ego', in R. Wollheim and J. Hopkins, eds., *Philosophical Essays on Freud* (Cambridge: Cambridge University Press, 1982), pp. 124–38, for valuable discussion of this topic (as it arises in Freud's thought).

21 Thus one way the infant initiates phantasy is by manipulation of his bodily sensations (as in masturbation phantasy); equally, he can take advantage of the occurrence of sensation (such as excretion) as the basis for a phantasy (of projection). See the entry on 'Unconscious Phantasy' in R. D. Hinshelwood, *A Dictionary of Kleinian Thought* (London: Free Association Books, 1984), pp. 32–46.

22 Freud's 'Some Psychical Consequences of the Anatomical Distinction between the Sexes' appeared in 1925. The question of female sexuality was much discussed during the 1920s and 1930s, with female analysts (such as Karen Horney) challenging Freudian orthodoxy.

23 Klein summarizes these feminine anxieties in 'The Oedipus Complex in the Light of Early Anxieties' (1945), *WMK* 1, pp. 370–419 (hereafter, 'Oedipus'), (pp. 413–15).

24 Ibid., p. 409.

25 Susan Isaacs, 'The Nature and Function of Phantasy', in M. Klein et al., *Developments in Psycho-Analysis* (London: Hogarth Press, 1952), pp. 67–121 (p. 83).

26 Hinshelwood (*Dictionary*, pp. 34–5) characterizes part-object phantasy as 'animistic', and suggests we can see the residue of this outlook in phrases like 'Hunger is gnawing at my stomach'.

27 Klein focuses especially on the aim of controlling the other person ('Notes', pp. 8, 11). More recent Kleinian work (for example, by Hanna Segal and Wilfred Bion) has identified other functions of projective identification, including benign ones.

28 See Klein's 'A Contribution to the Psychogenesis of Manic-Depressive States' (1935), in *WMK* 1, pp. 262–89, for detailed discussion of the depressive position. The term 'depressive' is not meant to imply that one is depressed in this position but that, in recognizing separation and loss, one has the *capacity* to be depressed.

29 Paula Heimann develops the narrative this way, in another Kleinian contribution to the 'Controversial Discussions': 'Certain Functions of Introjection and Projection in Early Infancy', reprinted in Klein et al., *Developments*, pp. 122–68.

30 Heimann, 'Certain Functions', p. 157.

31 Ibid., p. 158.

32 Segal, *Introduction*, p. 68.

33 These frustrations, conjoined with the increased awareness of the mother's separateness (and hence her possible involvement in relationships with others), bring to the depressive position experiences (such as jealousy and rivalry) that are bound up with the Oedipus complex. See Ronald Britton, 'The Oedipus Situation and the Depressive Position', in R. Anderson, ed., *Clinical Lectures on Klein and Bion* (London: Tavistock/Routledge, 1992), pp. 34–45, for discussion of the relationship between the two configurations.

34 Internal figures are not copies of their external 'counterparts'; some degree of affect will always distort their representation. Where an internal figure is wildly unrealistic, manifestations are likely to appear in the form, for example, of inhibitions in behaviour (in which, for the subject, this figure is symbolically implicated). I have concentrated, as Klein does, on the process, central to personality development, by which the internal mother is established. However, it is clear that several internal figures exist, corresponding to the real people of significance to the infant. (An interesting methodological question arises concerning the individuation and identification of these figures.) Moreover these figures can have relationships with each other: Klein encountered a commonly phantasized 'combined parent figure', in which the internal parents were

entwined in a gruesome type of intercourse, thereby exhibiting the form of the infant's oedipal anxieties about his (real) parents.

35 M. Klein, 'Envy and Gratitude' (1957), in *WMK* 3, pp. 176–235.

36 Chodorow's interest in the mother's role, for example, focuses on the transmission of gender identity, while Gilligan considers her influence in relation to the 'care' perspective.

37 The importance of the mother's ability to 'contain' and understand her child's mental states is a Kleinian theme that other thinkers (especially W. Bion and Donald Winnicott) have emphasized and explored.

38 Susie Orbach argues that this familial pattern is often the background to eating disorders such as anorexia (*Hunger Strike*, pp. 22–8).

39 C. Gilligan, *In A Different Voice*; S. Ruddick, 'Maternal Thinking', *Feminist Studies* 6 (1980), 342–67.

40 'Oedipus', *WMK* 1, p. 403.

41 Sigmund Freud, 'Femininity' (1933), in *The Standard Edition of The Complete Psychological Works of Sigmund Freud* (London: Hogarth Press, 1964), vol. XXII, pp. 112–35 (p. 129).

42 M. Klein, 'The Early Development of Conscience in the Child' (1933), in *WMK* 1, pp. 248–57 (p. 251).

43 Klein's work can inspire numerous further ideas about moral psychology. See Richard Wollheim's excellent discussion in ch. 7 of his *The Thread of Life* (Cambridge: Cambridge University Press, 1984), where he argues that moral obligation and value have their respective sources in introjection and projection.

44 'Oedipus', *WMK* 1, p. 403.

45 Some arguments for this redistribution are given by Chodorow (*Reproduction*) and Dinnerstein (*Mermaid*).

46 M. Klein, 'On Observing the Behaviour of Young Infants' (1952), *WMK* 3, pp. 94–121 (p. 117).

47 S. Firestone, *The Dialectic of Sex* (New York: William Morrow, 1970).

48 See D. Riley, *War in the Nursery* (London: Virago Press, 1983) for an excellent account of the ideological uses of theories of mother and child. I disagree with Riley, however, that 'the separation of "theory" from "use made of theory" . . . is . . . implausible to sustain' (p. 92).

49 I am grateful to the following people for help with (earlier versions of) this chapter: Helena Cronin, R. D. Hinshelwood, Véronique Munoz-Dardé, Lucy O'Brien, Maria Pozzi and Neil Vickers.

5

JENNIFER HORNSBY

Feminism in philosophy of language
Communicative speech acts

Some philosophical work about language and its use has been inspired by
feminist agenda, some by malestream philosophical agenda.[1] Reading work
in these two areas – in feminist-philosophy of language and in philosophy
of language, as I shall call them – one easily gets the impression that they
are totally separate enterprises. Here I hope to show that the impression is
partly due to habits of thought that pervade much analytical philosophy
and have done damage in philosophy of language. My claim will be that an
idea of communicative speech acts belongs in philosophy of language
(section 2). I think that the absence of such an idea from malestream
accounts of linguistic meaning might be explained by ways of thinking
which are arguably characteristically masculine (section 3). Once communicative speech acts are in place, various feminist (and other political)
themes can be explored (section 4).

1 Feminist-philosophy of language and philosophy of language

Language's relation to gender was at the centre of discussions from the
beginning of feminism's second wave.[2] Dale Spender, in a path-breaking
book, claimed that 'males, as the dominant group, have produced language,
thought and reality'.[3] Some feminists refused to share Spender's pessimism,
and questioned whether language could be the powerful controlling
influence that Spender represented.[4] But a view of language as a vehicle for
the perpetuation of women's subordination was prevalent in the 1980s,
even if it was often based upon less radical claims than Spender's. Writers
gave attention to the sexism implicit in language that contains purportedly
generic uses of masculine terms, especially the supposedly neutral 'man'
and male pronouns.[5] One question raised was whether concerted attempts
to avoid sexism in speech might themselves constitute a feminist advance,
or whether language's working to women's detriment is merely a symptom
of existing power relations.[6] On the assumption that language can be a site

of oppression in its own right, some argued that women's enfranchisement – whether as political subjects or as knowledgeable beings – required women to find a distinctive voice.[7] The use of language as it is passed down to her can seem to falsify a woman's experience, and present an obstacle to discussing it authentically.[8] Women have been described as 'silenced'.[9]

The drift of feminist-philosophy of language has been affected by a change in the agenda of feminist academic work since the early days. Speaking broadly and roughly, one might put this by saying that feminists have moved from the material to the symbolic – from sociological under-standings of patriarchy to explorations of the contingencies of gendered identities. Following the change, there has been work concerned with the need for female subjectivity to become symbolized.[10] The place of language in the make-up of the unconscious has occupied thinkers; and prominent feminists have been concerned with how 'male' and 'female' act as symbols.[11]

In all of this feminist work, the use of language is treated always in a social context, in which the presence of gendered beings is taken for granted. In philosophy of language, by contrast, when modality, say, or relative identity, or reference is the topic, the subject matter is apparently far removed from any social setting. Studying the products of the male-stream, it becomes very easy to forget that language is part of the fabric of human lives. And readers who come to philosophy of language unversed in its professional techniques and technicalities find themselves on the outside of an 'alien hermeneutical circle'.[12]

Questions about *meaning* belong in any philosophy of language. And when the topic is *meaning*, one might expect to find connections between malestream and feminists' agenda. Yet focus on semantic theories has actually helped to sustain the appearance of a gulf between philosophical treatment of language and the treatment of social phenomena. When semantic theories are constructed, languages appear to be treated as objects; the institution of language use, in which people participate, is set to one side. Some feminist writers in consequence have been hostile to the very idea of a semantic theory.[13]

Such hostility seems to me misplaced. I believe that the real objections should be targeted on the conception of the institution of language use that one finds in the malestream. I hope to demonstrate this by giving an account of *saying something to someone* which is intended to replace the standard account. It is a natural account for anyone guided by feminist methodology, and it can assist in the project of understanding language use as a phenomenon in the real social world.

2 Communicative speech acts

A leading question in contemporary English-speaking philosophy is how it is that elements of natural languages have meaning: what is it for words and sentences to be meaningful? The idea of a semantic theory is supposed to help with this question. But no one thinks that it can be answered by appealing to semantic theories alone. The account of *saying something to someone* to which I should want to appeal can be based in an idea I find in J. L. Austin, the originator of so-called speech act theory. I start with some of the Austinian background.[14]

2.1 *Speech acts*

Austin is famous for drawing attention to what he called performatives. When a performative is spoken in appropriate circumstances, a person manifestly *does something* using words. One of Austin's own examples (and he gave plenty) was 'I name this ship the *Queen Elizabeth*', in using which, in an appropriate setting and with an appropriate bottle to hand, a person manifestly *names a ship*. The idea of performativity has been picked up in many areas, including in feminist theory. But the present concern is not with performativity as such, but with a fact which examples of performatives bring to prominence – the fact that speech is action. In order to appreciate this, we need to look to the category of speech acts within which Austin located performatives, which is the category he named 'illocution'. Illocutionary acts are things a speaker does *in* speaking, 'such as informing, ordering, warning, undertaking etc.'.[15]

Illocutionary acts are one among three broad categories of things people do with words. Austin distinguished between locutionary, *il*locutionary and *per*locutionary acts – between speaking, things done *in* speaking and things done *by* speaking. His main interest was to 'fasten onto the illocutionary act and contrast it with the other two'.[16] Locutionary acts he thought of as belonging in the territory of those concerned with 'sense and reference' – of semantic theorists, that is;[17] and perlocutionary acts (such as *amusing*, or *threatening*, or *persuading*) he thought of as requiring effects of speaking which go beyond anything needed for a piece of language use. Illocutionary acts, which one can home in on by marking off the locutionary and the perlocutionary, are the central ones. They occupy the dimension of language use one has to know about in order to grasp what is special about the action that is speech.

2.2 *Semantic theories and linguistic meaning*

One doesn't need Austinian terminology to recognize that some idea of people doing things with words needs to be brought into a philosophical explication of linguistic meaning. Semantic theories are supposed to reveal *words and sentences* as the meaningful things they are; but we gain a conception of words and sentences as meaningful through an idea of *speakers'* using them.

A semantic theory is a formal and axiomatized thing that deals with a particular language.[18] The axioms of a semantic theory treat the individual words of the language; its inference rules allow for the derivation, in the case of any of its very many sentences, of a theorem that can be taken to specify that sentence's meaning.[19] The concept of linguistic meaning, though, has application not to one particular language but to any of a host of human languages. And if the idea of a semantic theory is to cast light on the general concept of linguistic meaning, then something general has to be said about the relations between languages (thought of now as the objects of semantic theories) and groups of speakers. We might say that a semantic theory for a language is correct only if it belongs inside an overall account of the lives and minds of the people who use the language – people who interact with one another, rational agents with their various bits of knowledge, and with thoughts and wants and hopes and fears. A very wide range of psychological and social concepts must be in play, then, if a semantic theory is to be assessable for correctness. Still the concepts on which one needs to focus, if the task is to explicate linguistic meaning, are those which make connections between what a semantic theory tells one about a language and what the speakers of that language *do* with its sentences – concepts for speech acts.

The aspect of linguistic meaningfulness that is missing when semantic theories are treated in detachment from language users is often studied under the heading of 'force'. 'Theories of force' of various kinds have been offered. And Austin's views about illocution can be taken to amount to his own account of force. Austin speaks of an utterance's '*illocutionary* force'; and he distinguishes as finely between the different forces that utterances may have as between different illocutionary acts that speakers may do. Thus if someone warns someone of something, her utterance has the force of a warning; if someone congratulates someone, her utterance has the force of congratulations . . . One might suggest that it is the same for saying: if someone says something to another, her utterance has the force of *saying*.

Austin's own project was not that of explicating linguistic meaning; and he offered no account of *saying*.[20] He was more interested in providing an exhaustive survey of species of illocutionary acts than in uncovering a unified account of the phenomenon of illocution. Wishing to show linguistic action off in all its great variety, Austin made many distinctions among sorts of illocutionary acts, and he paid special attention to particular conventionalized illocutionary acts (such as the example we noted of naming a ship). *Saying* would hardly have been the speech act of choice for Austin, given its humdrum character. But its very ordinariness ensures that *saying something to someone* will count as fundamental among the various things that speakers do in making meaningful noises.[21]

And it is plausible that an account of *saying something to someone* is part of what is needed in the explication of linguistic meaning. Whatever language she speaks, a person who utters a sentence which means that *p* is likely to be saying that *p* to someone. A connection is made here between something issuing from a semantic theory – namely, what a certain *sentence* means – and something that a *speaker* may do in giving voice to the sentence – namely say something. *Saying* is thus a speech act that comes to notice if one thinks about general connections between what sentences mean and what speakers do with them. (If we look to non-indicative sentences, as well as to indicative ones, then there will be other connections to think about. It is for simplicity's sake that I treat only *saying* here.[22])

2.3 Saying something to someone as communicative

Austin thought that people do things *in* speaking in virtue of their being understood by others. More precisely, he claimed that doing something illocutionary:

> involves the securing of uptake . . . [i.e. it involves] bringing about the understanding of the meaning and force of the locution.[23]

To see what this implies, suppose that Sue says something to Helen, and does so in uttering a sentence which (as a semantic theory might tell one) means that *p*. Then what Austin here calls the 'meaning' of the locution is that *p*; and what Austin calls the 'force' of the locution is *saying* (we saw that, for Austin, force is illocutionary force). According to Austin's claim, then, Sue's saying that *p* to Helen involves Helen's being brought to understand that *p* was said. When *saying something to someone* is treated as an illocutionary act in Austin's sense, it is thought of as something that a person does in bringing it about that she is taken to have done it.

In this account, the act of saying that *p* is characterized by reference to a certain type of effect. It is common enough to think of what a person does in terms of effects of her actions. (Someone who has broken the jug, for example, is someone an effect of whose action – in terms of which we think about what she did – is that the jug is now broken.) But in the case of an illocutionary act like *saying* we encounter something more than this common phenomenon. For here the effect a speaker must have is the effect of being taken by the hearer to have done *that very act*. The idea, then, is that what Austin called 'uptake' is an effect of a very special kind, which is peculiar to some linguistic acts. What is special about illocutionary effects is that our concepts for them (*saying to another*, for example) are just the speech act concepts of the actions whose effects they are. An illocutionary effect is someone's taking a piece of speech to be the sort of speech act that it (thereby) is. Illocutionary effects guarantee that speech is communication.

In accepting that *saying to another* is a communicative speech act, one allows that the idea of people saying things coexists with the idea of people understanding others as saying things to them. Austin probably didn't intend anyone to extract this from his claims. But it seems reasonable enough. A language user is a potential party to normal linguistic exchanges. A normal linguistic exchange involves (at least) two parties. So there being acts of saying requires not only abilities on the part of speakers but also co-ordinated abilities on the part of hearers who are receptive to things being said to them.

3 Against individualism in philosophical accounts of language

There will certainly be resistance to the account of *saying* I have just presented. I shan't be able to answer every objection that might be made. But I shall try to show that many of them spring from a common fount, and that this is a source of feminist dissatisfaction with much malestream philosophy – whether philosophy of mind, political theory, or epistemology.

3.1 Why invoke hearers?

It might be thought that *saying* as explicated here really can't belong in the Austinian category of *illocution*. For (as we saw) Austin wanted to use the idea of effects of speech to characterize *per*locutionary acts, and thereby to distinguish them from illocutionary ones. But now we find effects of speech – albeit effects of a special sort – used in the characterization of the illocutionary. Well, 'uptake' occurs often enough in what Austin has to say about *illocution* that there cannot be any doubt that he thought of what a speaker does *in* speaking as done by virtue of her speech impinging on a hearer. The question then is why Austin should have thought that effects only get in at the perlocutionary level. Why did he fail to acknowledge that he used effects to characterize *illocution*? One possible answer is that Austin supposed that the essence of what a speaker does is present in a self-contained account of a single individual. If this is the explanation of his inconsistency, then, despite his having pointed up the communicative character of speech, Austin was prone to a sort of individualism.

Questioning its fidelity to Austin will not be the only occasion for making objections to the account. Many philosophers will deny that *successfully saying something to another* could be a simple notion, or a fundamental one. (And they might say that if I have interpreted Austin correctly, then so much the worse for Austin.) They want to treat *saying something to another* as containing a basic speaker-related ingredient from which any reference to communication, or to hearers, can be separated off. They may allow that we need to think of speakers having intentions directed towards hearers. But they say, 'What one can do with a hearer-directed intention, one can also do without.' And from this they deduce that there must be two separable necessary conditions of a person's saying something to another. A piece of conceptual arithmetic is meant to ensure that an individualistic property attaching to an individual speaker is an extricable component of her communicating with someone else. But I should claim (in company with P. F. Strawson[24]) that the arithmetic of these philosophers is bogus.

Such conceptual arithmetic is the basis of a kind of 'decompositionalism', which can lead to accounts from which relations are extruded. In the present case, the relation lost through decomposition is the relation between one language user (a speaker) and another (a hearer). Decompositionalist thinking pervades analytic philosophy wherever 'necessary and sufficient conditions' for the applications of concepts are sought. Philosophy of mind is one of the areas in which such thinking has been called into question recently: many have come to doubt, for instance, that the attribution of the state of mind of 'seeing x' to a person is equivalent to any conjunction of something purely internal with something purely external.[25] In the philosophy of language, I suggest, we have similarly to acknowledge that the attribution of a piece of linguistic communication between two people is not equivalent to the conjunction of something purely speaker-related with something purely hearer-related.[26]

The decompositionalism to which I am objecting here might be regarded as a masculine way of thinking. For we are sometimes told that men – men in our culture, that is – 'prefer what is separable', and that women 'assign importance to relational characteristics'.[27] If it is true that, being women, we 'are less likely to think in terms of independent discrete units', then philosophers' failure to give an account of *saying something to someone* that introduces an idea of communication might be blamed on habits of thought which we should expect to strike us – culturally situated as we are – as male.

When it comes to linguistic communication, decompositionalist thinking underwrites a kind of individualism that has independently been castigated as male.[28] When 'seeing x' is treated as decomposable, subjects of experience are cut off from visible objects. But when communicative linguistic concepts are treated as decomposable, human beings are cut off from one another. The treatment of language then exhibits the kind of individualism which has been taken to be characteristic of liberal political theory – in which accounts of social arrangements are based in properties of individuals atomistically conceived. Such theory, which lacks a conception of politics which gender can easily mix with, does not suit feminists.[29]

One cannot make a case for communicative speech acts merely by showing that they emerge when habits of thought that may strike one as male are rejected. Of course not. If men are indeed acculturated to think in one way and women in another, then that is not yet to say that either style of thinking has a monopoly on the truth in any area. But in a culture where most philosophical writing has come from the pens of men, a certain significance is bound to attach to a criticism of a piece of philosophy if the target of the criticism is a male habit of thought. And the individualism to which decompositionalism leads goes deep in modern philosophy (as we shall see).

3.2 *Gricean intentions repudiated*

It might help to make a case for the communicative nature of some speech acts to show that alternative accounts ought not to be congenial to anyone.

Intentions of a sort which Grice first proposed are often supposed to be characteristic of language use.[30] On an orthodox (malestream) account, what is central to language use, which enables connections to be forged between semantic theories and accounts of speakers' lives and minds, is a particular kind of complex, hearer-directed intention on the part of speakers. Thus, it is claimed: someone who addresses a hearer, H, using an indicative sentence that means that p typically has a three-part intention. This comprises a primary intention to produce a belief in H by using an utterance whose content is that p, a secondary intention that the utterance should have a feature by means (in part) of which H recognizes the primary intention, and a further intention that recognition of the primary intention should be part of H's reason for believing that p. Such an intention is supposed to belong to a speaker who says something to H.[31]

I think that this ought to seem ludicrous. Real people regularly get things across with their utterances; but real people do not regularly possess, still less act upon, intentions of this sort. Developmental psychologists find it doubtful whether three-year-old children possess the concept of belief; but they do not find it doubtful that three-year-olds can, for instance, tell them things. And notice that an enormous amount would be demanded of hearers, as well as of speakers, if such complex intentions really were needed in order to say things. Unless a hearer H actually thinks, for example, that her (H's) recognition of S's primary intention is intended . . ., there could not be any point in S's intending that it should be so intended. And there would seem to be various things that a hearer would have *not* to think if speakers had these complex intentions. (It is often said to be necessary for S's saying something to H that S does not intend that H should think that she (S) lacks the intention that H's recognition of her primary intention should be part of H's reason for believing that *p*. But then H must surely *not* think that S lacks the intention that . . . .) So a person would have to achieve an extraordinary wariness in order to grasp that a speaker with Gricean intentions had said something to her. But surely one doesn't need to judge the extent of someone's complex intentions exactly aright in order to converse with her. I think that it should strike us as plainly incredible that it might be as difficult to participate in the ordinary communicative use of language as the orthodox account of saying would have it.

It requires explanation why such obviously implausible accounts have gained the acceptance they have. Part of the explanation would surely be found in philosophers' readiness to think individualistically, and another part in their unduly intellectualized conception of human beings, as 'men of reason'.[32]

3.3 Speech acts and semantics again

I have responded to those who doubt that *successfully saying something to someone* could be a simple and fundamental concept (section 3.1). But there will be further doubts when it is suggested that this concept has a place in an overall philosophical understanding of linguistic meaning.

Part of the point of attending to *saying* was to get into a position to understand better a connection between the deliverances of semantic theories and the practices of speakers. When the account I have offered is brought to bear, the suggestion must be that where a semantic theory tells one that a sentence *s* means that *p*, utterances of *s* are seen as fit for use to say that *p* to someone, and that an utterance is fit for such use only where a fellow language user's taking it to be so used could suffice for a speaker who uses it having said that *p*. The application of semantic concepts is now viewed as inseparable from the application of concepts of linguistic force; and a communicative concept, which has application only when speakers and hearers can find one another intelligible, is introduced into the account of force. No linguistic meaning without saying, and no saying without communication.

This view of the matter represents a departure from the usual one. Usually a semantic theory for a language is taken to correspond to an isolable psychological state belonging to each of the individual speakers of the language.[33] The conditions of a sentence's being fit for a certain use (its having a certain meaning) are then treated as something that could in principle be known by someone who never participates in speech acts – they are treated as separable from the conditions required for a sentence's actually being put to use. The usual view is supposed to be recommended by the fact that speakers of English, of Turkish, of Hindi, of Malay . . . have something in common. The thought then is that the theorist's task is to extract what is common, so that, in any particular case, what is left over corresponds to a theory for a particular language – for English, . . ., for Malay, etc. But the thought shows only the possibility of a theoretical piece of abstraction. What is in question here – which divides the communicative view from the usual one – is not the abstraction that semantic theories represent, but the idea that any real description of an individual person should be articulated along its lines.

The decompositionalism we were suspicious of earlier might encourage a conception of semantic knowledge as psychologically self-standing. And we should notice now that such a conception may be the product also of a certain philosophical frame of mind, which again has struck women as inimical to feminist thinking.[34] I mean a frame of mind which is characteristic of the sort of philosophy whose problems are generated in the first instance by inquiries into what relations might hold between a self-contained subject (on one hand) and a world of objects, or of other self-contained subjects (on the other). When it comes to language, alone in one's study one may think of one's own language as something one could know in isolation from others. The sentences of one's language can appear to equip one simply to 'express beliefs'; directing remarks to another person appears to be a separate matter, requiring 'other minds'. It then appears as if one could perfectly well have the knowledge that a semantic theory might be supposed to record one as possessing, but lack what it takes to communicate.

Appearances can be deceptive. It surely isn't plausible that it is possible actually to learn a first language except in interaction with other speakers. Why should it be thought possible even in principle to achieve the state of mind of someone who knows a language but cannot say anything to anyone? By what right does a philosopher in his study assume that a person could possess the skill that a semantic theory records but have no communicative abilities? Provided we avoid decompositionalist arithmetic, we can allow that the notion of 'expressing belief' that a person thinks she applies to herself in isolation actually depends upon notions picked up in the situation in which language is learnt. Then we shan't think that it is really possible that someone should know a language but be unable to communicate.[35]

Philosophers who think in isolation about language make an assumption about the self-sufficiency of the individual language user. Just such an assumption, about the self-sufficiency of the *epistemic* subject, has recently been brought to the surface in epistemology.[36] (Here we see that the individualism of liberal political theory is characteristic of much more than properly political thought.) In epistemology, the assumption has been put under pressure by inquiring into the function of knowledge, or into the point of having the concept.[37] And so it can be in philosophy of language. The philosopher who thinks about language in abstraction from use forgets about its function: he forgets what sentences are *for*. Sentences of course are for communicating with. Thus we make the function of language evident if we accord a central role to *saying something to another* in the explication of linguistic meaning.

When the assumption about the self-sufficiency of a speaker is renounced, philosophy of language can begin from the situation in which people are such as to get their thoughts across to one another. Understanding is then seen to be attuned not only to the significance of words but also to speakers' performances of acts like saying. A certain transparency between those who share a language is acknowledged.[38] But the possibility is admitted that relations of power and authority, which differentiate speakers, will affect which speech acts they are capable of performing.[39] The institution of language is social *au fond*.

4 Feminism and philosophy of language

I shall finish with an attempt at an illustration of the difference that it makes for feminists to recognize that language is social *au fond*. Elsewhere I have argued that when speech is treated as illocution, an egalitarian position about *free speech* is lent a distinctive content and argumentative foundation.[40] One conclusion I tried to establish is that upholding what libertarians cherish under the head of free speech will work to the advantage of those whose speech least needs protecting, and thus, in many current climates, to women's disadvantage. That conclusion may be reinforced, I think, by considering so-called hate speech.

4.1 'Hate speech'

Regulations that proscribe and penalize 'hate speech' have sometimes been in place on university campuses in the USA. 'Hate speech' can be the name for speech which is addressed to individuals whom it is intended to insult – to insult on the basis of their sex, race, handicap, sexual orientation etc. – and which makes use of hate words, i.e. words which are commonly understood to convey direct and visceral hatred or contempt.[41] 'Libertarian' can be the name for the position of those who claim that any regulation of hate speech is bound to be contrary to a defensible principle of free speech. I want to cast doubt on two of the libertarians' arguments. (I don't address the question of whether hate speech should ever be regulated.[42])

The first argument is meant to make us deny that speakers should be held responsible for hate speech's harmful effects. The libertarian's premise is that the effects of speech on a hearer are brought about through a certain kind of 'mental intermediation' (as it has been called in US courts).[43] The effects of speech are supposed to be mediated by the thinking and beliefs of the person to whom it is directed, so that the construction put upon the words is the responsibility of that person. When a word is construed as conveying visceral hatred, this construction is then (according to the libertarians) more the fault of the hearer than the speaker.

Well, the idea of such mental intermediation might find favour among philosophers who swallow the story about hearer recognition of Gricean intentions (see section 3.2 above). But one need only see that story for the fiction it is to be in a position to allow that (say) a woman who is called 'a slag' may be directly hurt and insulted through no fault of her own. When the phenomenon of illocution is recognized, we can better understand how hate speech works to convey contempt: hearer reactions to speech are attuned directly and simultaneously to the significance of words and to speakers' performances.[44]

The second argument is meant to make us accept that a victim of hate speech always has a remedy – in the form of more speech. What the libertarians claim now is that insofar as speech can cause hurt, the hurt can always be redressed: the injured party can always contradict, or answer back, it is said. And so (it is concluded) speech, though some of it may be hateful, is bound to be harmless overall.[45] In response to this, the first point to notice is that hate words don't have obverses in a certain sense. There are words for women (say) that are commonly understood to convey contempt, but no counterpart words for men. And so it seems to be for blacks vs. whites, gay people vs. straight people, non-nationals vs. nationals. In all of these cases, there is vocabulary enabling a member of the second group to vilify a member of the first, but not conversely. Of course in any of these cases the situation may change: a claim about asymmetries can concern only *common understandings at a particular time*. Still it is noteworthy that at any time, those who are objects of vilification are those who are then already at the losing end of discriminatory practices. The lack of an obverse for (say) 'slag', or 'nigger' or 'faggot' is not an accidental lexical gap.

The claim that hate speech can simply be redressed now seems plainly wrong. For if there is a word that you can use to insult me, but no word that I can use to insult you, then, in one straightforward sense, there is no such thing as my answering back. It isn't possible to answer back by contradicting what was said; for where a hate word adds to a neutral word an expression of contempt (as, in some quarters at present, 'nigger' adds to 'black'), there is no way in which the hatefulness can be gainsaid. (It is true that the retort 'I am not a nigger' is not itself a piece of *insulting* hate speech. But, like any other retort, it cannot serve to remove the contemptuousness conveyed in an insulting use.[46]) This explains the reaction of right-minded people to hate words that insult people in groups to which they don't themselves belong: they have no use for them.

A different reaction may be possible for people who do belong to groups that hate words insult. And it is a response that may be possible also for people who are well placed to evince solidarity with members of insulted groups, or, again, for people who have the medium of satire to play with. For such people the words can be put to a *new* use. If a word is used in a context in which there cannot be an intention to insult, then its use will not be a piece of hate speech. But words mean what they are used to mean. And uses of hate words, in enough new contexts, may serve to counteract the possibility of their hateful use, and thus to change their common understanding. When the libertarian said that 'more speech' was the remedy for hate speech, such cumulative non-hateful usage was not what he had in mind. Nevertheless, it seems that a hate word might, through benign usage, be deprived of its power to insult. We can probably all think of cases where re-signification seems to have happened through a political process of appropriation: 'gay' is one striking example. Examples in which a hate word has ceased to be a hate word are hard to find except within particular dialects. (In some dialects, perhaps, the power of 'dyke' to insult has been defused.)

4.2 *Meaning and change*

Hate words, then, may change their meanings. And so, of course, may other words: the phenomenon of meaning-change at the level of vocabulary is familiar enough. But it is theoretically quite challenging to account for. I suggested that 'mental intermediation' is an obstacle to appreciating how very simple it can be for one person to hurt another using words. I should also suggest that the usual individual and rationalistic model of the workings of language is an obstacle to appreciating the social mechanisms at work in meaning-change.

To recognize meaning-change is to recognize that the abstraction from social patterns to which a semantic theory corresponds is not an invariant thing. A much finer-grained understanding of 'a language' than I have worked with will be required to accommodate this. 'A language' is something shared by people who are readily intelligible to one another at that time. In my view, such intelligibility depends upon the sort of (normal, human) social environment that is illocution's *sine qua non*. Of course it depends on very much more than this. On any actual occasion of language use, there are many things that a speaker does, all of which would need to be specified to record her 'total speech act'.[47] The abstraction which corresponds to 'what the speaker's words meant then' is an abstraction from such total speech acts. And total speech acts depend in their turn upon (among other things) the attitudes of those whose acts they are.

When a pejorative term, whose application to a group of people is derogatory, comes to lose its negative associations, the attitudes expressed by those who use it change. Relevant changes of attitude, it seems, might be directly brought about in the use of language itself. But it may not be possible to make the right sort of allowance for this if one is required to think in independence about the speaker and the hearer on an occasion when a word is used in a slightly new sense. One wants to admit that the message conveyed with a piece of speech, in simple cases at least, can be something immediately shared between people. One wants, in a word, to allow that speech acts are communicative.

Conclusion

If communicative speech acts are admitted into philosophy, there could be more than one reason to count that a feminist advance. In section 3, I represented that a current of thought created by the feminist tide can lead to the repair to malestream philosophy of language that I should want to make – in which communicative speech acts are introduced at the place where Gricean intentions feature in the orthodoxy. And I have just suggested that the orthodox (unrepaired) account may be unable to accommodate meaning-change. If so, it is surely unfit to serve as the basis of accounts of actual social phenomena. (Some philosophers may claim that a philosophical account of language, being non-empirical, is no more obliged to illuminate the phenomenon of meaning-change than to speak directly to, say, questions about particular sexist usages. But if the idea of these philosophers is that philosophy never makes empirical commitments, then they should think about what flows from the supposition that linguistic meaning might be explained by crediting speakers with Gricean intentions. Empirical claims about the nature of the generic, but individua-listically conceived, human subject are rife in modern philosophy.)

At any rate, real-world social linguistic phenomena are bound to be neglected while philosophy of language is pursued along malestream lines. Not that even the repaired philosophical account makes any actual progress with practical political questions by itself. The account I advocate assumes that language users are socially related, but it does not speak to any of the actual properties, whether individual or social, of the socially related people who use languages. A realistic account of language use, by reference to which questions that concern feminists can be formulated, has to refine and extend, as well as instantiate, an abstract philosophical account. But the philosophical account must have the right ingredients before the gulf between philosophical treatment of language and the treatment of actual linguistic phenomena in the social world can be bridged.[48]

NOTES

1 'Malestream' – introduced at least twenty years ago (I don't know by whom) – remains a useful term for the preponderantly male mainstream. It might seem tendentious to identify a body of philosophical work by allusion to its maleness. But the claim need only be that the contributors are *de facto* nearly all men. (In the 1997–98 edition of *Philosophy Study Guide* (© Philosophy Panel, University of London), for example, around 98 per cent of the entries under 'Philosophy of Language' are written by men.)

2 I have had to ignore discussions in psychology and sociolinguistics here; and even within philosophical work, the brief overview that follows is very selective.

3 *Man Made Language* (London: Routledge & Kegan Paul, 1980).

4 E.g. Deborah Cameron, *Feminism and Linguistic Theory* (Andover: Macmillan, 1985).

5 E.g. Janice Moulton, 'The Myth of the Neutral "Man"' and Carolyn Korsmeyer,

'The Hidden Joke, Generic Uses of Masculine Terminology', in Mary Vetterling-Braggin, Frederick A. Elliston and Jane English, eds., *Feminism and Philosophy* (Totowa, NJ: Rowman & Allanhead, 1977), pp. 124–53; Adèle Mercier, 'A Perverse Case of the Contingent A Priori: On the Logic of Emasculating Language (A Reply to Dawkins and Dummett)', in Sally Haslanger, ed., *Feminist Perspectives*, special issue of *Philosophical Topics* 23:2 (1995), 221–59.

6 Virginia Valian, 'Linguistics and Feminism', in *Feminism and Philosophy*, pp. 154–66.

7 For a phenomenologically acute presentation of one such argument, see Carol Cohn, 'Nuclear Language and How We Learned to Pat the Bomb', reprinted in Evelyn Fox Keller and Helen Longino, eds., *Feminism and Science* (Oxford: Oxford University Press, 1996), pp. 173–84.

8 Alienation is discussed in chs. 6–8 of Cameron, *Feminism and Linguistic Theory*.

9 Cameron, *Feminism and Linguistic Theory*, chs. 6–8 are relevant again. And see T. Olsen, *Silences* (New York: Delacorte Press, 1978). One focus of debate has been Catharine MacKinnon's claim that 'pornography silences women': see 'Francis Biddle's Sister', in C. MacKinnon, *Feminism Unmodified: Discourses on Life and Law* (Cambridge, MA: Harvard University Press, 1987).

10 E.g. Patrizia Violi, 'Gender Subjectivity and Language', in Gisela Bock and Susan James, eds., *Beyond Equality and Difference: Citizenship, Feminist Politics and Female Subjectivity* (Routledge: London, 1992), pp. 164–76.

11 For references to ideas about how imagery and metaphor work in philosophical texts, see Lloyd's chapter in the present volume. For French feminism and the philosophy of language, see Andrea Nye, 'The Voice of the Serpent: French Feminism and the Philosophy of Language', in Ann Garry and Marilyn Pearsall, eds., *Women, Knowledge, and Reality: Explorations in Feminist Philosophy* (London: Unwin Hyman, 1989), pp. 233–49. And for relevant psychoanalytical material, see Further Reading under 'Feminism and Psychoanalysis' in this volume, p. 266.

12 See Andrea Nye, 'Semantics in a New Key', in Janet A. Kourany, ed., *Philosophy in a Feminist Voice: Critiques and Reconstructions* (Princeton: Princeton University Press, 1998).

13 An example is Deborah Cameron, whose criticisms I started to address in my 'Disempowered Speech', in Sally Haslanger, ed., *Feminist Perspectives*, special issue of *Philosophical Topics* 23:2 (1995), 127–47.

14 *How to do Things with Words*, 2nd edition (Oxford: Oxford University Press, 1975).

15 Ibid., p. 109.

16 Ibid., p. 103.

17 I rely at this point on what Austin says: 'a *locutionary act* is roughly equivalent to uttering a certain sentence with [something] roughly equivalent to "meaning" in the traditional sense' (ibid., p. 109). Austin had no single stable conception of the locutionary, and he often used 'say' for it (incorrectly in my opinion, cp. note 120). A defence of my reading of Austin, and an account of illocution (of which only a portion emerges here) is given in my 'Illocution and its Significance', in S. L. Tsohatzidis, ed., *The Foundations of Speech Act Theory: Philosophical and Linguistic Perspectives* (London: Routledge, 1994).

18 'A particular language' assumes that languages can be individuated. The assumption raises questions that I don't approach until section 4 below (see note 47). In the meantime, I assume that e.g. 'English' names a language.

19 It has been claimed (and I don't demur) that a Tarskian definition of 'true' for a language can serve as its semantic theory. The entrance of 'true' into the study of language has itself been a cause of feminist objection: see Nye, 'Semantics in a New Key'. In the present context, I hope it will be clear that if 'true' had a place in semantic theories, then that would not 'purge language of . . . communicative power'.

20 Austin initially contrasted performing with stating – as if stating (or saying) something was not a case of doing something – thus making it seem that 'state' (or 'say') could not be illocutionary. Although Austin (rightly) abandoned this contrast, he (unluckily) didn't follow through on the implications of abandoning it.

21 Ordinarily *assertion* is the speech act used to connect a semantic theory with speakers' practices (though Austin himself gave a special place to *stating*: see previous note). There are good questions about the relations between these various speech acts. The answers, I believe, need not be affected by claiming an illocutionary status for them all.

22 And for simplicity's sake, I allow myself to assume (as I have argued elsewhere) that force and mood can be correctly related when force is understood in terms of illocution. See my 'Things Done With Words', in J. Dancy et al., eds., *Human Agency: Language Duty and Value* (Stanford: Stanford University Press, 1988), pp. 27–46.

23 Ibid., pp. 160–1.

24 'Bogus arithmetic' is one of the resources of an opponent whom Strawson envisaged in his 1967 lecture 'Meaning and Truth' – an opponent keen to make much of the point that 'What we can do with an audience-directed intention, we can also do without any such intention', p. 185. The lecture is printed in *Logico-Linguistic Papers* (London: Methuen, 1974), pp. 170–89.

25 The challenge to decomposing *seeing* (which contests the extrusion of the relation between a subject of experience and a visible object) can be an instance of a very general claim that has led to the idea of '*broad* mental states'. (Mental states' breadth is the nub of the anti-individualism mentioned at note 28 below.) For a proof that conceptual arithmetic of the kind I am resisting is bogus (i.e. leads to demonstrably false conclusions), see Timothy Williamson, 'The Broadness of the Mental: Some Logical Considerations', forthcoming in *Philosophical Perspectives* 12, ed. James Tomberlin (1998), 389–410. Williamson's paper is useful for showing why non-decomposable concepts should be serviceable.

26 There is actually more at issue here. A speaker may be said to have gone in for an act of an illocutionary kind even though there was no uptake on the part of a hearer. For example, we can imagine someone reporting 'I warned him, but he didn't realize that I was serious'; or 'I said that – to him, but he didn't hear me.' So we have to allow that the verb 'say to someone' might apply to someone not taken by any hearer to have said anything. This is to allow that ordinary verbs like 'warn' and 'say to someone' do not stand for illocutionary acts as Austin defined them. Commentators on Austin have all responded by revising Austin's account, so as to make only 'the aim', not 'the achievement', necessary for an

illocutionary act's performance. But if one thinks that a speaker's aiming at uptake is not adequately understood except by reference to what it is for uptake to be achieved, then one has a reason to introduce a notion of illocutionary act like Austin's own, i.e. a notion designed to include the achievement. (See further my 'Illocution and its Significance'.)

27 See Merrill Hintikka and Jaakko Hintikka, 'How Can Language be Sexist?', in S. Harding and M. B. Hintikka, eds., *Discovering Reality: Feminist Perspectives in Epistemology, Metaphysics, Methodology, and the Philosophy of Science* (Dordrecht: Reidel, 1983). Sally Haslanger also cites this in the present volume; I am happy to take her reservations on board.

28 'Individualism' has recently been used for a number of different philosophical theses. I note that the present anti-individualism is different from one which Tyler Burge has demonstrated and which I also endorse – that propositional mental-state and event kind terms are *nonindividualistically individuated*. The difference between Burgean anti-individualism and that defended here might be put by saying that the Burgean sort bears on 'that *p*' in 'means that *p*' whereas the present sort bears on 'means that' in 'means that *p*'.

29 See Naomi Scheman, 'Individualism and the Objects of Psychology', in her *Engenderings* (London: Routledge, 1993), pp. 36–53 (p. 43). Much work in political philosophy plays variations on the theme that individualism, by eradicating gender, potentially excludes feminists' concerns from the political arena.

30 There is an enormous literature stemming from Grice's 'Meaning', *Philosophical Review* 66 (1957), 377–88. Here I should note that there is no single account accepted by all who believe in 'Gricean intentions', and that philosophers who have developed the various accounts have had different overall objectives.

31 Both Grice and Schiffer used intentions of this sort in an account specifically of *saying*. For the use of complex intentions to make what I have called 'the fundamental connection between semantic theories and speakers' practices', see e.g. section 5.1 of Martin Davies, 'Philosophy of Language', in N. Bunnin and E. P. Tsui-James, eds., *The Blackwell Companion to Philosophy* (Oxford: Blackwell, 1996), pp. 90–139.

32 *The Man of Reason*, by Genevieve Lloyd (London: Methuen, 1984), is mentioned in the 'Introduction' to this volume, and in many papers here.

33 Cp. John McDowell, 'Antirealism and the Epistemology of Understanding', in H. Parret and B. Bouverese, eds., *Meaning and Understanding* (Berlin, New York: Walter de Gruyter, 1981), pp. 225–48. McDowell shows that a semantic theory corresponds to an isolable psychological state in Dummett's view. I take the isolability claim to be endorsed by others than Dummett, even if others don't rely upon it to draw those anti-realist theses that McDowell was concerned to refute.

34 See e.g. Naomi Scheman, 'Confessions of an Analytical Philosopher Semi-Manqué', in her *Engenderings*, pp. 245–9.

35 Here one takes Wittgenstein's side. Many of the early remarks in *Philosophical Investigations* (trans. G. E. M. Anscombe, Oxford: Blackwell, 1976) are designed to free us from the standing temptation to think of language in abstraction from use.

36 I am concerned here with 'strong self-sufficiency' in the sense of Louise Antony's

'Sisters, Please, I'd Rather Do it Myself: A Defense of Individualism in Feminist Epistemology', in Sally Haslanger, ed., *Feminist Perspectives*, special issue of *Philosophical Topics* 23:2 (1995). (As Antony's title may suggest, she and I aren't on exactly the same side.)

37 An example would be the practical approach to explaining the concept of knowledge taken in Edward Craig's *Knowledge and the State of Nature: An Essay in Conceptual Synthesis* (Oxford: Clarendon Press, 1990).

38 In my 'Illocution and its Significance' I introduced 'reciprocity' as a name for the condition which is part of the background of any social human environment and which provides for such transparency. In emphasizing how relatively easy communication *can* be, I don't deny that (as Andrea Nye, in 'Semantics in a New Key', properly says, we must allow that communication can be difficult: see next note).

39 See, e.g. Sarah Richmond, 'Derrida and Analytical Philosophy: Speech Acts and their Force', *European Journal of Philosophy* 4:1 (1996), 38–62, esp. 'Conclusion'. The implications of differences between speakers that arise from social relations won't be appreciated until a much wider range of illocutionary acts than I have been able to look at here is considered.

40 See 'Free and Equal Speech', *Imprints* 1:2 (1996), 59–76. For the argument as it bears on feminist debate, see J. Hornsby and R. Langton, 'Free Speech and Illocution', *Legal Theory* 4:1 (1998), 21–37.

41 This (though not itself intended as a definition) is extracted from a definition that Thomas Gray formulated for use in a Code of Practice for Stanford University, which was struck down by the courts.

42 Questions about hate speech can arise outside any legislative context. I have spoken of 'a defensible principle of free speech' (rather than the First Amendment of the Constitution of the USA, from which American libertarians actually argue) not only because we are not all US citizens, but also to remind us that free speech can be a principle of political morality, and that when it comes to such a principle the legal interpretation of a particular country's legislation might be neither here nor there. For a discussion which acknowledges that questions about regulation cannot be disregarded in a full treatment, see Judith Butler, *Excitable Speech: A Politics of the Performative* (London: Routledge, 1997).

43 For an account of this, and a good discussion, see Susan J. Brison, 'Speech, Harm and the Mind-Body Problem', *Legal Theory* 4:1 (1998), 39–61.

44 One would need to be more precise about illocution than I have been able to be here to determine whether *insulting* might itself be an illocutionary act. The present point is only that hate speech relies upon there being some illocutionary act.

45 This conclusion – of overall harmlessness – requires that two wrongs can make a right. A less implausible conclusion (against which my arguments will also serve) would be that there are no *particular* groups of people who need be at the losing end where there are no impediments to hate speech.

46 One sees this clearly if one thinks of pejorative words as non-conservatively extending languages to which they are added: see Michael Dummett, *Frege: Philosophy of Language* (London: Duckworth, 1973), p. 454. (Not all hate words can be understood in this way, however.)

47 For an account of how much is properly involved in this notion, see my 'Disempowered Speech', where allowance is made for fine-grained individuation of languages, so that sense can be made e.g. of 'dialects'.
48 I thank my co-editor for her comments on an earlier draft.

6

SALLY HASLANGER

Feminism in metaphysics
Negotiating the natural

Introduction[1]

Metaphysics has never been without critics. Plato's efforts have repeatedly been a target of attack; Hume ranted against the metaphysicians of his day; and one of the founding missions of logical positivism was to show that metaphysical claims are meaningless. More recently, feminist theorists have joined the chorus. To reveal among academic feminists that one's specialization in philosophy is metaphysics is to invite responses of shock, confusion and sometimes dismissal. Once after I gave a presentation at an American Philosophical Association meeting on social construction, a noted senior feminist philosopher approached me and said, 'you are clearly very smart, and very feminist, so why are you wasting your time on this stuff?' Academic feminists, for the most part, view metaphysics as a dubious intellectual project, certainly irrelevant and probably worse; and often the further charge is levelled that it has pernicious political implications as well.[2]

Academic feminism has never been without critics either. If academic theorizing is an effort to achieve objective accounts of the world and its parts, and if feminism is a political movement guided by substantive moral and political values, then, some have suggested, the idea of academic feminism is oxymoronic.[3] Philosophers have been especially keen to discount the relevance of feminist thinking to research outside of normative moral and political theory, and the idea that feminism might have something to contribute to metaphysics is often regarded as ridiculous.[4] Reality is what it is, and the metaphysician's goal should be to discover what it is apart from the social and political values we bring to it.

These representations of metaphysics and of academic feminism are distorted and presuppose cartoon versions of contemporary research in the two areas. Yet even if we allow that there are more subtle understandings of metaphysics and feminist inquiry, the questions remain: is there a place within feminist inquiry for metaphysics? Does feminist theory have anything to offer metaphysicians? My goal in this chapter is to begin to answer these questions, with full awareness that both subject areas are too large, too multifaceted, and too contested to capture comprehensively. The best I can hope to do is make clear what facet of each I'm considering as we proceed. At the start I should make clear that my discussion will focus exclusively on Anglo-American metaphysics and Anglo-American feminism.

With this limitation in mind, we need to ask: what is metaphysics, anyway? Oversimplifying considerably, it can be organized into three main parts: (i) A study of what there is, or what is real. (This area is also known as *ontology*.) E.g. Are minds distinct from bodies? In addition to physical objects, does the world include properties, natural kinds, universals, essences? (ii) A study of the basic concepts employed in understanding ourselves and the world, e.g. existence, predication, identity, causation, necessity. (iii) A study of the presuppositions of inquiry, or first principles.

There has been significant feminist work addressing many substantive ontological issues: personal identity, mind/body, free will.[5] The question I will focus on here is how feminism might contribute to the more abstract issues in metaphysics. What would it mean to have a feminist theory of causation or modality? Can feminist inquiry help us discover the basic categories of being?

Feminists themselves disagree about whether and how feminist inquiry might engage with metaphysics. It is important to distinguish at least two different reasons behind their attitude of suspicion. Some have argued that the questions and claims of certain dominant metaphysical theories are male-biased, and recommend less male-biased replacements; whereas others have argued that feminists have good reason to reject the project of metaphysics altogether. Feminist critique of the second sort resists the temptation to engage in any metaphysical theorizing; though, as we shall see, metaphysical issues are not completely ignored.

I shall elaborate these critiques a bit further in the following sections, offering some examples. Both forms of critique, I believe, raise important questions, but are also flawed. After considering these flaws I will suggest some ways to build on their strengths to develop yet another approach to feminist metaphysics.

Androcentric versus gynocentric metaphysics

In the 1980s there was a surge of feminist work that looked behind the debates over concrete political issues such as sexual violence, reproductive rights, and equal pay, to consider how sexist beliefs are embedded in our theorizing.[6] Some of this work was motivated by the awareness that (supposed) reasoned debate was not always an effective tool for combating sexism because its epistemological and metaphysical assumptions were preventing certain points of view from being heard or taken seriously. It became clear that science and philosophy are at least as prone to sexism as any other social institution; what's worse, they often provide the tools to buttress the institutions that are the more immediate problem.

Blatantly sexist theories – ones that assert women's inferiority to men, claim that women's subordination is good or appropriate, or recommend gender-stereotyped behaviour – are not absent from philosophy. But feminist theorizing in this period also raised questions about the less obvious ways that philosophical theorizing contributes to women's subordination. One important form of such critique is directed at *andro-centrism*. Very briefly, a theory is androcentric if it takes males or masculinity to be the norm against which females and femininity are considered deviant,[7] or if it considers its subject matter from the point of view of men and simply ignores women or women's perspective.[8] Let me mention just two sample arguments that raised the question of androcentric bias in metaphysics.[9]

In their paper, 'How Can Language be Sexist?', Merrill and Jaakko Hintikka argue that an ontology of discrete particulars is biased towards males:

> [W]omen are generally more sensitive to, and likely to assign more impor-tance to, relational characteristics (e.g. interdependencies) than males, and less likely to think in terms of independent discrete units. Conversely, males generally prefer what is separable and manipulatable. If we put a premium on the former features, we are likely to end up with one kind of cross-identification and one kind of ontology, if we follow the guidance of the latter considerations, we end up with a different one.[10]

Hintikka and Hintikka go on to point out that 'Western philosophical thought' has emphasized an ontology of discrete objects 'individuated by their intrinsic or essential (non-relational) properties', and has been 'un-favorably disposed towards cross-identification by means of functional or other relational characteristics'. They ask, 'Is it to go too far to suspect a bias here? It seems to us that a bias is unmistakable in recent philosophical semantics and ontology.'[11] In response they recommend Jaakko Hintikka's contextually based methods for cross-identification.

Iris Young argues in her paper 'Pregnant Embodiment: Subjectivity and Alienation' that attention to the phenomenology of pregnancy 'jeopardizes dualistic metaphysics altogether. There remains no basis for preserving the mutual exclusivity of the categories of subject and object, inner and outer, I and world.'[12] For example, 'Pregnancy challenges the integration of my bodily experience by rendering fluid the boundary between what is within, myself, and what is outside, separate. I experience my insides as the space of another, yet my own body.'[13] Pregnancy does not only make vivid the 'externality of the inside',[14] however, but also challenges a disembodied conception of agency based in the 'dichotomy of subject and object'. In the experience of pregnancy, Young argues, awareness of the body need not be in tension with the accomplishment of one's aims. 'The pregnant woman experiences herself as a source and participant in a creative process. Though she does not plan and direct it, neither does it merely wash over her; rather she *is* this process, this change.'[15]

These critiques have in common the idea that metaphysical theorizing as we've known it tends to draw uncritically on experiences and patterns of thought that are characteristically male or masculine, and ignores or devalues those that are characteristically female or feminine, in a context where there is no reason to think that the male or masculine perspective deserves to be privileged. This charge of androcentrism is not simply a political charge, but concerns the epistemic credentials of a theory. If men and women do differ systematically in their perspectives on the basic features of reality (let's call these proposed perspectives 'androcentric' and 'gynocentric' perspectives), and if a particular metaphysical theory has reflected only the androcentric perspective, then it is right to charge it with male-bias. Likewise, theorizing entirely from a gynocentric perspective would not be warranted unless there were grounds for privileging a gynocentric perspective on the issue. Perhaps for this reason, this genre of feminist critique has been more effective in revealing the limitations of mainstream views than in defending gynocentric ontologies.

Note, however, that many feminists reject this form of critique. In the first place, it is very difficult to establish convincingly systematic differences between the perspectives of men and women on the kinds of phenomena in question. As feminist philosophers of science have often pointed out, research 'documenting' the differences between men and women along stereotypical lines has often been credited with accomplishing much more than the evidence warrants because it tells us what we've been taught to expect.[16] Because the stereotypes also serve socially to keep women in their place (marking those who fail to fit the stereotype as deviant), this research requires heightened scrutiny.[17]

One major difficulty in establishing that there are systematic differences between men's and women's perspectives is that men and women are so tremendously varied as individuals, and across race, class, culture and historical period. As a result it becomes very difficult to describe the experiences of women 'as a group'. Consider Young's reports of the phenomenology of pregnancy. The problematic of embodied agency that her experience eloquently refutes is actually culturally specific. It is not hard to imagine a different scenario in which the extent of agency involved in being pregnant is simply not an issue, or in which the mother does not experience herself as an agent in the process. This might occur either because the cultural meanings of pregnancy do not engage the issue of agency, or because of the individual history of the woman or the pregnancy in question. A single experience of the breakdown of subject/object or inner/outer in pregnancy (such as Young's) can be enough to challenge the reigning metaphysical dichotomies. But in such a case it is difficult to charge the dominant view with *androcentrism* if the claim is only that it is insensitive to the experiences of some pregnant women. In short, we need to ask: what exactly is a 'gynocentric' perspective? Must a 'gynocentric' perspective capture the experiences of all or most women? And if not all women have access to a 'gynocentric' perspective, do efforts to describe such a perspective rely on problematic normative stereotypes about how women *should* be?

It is plausible that gender is a factor affecting one's perspective on the world. But if gender itself is a culturally variable phenomenon, then it may not be possible to capture *the* mediating force of gender in terms of a shared content to be found in women's thought. This being said, however, it would be wrong to neglect the failings of a theory that systematically ignored or devalued a female or feminine perspective, as it appears in context. Consider for example a context where women are socialized to be sensitive readers of emotions and men are socialized to be emotionally insensitive. A theory constructed in that context (by those who are socialized in this way) that denied the reality of emotion would be at least *contextually androcentric*. In making the charge of 'contextual' androcentrism, however, care must always be taken to look carefully at the potentially complex meanings of gender in the context, as well as variations across contexts.

To sustain a distinctively gynocentric metaphysics, one would have to argue that either having a female body, or being socialized as a female, provides one with better access to reality.[18] However, those who are committed to the idea that there are distinctive (and competing?) androcentric and gynocentric perspectives, and yet are wary of privileging any perspective, may opt instead for the idea that neither men nor women know what is real because it is impossible to overcome the distorting effects of gender (and other social factors) on our thinking. This is the direction Jane Flax takes:

> To the degree that thought depends upon and is articulated (to ourselves and others) in language, thought and the 'mind' itself will be socially and historically constituted. No ahistorical or transcendental standpoint exists from and by which the Real can be directly and without construction/distortion apprehended and reported in or by thought.[19]

The idea seems to be that once gender (and other social factors) mediates our access to reality, it does not make sense to claim privilege for a gynocentric perspective; no perspective can tell us what's 'Real'.

Many metaphysicians are likely to hear this as a bold metaphysical view (how can you tell what would distort reality without some access to undistorted reality as a basis for comparison?). Setting such concerns aside, however, the thought is clear enough: because our thinking is culturally conditioned, we are not able to discover what is really 'Real'. So any scheme of metaphysics that attempted such a project of discovery would be profoundly misguided. If one adopted this view, one might then go on to argue that a gynocentric perspective is preferable, not because women have privileged access to reality, but on the basis of other virtues, perhaps epistemic, perhaps political. This challenge goes well beyond a critique of particular metaphysical claims. So let us now turn to the broader critiques of metaphysics as a whole.

Feminist anti-foundationalism

In describing the subject area of metaphysics (in my introduction), I set out what I take to be the central questions without saying much about the method for addressing them, or more generally, the epistemology of metaphysical inquiry. What methods should we employ to analyse our basic concepts or to discover the categories of being? Suppose it is true that we don't have 'direct' access to reality. Does it follow that the project of metaphysics is impossible or indefensible?

It is difficult to emphasize too strongly that method has always been a matter of controversy within metaphysics. Unsurprisingly, method in metaphysics has reflected the influence of broader trends in epistemology. In periods where foundationalist epistemology was dominant, foundationalism tended to be dominant in metaphysics. (By *foundationalism* I mean here the philosophical view that a belief is justified only if it is itself certain, or is derivable from premises that are certain.) But in periods where foundationalism has been questioned, metaphysicians have worked with other epistemic frameworks. In mid century, ordinary language philosophers were keen both to address questions about what there is and to provide conceptual analyses of basic metaphysical concepts through subtle reflection on ordinary language; and linguistic/semantic analysis is to this day an important and much-used tool in addressing metaphysical questions. Language is assumed to be a medium through which we have access to what there is; and there is no assumption that the truths being analysed are known with certainty. In the context of post-Quinean metaphysical debate, the thought that we might have *or need* certainty, or direct access to reality, in order to make legitimate ontological claims, has been rejected.

Despite this, it is not uncommon to find feminist theorists criticizing metaphysics because of its 'foundationalism'. There are two strands to this critique (though some theorists focus on one strand, others on the other). The first concerns the nature of our access to reality. Do we have direct access to reality, e.g. unmediated by gender socialization or other cultural norms, and does the project of metaphysics assume that we do? The second concerns the 'foundational' role of metaphysical claims in non-metaphysical theorizing. Does metaphysics function to constrain our theorizing within patriarchal limits by setting unquestioned and unquestionable starting points? The two issues can be linked; for if metaphysicians wrongly assume that we have unmediated access to reality when in fact our access is culturally conditioned by background sexist and racist beliefs, and if metaphysics also functions to constrain our theorizing within the limits it sets, then this poses a very serious problem for any effort to overcome oppressive attitudes and practices.

I'll return in the next section to consider the first strand of this critique in more detail. A more pressing issue is that the critique has as its target a very substantive conception of metaphysics that is, as far as I can tell, completely outdated. Let me sketch what I take to be a very widely endorsed approach to metaphysics in the contemporary Anglo-American tradition, which I'll call the *aporematic* approach. Here one begins inquiry by asking a question and looking for answers. Theorizing starts when one finds a particular puzzle, tension, or contradiction in the answers, either in one's beliefs on the question or, more generally, in the claims made on a certain topic. The goal is to resolve these puzzles in order to achieve a broadly consistent set of beliefs, allowing beliefs to be weighted according to plausibility. Other theoretical virtues may also play a role, though the question of which virtues and what role is controversial and should itself be explored through an aporematic inquiry. Sometimes resolution of the puzzle comes by rejecting the original question as ill-formed or confused; sometimes it comes in rejecting one or another of the conflicting claims as unwarranted.

Puzzles from different subject areas interact with each other, so that in theorizing about metaphysical topics, for example, attention to the broader picture is required. Any results achieved will be revisable as inquiry proceeds.

On this view metaphysics is not, at least in the traditional philosophical sense, a foundational project at all: it is not a quest for self-evident premises on which one can build the edifice of knowledge. Aporematic metaphysics might reasonably be considered immanent metaphysics: the questions, the puzzles, and the proposed answers arise within our thinking in response to current theoretical and practical demands. My sketch is rough enough to accommodate a variety of different non-foundational epistemologies; but it is certainly common for theorists working in this model to adopt an account of justification that is *holist* – a belief is justified if it coheres widely with other beliefs one has – and is, in two senses, *fallibilist* – all beliefs are revisable, and one might be epistemically justified in believing something that is nonetheless false.

Moreover, there is no suggestion that an aporematic approach to metaphysics need be foundational in the senses suggested by the feminist critique briefly mentioned. On an aporematic approach, making justified claims about the world does not require direct access to it; and metaphysics makes no claim to authority over other forms of inquiry: it is perfectly consistent with, and is in fact required by this approach that our metaphysical inquiry should be responsive to a broad range of experience as well as theoretical pressures from other domains, including normative inquiry in epistemology and moral theory.

It is in this last respect, I believe, that contemporary Anglophone metaphysics tends, in practice, to fall short of its epistemic responsibilities: the common strategy of 'analytic' philosophy to break down questions to simpler ones and to focus on everyday examples masks the selectivity involved in prioritizing the phenomena the theory needs to accommodate. Feminist and anti-racist theorizing is especially attentive to phenomena that have been eclipsed both by dominant theorizing and 'common sense', and is highly sensitive to unstated priorities; for these reasons metaphysical discussion would more fully approximate the aporematic ideal by attending to and engaging with the feminist and anti-racist literature.

Still, it should be recognized that feminist theorists are not merely tilting at windmills when they argue against metaphysics as a 'foundational' project. Feminist theory is an interdisciplinary field, and often theorists are responding to philosophical claims or assumptions made in their field, rather than to current work in philosophy. Consider, for example, Joan Scott's characterization of history:

History has been largely a foundationalist discourse. By this I mean that its explanations seem to be unthinkable if they do not take for granted some primary premises, categories, or presumptions. These foundations (however varied, whatever they are at a particular moment) are unquestioned and unquestionable; they are considered permanent and transcendent . . . In the minds of some foundationalists, in fact, nihilism, anarchy, and moral confusion are the sure alternatives to these givens, which have the status (if not the philosophical definition) of eternal truths.[20]

In many cases the feminist challenge to foundationalism is a request to reconsider the starting points of the author's field, to ask whether these starting points are biased, and what purposes have been served by treating these assumptions as unquestionable. Because very often the starting points take the form of a commitment to certain kinds of entities, to certain kinds of explanation, to a certain basic conceptual framework, and because these are entities, explanations and concepts that also fall within the subject matter of metaphysics, the critique is reasonably lodged against the use of metaphysical assumptions in the field in question. But this does not make it a critique of metaphysical inquiry within academic philosophy.

If we take an aporematic approach to metaphysics, then we must acknowledge that what questions we ask, and what puzzles arise in our attempts to give answers is going to be, to some significant extent, a parochial matter: it will depend on cultural and historical context, broader theoretical needs, etc. In a social context in which sexist and racist views are widely held and institutionalized, there is a compelling need for theories that diagnose, explain, and replace the sexist and racist beliefs. We need not suppose that these theories will be gynocentric – in the sense that they privilege a special female or feminine perspective; rather, they are feminist insofar as they engage the realities of women's oppression with the goal of ending it.[21] As these theories emerge, they may be relevant to metaphysics in two ways: feminist theories – including feminist moral and political theory and epistemology – may have repercussions that must be accommodated in our metaphysics; and feminist insights into the cultural/historical context of the metaphysical puzzles we consider may defuse and/or replace them.

Admittedly, all this remains very vague and abstract. To enrich the discussion, let us return to the issue of 'direct access' and consider a topic of considerable importance in both metaphysical and feminist theorizing: natural kinds.

Feminist metaphysics: natural and social kinds

One of the major preoccupations of traditional metaphysics is the extent to which the mind is involved in constructing the world. Is there a structured world existing independent of us, whose 'joints' we can sometimes capture in our theorizing? Or is the appearance of structure entirely dependent on us?

The question of the mind's involvement with the world is also of primary concern to feminists theorizing gender (and race). Traditional efforts to justify what we now view as racist and sexist institutions have portrayed women and people of colour as 'different', and often explicitly 'inferior', *by nature*. In these contexts there is an unmistakable pattern of projecting onto women and people of colour, as their 'nature' or as 'natural', features that are instead (if manifested at all) a product of social forces. This projective error has led feminists to be extremely suspicious of natural kinds and objective types: if one function of references to 'nature' or 'natures' is to mark the boundaries of what is socially possible, thereby 'justifying' pernicious institutions, we must be wary of the suggestion that any category is 'natural'.[22] Yet feminists have also recognized that there are some limits on what social arrangements are possible for human agents. So we are left with a host of questions. Is there any meaningful (and politically viable) distinction between the natural and the social, and if so, where does the line fall? Is there any way to theorize about what's natural that does not depend on the projection of our political biases? If so, how?

The terminology of 'natural kind' is used in several different ways, so it will be helpful to draw a couple of distinctions. The term 'kind' is sometimes used in the classification of substances, where the paradigm substances are ordinary (physical) objects. Substances are to be classified according to their essence, so kinds consist of groups of objects with a common essence. For example, tigers constitute a kind of thing because each tiger has essentially a certain cluster of properties that define the kind. On other occasions, the term 'kind' is used to refer to what I'd like to call here *types*. Types are groups of things, sometimes substances, but possibly (e.g. in the case of higher-order types) non-substances, that have a certain unity. This unity is typically not a matter of sharing essential properties. So, for instance, red things constitute a type (their unity consists in their all being red), even though redness is seldom an essential property of the things that have it. Unity seems to come in different degrees, so, for instance, the things on my desk might be thought to constitute a weak sort of type (they have in common the fact that they are on my desk), and at the limit there are highly gerrymandered sets of things that have no unity at all and so fail to constitute a type.

Given these different uses of the notion of 'kind', the problem of 'natural kinds' appears in different forms. One version concerns whether there are groups of things, in particular, substances, that share a common essence.

(This debate links directly to debates over 'Aristotelian' essentialism.) Another version is whether there are what I will call *objective types*. Assuming that there is a distinction between types and random gerrymandered sets, the question is what distinguishes types from the rest? A realist about objective types is someone committed to there being a kind of unity independent of us that distinguishes certain groups of individuals – the objective types – from others. Anti-realists may simply be *sceptical*, arguing that we cannot know whether there are objective unities, or they may be *nominalist*, granting that there is a distinction between types and random sets of things, but maintaining that the basis for being a type is non-objective, i.e., dependent on us. In the context of feminist theory, *realism* about both kinds and types – the view that there are natural kinds/types and that we can come to know what they are (or at least what some of them are) – is generally assumed not to be an option. Forms of scepticism and nominalism are by far the preferred positions. This, I think, is a mistake. In what follows I'll look briefly at some feminist concerns about kinds, but will concentrate on the issue of types. My goal is to indicate why a modest realism about types is compatible with feminist insights into the problematic political rhetoric of 'natures' and what's 'natural'.

The social construction of the body

For some time feminists have been concerned to challenge the idea that there is such a thing as 'women's nature' (or 'men's nature'). Historically dominant views about men and women assume that anatomical sex, social position and sexual preference come in two distinct packages: there are those who are anatomically male, socially men and sexually desire (only) women; and there are those who are anatomically female, socially women and sexually desire (only) men. Those who don't fit into one or the other of these packages are considered deviant, and are devalued and abused. The picture driving this package deal seems to be one in which individuals have gendered natures or essences that explain the 'normal' combinations of anatomy, social position and sexuality; and various institutions (from medicine to the law) justify their treatment of individuals by taking the alleged natures as normative – the law protects individuals who are appropriately expressing their gendered/sexual nature, and it punishes those who are not; medicine is framed with the 'normal' packages in mind and undertakes to rebuild those who aren't normal in this sense.

It has been a primary goal of feminist theory to challenge the givenness, naturalness and stability of this picture. Judith Butler, for example – along with many others – argues that the normalized conjunctions of body/

gender/sexuality are not grounded in natures or essences (as she puts it: genders are not substances); rather, we are to think of these conjunctions as natures through participating in social institutions that are structured to take advantage of the limitations they also impose upon us.[23] Butler, in particular, suggests that we should work to break up the dominant model by proliferating alternative bodily possibilities, and specifically encourages gender crossings that parody the assumption of natural gender configurations (such as drag).

These arguments at the very least provide an important case study for debates about essentialism and natural kinds (in the first sense mentioned). If our investment in gendered natures is as politically grounded and as misguided as suggested, then we need to reflect carefully on our broader commitments in the area to determine whether our inquiry has been biased in favour of an ontology that serves particular political ends. What other ontologies have been ignored? Why? And at what cost?

Recent feminist discussion has gone on to question not only our commitment to natures, but also objective types. Turning again to Butler, it is clear that simply rejecting the idea of gendered natures wouldn't by itself destabilize the idea that there are two acceptable sexes (male/female) with two acceptable sexualities (male desire for female; female desire for male). One can grant that gender is constructed and still maintain that there are right and wrong ways for bodies to be, and to be sexual. Butler's somewhat unexpected next move is to reconsider the category of sex:

> And what is 'sex' anyway? Is it natural, anatomical, or hormonal, and how is a feminist critic to assess the scientific discourses which purport to establish such 'facts' for us? Is there a history of how the duality of sex was established, a genealogy that might expose the binary options as a variable construction? If the immutable character of sex is contested, perhaps this construct called 'sex' is as culturally constructed as gender . . .[24]

The point of her rhetorical questions here is to suggest that sex, i.e. the distinction between male and female, is not a natural 'given', but a construction, and moreover, a construction parasitic on the social categories of gender. Roughly, the idea is that if we ask why we divide human beings into the two groups we do, along the lines of 'sex', then the answer can't simply be: because bodies naturally come in these two forms; a complete answer will have to make reference to the gendered structure of our social worlds.

To illustrate this point, consider Monique Wittig's analysis of the social category of gender.[25] On Wittig's account, gender is defined in terms of the social/sexual positions made available under regimes of compulsory heterosexuality: *very roughly*, one is a woman by virtue of serving the hetero-sexual and reproductive needs of others; and one is a man by having one's heterosexual and reproductive needs served. Compulsory heterosexuality in this context is understood as a social institution regulating what sorts of bodies we recognize – and it does so by treating one of many anatomical distinctions between people as fundamental and, importantly, casting this choice of distinctions as determined entirely by natural facts about our bodies. Under such regimes, what matters most in thinking about human bodies is who has a penis and who has a vagina, and so these are the markers we focus on in making our basic distinction between kinds of human beings.[26]

Butler's discussion of sex suggests that the distinction between males and females is not objectively grounded even in non-essential facts, and instead is motivated by forces that are politically problematic; in particular, by the forces sustaining compulsory heterosexuality. In other words, we're not (or not simply?) mapping nature's joints in distinguishing males and females; we're enforcing a political regime.

Anti-realist commitments?

There is no doubt that oppressive regimes justify themselves and eclipse alternative political arrangements by casting their representation of the world as revealing nature's real structure. This motivates Butler's broad argumentative strategy: when an oppressive regime purports to be grounded in objective or independent facts, show that the supposed facts are neither objective nor independent, but are 'constructed' by the regime itself. Then add to this critical project positive suggestions for new sorts of distinctions that would at least provide the conceptual space for alternative social arrangements. This strategy is in many respects familiar and appealing; and the creativity and insight feminists have demonstrated in challenging the objectivity of entrenched categories is remarkable. But it is not clear that this line of thought provides reasons for accepting an anti-realist approach to objective types; if anything, it seems to presuppose such an anti-realism (otherwise, how can one be confident that an effort to challenge the supposed objectivity of the regime's grounding will be successful?). What is the basis for such an assumption?

It will help to return to the idea that our access to reality is mediated. Let's grant for the moment that there are many social and cultural factors – notably gender among them – that affect how we conceptualize the world, and that there is no way we can 'step outside' all conceptualization to determine which, if any, will provide the resources to capture how the world really is. Gripped by these insights, it is tempting to locate ourselves once again behind a 'veil of ideas', not a veil as opaque as Descartes supposed necessarily, but one at least that filters any information we might receive. A translucent veil, however, would seem to be little help so long as we're not in a position to compare what we experience through the veil with the reality behind it; we still have no way to distinguish in experience between what is real and what is a result of the veil's filtering effects. The best we can hope to accomplish is to describe the world-as-it-appears-through-the-veil, and to offer each other new veils that filter the world in different ways, hoping for ways that will invite us to restructure our political arrangements to be less oppressive. So, for example, a world consisting of males and females appears when we wear one veil, but if we change our veil we find a much more complex array of human bodies. On this view, the claim that the world itself (i.e. unveiled) really contains males and females should be regarded as suspect, for no one has access to unveiled reality. An insistence on the reality of males and females is instead serving a political function, normatively positioning certain bodies as preferable to others.

This picture, I think, guides a lot of feminist thinking about metaphysics and epistemology. Within this picture the suggestion that there are objective types of which we can gain knowledge makes little sense: perhaps we can have knowledge of types-as-they-appear-through-the-veil, but this is knowledge of types constituted in part by us, not objective types. Of objective types we must remain, at best, sceptical. I believe this picture is misguided in several ways.

Consider an argument that would seem to support it. In *Bodies That Matter*, Butler maintains that discourse does not 'construct' things (such as the sexes) in the sense of bringing them (wholly) into existence; nonetheless we can only refer to things that have been partly constituted by discourse:

> To concede the undeniability of 'sex' or its 'materiality' is always to concede some version of 'sex,' some of 'materiality'. ... To claim that discourse is formative is not to claim that it originates, causes, or exhaustively composes that which it concedes; rather, it is to claim that there is no reference to a pure body which is not at the same time a further formation of that body. In this sense, the linguistic capacity to refer to sexed bodies is not denied, but the very meaning of referentiality is altered.[27]

> Indeed, to 'refer' naively or directly to such an extra-discursive object will always require the prior delimitation of the extra-discursive. And insofar as the extra-discursive is delimited, it is formed by the very discourse from which it seeks to free itself. This delimitation ... marks a boundary that

includes and excludes, that decides, as it were, what will and will not be the stuff of the object to which we then refer.[28]

In short, our discursive practices mediate our relation to the world in such a way that any attempt we might make to refer to something independent of discourse compromises the independence of that to which we 'refer'. Why? Because any act of reference depends upon a boundary that we set (to refer to an object or a kind is to refer to something with the particular boundaries we determine), the boundaries of the objects and kinds we refer to are constituted by us. Therefore, the things we can know or refer to are not 'pregiven', or 'extra-discursive', i.e., their boundaries are not objective. But this argument is fallacious.

One way to capture the fallacy is to see it as ignoring a crucial scope distinction. The following claim is ambiguous:

(i) We make it the case (through our discursive practices, etc.) that the things we refer to have the boundaries they do.

On one reading (i) makes a relatively uncontroversial point:

(i_a) We make it the case (through our discursive practices, etc.) that *the boundaries of our reference*, i.e., our referents *qua* things referred to, are what they are.

On (i)'s other reading, the point is highly controversial:

(i_b) We make it the case (through our discursive practices, etc.) that *the boundaries of objects we refer to* , i.e., our referents *qua* individuals, are what they are.

Butler's argument seems to slide from (i_a) to (i_b). But if we reject that inference, then it is possible to grant that our acts of reference depend upon often problematic background presuppositions, while also maintaining that some things and some kinds have objective boundaries. In other words, we can eagerly develop the political potential of (i_a), without relinquishing the belief that the world includes some 'pregiven' and 'extra-discursive' objects.

Two main questions underlie what is at issue here. First, does it follow from the fact that our epistemic relation to the world is mediated (by language, by concepts, by our sensory system, etc.) that we cannot refer to things independent of us? Certainly not. Intermediaries do not necessarily block access: when I speak to my sister on the phone, our contact is mediated by a complicated phone system, but I still manage to speak *to her*. And intermediaries sometimes improve access: there are many things in the world I cannot see without my glasses, and there are many things I cannot recognize without my concepts. Donna Haraway reminds us of the amazing prosthetic devices – telescopes, microscopes, listening devices, cyborgs – that enhance our access to the world through their mediation.[29] If we aren't in a position to compare our experience with the reality 'behind it', then is it not as contentious to hold that our experience/discourse is a 'further formation' of that reality as it is to say that it aptly captures it?

Second, does it follow from the fact that I cannot get outside of myself to 'check' my experience against reality that I cannot know what's real or what's true? Again, no. This takes us back to the epistemological issues raised in the previous section. Admittedly, some philosophers have insisted on certainty as a condition for knowledge. But there are many other conceptions of knowledge that accept this limitation and set alternative, satisfiable conditions on justification. There is a temptation to think that if we cannot 'get outside' of ourselves to test our beliefs against reality, then there's nothing further we can do epistemically to regulate belief; we're left with only political negotiation. But there are other epistemic considerations that can be brought to bear on belief, and provide grounds for claims to truth, for example coherence, evidential support, fruitfulness, etc. Oddly, many feminists feel pressed to scepticism about an independent reality because they implicitly endorse a traditional conception that requires certainty or direct access to reality in order to have knowledge of it, while at the same time they often find the traditional conception of knowledge problematic. In fact, metaphysical inquiry should be no more problematic than other forms of inquiry if certainty/direct access is not required for legitimate claims about what's real, and if an alternative epistemology – a feminist social empiricism, say – can be developed to replace the traditional one.

Is there now any further reason why someone sympathetic to a feminist political agenda need adopt either a nominalist or sceptical stance towards objective types? More specifically, if we acknowledge that our ways of classifying human bodies are motivated by problematic sexist, racist and heterosexist concerns, must we deny that there is an objective difference (or a knowable objective difference), say, between males and females? I don't think so. Remember how the move to nominalism functions in the structure of Butler's strategy: if there is no objective basis for distinguishing one group from another, then no political regime – especially the dominant one – can claim authority by grounding itself in 'the way the world is'; instead (I assume) the choice between political regimes will have to be made on the basis of normative argument. The worry seems to be that if we allow objective types, then we are politically constrained to design our social institutions to honour and sustain them.

But that worry is unfounded. One can easily maintain that the choice between political regimes requires normative debate while accepting a form of realism about types. Even if there are objective types, the question remains which of them are morally and politically relevant. The realism I've been defending is an ontological view: the idea is that some properties are more important than others in structuring the world, and it's not up to us, so to speak, which these are.[30] More precisely, some properties, in themselves and not in relation to us, play a fundamental role in determining what the world (as a whole) is like and how it evolves. There are a number of factors that might be relevant to whether a property should count as fundamental – and it is certainly not settled – but traditionally philosophers have pointed to the need to account for non-trivial similarity relations and causal laws. So, if we compare the set of all hydrogen atoms with a gerrymandered set (e.g. that consisting of the Statue of Liberty, the cars currently parked in the lot at the San Diego Zoo, and the last sentence of each of Toni Morrison's novels), both may be the extension of some property, but the property determining the former set is more fundamental than the property determining the latter.

Realists and non-realists can agree that any grouping of things, however miscellaneous, constitutes a set; and they can also agree that some sets are more important to us than others. What makes a set important *to us* will depend on our purposes.[31] For example, the miscellaneous set of things in my refrigerator is important to me when I'm trying to decide what to make for dinner; the set of things on the top of my desk is important when I'm trying to pack my office to move. Depending on what I want to know and why, different properties of things are relevant, and how fundamental they are usually matters little. Some decisions, moreover – about who counts as an American citizen, or who counts as a mother – are politically and legally important, and cannot be settled simply by deciding what divisions are to be found in 'nature'. The realist can agree with the non-realist that our classification schemes are often motivated by interest-laden concerns, and that we need to look beyond questions of what is ontologically fundamental to determine how to structure our lives socially and politically; these issues are not ones that divide the two sides of the debate. The realist begins to diverge from the non-realist, however, when she claims that in some cases it is important to know what sets are fundamental, e.g. what properties are causally significant, in order to effectively interact with or understand the world.

The strategy of challenging oppressive regimes by arguing that their representation of the world is inadequate is a good one, and introducing alternative conceptual frameworks on which to construct new political arrangements is essential to social change. But these political insights don't provide a basis for accepting an anti-realism about types. Even the most extreme realist about classification may grant that social factors play a role in determining what classification scheme we use, and that it is appropriate that they do so. In the case at hand, a realist could argue that there are lots of relatively objective unities to choose from in thinking about human bodies, and any one we mark will be marked for social reasons. Or she could argue that the categories of male and female are not objectively unified to any significant degree, but that we have been simply taught to think they are for political reasons. Or again, she could argue that the distinction between males and females is fundamental, but that it should still not be a basis for drawing moral or political distinctions. Any of these options allows for the social change Butler is concerned to promote. None of them denies the existence of objective types.

Conclusion

The previous section is an example, I hope, of feminist metaphysical debate. What makes the discussion feminist is not that it claims privilege for a woman's perspective, or that it assumes that women have different access to reality than men. It is feminist in its concern with the ways in which our views about the mind and reality either sustain or challenge oppressive patterns of thought and behaviour. It is also, I hope, an example of aporematic metaphysics. The background issue is whether ontological realism is compatible with the feminist insight that oppressive regimes mistakenly justify themselves by claiming that their political arrangements are grounded in 'nature' or are based in 'the way the world really is'. If one's metaphysical views must fit with other well-justified claims to be justified themselves, and if feminist argument suggests that there isn't 'a way the world really is' or that we could never know what way that is, then one's realism must be put to the test. I've argued that feminist doubts need not lead one to an anti-realism about types, and in doing so I've also touched on the question whether feminist metaphysics itself – understood as a feminist inquiry into what there is – might be possible.

NOTES

1 For valuable discussion on related topics, many thanks to Elizabeth Anderson, Richard Holton, Rae Langton, Mary Kate McGowan and Sam Ruhmkorff. For that and comments on an earlier draft, thanks to Miranda Fricker, Jennifer Hornsby and Stephen Yablo. Special thanks to Miranda and Jen for their patience and excellent editorial advice.

2 E.g. N. Fraser and L. Nicholson, 'Social Criticism without Philosophy: An

Encounter Between Feminism and Post-modernism', in L. Nicholson, ed., *Feminism/Postmodernism* (New York: Routledge, 1990), pp. 19–38; J. Butler, 'Contingent Foundations', in J. Butler and J. Scott, eds., *Feminists Theorize the Political* (London and New York: Routledge, 1992), pp. 3–21.

3 E.g. S. Haack, 'Epistemological Reflections of an Old Feminist', *Reason Papers* 18 (Fall 1993), 31–43.

4 E.g. J. Searle, 'Rationality and Realism: What Is at Stake?', *Daedalus* 122 (1993), 55–83.

5 See e.g. S. James, 'Feminism in Philosophy of Mind: The Question of Personal Identity', and N. Scheman, 'Against Physicalism', in this volume.

6 E.g. S. Harding and M. Hintikka, eds., *Discovering Reality* (Dordrecht: D. Reidel, 1983).

7 As is common, I use the terms 'male' and 'female' to refer to the two standard anatomical sexes, 'man' and 'woman' to refer to the two standard genders (understood as social positions), and 'masculine' and 'feminine' for the norms associated with the genders.

8 See E. Anderson, 'Feminist Epistemology: An Interpretation and Defense', *Hypatia* 10 (Summer 1995), 58–9.

9 Psychoanalytic feminism offers another sort of androcentric critique not discussed here. See, e.g. J. Flax, 'Political Philosophy and the Patriarchal Unconscious', in Harding and Hintikka, eds., *Discovering Reality*.

10 M. Hintikka and J. Hintikka, 'How Can Language Be Sexist?' in Harding and Hintikka, eds., *Discovering Reality*, p. 146.

11 Ibid., p. 146.

12 I. Young, 'Pregnant Embodiment', in her *Throwing Like a Girl and Other Essays* (Indianapolis: Indiana University Press, 1990), p. 161; see also I. Young, 'Breasted Experience', in *Throwing Like a Girl*, pp. 189–209.

13 'Pregnant Embodiment', p. 163.

14 Ibid., p. 163.

15 Ibid., p. 167.

16 See C. Tavris, *The Mismeasure of Woman* (New York: Simon and Schuster, 1992).

17 Note, e.g. that Hintikka and Hintikka cite as the basis for their claim about cognitive differences between the sexes a study on children in second to fourth grades that was already twenty years old when they published their paper. When they generalize the result to 'women', they cite a paper that still only surveys research on children, and moreover, questions their empirical premise: E. E. Maccoby, 'Sex Differences in Intellectual Functioning', in E. E. Maccoby, ed., *The Development of Sex Differences* (Stanford: Stanford University Press, 1966), esp. pp. 27, 41–2.

18 See, e.g. N. Hartsock, 'The Feminist Standpoint: Developing the Ground for a Specifically Feminist Historical Materialism', in Harding and Hintikka, eds., *Discovering Reality*, pp. 283–310; and S. B. Hardy, 'Empathy, Polyandry, and the Myth of the Coy Female', in Ruth Bleier, ed., *Feminist Approaches to Science* (New York: Pergamon, 1986), pp. 119–46.

19 J. Flax, 'The End of Innocence', in Butler and Scott, eds., *Feminists Theorize the Political*, p. 453.

20 J. Scott, 'Experience', in Butler and Scott, eds., *Feminists Theorize the Political*, p. 26.

21 See H. Longino, 'In Search of Feminist Epistemology', *The Monist* 77 (1994), 472–85.
22 See my 'On Being Objective and Being Objectified', in L. Antony and C. Witt, eds., *A Mind of One's Own: Feminist Essays on Reason and Objectivity* (Boulder, CO: Westview Press, 1993), pp. 85–125, and 'Ontology and Social Construction', in Sally Haslanger, ed., *Feminist Perspectives on Language, Knowledge and Reality*, special issue of *Philosophical Topics* 23:2 (1995), 95–125.
23 J. Butler, *Gender Trouble* (New York: Routledge, 1990), and *Bodies That Matter* (New York: Routledge, 1993).
24 *Gender Trouble*, p. 7.
25 M. Wittig, 'The Category of Sex', in *The Straight Mind* (Boston: Beacon Press, 1992), pp. 1–8.
26 Controversy in defining sex may emerge because reproductive and heterosexual needs focus on different body parts: heterosexual concerns with sexuality highlight perceptible bodily organs; concerns with reproduction highlight reproductive function, including hormonal/chromosomal factors.
27 *Bodies That Matter*, pp. 10–11.
28 Ibid., p. 11.
29 D. Haraway, 'Situated Knowledges: the Science Question in Feminism and the Privilege of Partial Perspective', *Feminist Studies* 14: 3 (Fall 1988), 575–99.
30 See M. K. McGowan, 'Realism or Non-Realism: Undecidable in Theory, Decidable in Practice', PhD Thesis, Princeton University, 1996; and D. Lewis, 'New Work for a Theory of Universals', *Australasian Journal of Philosophy* 61:4 (December 1983), 343–77.
31 See E. Anderson, 'Knowledge, Human Interests, and Objectivity in Feminist Epistemology', in Haslanger, ed., *Feminist Perspectives*, pp. 27–58.

7

RAE LANGTON

Feminism in epistemology
Exclusion and objectification

Introduction

Philosophy leaves everything as it is, or so it has been said.[1] Feminists do not leave everything as it is. We are always interfering, always fighting for something, always wanting things to be otherwise and better – even in philosophy itself. But if philosophy leaves everything as it is, shouldn't feminists leave philosophy as it is? If philosophy leaves everything as it is, then it cannot hurt women, and it cannot help women. To be sure, if philosophy leaves everything as it is, it leaves oppression as it is, but one should no more hope otherwise than one should hope for the stones to cry out for justice. Shouldn't feminists let philosophy be? Well, not everyone agrees with the one who said philosophy leaves everything as it is. Someone else began his meditations thus:

> Some years ago I was struck by the large number of falsehoods that I had accepted as true in my childhood, and by the highly doubtful nature of the whole edifice that I had subsequently based on them. I realized it was necessary, once in the course of my life, to demolish everything completely and start again . . .

He thought that philosophy can shore up prejudice – but can also uproot it, 'demolish everything completely', destroy 'the habit of holding on to old opinions'.[2] Descartes has been a villain of the story for many feminists, but on this question at least – on the question of philosophy's passivity or power – we are perhaps on the same side.

Many a woman has experienced vividly at first hand that demolition, that shaking of established belief, which Descartes thought necessary for the acquisition of knowledge – and it has happened not because she is a philosopher, retreating to a room of her own, but because she is a woman in the wide world. At some, usually early, point in her life, the news of women's oppression arrives as a shock, a sudden discovery that things are not as they had seemed to be. The discovery can be an exhilarating one for someone to whom the world had seemed gloomy. Life had seemed to offer little opportunity and adventure, no future fate but keeping house and raising babies, and then all of a sudden something – a friendship made, a scholarship won, a mountain scaled – reveals the perception of fate to be an artifact of oppression. Things are much better than they had seemed to be. The same discovery can also be a depressing one for someone to whom the world had seemed rosy. Life had seemed to offer a level playing field, full of opportunity and adventure, and then all of a sudden something – exclusion from the team, rape, unexpected pregnancy – reveals that the cards are stacked. Things are much worse than they had seemed to be. Foundations in either case are shaken, not by reflections on demons and sensory delusion, but by a life under inequality or oppression – a life which suddenly reveals for what they are those many falsehoods one had accepted as true. If doxastic shock is supposed to have the therapeutic effect Descartes ascribed to it, one might expect women to have an antecedent advantage as knowers. Perhaps oppression is a help to knowledge.[3]

The questioning of prejudice, and the philosophical method itself, have seemed to some feminists to go hand in hand. Mary Astell, writing in 1700, confronted the 'error' underpinning women's oppression, the '*Natural Inferiority* of our Sex, which our Masters lay down as . . . Self-Evident and Fundamental', and presented with typical eloquence the philosophical remedy for it.

> Error, be it as antient as it may, [cannot] ever plead Prescription against Truth. And since the only way to remove all Doubts, to answer all Objections, and to give the Mind entire Satisfaction, is not by *Affirming*, but by *Proving*, so that every one may see with their own Eyes, and Judge according to the best of their own Understandings, [the author] hopes it is no presumption to insist on this Natural Right of Judging for her self . . . Allow us then as many Glasses as you please to help our Sight, and as many good Arguments as you can afford to Convince our Understandings: but don't exact of us we beseech you, to affirm that we see such things as are only the Discovery of Men who have quicker Senses; or that we understand and Know what we have by Hear-say only; for to be so excessively Complaisant is neither to see nor to understand.[4]

More recently Michèle Le Dœuff has said that '"thinking philosophically" and "being a feminist" appear as one and the same attitude: a desire to judge by and for oneself'.[5] These are feminists who see that an insistence on judging for oneself can be a powerful tool against prejudice, whether of the sort challenged by foundational philosophy or the sort challenged by feminism.[6] Viewed this way, epistemology is a friend to feminism, in its ability to uproot 'the habit of holding on to old opinions', and to reveal women as rational knowers. The discovery of one's ability to judge for oneself – and the subsequent discovery that one is a thinking thing – can be at the same time a discovery that women are not made for servitude. Astell drew a feminist moral from her own Cartesian reflections, and drew it with her usual irreverence:

> [A] Rational Mind is too noble a Being to be Made for the Sake and Service of any Creature. The Service [a woman] at any time becomes oblig'd to pay to a Man, is only a Business by the Bye. Just as it may be any Man's Business and Duty to keep Hogs . . .[7]

The duties a woman might owe to a man are like the duties of a swineherd to his charges, a 'Business by the Bye', and not what she is made for. Astell is not simply a feminist who happens to be a philosopher, or a philosopher who happens to be a feminist: her feminism and her philosophy are allies. When what stands between oppression and liberty is 'the habit of holding on to old opinions', especially when the opinion that women are incapable of rational thought is an old one, rationalist methodology can be revolutionary. Given the non-accidental connection between her epistemology and her feminism, it would be churlish to deny that Astell is doing one sort of feminist epistemology.

If relations between feminism and epistemology were entirely friendly, then feminism's contribution to the subject would be to point this out, as Astell did. 'Feminist epistemology' would be epistemology aware of its own feminist implications. But there is more to the story than this, and there are many ways in which relations have not been entirely friendly. One central strand of the feminist contribution to epistemology has been to show how, when it comes to knowledge, women get left out. Another has been to show how, when it comes to knowledge, women get hurt. These partly overlap, since women may be hurt by being left out, but may be hurt in other ways too. To say that women get left out when it comes to knowledge is to say something vague, to say something that does duty for many things – which suggests already that we have here not so much a strand, but a rope, whose strands tend in the same direction; or not a rope, but a web, whose strands tend in different directions. Likewise for the second claim: to say that when it comes to knowledge women get hurt is to say something vague, something that does duty for many things. In what follows, these two claims – that women get left out, and that women get hurt – form the topics of the following two sections.

Knowledge and how women might be left out

A first way in which women might be left out is that women might *fail to be known*. Women might get left out, as objects of knowledge, in its various institutionalized branches. Women's lives may be rendered invisible by particular bodies of knowledge, such as history, economics, medicine and philosophy itself.[8] When historians chronicle only kings and dates and battles, women are left out. When economists analyse the relations between capital and labour, ignoring unpaid labour in the home, women are left out. When scientists study heart disease using male-only samples, women are left out. When philosophers define human beings as rational animals, assuming all the while that women are not rational, women are left out. To the extent that these things happen, women remain a kind of *terra incognita*.

This status of *terra incognita* has sometimes been viewed as distinctive of, even essential to, one's being as a woman. On this way of thinking it will appear no accident that women are unknown, for women appear as unknowable. Simone de Beauvoir wrote that of all myths about women,

> none is more firmly anchored in masculine hearts than that of the feminine 'mystery'. It has numerous advantages. And first of all it permits an easy explanation of all that appears inexplicable; the man who 'does not understand' a woman is happy to substitute an objective resistance for a subjective deficiency of mind; instead of admitting his ignorance, he perceives the presence of a 'mystery' outside himself: an alibi, indeed, that flatters laziness and vanity at once ... [I]n the company of a living enigma man remains alone ... [This] is for many a more attractive experience than an authentic relationship with a human being.[9]

When women are not known, there is ignorance on the part of men – 'a subjective deficiency of mind', as de Beauvoir puts it. The lazy way out is to say that the ignorance is not the fault of the ignorant subject, but of the unknown object: woman is a living enigma. If women are *terra incognita*, that is not the fault of ignorant men, but of unknowable women. An objective resistance is substituted for a subjective deficiency, and women's absence from the objects of knowledge appears to be an inevitability. De Beauvoir describes this as a kind of solipsism. The bridge to other minds – the bridge to women's minds – remains unbuilt. Solipsism is not simply a problem in epistemology, but a political problem: in the company of a living enigma, man remains alone.

A second way that women might get left out is by *failing to be knowers*: women might get left out as subjects of knowledge, rather than as objects of it. Here are some ways this might happen.

Women might fail to be knowers because they are deprived of the knowledge men have. From the earliest days of feminism it has been eloquently argued that women's subordination is constituted in part by barriers to the knowledge to which men have access. Here is Astell once again:

> Boys have much Time and Pains, Care and Cost bestow'd on their Education, Girls have little or none. The former are early initiated in the Sciences, are made acquainted with Antient and Modern Discoveries, they Study Books and Men, have all imaginable encouragement . . . The latter are restrain'd, frown'd upon, and beat, not for but from the Muses; Laughter and Ridicule that never-failing Scare-Crow is set up to drive them from the Tree of Knowledge. But if in spite of all Difficulties Nature prevails, and they can't be kept so ignorant as their Masters wou'd have them, they are star'd upon as Monsters . . .[10]

If some of us are more fortunate today, the complaint will remain that many women still lack knowledge: that women are deprived of the epistemological resources of the written word through lack of the requisite language, literacy, time, power, or economic resources; or that women are excluded, overtly or covertly, from particular fields of knowledge such as medicine or physics; or (more subtly) that a woman's under-confidence – her lack of what we might call subjective authority – means that even when she apparently knows, she does not know she knows, and therefore (given a certain principle about knowledge) does not really know.[11] The remedy for the complaint that women lack knowledge would be to remove the barriers to knowledge, whatever they may be. It would mean working for women's literacy and education, and removing the overt and covert discrimination which excludes women from particular fields of knowledge. It would mean creating the conditions that allow women to gain confidence, to gain the subjective authority required for knowledge, so that they can indeed 'see with their own Eyes, and Judge according to the best of their own Understandings', as Astell put it. A special role has been ascribed by some feminists to this claiming of subjective authority, with Marilyn Frye going so far as to call it 'the first and most fundamental act of our own emancipation'.[12]

Women may be left out both as subjects and as objects of knowledge if they are deprived of knowledge of themselves. One important strand in feminist thinking has been an argument that women lack knowledge of their own lives and experiences as women – precisely the knowledge one might antecedently expect to be the most accessible. Here the deprivation is not a lack of what men already have, for men lack it too. It is a lack of what women should be the first to have. Thus Betty Friedan wrote of an amorphous and gnawing 'problem that has no name'. She wrote of the desperation of women who felt the problem obscurely, though lacked the conceptual resources to bring it to full awareness – until, that is, they learned to communicate with one another and learned to name the hitherto nameless.[13]

Opinions about the appropriate remedy to this problem differ; opinions differ as to how one can come to name the hitherto nameless. Part of the solution will be the achievement of the confidence and authority just alluded to. But to the extent that there are conceptual constraints on what women can know, more will be needed. Some feminists suppose that women's ignorance of their own lives and experiences can be remedied by the ordinary talk that takes place among women at a grass-roots level, the sort that sometimes goes by the name of 'consciousness raising'. Others think that the conceptual resources for such knowledge will only become available with radical reforms of language, or with radical reforms of the symbolic order of the imagination. They say that if the words we use, or the symbols with which we think, come from a 'man-made' language, or a 'language of the fathers', then that will be a bar to women's knowledge of themselves as women. At this point feminist questions in epistemology will overlap with their cousins in philosophy of language and psychoanalysis.[14]

These are ways in which women get left out as subjects of knowledge because they really fail to be knowers. But women may be left out as subjects not by failing to be knowers, but by *failing to be counted as knowers*, even when they do know. Here are some of the ways in which women may fail to be counted as knowers.

Women may fail to be counted as knowers because of a lack of credibility – a lack of what we might call intersubjective authority. Because of this lack, even when women are knowers, they are not known by others to be knowers. Some philosophers say that credibility is of more than incidental interest to an account of knowledge as such. Miranda Fricker argues that the notion of credibility is crucial to the concept of a knower, properly understood.[15] Once one acknowledges that where there are unequal distributions of social power, the distribution of credibility is likely to be distorted, one sees that an understanding of social power is crucial to a proper understanding of the concept of a knower. This in turn enables one to identify a phenomenon of epistemic injustice, which can arise from an unjust distribution of credibility, and which could serve to exclude women from the class of those who fully function as knowers.[16] The remedy for this problem is not to remove barriers to women's knowledge, but to remove the barriers to credibility.[17]

Women may fail to be counted as knowers in a different way – because of a spurious universality ascribed to a merely partial story of the world as told by men, which means that even when women know, they are not known by men to know. Women are left out, because women's perspectives on the world are left out. Marilyn Frye says,

> Imagine that a single individual had written up an exhaustive description of a sedated elephant as observed from one spot for one hour and then, with delighted self-satisfaction, had heralded that achievement as a complete, accurate and profound account of The Elephant.

That story of the elephant is, she says, like the traditional story of the world.

> The androcentrism of the accumulated philosophy and science of the 'western' world is like that. A few, a few men, have with a like satisfaction told the story of the world and human experience – have created what pretends to be progressively a more and more complete, accurate and profound account of what they call 'Man and his World'.[18]

What women know about the world fails to enter this official story about life, the universe, and everything, and the incompleteness and partiality of the story goes unnoticed. So even when women do achieve knowledge – do break free from the various material and conceptual constraints on knowledge described above – their knowledge may fail to look like knowledge to men, so that women, again, fail to be counted as knowers. Seen this way, one goal of feminism is to correct the partiality of existing knowledge:

> The project of feminist theory is to write a new Encyclopaedia. Its title: The World, According to Women.[19]

There is yet a different way in which women may fail to be counted as knowers, which has not so much to do with women, or with the incompleteness of knowledge, but with a conception of knowledge itself. Women may fail to be counted as knowers because there is something wrong with traditional conceptions, or traditional ideals, of knowledge. Something about knowledge, as it is traditionally understood, is mistaken, and it is this mistake – not women's ignorance, or women's lack of credibility, or the omission of women's perspectives on the world – which prevents women from counting as the knowers they really are. Just what the mistake is will depend on what the traditional conception is interpreted to be, and the remedy likewise. It is at this point that feminist critique of reason becomes more radical, and – sometimes questioning the uncritical use of notions of truth, knowledge, and reason, with which early feminists like Astell argued for liberation – advocates reform, supplementation, or outright rejection of the epistemological status quo. To take one example, made famous by Carol Gilligan, it may be that moral knowledge is defined by some theorists in such a way that women and girls are made to seem ignorant or immature, and the remedy might not be to change women, but to change the conception of knowledge. Once it is recognized that women have a 'different voice' when it comes to moral knowledge, which speaks in an idiom of care rather than justice, and that this voice is as good as if not better than its male counterpart, then women and girls will be recognized for the moral knowers they are.[20] Or, to take an example discussed by Vrinda Dalmeyer and Linda Alcoff, it may be that assumptions about the propositional character of knowledge have served to discredit the knowledge of illiterate midwives whose knowledge is more a matter of knowing how than knowing that.[21]

What have these claims to do with the idea that when it comes to knowledge, women get hurt? To the extent that women are left out in any of the ways just described, women are also hurt. If women are left out as objects of knowledge, whether in the history books or in medical research, that is one of the ways in which women are hurt; and if women are viewed as essentially mysterious and unknowable, then that too is a way in which women get hurt. In addition there will be the hurts arising from these, when ignorance of women is acted upon. If women get left out as subjects of knowledge – whether because they lack the knowledge men have, or because they lack knowledge of themselves as women, or because they lack credibility, or because their perspectives on the world are omitted, or because they are excluded by a mistaken traditional conception of knowledge – these are all ways in which women get hurt. In addition there will be the hurts arising from these, when women's exclusion as subjects of knowledge has consequences for their wider social lives – for example when lack of knowledge, or of credibility, undermines their status and their job prospects. In so far as the problem is one of women being left out (and of the consequences of being left out) the sin looks to be a sin of omission, whose remedy is simple: let women in. Let women into the stories of those who are known – let women into the history books, and the rest. Let women in to the treasures of knowledge, let women in to the club of the credible, let women's knowledge count as the knowledge it is.

However, there might be hurts that accrue to someone which go beyond the hurt of being left out, and its consequences. Perhaps there could be something about knowledge – as traditionally pursued, under patriarchal conditions – that does not merely leave women out, but hurts women in a more active way. Some feminist writers have claimed that some traditional norms of knowledge objectify women. If this is so, we have here not a sin of omission, but a sin of commission which cannot be remedied simply by letting women in.

Knowledge and how women might be hurt

The thought that some traditional ideals of knowledge objectify women finds one expression in the work of Catharine MacKinnon.

> The stance of the 'knower' . . . is . . . the neutral posture, which I will be calling objectivity – that is, the nonsituated distanced standpoint . . . [This] is the male standpoint socially . . . [The] relationship between objectivity as the stance from which the world is known and the world that is apprehended in this way is the relationship of objectification. Objectivity is the epistemological stance of which objectification is the social process, of which male dominance is the politics, the acted out social practice. That is, to look at the world objectively is to objectify it.[22]

MacKinnon says there is something wrong with knowledge as it is traditionally pursued or understood, and to that extent her complaint belongs with those just discussed. But there is more, for her complaint is also that women are actively hurt. Objectivity, she says, is the stance of the traditional male knower; and objectivity objectifies. Now MacKinnon's point may be overstated, but there is something right about it, and it is worth thinking about how an assumption of objectivity might help to objectify women.[23] To do this we would need a clearer sense of what might be meant by objectivity, and what might be meant by objectification. Sally Haslanger has suggested an interpretation of MacKinnon which offers a more detailed grasp of each of these, which she puts to use in defending MacKinnon's claim.[24]

Objectivity – that 'non-situated distanced standpoint' – can be thought of as an epistemological norm that has its place in a familiar picture of the world, says Haslanger. Things in the world are independent of us, and their behaviour is constrained and determined by their natures. We can best discover those natures by looking for the regularities that reveal them in normal circumstances. In abnormal circumstances things may be distorted, and the regularities we see may not reveal their natures. But the usual circumstances are the normal circumstances, so we should infer the natures of things from how things usually are. When it comes to practical matters, our actions will of course need to accommodate the natures of things, if we are to achieve our practical goals.

Thus understood, objectivity seems to be an innocuous enough collection of epistemic and practical norms governing one's reasoning about the world and how to get about in it. In so far as it has any distinctive feature, it is the default assumption that one's epistemic circumstances are normal – which is why Haslanger dubs it 'Assumed Objectivity'. The collection of norms, she says, consists of these:

(i) epistemic neutrality: take a genuine regularity in the behaviour of something to be a consequence of its nature;

(ii) practical neutrality: constrain your decision making and action to accommodate things' natures;

(iii) absolute aperspectivity: count observed regularities as genuine regularities just in case the observations occur under normal circumstances;

(iv) assumed aperspectivity: if a regularity is observed, assume that circumstances are normal.[25]

Attending to the notion of 'normal circumstances' that appears in conditions (iii) and (iv), we can note that there are many ways in which observational circumstances could fail to be normal, an important one among them being that the regularities observed fail to be independent of the observer – that they are an artifact, created by, or conditioned by, the observer or the process of observation. The observer may render the circumstances abnormal in a variety of different ways: the properties of the observed items may be altered by the observer's sheer physical presence; by his social features, for example his power or rank; by his propositional attitudes, his beliefs and desires. So when the norm directs one to assume, among other things, the observer-independence of what is observed, it directs one to assume that the observer is not rendering the circumstances abnormal in any of these ways.

The norm of Assumed Objectivity directs an observer to assume that circumstances are normal. But if an observer's *beliefs* can render observational circumstances abnormal by helping to alter the properties of the observed, then implicit in the norm is an assumption about *direction of fit*: that one's belief about perceived regularities conforms to the world. By that I do not mean simply that the belief corresponds to how the world is – for short, that it is true. For there are two ways in which a belief could correspond to how the world is: the belief might conform to the world; or the world might conform to the belief. A believer might believe that p because p is the case – her belief thus conforming to the world; or p might be the case because the believer believes it – the world thus conforming to her belief. In the latter situation there would be something self-fulfilling about the belief: there would be a belief whose direction of fit was the reverse of the normal case, 'normal' in a sense to be considered in a moment.

Elizabeth Anscombe used a nice example to explain the notion of what has come to be called direction of fit. Imagine a shopper, filling his trolley with the things on his shopping list, and a detective following him, writing a list of the things in the trolley. The shopper's list and the detective's list both match the things exactly, but there is a difference in direction of fit.[26] If the things in the trolley fail to correspond to the shopper's list, the mistake is in his performance: he ought to make the world fit his list. If the things in the trolley fail to correspond to the detective's list, the mistake is in the list: he ought to make his list fit the world. Assuming there are no mistakes, the things in the trolley conform to the shopper's list; and the detective's list conforms to the things in the trolley. Another difference: the shopper's list is a list of the things he *wants* to be there; the detective's list is a list of the things he *believes* are there. These latter differences are no accident: a difference in direction of fit is widely thought to be constitutive of the difference between belief and desire. Belief aims to fit the world; desire aims for the world to fit it. There is an assumption in epistemology generally – and in the norm of Assumed Objectivity in particular – that the knowing subject is like the detective, moulding his list to the way the world is, and not like the shopper, moulding the world to the way his list is. And that makes sense, because the subject matter of epistemology is not desire, but belief, and whether or not belief is true and justified. The norm of Assumed Objectivity directs one to assume, among other things, that one's observations about the world have the normal direction of fit – which is to say, the direction of fit that beliefs aim to have.

But even if beliefs do aim to fit the world, beliefs sometimes fail to fit the world, sometimes for the ordinary reason that they are false, as when the detective makes a mistake; and sometimes for the more complicated reason that they have an anomalous direction of fit – perhaps the belief has come to fit something other than the world, or perhaps the world has come to fit the belief, or perhaps both. Here are the sorts of anomalies I have in mind.

Sometimes beliefs arrange themselves to fit desires. I want to believe I can jump across a crevasse, and, gritting my teeth, come to believe it.[27] Pascal wants to believe there is a God, goes to church, and ends up believing it. I want to believe that every day, in every way, I am getting better and better, and – with the help of some New Age motivational tapes – talk myself into believing it. There is something odd about these examples, because of belief's 'normal' direction of fit: if belief aims to fit the world, how can it be produced by desire rather than by perception of the world? Such cases tend to be relegated to the margins of epistemology, where they are discussed, if at all, under the heading of wishful thinking and self-deception.

Sometimes the world arranges itself to fit beliefs. I believe I can jump across the river, and, freshly emboldened, do indeed jump across the river. I believe that every day, in every way, I am getting better and better, and – with luck, and with the help again of my New Age motivational tapes – do indeed get better and better. There is something odd about these examples too, again because of belief's 'normal' direction of fit: if belief aims to fit the world, how can there be a belief whose direction of fit has the pattern distinctive of desire – how can there be a belief which alters the world, so as to make the world fit the belief? Such cases again tend to be relegated to the margins of epistemology, and discussed, if at all, under the heading of the psychology of self-fulfilling belief.

The ordinary reason for failure of fit in a belief – namely outright falsehood – receives plenty of attention in epistemology; these more complicated anomalies receive less. But it is these which will be of special interest to anyone who wants to think about how an assumption of objectivity may help to objectify women.

If objectivity is about how mind conforms to world, objectification is about the opposite: objectification is, roughly, about some of the ways in which world conforms to mind. Objectification is a process in which the social world comes to be shaped by perception, desire and belief: a process in which women, for example, are made objects because of men's perceptions and desires and beliefs. To say that women are made objects is to speak in metaphors, albeit familiar ones; but, to make a start, it has something to do with how some men see women. MacKinnon says,

> Men treat women as who they see women as being . . . Men's power over women means that the way men see women defines who women can be.[28]

Marilyn Frye describes something similar, and calls it 'The Arrogant Eye'.

> The arrogant perceiver . . . coerces the objects of his perception into satisfying the conditions his perception imposes . . . He manipulates the environment, perception and judgment of her whom he perceives, so that her recognized options are limited, and the course she chooses will be such as coheres with his purposes. The seer is himself an element of her environment. The structures of his perception are as solid a fact in her situation as are the structures of a chair which seats her too low or of gestures which threaten. How one sees another and how one expects the other to behave are in tight interdependence, and how one expects the other to behave is a large factor in determining how the other does behave.[29]

MacKinnon and Frye describe a sort of perception that works to objectify women, where seeing women as subordinate makes women subordinate: a kind of self-fulfilling perception, where seeing it as so makes it so, when it is backed up by power. The perception does not work in isolation from other things. It is there because of what men believe, and in that sense it is a theory-laden perception. And to the extent that the perception is self-fulfilling, the underlying belief is too. MacKinnon says,

[The] beliefs of the powerful become [proven], in part because the world actually arranges itself to affirm what the powerful want to see. If you perceive this as a process, you might call it force, or at least pressure or socialization or what money can buy. If it is imperceptible as a process, you may consider it voluntary or consensual or free will or human nature, or just the way things are. Beneath this, though, the world is not entirely the way the powerful say it is or want to believe it is.[30]

The world 'arranges itself' – at least in part – to fit what the powerful believe. Believing women to be subordinate can make women subordinate: thinking so can make it so, when it is backed up by power.

Such beliefs have an anomalous direction of fit, anomalous in both of the ways considered earlier. Instead of belief arranging itself to fit the world, it arranges itself to fit desire. On MacKinnon's description, when the powerful desire that p, they come to believe that p – in the manner of the wishful thinker. And instead of belief arranging itself to fit the world, the world arranges itself to fit belief. When the powerful believe that p, things alter to make it the case that p. Unlike most examples of wishful thinking, the result here is not mere projection accompanied by self-deception, for there is a sense in which the wishfully thought beliefs become *true*. The powerful are described as doing what the unusually fortunate wishful thinker does: for example, the crevasse-leaper of William James's example, who desires that p, consequently believes that p, consequently makes it the case that p.

This difference between objectification and ordinary wishful thinking is an important one, for it explains what would otherwise be inexplicable: how an objectifier's beliefs can have the direction of fit constitutive of belief – how they can aim to fit the world. This task of explanation is often left aside by feminists who think the self-interest of the objectifier a sufficient motive. But philosophers think that self-interest is not, in general, a sufficient motive for belief, and they are surely right: you cannot get me to believe I am Elvis by offering me twenty, or even twenty million pounds.[31] But if there is a self-fulfilling aspect to the belief in question, that makes an important difference. The wishful thinker whose belief is outright false – the wishful thinker whose belief is *mere* projection – must keep turning a blind eye to the evidence, which is what makes it difficult to see how it can even *aim* to fit the world, and hence how it can even be a belief at all. But to the extent that an objectifier's belief is self-fulfillingly true, he need turn no blind eye: since the evidence will, for the most part, confirm the belief, the belief can aim to fit the world. The objectifier's self-fulfilling belief will be rational – or at any rate, more rational than the beliefs of the ordinary wishful thinker.

How does the world 'arrange itself' to conform to what is seen or believed? Men *treat* women as who they see women as being, says MacKinnon. How men treat women is affected by men's perceptions, desires and beliefs about women. Part of the treatment will just be a matter of making known one's beliefs – making known one's expectations. Those expectations can exert the sort of pressure that Frye described so vividly in the passage quoted above, so that how women are will come to fit what is believed about women – what is expected of women. Part of the treatment will be a matter of what men *say* to women and about women. This brings us to questions about language, thus to questions beyond our present project, but a brief glance in their direction suggests that here again one would discover the same anomalous direction of fit: that saying so can, in conditions of oppression, make it so.[32]

Described this way, objectification is a process of projection supplemented by force, whose result is that women are made subordinate. The projection involves desire, belief and perception all working together: men desire certain qualities in women, believe women have them, see women as having them. But this projection, says MacKinnon, 'is not just an illusion or a fantasy or a mistake. It becomes embodied because it is enforced'.[33] Women really come to have at least some of the qualities that are projected onto them. Haslanger draws on these ideas in MacKinnon's work to reach a general view of what it is to objectify someone or something. One objectifies a thing or person when one satisfies these conditions:

(i)   One views it and treats it as an object for the satisfaction of one's desire;
(ii) where one desires it to have some property, one forces it to have that property;
(iii) one believes that it has that property;
(iv) one believes that it has that property by nature.[34]

For example, men objectify women if they view and treat them as objects of male sexual desire; they desire them to be submissive, and force them to submit; they believe that women are in fact submissive; and they believe that they are submissive by nature. The belief of the final condition – namely the belief that women are submissive by nature – is quite illusory. But there is something interesting about the belief of the third condition. Under conditions of oppression, that belief – the belief that women are submissive – will be a true belief, an accurate descriptive belief. That belief is, as MacKinnon says, 'not just an illusion or a fantasy or a mistake': it is a belief that corresponds to the world. It is not, though, a belief that conforms to the world: it is a belief to which the world has conformed. The belief of the third condition is part of the force of the second condition. Thinking that women are so has – suitably supplemented by power – made women so.

MacKinnon says that objectivity and objectification go hand in hand: to look at the world objectively is to objectify it. Well, we can see now that there is something right about this: to look at the world objectively can certainly *help* one to objectify it. For suppose a man were to look at the social world objectively: that is, suppose he were to follow the norm of Assumed Objectivity in his dealings with the social world. Suppose it is a world in which gender hierarchy exists. Such a man will observe that women appear, in general, to be sexually submissive. Following (iv), the norm of assumed aperspectivity, he assumes that circumstances are normal. Following (iii), the norm of absolute aperspectivity, he concludes that this is a genuine regularity. Following (i), the norm of epistemic neutrality, he attributes the regularity to the workings of the nature of women. Following (ii), the norm of practical neutrality, he structures social arrangements to accommodate those natures, and, for example, dominates women in sexual encounters. Will this help him objectify women? Yes – to a degree. If he is an objectifier, following the norm of Assumed Objectivity will help to make him a more successful one. His interpretations of the regularities he encounters will lead him to the sorts of beliefs possessed by the objectifier: he will satisfy the third and fourth conditions that the objectifier satisfies, because he will believe that women are submissive, and believe that women are submissive by nature. Moreover, acting on those beliefs will help him satisfy the second condition: acting on the beliefs that women are submissive by nature, he will make women submissive. In acting on the assumption that his mind conforms to an independent world, he will play his part in making that world conform to his mind – and to the minds of other objectifiers. Being objective helps to make him a successful objectifier.

When objectification is going on, in place of a world-sensitive observer there is an observer-sensitive world: a social world distorted by the physical, social and mental properties of those who are doing the observing. When that social world is distorted by the beliefs of the observers to the extent that the world comes to fit the observers' beliefs, the knowing subject is less like the detective of Anscombe's example, moulding his mind (his mental 'list') to the way the world is, and more like the shopper, moulding the world to the way his mind is. And Assumed Objectivity masks all this: it allows the observer to rest secure in an assumption that his beliefs are a mirror, not a template.

The conclusion that objectivity can help the objectifier is more modest than MacKinnon's, as Haslanger points out: although being objective can help one be an objectifier, one can be objective without being an objectifier. Following the norm of Assumed Objectivity in other everyday activities – gardening, for instance – will have no untoward results.[35] But if being objective can even help one be an objectifier, surely that is bad enough. We have grounds, surely, for a political critique of a certain epistemological norm: when men follow it under conditions of oppression, women get hurt.

Understood this way, the feminist critique is a practical one: Assumed Objectivity has bad consequences for women. A merely pragmatic critique has its shortcomings, though. For one thing, if feminists use pragmatic arguments, we can hardly complain when others do. Objectified women may complain, it's bad for us; and objectifiers may respond, yes, but it's good for us. We can add to this pragmatic critique a philosophical one: the norm of Assumed Objectivity is not just bad for women, it is simply *bad*. Applied in conditions of gender hierarchy, although it leads some objectifiers to self-fulfillingly *true* beliefs, it also reliably leads them to *false* beliefs. As MacKinnon says, 'the world is not entirely the way the powerful say it is or want to believe it is'. It is only in part that 'the world actually arranges itself to affirm what the powerful want to see'. Something about the world is different to what the powerful say and believe.

Some of their ordinary beliefs *about women* are false. Guided by Assumed Objectivity, objectifiers believe falsely that women possess by *nature* the properties they acquire through objectification.[36] For example, they believe falsely that women are submissive by nature. That is one way in which their beliefs fail to fit the world. Moreover, some of their more complex beliefs are false: some of their beliefs *about their beliefs* are false. Guided by Assumed Objectivity, objectifiers believe that their true beliefs have come to fit the world, when in fact it is the world that has come to fit their beliefs. For example, while they believe truly that women are submissive, their belief about that belief is false. They believe they believe it because women are submissive. Wrong: they do not believe it because women are submissive; women are submissive because they believe it. Believing so, with the aid of structures and practices of power, has made it so. That is another way in which their beliefs fail to fit the world. Assumed Objectivity has led them away from the truth – the truth about women, and the truth about their own beliefs.

Armed now with two critiques, a practical and a philosophical, we can say that the epistemological norm of Assumed Objectivity is a bad one: it hurts women, and it gets in the way of *knowledge*. To say that it is bad because it gets in the way of knowledge is to suppose knowledge to be a good thing – just as Mary Astell supposed when she argued so eloquently against the ancient error, and for the truth. Is this to fall prey once again to an uncritical allegiance to knowledge, of the sort that feminists are supposed to question? I hope not. Astell is right: what has hurt women is not knowledge but ignorance masked as knowledge. What has hurt women is not objectivity after all, but pretended objectivity. The hurt is in the complacent assumption, and not, surely, in the ambition.

NOTES

1 Ludwig Wittgenstein, *Philosophical Investigations* §124, trans. G. E. M. Anscombe (Oxford: Blackwell, 1958).
2 René Descartes, *Meditations on First Philosophy*, 12, 34, trans. John Cottingham (Cambridge: Cambridge University Press, 1986).
3 This thought motivates feminist standpoint epistemology: see Miranda Fricker's and Diemut Bubeck's chapters in this volume.
4 Mary Astell, *Reflections Upon Marriage* (London: John Nutt, 1700), reprinted in *Astell's Political Writings*, ed. Patricia Springborg (Cambridge: Cambridge University Press, 1996), pp. 9, 10.
5 Michèle Le Dœuff, *Hipparchia's Choice*, trans. Trista Selous (Oxford: Blackwell, 1990), p. 9, also discussed by Linda Martin Alcoff, in 'Is the Feminist Critique of Reason Rational?', in Sally Haslanger, ed., *Feminist Perspectives on Language, Knowledge and Reality*, special issue of *Philosophical Topics* 23:2 (1995), 1.
6 See also Louise Antony, 'Sisters, Please, I'd Rather Do it Myself: a Defense of Individualism in Feminist Epistemology', in Haslanger, ed., *Feminist Perspectives*, pp. 59–94.
7 *Reflections*, p. 11. The passage continues: 'he was not Made for this, but if he hires himself out to such an Employment, he ought conscientiously to perform it'. Astell took the Cartesian meditations to reveal women as essentially thinking things – and hence as beings entitled to an education. On feminism and Cartesian rationalism see Margaret Atherton, 'Cartesian Reason and Gendered Reason', in Louise Antony and Charlotte Witt, eds., *A Mind of One's Own: Feminist Essays on Reason and Objectivity* (Boulder, CO, and Oxford: Westview Press, 1993), pp. 19–34.
8 See for example Dale Spender's *Women of Ideas and What Men Have Done to Them* (London: Routledge & Kegan Paul, 1982).
9 Simone de Beauvoir, *The Second Sex* (1949; reprint, London: Pan, 1988) pp. 285–6. See also Le Dœuff, *Hipparchia's Choice*, pp. 52, 102; Langton, 'Love and Solipsism', in Roger Lamb, ed., *Love Analyzed* (Boulder, CO: Westview Press 1996), and 'Sexual Solipsism', in Haslanger, ed., *Feminist Perspectives*, pp. 149–87.
10 *Reflections*, p. 28.
11 According to the so called KK Principle you know something only if you know that you know it.
12 'For feminist thinkers of the present era the first and most fundamental act of our own emancipation was granting ourselves authority as perceivers', 'The Possibility of Feminist Theory', reprinted in Ann Garry and Marilyn Pearsall,

eds., *Women, Knowledge and Reality* (2nd edition, London and New York: Routledge, 1996), pp. 34–47 (quotation from p. 35).

13 Betty Friedan, *The Feminine Mystique* (New York: Dell, 1964).

14 See in this volume the chapters by Jennifer Hornsby, Susan James and Sarah Richmond.

15 'Rational Authority and Social Power: Towards a Truly Social Epistemology', *Proceedings of the Aristotelian Society* (1998), 159–77.

16 Fricker draws on Edward Craig's *Knowledge and the State of Nature: An Essay in Conceptual Synthesis* (Oxford: Clarendon Press, 1990) in arguing that being a participant in the spread of knowledge is central to our conception of knowledge, and uses this framework to develop her notion of epistemic injustice. See also Marilyn Frye, *The Politics of Reality: Essays in Feminist Theory* (Freedom, CA: The Crossing Press, 1983), especially, 'In and Out of Harm's Way: Arrogance and Love'.

17 Louise Antony suggests a kind of epistemic affirmative action as a remedy, 'Sisters, Please, I'd Rather Do It Myself', p. 89.

18 Frye, 'Feminist Theory', p. 34.

19 Ibid., p. 35.

20 Carol Gilligan, 'In a Different Voice: Women's Conceptions of Self and of Morality', in Hester Eisenstein and Alice Jardine, eds., *The Future of Difference* (Boston: G. K. Hall and Co., 1980), pp. 247–317.

21 Vrinda Dalmeyer and Linda Alcoff, 'Are "Old Wives'" Tales Justified?', in Linda Alcoff and Elizabeth Potter, eds., *Feminist Epistemologies* (London and New York: Routledge, 1993), pp. 217–44; the authors draw on work by Lorraine Code, e.g. in 'Taking Subjectivity into Account', ibid., pp. 15–48.

22 *Feminism Unmodified* (Cambridge, MA: Harvard University Press,1987), p. 50.

23 The argument of this section draws on Langton, 'Beyond a Pragmatic Critique of Reason', *Australasian Journal of Philosophy* 71 (1993), 364–84.

24 Haslanger, 'On Being Objective and Being Objectified', in Antony and Witt, eds., *Mind of One's Own*, pp. 85–125.

25 Ibid., p. 107. I have abbreviated and slightly paraphrased the conditions. Haslanger adds to the notion of normal circumstances what I take to be included in that notion, namely that the observations are not conditioned by the observer's social position, and that the observer has not influenced the behaviour of the items under observation.

26 Elizabeth Anscombe, *Intention* (Oxford: Blackwell, 1957), p. 56. See also Lloyd Humberstone, 'Direction of Fit', *Mind* 101 (1992), 59–83.

27 The example is from William James, *The Will to Believe and Other Essays in Popular Philosophy* (London: Longman's and Green, 1891).

28 MacKinnon, *Feminism Unmodified*, p. 172.

29 Frye, 'In and Out of Harm's Way', p. 67.

30 MacKinnon, *Feminism Unmodified*, pp. 58–9. I follow Haslanger in substituting 'proven' for 'proof'.

31 Non-voluntarism about belief, with its implications for feminist critiques of reason, is a topic of Langton, 'Beyond a Pragmatic Critique of Reason'.

32 Many speech acts have a direction of fit which is the reverse of the 'normal' direction associated with assertion – e.g. imperatives, exercitives, and (sometimes) verdictives – altering the world in different ways, some causal, others not.

See Langton, 'Subordination, Silence and Pornography's Authority', in Robert Post, ed., *Censorship and Silencing* (New York: Getty Center and Oxford University Press, 1998), 'Speech Acts and Unspeakable Acts', *Philosophy and Public Affairs* 22 (1993), 305–30. Cf. Frye, 'The voice of the men's world story is the voice of the speaker who does not have to fit his words to the truth, because the truth will fit his words', *Feminist Theory*, p. 44. See also MacKinnon, *Feminism Unmodified*, p. 131.

33 *Feminism Unmodified*, p. 119.

34 Haslanger, 'On Being Objective', pp. 100–4, 109. Again, I have paraphrased her analysis, and drawn on an earlier version seen in manuscript.

35 Haslanger also suggests that following the norm could help one be a collaborator in, rather than an initiator of objectification. For example, a woman following the norm would observe the same regularities about women, and interpret women's subordination as natural and inevitable, without herself desiring it or forcing it to be that way (ibid., pp. 109–10).

36 Haslanger identifies this as the major illusion generated by the norm, ibid., pp. 103–4.

8

MIRANDA FRICKER

Feminism in epistemology
Pluralism without postmodernism

Those Greeks were superficial – *out of profundity.*
Nietzsche[1]

Introduction

Someone might wonder how there can be feminist epistemology – 'knowledge is simply *knowledge*, regardless of gender, and that's all there is to it'. There are philosophers of a relativistic mindset, some feminists among them, who would challenge the idea that knowledge is 'simply' knowledge, believing it to be both less and more than it seems. Those, for instance, who regard 'true' as an 'empty compliment'[2] that we pay to propositions we want to endorse, or as part of a philosophical 'discourse of legitimation',[3] will regard 'knowledge' too as a metaphysically empty stamp of approval. Metaphysically speaking, then, they believe knowledge to be less than it seems. But politically speaking, they believe it to be more than it seems; for once their view of knowledge is in place, it is only a small step to the suggestion that propositions approved as knowledge are likely to reflect the perspectives and even serve the interests of those whose social power shapes the practices of approval. Since being female has placed one historically at the less powerful end of gender relations, it would be easy then to see how there could be a role for feminism in the theory of knowledge. Feminism would have a ready-made task in counter-acting and protecting against gender bias in the processes and institutions of approval.

There are also, of course, philosophers of a more realist mindset, some feminists among them, who find the relativistic conception of knowledge quite unconvincing. But they need not agree with the person who says that knowledge is 'simply knowledge, regardless of gender'. They may have their own reasons for considering gender to be relevant to the epistemologist's task. Although a good deal of feminist work is aligned with anti-epistemological strains of thought, there is also a growing corpus of feminist work which makes a critical contribution to epistemology, radicalizing it from the inside, as opposed to engaging in a critique of it as if from the outside.

A central example is feminist standpoint theory, which originates in Marx's historical materialism.[4] The key Marxian idea is that different social groups have different epistemic 'standpoints', where the material positioning (the relation to production) of one of the groups is said to bestow an epistemic privilege. In Marxism we find the idea that the position of the proletariat makes available the correct view of material relations (though it was Lukács who emphasized and developed the significance of the Marxist notion of standpoint[5]). Feminists have taken from Marxism the intuitive idea that a life led at the sharp end of any given set of power relations provides for critical understanding (of the social world, in the first instance) where a life cushioned by the possession of power does not. Here, then, is a first way in which social identity and power relations (e.g. gender and gender ideology) may be relevant in epistemology: they may influence epistemic access to the world.

A second way is that social identity may constrain participation in epistemic practices – practices of asserting, denying, telling, asking, giving reasons etc. Such practices are in large measure interactive, so that a person's full participation in them depends upon certain reciprocating background attitudes on the part of fellow participants – attitudes which, for instance, provide for the appropriate distributions of trust and of credibility. If relations of gender, class, or race cause distortion in these background attitudes, then social identity and power have intervened in a manner that can be the concern not merely of the sociologist of knowledge but of the epistemologist.

The picture I have just presented is, I hope, useful; but it is somewhat artificial. In it, feminism's engagement with epistemology takes one of two different forms: either it is aligned with postmodernism, in which case the order of the day is 'endist'[6] and anti-epistemological, or it is aligned with epistemology, in which case it works for a more fully socialized and thus[7] a more politically aware epistemology. The label 'feminist epistemology' naturally attaches to the latter sort of work. But, as the label would suggest, feminist epistemology has something important in common with feminist anti-epistemological lines of thought – a commitment to theorizing social difference, at the very least – so that there is an ongoing, vitalizing tension within feminist epistemology in virtue of which it considers itself answerable to its more philosophically radical[8] sister. This chapter attempts to answer and be answerable to the anti-epistemological strains of feminist postmodernism, by engaging in a critical, but I hope not merely antipathetic, diagnosis of the postmodern impulse.

A postmodern approach

Nancy Fraser and Linda Nicholson say that a feminist postmodernism would

> replace unitary notions of woman and feminine gender identity with plural and complexly constructed conceptions of social identity, treating gender as one relevant strand among others, attending also to class, race, ethnicity, age, and sexual orientation.[9]

Feminist postmodernism is to be credited with making important intellectual currency of the insight that social identity is multiply fragmented. The insight certainly fits with 'postmodernism's big-bang logic of expansion',[10] but a conception of social identity as fragmented is not indissolubly linked with the postmodernist outlook. Postmodernism does not have a monopoly on the idea that social identity is complex. Indeed, that which commends the idea to us is really something of an anathema to postmodernism – the aspiration to represent the world truly, to capture the facts. One has a reason to adopt a social ontology of fragmentation if one thinks that it makes for an accurate representation of how things are – more accurate, for instance, than a social ontology which mentions only class.

Postmodernists typically advocate a social ontology of fragmentation not on grounds of sociological accuracy, but on the political ground that any other ontology would be exclusionary. The suspicion is that any general categories of identity will not be fit to capture the indefinitely many and shifting combinations of social positionings which real people occupy: 'Consciousness of exclusion through naming is acute. Identities seem contradictory, partial and strategic.'[11] In feminist postmodernism, then, to recognize difference is to meet an obligation to political inclusiveness rather than to empirical accuracy.

There is reason, however, to doubt the political adequacy of a postmodernist formulation. When the call for a sensitivity to difference is given in terms of 'exclusion', it is implied that the objection to general social categories of class, gender and race is that they leave some people out. But the notion of exclusion on its own cannot possibly capture all that is wrong with over-generalizations employing these categories. The point has often been made, and remains true, that an adequate feminist politics will represent more than a demand to be included; it will represent a demand for change. Thus the feminist postmodernist formulation of the problem of difference, with its anaemic political lexicon of exclusion, risks falling short of a genuinely political stance. Susan Strickland puts the point well:

> [D]ominant theories and categories were wrong not simply in universalizing beyond their scope, i.e., that they were partial in the sense of being limited, not universally applicable, but that they were also partial in the sense of being ideological, interested and distorted; in short to a greater or lesser extent false . . . The assertion of feminist 'difference' was and is, basically a challenge and critique.[12]

Feminism's concern with difference is driven by a political commitment to robust critical thought and indeed to political action; whereas the distinctively postmodernist concern with the fragmentation of social identity primarily speaks to the quite general theoretical commitment to the 'big-bang logic of expansion'. This is how the familiar yet unresolved question is raised as to whether postmodernism possesses the epistemological resources to fuel genuinely critical thought. If not, it courts conservatism.

An appropriate touchstone for a working conception of postmodernism is Jean-François Lyotard's *The Postmodern Condition* – the original, and very influential, postmodernist philosophical text. Here we find it is a definitive commitment of the anti-epistemological strand of postmodernist thought that the rules of 'language games' are strictly 'local'. There are no trans-local norms of rationality and justification; any attempt to impose constraints on thought by way of an appeal to reason as such is judged to be an act of 'terror':

> We must . . . arrive at an idea and practice of justice that is not linked to that of consensus.
> A recognition of the heteromorphous nature of language games is a first step in that direction. This obviously implies a renunciation of terror, which assumes that they are isomorphic and tries to make them so. The second step is the principle that any consensus on the rules defining a game and the 'moves' playable within it *must* be local, in other words, agreed on by its present players and subject to eventual cancellation.[13]

Lyotard's idea of locality is not a locality to culture, or even to social group. The authority of the rules of a given 'language game', we are told, resides only in a fleeting agreement by 'present players'. Thus the postmodernist 'war on totality'[14] brings a bizarrely voluntaristic brand of relativism. Here 'language game' signifies something fleeting and voluntaristically conceived – something closer to a single conversation than to an entrenched and historically stable discursive practice. Of course not all forms of postmodernism need imitate Lyotard's rhetorical extremes, but his text can serve here as a model for the trenchantly anti-epistemological current in postmodernism which more moderate positions will resist.

Any political inadequacy we may suspect of postmodernism is likely to flow from an epistemological source. That source is now in view. The insistence on the localness of all norms of judgement renders postmodernism incapable of sustaining ordinary critical judgements, such as the judgement that some forms of social organization are plain unjust, or that some beliefs are plain false. The question whether any particular critical judgement is reasonable cannot depend on the 'agreement' of those who happen to be one's interlocutors – their interests may be served very nicely by the discursive *status quo*. Yet if we try to change the *status quo* by appeal to any general standards of reason, apparently it is we who are guilty of discursive terrorism. At an aesthetic level, postmodernism may be a champion of creativity, playfulness and perpetual movement, but this should not conceal the fact that at the level of critical thought, it replaces the progressive dynamic of reason with a lugubrious critical stasis.

Feminist postmodernists who are aligned with the anti-epistemological strand of postmodernism under attack here may, ever-resourceful, adopt a strategy of insisting, against the charge of conservatism, that genuinely critical and evaluative thought *can* be purely local. Perhaps they will exploit Lyotard's idea of a language game fleetingly played, or some related idea of 'situated criticism', or of epistemic 'nomadism',[15] or some other idea designed to ensure both that the boundaries of the local are respected and that genuine critical judgements are seen to issue from positionings that are transient, strategic, or pragmatic. But would such judgements be genuine critical judgements? Suppose someone protests 'Equal pay for equal work!', or 'Slavery is wrong!'. And suppose the protest is met with a shrug of cynical insouciance from the powers that be. Postmodernism is unfit to characterize that response as unreasonable, or unjustified, or even inappropriate, for who is to say which 'language game' the authorities may provisionally have 'agreed' to play? Of course, no other epistemological view can guarantee that dissenting voices are given their due: the practical prospect of discursive injustice spans the gamut of theoretical positions. What is at issue is the authority of the critical thoughts we may voice and of others' responses to them. (The question of authority is crucial, and I confront it in the next section.)

If the postmodernist should try to defend the radical credentials of local/situated/nomadic criticism by pointing to our ordinary discursive resources and proposing that they already provide all we need for critical thought, then she surely looks naive. As Seyla Benhabib has said, it is a 'defect of "situated criticism" . . . to assume that the constitutive norms of a given culture, society, and tradition will be sufficient to enable one to exercise criticism in the name of a desirable future'.[16]

On a more sinister note, our worry about conservatism must be seen to go beyond a concern that postmodernism brings an inadvertent conservatism of critical inertia. We have to be suspicious that it is motivated, in some quarters at least, by a more energetic type of conservatism. As Sabina Lovibond asks:

> What . . . are we to make of suggestions that the [modernist] project has run out of steam and that the moment has passed for remaking society on rational, egalitarian lines? It would be only natural for anyone placed at the sharp end of one or more of the existing power structures . . . to feel a pang of disappointment at this news. But wouldn't it also be in order to feel *suspicion*? How can any one ask me to say goodbye to 'emancipatory metanarratives' when my own emancipation is still such a patchy, hit-and-miss affair?[17]

In response to a 'suspicious' reading of this kind, the postmodernist might say that her insistence on seeing trans-local critical judgement as terroristic is motivated only by a desire to castigate attempts on the part of the powerful to lay down the law about how the world is. But even if this were the driving motivation, the insistence would retain its sinister aspect. For it equally has the effect of robbing the powerless of the right to regard their own counter-claims as grounded in something which is of itself authoritative, something whose authority is not diminished by the cynical insouciance of others. If the powerful are merely *expressing* themselves when they tell others how the world is, then so too are the powerless – only in the case of the powerless nobody is listening. The problem with the postmodernist charge of terrorism (or imperialism, or authoritarianism) against a practice of reason is that it is hopelessly indiscriminate.

A different, familiar criticism of postmodernism, but one from which I shall suggest the postmodernist is ultimately immune, is the charge of self-refutation.[18] Isn't a position that vilifies all 'grand narratives' itself a grand narrative? Isn't anti-epistemology yet another species of epistemological position (even if it refuses to be pinned down to any stable determinate thesis)? On the face of it, the answer is Yes. But postmodernism can achieve an artful dodge away from this charge, by exploiting the idea of irony. The historical self-consciousness of the postmodern era is understood to impose on the subject an ironical attitude of detachment, so that she is semi-disengaged from even her most keenly held beliefs and values.[19] Richard Rorty affectionately describes 'ironists' as never being 'quite able to take themselves seriously because always aware that the terms in which they describe themselves are subject to change, always aware of the contingency and fragility of their final vocabularies, and thus of their selves'.[20] Rorty's ironism invites us to live with a tension, even a conflict, between our attitude towards the things we take seriously and our ironist's lack of seriousness. The will to tolerate this sort of dissonance is also explicit in Donna Haraway's characterization of postmodernist irony: 'Irony is about contradictions that do not resolve into larger wholes, even dialectically, about the tension of holding incompatible things together because both or all are necessary and true.'[21] Provided that the ironical attitude can be said to extend to the theoretical pronouncements that are expressive of the postmodernist outlook itself, then the postmodernist does not contradict herself in stating her position. The 'statement' is itself provisional, not ultimately taken seriously, not understood as having any sway beyond the discursive locality of this conversation, this 'language game'.

Or so the vigilant ironist will *say*. But even if she wins a technical victory for postmodernism in the face of accusations of self-refutation, there is still a case to be answered in respect of the practical psychological viability of ironism. We may well doubt our prospects for psychological health in a life where we cannot quite take 'seriously' even our most deeply held beliefs and values. We are entitled to doubt the livability (not to mention the desirability) of a life in which the historical achievement of self-consciousness has degenerated into a knowing disingenuousness.

We can see, then, that postmodernism is dogged by problems of conservatism and of psychological viability. But there remains a powerful and profound philosophical motivation for it which we have not yet reckoned with: the problem of the authority of reason. We all know that postmodernism is a response to a 'crisis' of reason (the crisis produced by modernity[22]). But perhaps we can come to a better understanding of the postmodern rational malaise by venturing a more specific diagnostic interpretation. I now turn to that heuristic exercise. I shall propose a speculative reconstruction which is designed to explain the malaise, by making plain both its intelligibility and its needlessness.

A genealogy of postmodernism

The idea that there could be a problem surrounding the question of reason's authority has arisen in various forms at different points in the history of philosophy.[23] The problem can be seen in its modern form, perhaps most relevantly and most vividly, at the heart of Kant's philosophy. One quick – too quick – way of generating an apparent crisis of reason would be achieved in four steps. First, accept the fundamental Kantian distinction between a wholly unconditioned reason on the one hand, and merely heteronomous forces on the other. Second, accept that the authority of reason derives from the fact that reason is empirically unconditioned. Third, reflect that the idea of a wholly unconditioned reason is dubious. Fourth, conclude that reason is just force by another name.

This would be too quick on several scores, not least that of Kantian exegesis. But more careful and more subtle routes to rational crisis may nonetheless take roughly this form. I shall suggest – in postmodernism's favour – that even on a constructivist reading of Kant, the question of reason's vindication remains problematical; but I shall also suggest – against postmodernism – that the above crisis-producing argument contains a false move which is preserved in sublimated form in the intellectual background to the postmodernist rational malaise. The false move is made when the acceptance of (something like) the Kantian standard for reason's vindication is held on to, even while the outlook that produced it is disowned. Once we make the move explicit we are better placed to find a philosophical means of staving off the malaise. Many philosophers of an analytic persuasion meet postmodernism with bafflement, or doubt that it has any genuine philosophical motivations. I aim to present a philosophical motivation for postmodernism which can lead us to understand precisely how the postmodernist view of reason goes awry, and also to appreciate that it is an interestingly (and not merely influentially) mistaken response to a deep philosophical problem.

The postmodernist acquiescence in rational crisis can be generated not only in the quick four-step manner rehearsed above, in which Kant figures as embarked on a doomed foundationalism. It can also be generated, or so I will suggest, from an interpretation of Kant which takes his vindicatory project as a piece of constructivism. This is important, because if the postmodernist acquiescence in crisis were dependent on an acceptance of foundationalism, then postmodernism would surely be far easier to dispense with than it is. A constructivist interpretation of Kant's vindication of reason is given by Onora O'Neill. She has argued that we should understand Kant as pitched against the foundationalism of his rationalist predecessors, and as offering a constructivist vindication that depends upon (a historical progression towards) an ideal discursive practice which is governed entirely by principles of reason that anyone could accept – an ideal of perfect Enlightenment.[24] In O'Neill's reading, the dependence of reason upon freedom which we find in Kant takes on a political aspect. The freedom on which reason relies for its authority is conceived in the politically demanding sense of communication with (rather than mere toleration of) dissent. This demanding conception is required to provide the conditions for historical progress towards the ideal of perfect inclusiveness.

O'Neill's interpretation is borne out by the emphasis Kant places in 'What is Enlightenment?' on the distinction between 'private' and 'public' uses of reason. She explains:

> A 'public' use of reason is not defined by its large audience, and cannot take place in the public service, where relations of command and obedience permit only 'private' uses of reason. The reason Kant attaches importance to 'public' uses of reason is rather that these alone are not premised on accepting some rationally ungrounded [authorities] – 'alien' authorities (e.g. Frederick II, or the teachings of a church). Hence they alone are full uses of reason, and 'private' uses of reason are to be understood as defective, deprived or *privatus* . . .[25]

What makes private uses of reason 'private', then, is that they have a delimited jurisdiction: their audience is confined to and defined by some external authority. They issue from an imperfectly inclusive discursive situation so that, as one might put it, there are points of view which are neglected by that use of reason – points of view which have in one way or another been excluded or suppressed.

O'Neill's appealing constructivist reading distances Kant from his rationalist predecessors, so that he is seen to occupy a position somewhere between their foundationalism and the reductivism of the postmodernists. The reductivist position is captured in the view that reason is just another form of social power – or alternatively, in Foucauldian terms, the view that reason is a fundamentally 'disciplinary' authority in the service of a 'régime of truth'.[26] O'Neill herself suggests that a virtue of Kant's position is that it avoids both rationalist Scylla and postmodernist Charybdis. But while the constructivist interpretation clearly pre-empts the quick four-step argument to crisis, I would suggest – without detriment to O'Neill's exegetical strategy – that there is a route to postmodernism which such a constructivism cannot block. For it remains reasonable that someone should come to doubt the appropriateness of the ideal of a perfectly free and inclusive discursive situation in which no '"alien" authorities' are present to impugn the spontaneity of critical thought. One might come to doubt its appropriateness on the basis of Foucauldian considerations about the place of power in discursive relations:

> Relations of power are not in a position of exteriority with respect to other types of relationships (economic processes, knowledge relationships, sexual relations), but are immanent in the latter; they are the immediate effects of the divisions, inequalities, and disequilibriums which occur in the latter, and conversely they are the internal conditions of these differentiations; relations of power are not in superstructural positions, with merely a role of prohibi-

tion or accompaniment; they have a directly productive role, wherever they come into play.[27]

If power is a 'productive' force that helps to constitute discursive relations, rather than an alien force that threatens to interfere with them from the outside, then the Kantian conception – ideal or not – of discursive relations looks to be a false one. Power is certainly a heteronomous force. So the Kantian ideal must be of a discursive situation from which the operation of power is entirely absent. Yet this is impossible if power is partially constitutive of discursive relations. Given the Foucauldian insight, we cannot make sense of the idea of a discursive situation in which the non-suppression of any critical thought is secured by an *absence* of power. Confronted with any discursive situation, there will have been many an undetectable suppression in advance of the point at which we could ask the question: is every thought out in the open?

Someone who is justly influenced by this Foucauldian line of thought is entitled to a certain pessimism as to reason's susceptibility to the Kantian vindication. The pessimism seems appropriate even on the constructivist reading, because the idealization on which the vindication relies is an idealization of a false conception of discursive relations. The Kantian conception characterizes the workings of power as external to discursive relations, as if we could extrude the dynamics of power – the influence of '"alien" authorities' – from discursive relations *per se*.

In light of the Foucauldian conception of power's constitutive role in discursive relations, someone with a commitment to the Kantian standard for reason's vindication is likely to seek a counsel of despair. Disillusionment leads her to reject reason's authority – where she might instead have rejected the Kantian standard – and she comes to regard all uses of reason as on all fours with the operations of obviously heteronomous, worldly species of power. She may not go so far as to declare that reason's operation is morally equivalent to 'terrorizing' someone into believing that p, but she may come to the conclusion that the use of reason is no different from the exercise of social power – as Frederick II, or as the head of a church – to bring someone to believe that p. So far as she is concerned, all uses of reason are, in the Kantian terminology, private uses. She despairs of the possibility of the genuinely public uses on which the vindication of reason proper was seen to depend.

I do not deny that there may yet be room to show that something like a Kantian vindication of reason remains available. Perhaps it could be shown that a Kantian has no need to rely on a conception of discursive freedom that requires the complete absence of power's influence. A Kantian might adjust her conception of the conditions under which we can say that no critical thought is suppressed, so that only the absence of certain, corrupting operations of power is required. (This possibility surely provides a promising strategy for the Kantian impressed by the Foucauldian thought, and it is close to the strategy I shall eventually be recommending.) My purpose is simply to offer a reconstruction of a genuine philosophical motivation for even the most extreme postmodernist rational scepticism – scepticism whose object is the special authority that is supposed to attach to the force of reason.[28] Inasmuch as the Kantian conception of reason's authority is dependent on an ideal of political freedom, disillusionment with the possibility of vindicating it in the Kantian manner can be expected to find expression in specifically political terms. If the postmodernist anti-epistemological stance is motivated in the manner I have suggested, then its rhetoric of 'terror', 'authoritarianism' and 'imperialism' is, hyperbole notwithstanding, perfectly apt.

This is not to say that the postmodernist rational malaise is, all things considered, well-motivated. On the contrary, I have characterized it as a counsel of despair, and as an expression of disillusion. And I have suggested that the disillusionment might be blamed not on reason itself but on an unacknowledged continued commitment to a peculiarly unreachable (Kantian) standard for reason's vindication.[29] The little genealogy I have presented allows us to identify the crux of the postmodernist rational malaise: postmodernism despairs of the possibility of distinguishing authoritative from authoritarian uses of reason.

I think that this is not always appreciated. It is clear from Thomas Nagel's Introduction to *The Last Word* that he was prompted to write it partly by the prevalence of postmodernist thought. He never uses that term, and his book is not a *response* to postmodernism, but he says that the climate of subjectivist and relativist habits of thought is 'there as a source of irritation in the background', and it is manifestly an aim of the book to erect defences for reason fit to protect it against onslaughts from postmodernists. But Nagel does not appreciate the distinctively political character of postmodernists' rational scepticism. Their scepticism is not a response to familiar problems in metaphysics or philosophy of mind about the place of reason in nature or the relation of mentality to the physical realm. It is a response first and foremost to a problem which cuts across epistemology, metaphysics and ethics:[30] the problem of discursive authority. Nagel's neglect of the ethical-political impetus behind the irritating subjectivist climate is a disappointment. It ensures that his book's (surely correct) message – that reason, and not something else to which it is reduced, must have the last word – is not put in terms that could impact on the debates which have created the climate. It is not that Nagel hopes to persuade any relativist of reason's dominion – on the contrary, he says 'I don't seriously hope that work on the question of how reason is possible will make relativism any less fashionable'.[31] My point is simply that it is a pity, when reacting to an enormously influential *Zeitgeist*, not to diagnose it exactly right.

The diagnosis I have offered brings two points into view. First, it allows us to see that a policy of ironism, localness, or nomadism can provide no solution at all to the problem of how to refrain from discursive terrorism. If the source of the problem resides in the idea that rational persuasion is *au fond* just another form of coercion, then it changes nothing to reason – or, more neutrally perhaps, to communicate thoughts – fleetingly, ironically, locally, changeably. No matter how the postmodern subject is personified – in the figure of the cyborg, the nomad, the private ironist – we now see that it can provide no solace. If the reasoner is a discursive authoritarian who trades in a kind of terror, then the ironic and nomadic strategies merely add cynicism and capriciousness to the list of her vices.

Secondly, our diagnosis points to a suitable therapy for the despair. Something we may see as *the Kantian problem* – a foundational problem – may be insoluble. But perhaps we can show that the foundational problem arises only on a historically specific, and so non-compulsory, understanding of what is required for a proper distinction between authoritative and authoritarian uses of reason. In short, we may be able to prescribe a means of staving off disillusionment by posing the problem more superficially – at ground level, so to speak. If so, a broadly epistemological question will find its answer through being posed as a first-order question in the ethics of discursive practice. (The question relieved of its foundational aspect remains an epistemological one, because the practices whose ethics we are concerned with are epistemic practices.)

What the feminist, or otherwise politicized, epistemologist should be concerned to bring to light are cases of discursive authoritarianism. It is a condition of our being able to do this that our conception of rational authoritarianism permits a contrast with other discursive behaviours that we can regard as all right, as non-authoritarian. It is politically futile – indeed it is ultimately senseless – to say that all reasoned discourse is authoritarian or terrorist. If we say that, then we deprive ourselves of the required point of contrast. (We have just seen that the freeform ironic discursive attitude can provide no adequate contrast.) Meanwhile, the everyday ethical and meta-physical question of what constitutes an authoritarian use of reason has been obscured by the foundational, grand-metaphysical one – a consequence which is, once again, congenial to conservatism.

The question of reason's authority is one of the problems of freedom, where another such problem is that of free will. The two problems have a similar structure. The debate surrounding the former invokes a contrast with authoritarianism – mere social power; and the debate surrounding the latter invokes a contrast with causal determinism – mere causal power. My strategy here, then, can be seen as a Humean one. Where Hume argues that the relevant contrast with free will is not causal determination as such but only constraint, I am arguing that the relevant contrast with the authority we want for reason is not social power as such but only certain operations of power – authoritarian ones.[32]

If we succeed in transforming the question of rational authority from the excessively deep foundational one to the ground-level ethical one, then we shall perhaps have succeeded in being 'superficial out of profundity'.[33] Being suitably superficial here will require us to take the everyday ethical distinction between authoritative and authoritarian uses of reason at face value. We do not put the distinction in these terms every day, but we make such judgements nonetheless. It is surely one of the achievements of feminism that we have grown more attuned to the ethical and political aspects of discursive practice – though I do not deny that we need to get better at recognizing rational authoritarianism when we are confronted with it. Indeed, equipping ourselves with the right philosophical conception is meant to help. Feminism calls upon us to be concerned above all with the politics of lived experience. And this should lead us to focus on the practical, so that we aim to do philosophy in a way that is informed by and informs our best everyday judgements about the character of discursive transactions.

Our theoretical energies ought, then, to be directed to the important and novel task of using the distinction between 'authoritative' and 'authoritarian' in order to bring to light the first-order ethical and political aspects of epistemic practice. In bringing them into view we shall be exploring some ways in which ethical and political concepts can be literally, not merely metaphorically, applicable to epistemic practice.[34] When it is contrasted with this straightforward theoretical engagement with the ethics and politics of reason, postmodernism may seem to offer us little besides an opportunity to be profound out of superficiality.

This is a little unfair of course. In the postmodernist rhetoric of terror – and certainly in the feminist postmodernist rhetoric of exclusion – one should doubtless recognize the expression of a genuinely radical aspiration. Most relevantly here, postmodernists are impelled by a concern to build into epistemology the space for an epistemic pluralism. (Recall the earlier suggestion that the feminist postmodernist's concern with difference is driven by a political commitment to inclusiveness – an inclusiveness which she might once have hoped Kant could guarantee.) Insisting on 'permanent partiality' and on the multiplicity of epistemic perspectives is part of an attempt to secure a kind of expressive freedom which the discourse of traditional epistemology can seem designed to suppress. Sandra Harding captures the pluralist spirit in feminist postmodernism thus: 'Contrary to the assumption of "a" world out there . . . there are as many interrelated and smoothly connected realities as there are kinds of oppositional consciousness. By giving up the goal of telling "one true story", we embrace instead the permanent partiality of feminist inquiry.'[35] Postmodernism's credentials as the defender of plurality against epistemology's will to unification is one of its attractions for feminists, who are rightly concerned to honour the reality of epistemic difference at the level of theory. That is why postmodernism can appear as an ally. But I have been arguing that the apparent alliance is an illusion – and a treacherous one.

First, we found postmodernism to be troubled by conservatism and by psychological unviability. Then we saw that it presents us with a view about *the very idea* of rational authority (a view diagnosed as an expression of disillusionment) when what we need is a view about how we should conduct ourselves as reasoners – as participants in discursive or epistemic practice. Now we are reminded that postmodernism can seem attractive to feminists in virtue of its being a champion of pluralism. And I shall finish by arguing that, so far as feminism's commitment to theorizing epistemic difference is concerned, the ways in which postmodernism champions pluralism are the wrong ways.

Pluralism within reason – a perspectival realism

If the right level for pluralism is ground level, the level of practice, then what epistemology needs to be brought to accommodate is a first-order epistemic pluralism. It is that sort of pluralism which acknowledges the existence of many different perspectives on a shared world. And, assuming we are speaking literally, there must be a shared world. If there are ethical-political aspects of epistemic practice that arise as a result of the participants having different epistemic perspectives, then the participants stand to each other in ethical-political relations of one or another kind. This presupposes that they inhabit the same world – a world in which there may be authoritarian practices to be brought to light. The pluralism we need, then, is the ordinary first-order kind, a pluralism in practice: 'To acquiesce in a diversity of opinions – to tolerate dissensus – is to accept pluralism.'[36]

Inasmuch as postmodernists' urge to pluralism is explained by reference to a commitment to making epistemology reflect the reality of epistemic difference and epistemic authoritarianism, postmodernism imposes pluralism at every level except the right one. Pluralism gets expressed as an ontological thesis about multiple realities, as a metaphysical thesis about multiple truths, and as an epistemological thesis about the 'permanent partiality of perspectives'.[37] Meanwhile, the prospect of theorizing any first-order epistemic pluralism has been obliterated in the big-bang-style expansion.

The pluralism for which there is a genuine motivation is one that is capable of honouring the everyday insight (whose feminist theoretical expression originates in standpoint theory) that social differences give rise to differences in the perspectives in which the world is viewed, and that power can be an influence in whose perspectives seem rational. The aspiration to secure the legitimacy of a pluralism of perspectives is closely related both to the discursive practice which Kant idealized, and to the kind which feminists attracted by postmodernism might be hoping for. But our pluralism arises from a conception of discursive relations which, unlike Kant's, is informed by the idea of power's immanence in those relations. And our pluralism, unlike postmodernism's, promotes a practice of reason that permits different perspectives to come to the fore not merely in order that they should gain expression, but in order that they should contribute to an ongoing critical discursive practice.[38]

We have seen, then, that a critical awareness of the phenomenon of discursive authoritarianism should motivate us to make explicit provision for a first-order epistemic pluralism. This is not the place to attempt to do that, but a gesture at least can be made towards the possibility of what I have called a 'perspectival realism'.[39] According to perspectival realism, the right conception of social reality is such that, at any given historical moment, many of the facts that constitute it permit of being viewed rationally in more than one perspective. I think this is a thoroughly commonplace idea, but one that has not found much expression in epistemology. When informed by the Foucauldian insight about power's constitutive role in discursive relations, perspectival realism furnishes a rationale for a truly radicalized ethics of discursive practice. It is radicalized because our conception of authoritarianism is now informed by an awareness of how discursive transactions are permeated by operations of power. And also because it is informed by an awareness that the perspectives in which the powerless may view the world can appear less rational than they are, owing to an uneven discursive terrain. When this happens, there *is* a kind of epistemic tyranny – a tyranny which we are unable to identify if we take the postmodernist view that all uses of reason are tyrannical.

Conclusion

I have argued that the right way to set about answering the question of reason's authority is by posing it at ground level in the form of an ethical question about epistemic practice: which uses of reason are authoritarian, as opposed to simply authoritative? The Foucauldian insight – and indeed feminism's own insight into power's permeation of social and personal relationships, as captured in the slogan 'the personal is political' – must inform our first-order judgements so that our ethics of discursive practice emerges in a state of political awareness. We may refine our appreciation of what is at stake in the distinction between 'authoritarian' and 'authoritative' by way of comparisons with other, similarly subtle distinctions which are nonetheless thoroughly familiar to us. We exploit such distinctions when, for instance, we judge someone's outlook to be moral but not moralistic, or their words to be full of sentiment but not sentimental.[40] I have also argued that epistemology should be made accountable to difference by incorporating an epistemic pluralism into it, not an ontological or a metaphysical or an epistemological one. As in the case of reason's authority, the right level to accommodate difference is ground level.

Nagel gives the last word to reason. If the ethics and politics of reason are to be made visible, then we must understand reason in practical terms. Such an emphasis on the practical character of rationality inevitably summons the image of Wittgenstein, and we are reminded that it is a philosophical skill to know *at what point* simply to say 'This is where my spade is turned. This is what I do, this is what I say.'[41] The shadow of conservatism hovers over us in the risk of saying it too soon. But there is an equal risk – and one which has turned out to be equally hospitable to conservatism – in saying it too late. I have tried to show that, over the question of reason, postmodernists draw the discussion to a close too late. They want to give the last word not to our practice of reason but to the operations of social power, the defiant antidote to which is an excessively radical brand of expressive freedom. What makes the question of reason's authority important to the politically conscious epistemologist is its implications for the ethics of epistemic practice. It is for good reason, then, that the last word here shall be practical.[42]

NOTES

1 Friedrich Nietzsche, *The Gay Science*, Preface to the second edition; trans. Walter Kaufmann (New York: Vintage Books, 1974), p. 38.
2 Richard Rorty, *Philosophy and the Mirror of Nature* (Oxford: Blackwell, 1980), p. 10.

3 Jean-François Lyotard, *The Postmodern Condition: A Report on Knowledge*, trans. G. Bennington and B. Massumi (Manchester: Manchester University Press, 1984), p. xxiii.

4 See the work cited in Further Reading under 'Feminist Standpoint Theory', p. 269.

5 'The self-understanding of the proletariat is . . . simultaneously the objective understanding of the nature of society' (Georgy Lukács, 'The Standpoint of the Proletariat', in *History and Class Consciousness: Studies in Marxist Dialectics*, trans. Rodney Livingstone (London: Merlin Press, 1971; first published 1923), pp. 149–209 (p. 149)).

6 I borrow this term from Sabina Lovibond, who attributes it to Paul Hirst. See Lovibond, 'The End of Morality', in Kathleen Lennon and Margaret Whitford, eds., *Knowing the Difference: Feminist Perspectives in Epistemology* (London and New York: Routledge, 1994), p. 63.

7 To conceive epistemic subjects as social subjects *is* – for the socially non-myopic – to conceive them as placed in relations of power.

8 The question whether a given piece of philosophical radicalism is aligned with political radicalism is entirely contingent. Any use of the word 'radicalism' however carries a Leftist political association, and I believe that in some quarters this has led to an undue confidence in the political credentials of philosophical extremism.

9 'Social Criticism without Philosophy: An Encounter between Feminism and Postmodernism', in Linda J. Nicholson, ed., *Feminism/Postmodernism* (London and New York: Routledge, 1990), pp. 34–5.

10 Andreas Huyssen, 'Mapping the Postmodern', in Nicholson, ed., *Feminism/Postmodernism*, pp. 234–77 (p. 237).

11 Donna Haraway, 'A Manifesto for Cyborgs: Science, Technology, and Socialist Feminism in the 1980s', in Nicholson, ed., *Feminism/Postmodernism*, pp. 196–7.

12 Susan Strickland, 'Feminism, Postmodernism and Difference', in Lennon and Whitford, eds., *Knowing the Difference*, p. 267.

13 Jean-François Lyotard, *The Postmodern Condition: A Report on Knowledge*, trans. G. Bennington and B. Massumi (Manchester: Manchester University Press, 1984), p. 66.

14 In his concluding rhetorical flourish, Lyotard writes: 'Let us wage a war on totality; let us be witnesses to the unpresentable; let us activate the differences and save the honor of the name' (ibid., p. 82).

15 Rosi Braidotti uses Gilles Deleuze's idea of the nomadic subject in her conception of feminist philosophy as a 'new nomadism'; see her *Patterns of Dissonance: A Study of Women in Contemporary Philosophy* (Cambridge: Polity Press, 1991), e.g. pp. 277–8.

16 Seyla Benhabib, 'Feminism and Postmodernism: An Uneasy Alliance', in Seyla Benhabib et al., *Feminist Contentions: A Philosophical Exchange* (London and New York: Routledge, 1995), p. 27.

17 Sabina Lovibond, 'Feminism and Postmodernism', *New Left Review* 178 (1989), 5–28 (p. 12).

18 See Hilary Putnam, 'Why Reason Can't Be Naturalized', in Kenneth Baynes, James Bohman and Thomas McCarthy, eds., *After Philosophy: End or Transformation?* (Cambridge, MA: MIT Press, 1987).

19 The brand of irony distinctive of the postmodern is essentially sceptical, hence the psychological disengagement. This contrasts with the irony of modernism which is essentially the irony of the avant-garde – that of tireless self-conscious self-creation. For an undatingly illuminating discussion of modernism as a diversified cultural movement see Marshall Berman's *All That Is Solid Melts Into Air: The Experience of Modernity* (London and New York: Verso, 1982). For a critical discussion of modernism from a feminist point of view (including a discussion of Berman) see Rita Selski, *The Gender of Modernity* (Cambridge, MA, and London: Harvard University Press, 1995).

20 Richard Rorty, *Contingency, Irony, and Solidarity* (Cambridge: Cambridge University Press, 1989), pp. 73–4.

21 Donna Haraway, 'A Manifesto for Cyborgs', in Nicholson, ed., *Feminism/Postmodernism*, p. 190.

22 'Modernity can and will no longer borrow the criteria by which it takes its orientation from the models supplied by another epoch; *it has to create its normativity out of itself*' (Jürgen Habermas, *The Philosophical Discourse of Modernity* (Cambridge: Polity Press, 1985), p. 7, original italics. The quotation is from Lecture 1, whose title is also germane: 'Modernity's Consciousness of Time and Its Need for Self-Reassurance').

23 'I often used to hear from Gorgias that the art of persuasion is very different from other arts, since everything is enslaved by it willingly and not by force', Protarchus says in Plato's *Philebus*, quoted in Bernard Williams, *Shame and Necessity* (Berkeley: University of California Press, 1993), p. 154. On the origins of our many ideas of rhetoric and persuasion (including 'the terrifying, exhilarating possibility that persuasion is just power'), see Robert Wardy, *The Birth of Rhetoric: Gorgias, Plato and Their Successors* (London and New York: Routledge, 1996), p. 2.

24 Note that O'Neill's Kant 'offers an account of what it is to vindicate reason quite different from the foundationalist account that critics of "the Enlightenment project" target, and usually attribute to Kant' ('Vindicating Reason', in Paul Guyer, ed., *The Cambridge Companion to Kant* (Cambridge: Cambridge University Press, 1992), pp. 280–308 (p. 281). See also, her *Constructions of Reason: Explorations of Kant's Practical Philosophy* (Cambridge: Cambridge University Press, 1989), chs. 1 and 2.

25 O'Neill, 'Vindicating Reason', p. 298.

26 'Truth is a thing of this world: it is produced only by virtue of multiple forms of constraint. And it induces regular effects of power. Each society has its régime of truth, its "general politics" of truth' (*Power/Knowledge: Selected Interviews & Other Writings 1972–77*, ed. Colin Gordon, trans. Colin Gordon, Leo Marshall, John Mepham and Kate Soper (London: Harvester Wheatsheaf, 1980), p. 131).

27 Michel Foucault, *The History of Sexuality*, vol. 1: *An Introduction* (London: Pelican Books, 1981), p. 94.

28 For a historical (as opposed to merely reconstructive) account of motivations for poststructuralist and postmodernist philosophy, see Jürgen Habermas, *The Philosophical Discourse of Modernity*, trans. Frederick Lawrence (Cambridge: Polity Press, 1987). For a feminist account of the crisis of reason, see Elizabeth Grosz's 'Bodies and Knowledges: Feminism and the Crisis of Reason', in Linda

Alcoff and Elizabeth Potter, eds., *Feminist Epistemologies* (London and New York: Routledge, 1993), pp. 187–215.

29 There is a parallel between the present view of the Kantian legacy for rational authority and a view of the Kantian legacy in moral (sic) philosophy. At the end of the last chapter of *Ethics and the Limits of Philosophy*, Bernard Williams writes: 'morality makes people think that, without its very special obligation, there is only inclination; without its utter voluntariness, there is only force; without its ultimately pure justice, there is no justice. Its philosophical errors are only the most abstract expressions of a deeply rooted and still powerful misconception of life' (London: Fontana/Collins, 1985), p. 196.

30 It goes without saying that the ethics of discursive practice will cover the influence of power in discursive transactions, and will in that sense be simultaneously a discursive politics.

31 Thomas Nagel, *The Last Word* (Oxford and New York: Oxford University Press, 1997), p. 6.

32 David Hume, *An Enquiry Concerning Human Understanding*, 3rd edition (Oxford: Clarendon Press, 1975), section VIII. It is interesting to reflect that more recent empiricists have gone in for a reductive naturalism that reduces norms to causes in a manner which parallels the reductive programme of the postmodernists. The former reduce norms to causal operations in nature; the latter reduce them to operations of power in the social realm. Each has a problem fitting the normative into the world as they find it. (For a critical account of reductive or 'bald' naturalism, see John McDowell, *Mind and World* (Cambridge, MA and London: Harvard University Press, 1994), lecture IV; for a classic statement of a reductive naturalism in epistemology, see W. V. O. Quine, 'Epistemology Naturalized', *Ontological Relativity and Other Essays* (New York: Columbia University Press, 1969), pp. 69–90.)

33 Reading Bernard Williams's discussion of responsibility and intentional action in *Shame and Necessity* (Berkeley: University of California Press, 1993), and also Sabina Lovibond's 'Meaning What We Say: Feminist Ethics and the Critique of Humanism', *New Left Review* 220 (1996), 98–115, prompted me to put the issue this way. Williams alludes to Nietzsche's idea of being superficial out of profundity in the question of the Greeks' attitude to the voluntary in the sense of authorship of one's actions (pp. 66–70); and Lovibond refers (pp. 108–10) to Williams in order to suggest that the same idea may be applied to the question of authorship of one's thoughts. In effect, my own suggestion is that the same point can again be made in respect of authorship of one's reasons. Being the author of one's reasons requires standing by them – 'owning' them – beyond the fleeting context of the here and now. This attitude contrasts with the attitude of semi-disownment which ironism imposes.

34 See 'Incredulity, Experientialism, and the Politics of Knowledge', in Lorraine Code's *Rhetorical Spaces: Essays On Gendered Locations* (London and New York: Routledge, 1995), pp. 58–82. For arguments developing the idea of 'epistemic injustice', see my 'Rational Authority and Social Power: Towards a Truly Social Epistemology', *Proceedings of the Aristotelian Society* 98, part 2 (1998), 159–77.

35 Sandra Harding, *The Science Question in Feminism* (Milton Keynes: Open University Press, 1986), p. 194.

36 Nicholas Rescher, *Pluralism: Against the Demand for Consensus* (Oxford: Clarendon Press, 1995), p. 64.

37 I say more about what is wrong with the idea of permanent partiality in 'Knowledge as Construct: Theorizing the Role of Gender in Knowledge', in Lennon and Whitford, eds., *Knowing the Difference*, pp. 95–109 (pp. 100–3).

38 In this particular, the proposed view is allied with the view of communicative practice found in Habermas. Although the original idea of an 'ideal speech situation' is surely subject to the Foucauldian objection raised here against Kant, Habermas's idea of a 'constraint-free understanding among individuals' might permit of a suitably superficial reading which would free it from that objection (Jürgen Habermas, *Postmetaphysical Thinking: Philosophical Essays* (Cambridge, MA: MIT Press, 1992), p. 145).

39 In my 'Perspectival Realism: Towards a Pluralist Theory of Knowledge', D.Phil thesis, Oxford 1996.

40 I borrow this comparison from Sabina Lovibond's inspiring paper 'The End of Morality?' in which she conceives a philosophical task 'of distinguishing – though not necessarily in an abstract, criteriological way – between rationality and "ratiofascism"' and compares this task 'to that of distinguishing between morality and moralism' (p. 71).

41 Ludwig Wittgenstein, *Philosophical Investigations* (Oxford: Blackwell, 1953), §217.

42 My thanks to Sebastian Gardner, Melissa Lane, Sabina Lovibond and (especially) to my co-editor Jennifer Hornsby, for commenting on an earlier draft.

9

ALISON WYLIE

Feminism in philosophy of science
Making sense of contingency and
constraint

Introduction

Feminist philosophy of science is situated at the intersection between feminist interests in science and philosophical studies of science as these have developed in the last twenty years. Feminists have long regarded the sciences as a key resource for understanding the conditions that affect women's lives and, in this connection, they have pursued a number of highly productive programmes of research, especially in the social and life sciences. At the same time, however, feminists see the sciences as an important locus of gender inequality and as a key source of legitimation for this inequality; feminists both within and outside the sciences have developed close critical analyses of the androcentrism they find inherent in the institutions, practices and content of science. Both kinds of feminist engagement with science – constructive and critical – raise epistemological questions about ideals of objectivity, the status of evidence and the role of orienting (often unacknowledged) contextual values.

Despite substantial overlap between philosophical and feminist interests in science, a number of outspoken critics argue that the very idea of feminist philosophy of science (or, more generally, feminist epistemology), is a contradiction in terms.[1] Insofar as feminism is an explicitly partisan, political standpoint, they insist, it can have no bearing on the practice or understanding of science, the hallmark of which is value neutrality and objectivity. In response to objections of this sort, feminist philosophers of science argue that their critics make a number of highly problematic assumptions about science. Arguments that were well established by the late 1970s – arguments from the theory-ladenness of evidence, the underdetermination of theory by evidence, and various forms of holism – substantially undermine confidence in the central tenets of 'received view' theories of scientific knowledge; they make it clear that the empirical basis of science cannot be treated as a foundational given in any straightforward sense, and that objectivity cannot be identified with strict value neutrality and the context independence of epistemic standards.[2]

The conclusions that emerged from these internal critiques of positivism in the 1960s and 1970s have been reinforced by twenty years of post-positivist research in which philosophers have turned increasingly to fine-grained, discipline- and practice-specific studies of science. The inspiration for much of this work is a commitment to ground philosophical analyses in a detailed understanding of the content and practice of actual science.[3] Time and again, the result has been increased recognition that the sciences are complex and contingent in ways that resist explanation in conventional philosophical terms. 'Contextual' (external, non-cognitive) factors play a crucial role not only in decisions about what questions to pursue and how to apply the results of inquiry, but also in the intellectual and methodological judgements that shape the content of science; they influence how scientists conceptualize their subject domain, what hypotheses they consider plausible, and what will count as evidence and 'good reasons' in the evaluation of these hypotheses. It is a short step from the insights central to the work of this new generation of contextualizing philosophers of science to a recognition that the gendered dimensions of scientific practice – the gender structures inherent in its institutions, the gender symbolism associated with its practice and its products, the gendered interests and identities of its practitioners – may well be among the contextual factors that are relevant for answering philosophical questions about science.

In what follows, I begin with a general account of the difference that feminist perspectives have made to the practice of science. I then consider a number of responses to the philosophical questions raised by feminist critiques of science and feminist research initiatives, and describe the range of theories developed by feminist philosophers of science. I will focus, in conclusion, on recent developments in feminist empiricism and feminist standpoint theory as examples of work in feminist philosophy of science that illustrate both its unique contributions to and its continuities with the growing tradition of naturalizing and contextualizing research in philosophy of science.

Feminism and science

Where science is concerned, feminists are perhaps best known for sharply critical assessments of various ways in which sexist or androcentric values and assumptions are reproduced in the institutional structures, the practice, the research agendas and the resulting content of even the most credible and well-established sciences. Often feminist critics begin by documenting gender inequalities in the training, representation and recognition of women in the sciences, a pattern of marginalization that continues into the present even as increasing numbers of women demonstrate their aptitude for scientific training and their capacity to make substantial contributions to virtually all fields of scientific research. Londa Shiebinger, a feminist historian of science, argues that these long-established patterns of exclusion were by no means inevitable; elite women and women involved in traditions of craft production in the seventeenth and eighteenth centuries played an active role in the early formation of the sciences but were systematically marginalized as these disciplines assumed the institutional forms that have since become familiar.[4] Women were rarely admitted to the major scientific academies and universities responsible for training scientists until the last fifty years, whatever their talents or contributions and, despite their growing representation in graduate programmes, they remain a striking minority in most fields. The resulting under-representation of women in the sciences is both reflected in and reinforced by representations of science (popular and internal) that define it as a stereotypically masculine enterprise. The circle is closed when the tools of science are used to demonstrate that women, along with a variety of other unsavoury outsiders (e.g., criminals, the 'lower classes', a shifting catalogue of racial, ethnic and national groups) lack the cognitive capacities necessary to succeed at disciplined, scientific inquiry.[5]

While these 'equity' critiques challenge the democratic, meritocratic ideals associated with science, on their own they do not call into question its content or credibility. This requires a further programme of critical analysis that focuses on ways in which persistent, deeply rooted gender inequities compromise not only the fairness and effectiveness of science as an institution, but also its epistemic integrity. These 'content' critiques take quite different forms depending on the subject matter and practice of the field (or subfield) in question.[6]

In cases where the subject of inquiry is explicitly gendered – in the social sciences and some areas of the life sciences – feminists have pursued two broad strategies of analysis. On one hand, they draw attention to gaps in understanding that arise when researchers exclude women and gender as a subject of inquiry, or treat the experience and attributes of men as normative. Consider, for example, recurrent critiques of medical research that decry the preoccupation with ailments of special concern to men as opposed to those that primarily affect women, and the associated practice of generalizing the results of male-specific studies to women. The relative dearth of research on common forms of breast cancer has been a matter of intense public debate in the last decade, as are the results of recent studies which suggest that women may be routinely misdiagnosed when it is assumed that they suffer from the same (well-studied) forms of heart disease as afflict men. In a parallel critique from psychology, Carol Gilligan shows what is missed when the moral development of children is modelled exclusively on samples of boys.[7] And in history and anthropology feminists call into question the androcentrism of quite fundamental subject-defining assumptions. The Renaissance proves to be anything but a period of cultural 'rebirth' if you consider the fortunes of women,[8] while the activities of women 'gatherers' are frequently the primary source of dietary intake in 'hunter-gatherer' societies, a finding that reinforced the need to rethink 'man the hunter' models of human evolution.[9]

On the other hand, feminists are also concerned to identify systematic distortions that arise when gender differences are taken seriously but are conceptualized in terms of stereotypes that impose sharply polarized, static categories on what are often quite complex and highly variable constructs. Assumptions of this kind are most obviously at work in the long history of sex difference studies that have been dedicated to documenting gender differences in intelligence and other cognitive capacities, and to isolating their genetic or hormonal or other biophysical foundations.[10] Even if the contingency of cultural or historical subjects is explicitly recognized, parallel problems arise when investigators project gender categories derived from their own experience onto culturally and historically distant subjects. Assumptions about the passivity and dependence of women, by contrast to the active, publicly dominant roles of men, pervade archaeological and palaeontological reconstructions, and aligned theories of human evolution.[11] Feminists have themselves wrestled with the influence of these stereotypes from the time they initiated research programmes of their own. A number of auto-critiques appeared in the early 1980s in which feminist ethnographers and historians took stock of their early labours, concluding that, in refocusing attention on the activities and experiences distinctive of women, they had often simply inverted dominant assumptions about gender difference that, on closer inspection, require more fundamental reassessment.[12]

Sometimes this last type of critique proves salient in fields concerned with subject domains that are not overtly gendered, but that lend themselves to being projectively gendered and investigated in light of familiar sex/gender stereotypes. One widely publicized example is that of primatology where recent research suggests that, contrary to deeply entrenched assumptions about what counts as 'natural' in the domain of sex/gender relations, wild primate populations exemplify more flexible and, in many cases, more female-centred patterns of social organization than previously recognized.[13] Famously, studies of reproductive physiology were long structured by assumptions that arose from the attribution of stereotypically masculine traits to sperm (as active agents) and feminine traits to eggs (as passive), sometimes at considerable cost to empirical adequacy and explanatory power. And by extension of these most obvious cases, there are a number of areas of biological research in which even subjects of micro- and molecular biology are projectively gendered.[14]

Finally, a different kind of case is sometimes made for recognizing gender bias even in fields whose subject matter is neither inherently nor projectively gendered. This often depends on an argument to the effect that the whole orientation of fields like mathematics and theoretical physics, or the dominant concern with 'master molecule' theories in micro-biology, is ideologically masculine in its preoccupation with abstraction, control and an idealized 'culture of no culture'.[15] In the early 1980s, some feminists writing on science considered the possibility that the sciences, dominated as they are by men, may reflect a distinctively masculine cognitive orientation. Some drew on psychoanalytic accounts of early childhood socialization ('object relations' theory) and argued, on this basis, that girls tend to grow up with less sharply defined identity boundaries, less dissociation from objects of knowledge, less compulsion to control and manipulate, and a greater capacity for empathetic engagement, while boys develop the cognitive styles that have come to be associated with dominant, scientific forms of knowledge – the characteristically 'masculine' traits of detachment, objectivity, and a preoccupation with intervention and control of the objects of knowledge.[16]

The essentialism inherent in this line of argument has been as sharply criticized internally, by feminist theorists, as by their critics.[17] In recent discussions it has been reconceptualized as a thesis that concerns not actual gender differences in cognitive orientation, but the symbolic conventions by which the cognitive styles associated with science are represented and valued; the claim here is that the attributes of good scientific practice are assimilated symbolically to masculine stereotypes.[18] It should be noted, however, that this turn away from appeals to a distinctive women's or men's 'way of knowing' by no means establishes that gender is irrelevant to the understanding of sciences that investigate non-gendered subjects. One of the central insights to emerge from recent sociology of science is that class and national bias are evident not just in notorious instances of propagandistic science such as Nazi science, but in the conceptual foundations and preferred modes of practice typical even of those research programmes that were acclaimed as the best examples of natural science and mathematics in their day. The question of how the gendered dimensions of practice shape various of these fields is one that a number of feminists are actively exploring with reference, increasingly, to specific research programmes and practices in the physical and life sciences where the subjects of inquiry are not explicitly or projectively gendered.[19]

On not 'disappearing' gender: philosophical responses

Feminist practitioners and philosophers of science grapple with epistemological issues as soon as they ask how it is possible that many of our best and most authoritative sciences have been compromised by sexist and androcentric bias. Is the problem one of correcting surprisingly widespread instances of 'bad science', or must we reconsider the scope and powers of 'science as usual', good science, even our best science?[20] Even more perplexing, how are we to understand the contributions of feminist critics and practitioners? Androcentric and sexist presuppositions remained unrecognized in many fields until feminists drew attention to them and insisted that they be subjected to empirical and critical scrutiny. In this case it seems to have been the political engagement of feminist practitioners – the contextual values that comprise their distinctive 'angle of vision' – that put them in a position to notice 'things about research methods and interpretations that many others have missed',[21] and to formulate fruitful new lines of inquiry, both critical and constructive, that frequently improve upon the supposedly value-neutral research traditions they call into question.

These questions make clear the limitations of the traditional, positivist/empiricist conceptions of science that still define, for many, what it is to do science. In particular, they challenge us to rethink the relationship between the range of broadly 'internal', epistemic (cognitive) values that are generally taken to be constitutive of science, and the various contextual (non-cognitive, sociopolitical) factors that have conventionally been treated as properly 'external' to science.[22] They illustrate in concrete terms the extent to which the import of evidence is a function of the background theory and interpretive assumptions researchers bring to it. And they throw into relief the contingency of the decisions scientists make when they determine what questions to pursue, what categories of description and analysis to employ, what forms of evidence to seek, and what range of hypotheses and background assumptions to consider in connection with any given research project. Evidence alone cannot determine the adequacy of the interesting knowledge claims considered by scientists, and evidence itself cannot be treated as a self-warranting foundation, autonomous from the theoretical assumptions that frame research (internally) and from the contextual values and interests that are supposed to remain external to it.[23]

Feminist engagements with science reinforce the further point, central to much post-positivist philosophy of science, that even such core epistemic requirements as empirical adequacy, as well as a wide range of other constitutive values typically cited in this connection – internal coherence and external consistency, explanatory power, simplicity, unity – must be understood as evolving standards of practice, subject to interpretation and to historically situated, pragmatic considerations that determine how these virtues will be weighed against one another. They are not transcendent and universal; they are neither given by the subject domain (or evidence derived from it) nor by universal principles of rationality. These issues have been a central concern for post-positivist philosophy of science throughout the period when feminist philosophy of science has taken shape.

The epistemological challenge taken up by feminist philosophers of science is, then, to understand both the enabling and the compromising role that contextual factors play in science, in particular, those that arise from the gendered dimensions of scientific practice: gender relations, gendered identities, sex/gender systems, gender ideology. Although feminists hold widely divergent views about science, typically they share what Longino has described in another connection as a 'bottom line maxim' not to 'disappear' gender.[24] They do not assume that considerations of gender must be relevant, much less fundamental, but they do insist that gender cannot be assumed, in advance, to be irrelevant to the understanding of science.

This open-ended feminist commitment to a gender-sensitive contextualism has generated a diverse range of philosophical responses. At the conservative end of the spectrum, it has been sharply condemned by philosophical traditionalists who insist that it represents a pernicious concession to irrationalism. As Haack makes the case, when feminists take seriously the possibility that gender (among other contextual factors) may shape scientific understanding, they undermine crucial distinctions between 'truth seeking' inquiry – inquiry that is motivated by a 'genuine desire to find out how things are' and is 'not informed by political ideas at all'[25] – and various forms of 'sham' research undertaken by those who are bent on 'politiciz[ing] science' and therefore 'are not really engaged in inquiry at all'.[26] Haack insists that we must hold the line against social constructivism of all kinds which she identifies, as an undifferentiated whole, with the view that science is (nothing but) 'a value-permeated social institution'; politics or idiosyncratic preference, not evidence, determines what theories are accepted, indeed, reality itself may be seen as 'constructed by us'.[27]

Haack fails to distinguish between the wide range of positions articulated by feminists and by the growing number of philosophers of science who have, as she suggests, confronted the limitations of science and recognized that its epistemic authority should be scrutinized.[28] Broadly contextualist, anti-foundationalist and fallibilist positions take a number of different forms; by no means do all advocates of these positions assume that the only alternative to 'romantic' idealization is wholesale rejection of science and its orienting (epistemic) values. In fact, a great many feminist philosophers of science, and most feminist scientists, strongly resist corrosive post- or anti-modern critiques because there is much they need to know (as feminists) about 'how things [really] are' that requires the kind of systematic, empirical investigation best accomplished by scientific means. As clearly as feminists understand that science is a deeply social enterprise, they also recognize it to be hard and profitable work; scientific inquiry is a matter of sustained engagement with recalcitrant (if never uninterpreted) empirical realities which, time and again, reshapes our settled assumptions about how the world is, or must be. If anything, feminist philosophers and scientists are precisely those for whom the epistemic stakes valued by Haack are highest; they know first hand the cost of self-delusion and error in understanding the conditions they seek to change.[29]

Sometimes feminist analyses are rejected as antithetical to philosophical interests in science even by those who embrace the range of constructivist and contextualist positions to which Haack assimilates feminist theories of science.[30] More often they are simply ignored. Elisabeth Lloyd[31] argues that a wide range of influential (recognizably mainstream) philosophers have been prepared to question key elements of the 'philosophical folk view' underlying traditional epistemology; they recognize the 'essential sociality of science and its relations to our community's purposes and goals' and take seriously the role of community-based, intersubjective assumptions and values in science.[32] But when it comes to feminist work along these lines, they maintain a pervasive 'double standard'; they seem prepared to consider 'everything but the kitchen sink as potentially relevant to our conceptions of objectivity, truth, knowledge, and meaning – but not sex and gender'.[33]

At the other end of this spectrum lie the responses of feminists, some of whom are just as deeply sceptical as Haack about the prospects for making any fruitful connection between feminist analysis and philosophy of science.[34] Lorraine Code argues that the questions feminists raise about knowledge and science cannot be adequately addressed within the framework of any of the dominant traditions of epistemological research, perhaps most especially those central to contemporary philosophy of science. Whatever liberalizing trends may be evident, epistemology, 'for all its variations',[35] continues to be dominated by the quest for 'a monolithic, comprehensive epistemological *theory* removed from the practical-political issues a theory of knowledge has to address'.[36] As such, it is inimical to feminist interests in understanding the gendered contexts and contingencies of knowledge. Feminists must be prepared, Code concludes, to undertake a radical 'remapping of the epistemological terrain'.[37] Many feminists agree that philosophical questions about knowledge and science must be substantially reframed, but find rich resources and useful precedents for such a project within contemporary (post-positivist) philosophy of science.

The growing body of literature that constitutes feminist philosophy of science occupies a conceptual space between these sharply polarized expressions of scepticism about 'the very idea' of feminist philosophy of science. It is predicated on the conviction that feminist perspectives and philosophy of science have much to gain from one another. Indeed, as Lloyd's analysis suggests, the most innovative work by feminist philosophers of science frequently arises as much from the careful extension of insights central to post-positivist philosophy of science as from critical reaction against it.[38]

Feminist philosophy of science

In a now classic taxonomy of the epistemological positions embraced by feminist analysts of science that appeared in 1986, Sandra Harding distinguishes between feminist empiricism, feminist standpoint theory and emergent forms of feminist postmodernism.[39] In its most straightforward 'spontaneous' form feminist empiricism is often the position adopted by feminist scientists. As practitioners, many accept the objectivist and foundationalist ideals constitutive of their disciplines and argue not for a reassessment of these entrenched epistemic values (at least, not immediately), but for more systematic, rigorous application of the existing methods of science; many use these to good effect to identify and correct androcentric biases of content that must be understood to arise, on an empiricist account, from a contingent failure to counter the effects of intrusive external interests. More sophisticated forms of liberal empiricism have been developed by a number of feminist philosophers of science (I consider some of these below), but when Harding characterized this family of positions over a decade ago, she tended to the view later articulated by Code. As forms of empiricism, she argued, they lack the resources to account for the persistence of gender bias in many otherwise exemplary sciences, or to explain the corrective insights made possible by bringing feminist perspectives to bear on the sciences.[40]

By contrast, feminist standpoint theory gives central importance to the social and political contexts of inquiry. Its roots are Marxist; in its earliest formulations feminist standpoint theory turned on the argument that, just as the proletariat are in a position, by virtue of their class location, to see with particular clarity the exploitative relations of production that structure capitalist society, so too are women in a particularly good position to understand the inequitable social relations that constitute patriarchal social systems.[41] The central insight here is that, as 'embodied' social-natural beings, our understandings of the world and, more broadly, our capacities for epistemic engagement,[42] are to varying degrees partial and 'perverse' depending on the material conditions of our lives, and these conditions are, in part, a function of sex/gender systems. The mechanisms by which gender relations affect our epistemic standpoint are necessarily different in important respects from those which might account for the distinctive insights of an under-class. The complexity of sexual divisions of labour, both productive and reproductive, figure centrally in these accounts. Dorothy Smith and Nancy Hartsock argue (in rather different ways) that women do distinctive kinds of work – various forms of domestic labour and other types of service and support 'behind the scenes' – which are systematically obscured from public view.[43] As a result, women are often in a position to know how the social order is actually produced and maintained, and to recognize the ideological distortions in received knowledge that sustain conventional sex/gender systems.

These lines of argument are meant to show that, although women often lack epistemic authority, in fact they may occupy a privileged epistemic standpoint when it comes to recognizing the partiality of a dominant androcentric or sexist world view and to grasping the underlying realities of life that this world view obscures. Where scientific inquiry is concerned, standpoint theory suggests that androcentric bias of various kinds is to be expected. Science is likely to reflect assumptions that predominantly male practitioners take for granted, the limitations of which will be most clearly visible to practitioners who bring to bear not just the standpoint of women, but the analysis afforded by an explicitly feminist consciousness of gender relations.

From the outset, even those most closely associated with standpoint theory have raised probing questions about its central assumptions. Hartsock was clear about the difficulties involved in conceptualizing the standpoint of women by analogy to that of a political-economic class; and Harding called into question the viability of any appeal to a distinctive 'woman's' (or 'feminist's') standpoint, whether construed in psychoanalytic or political-economic terms.[44] Harding's reservations have been reinforced by well over a decade of intense critique of essentialism by feminist theorists and activists who draw attention to the enormous diversity of women's experience and circumstances and argue, on this basis, that it makes no sense to speak of the attributes of a gendered standpoint distinct from all the other factors that structure our identities, opportunities and social relations. In a recent reassessment of standpoint theory, Hekman notes that for these reasons (among others) it is 'frequently regarded as a quaint relic of feminism's less sophisticated past'.[45]

When Harding assessed standpoint theory in the mid 1980s, she characterized it as an unstable position located dialectically between feminist empiricism and various forms of feminist postmodernism. She argued that if feminist standpoint theorists were consistent in maintaining their central contextualizing insight – that all knowledge is 'situated and perspectival',[46] and all science 'irreducibly social'[47] – they must accept the thoroughgoing relativism of a postmodern stance that abandons or, at least, regards with ironic scepticism all claims of epistemic privilege. If, on the other hand, standpoint theorists are committed to the claim that feminists' (or women's) standpoints are epistemically privileged, they often revert to justificatory arguments that invoke transcendent epistemic standards (of rationality or credibility) of the sort associated with conventional empiricism. At the time, Harding urged strategic ambivalence. She embraced the visionary potential of postmodernism, but also acknowledged that feminists cannot afford to abandon the resources of the successor science projects that grow out of feminist empiricism and the more conservative forms of standpoint theory.[48]

I have argued that this is an inherently unsatisfying position,[49] and it is one that Harding has moved away from in recent work in which she has renewed her interest in standpoint theory.[50] The problem with it is the assumption, which animates Haack's defence of objectivism as much as arguments for postmodern conclusions, that contextualizing moves of any kind lead inexorably to corrosive relativism; if knowledge claims are recognized to be constructed and situated, it seems that there can be no ground for assessing their credibility, and no justification for claiming that any have epistemic authority. Neither horn of this implied dilemma has been acceptable to feminists engaged in science for all the reasons outlined above. They urge a realistic and pragmatic assessment of the (human) capacity of science to provide reliable, probative knowledge of the natural and social worlds in which we live and act. Feminists on both sides of the artificial divide insist that 'there are cultural *and* natural/material causes for knowledge claims', and both need to be considered if we are to understand the powers and limitations of real-world science: 'the fact that scientific knowledge is socially constructed does not imply that science doesn't "work"', and the fact that it 'works' is not grounds for reverting to objectivist ideals that disappear its essential contingency and contextual rootedness.[51] In short, feminist philosophers of science have been acutely aware of the hybridity of their subject. Those who work within the framework of philosophy of science have been centrally concerned to show that the sociopolitical dimensions of key features of science – the nature of evidence, ideals of objectivity – can be understood using the resources of liberal empiricism and post-positivist contextualism.

Consider, for example, the sophisticated feminist empiricisms developed by Lynn Hankinson Nelson[52] and Helen Longino.[53] They retain from the empiricist tradition the thesis that authoritative knowledge is evidentially grounded but make the case for a quite fundamental reformulation of what counts as evidence and as epistemic agents. Nelson argues, by careful extension of Quine's holism, that it implies not only that hypotheses are always embedded in networks of assumptions, but that individual epistemic agents are always (likewise) interdependent; they never produce or hold knowledge in isolation from one another. Consequently evidence, and the knowledge based on it, should be regarded as a collective achievement, and epistemic agents should be conceived as communities whose shared conventions of practice play a crucial role in determining what counts as an observation and what bearing it has on explanatory or generalizing knowledge claims.

Longino exploits a rather different strategy for building a recognition of the social dimensions of science into the core of a neo-empiricist theory of science. She draws on well-established arguments for the inferential complexity of evidential claims – Quinean holism, theory-ladenness, underdeterminism – to establish that contextual values deeply structure science; they do not displace epistemic considerations but necessarily supplement them at every point.[54] Given this, she argues that the central goals of science – producing empirically adequate, objective, explanatorily powerful theories – are best served not by ignoring or suppressing contextual values, but by making them explicit and subjecting them to critical scrutiny as an integral part of scientific inquiry. For example, Longino makes a case for 'democratizing' science on grounds that the best way to discover the errors and limitations of prospective knowledge claims is to subject them to critical assessment from as many different angles as possible. By extension, Longino's social empiricism suggests that it should be part of the mandate of science itself to ensure that its institutions foster the forms of rigorous, critical evaluation of knowledge claims, and open, inclusive debate that are called for by the constitutive ideals of scientific practice.

Although feminist standpoint theory has often been represented as incompatible with feminist empiricism, it is being reformulated in terms that reflect a common interest in resisting single-factor, reductive theories of science, whether these privilege internal (epistemological) or external (sociological) factors. Those who have been concerned recently to 'reassess' feminist standpoint theory are mindful of critiques of essentialism in characterizing epistemic standpoints, and repudiate any thesis of automatic privilege. Their central claim is that gender institutions and conventions define, in part, the standpoint of epistemic agents (or epistemic communities) and, in doing this, make a *contingent* difference to what these agents are in a position to learn or to know. In concrete terms, what kinds of empirical evidence an epistemic agent has access to, what sense they make of this evidence, what capacity they have to discern the limitations of dominant views about the social and natural world, and what new possibilities for inquiry they envision, may be both enhanced and limited by features of their social location (e.g., the experience, resources, values, and interests that comprise their standpoint).

Some of the most compelling examples of analysis along these lines have been developed by feminists who consider the kinds of contingent epistemic advantage and disadvantage that accrue to women who are 'insider-outsiders' to privilege in many other respects than gender alone.[55] An 'insider-outsider' who straddles class and race lines, for example, may be in a position to recognize anomalies, contradictions and implausibilities that have gone unnoticed in the assumptions or explanatory models taken for granted by those who operate exclusively within a dominant epistemic community. As Patricia Hill Collins describes her experience, the gaps and distortions inherent in standard explanations of race difference in employment patterns and household composition were patently obvious to her as one who brought to her professional training in sociology a grounding in the culture, history and experience of the black community.[56]

The insight central to feminist standpoint theory as it emerges in these accounts is that those who are marginal to established structures of privilege for any number of socioeconomic, political, or cultural reasons, including their gender, may prove to be better positioned to understand a given subject domain (natural or social) than those who are comparatively privileged. What counts as compromising baggage on standard objectivist accounts may confer crucial advantage in maximizing standard epistemic virtues. These epistemic advantages or disadvantages are understood to be contingent and specific both to subject matter and to purpose; no standpoint confers automatic or global epistemic privilege. Here the interests of feminist philosophers of science converge on various of the (social) naturalizing projects that have been so vigorously developed by philosophers of science in recent years. If we are to understand how contextual factors both enable and limit the knowledge-producing capacities of the sciences, it will be necessary to make extensive use of the tools of empirical inquiry – including those of the historical and social, as well as the behavioural, sciences – to determine exactly what features of 'location' or 'context' shape the practice of science and to what effect.[57] This has implications not only for feminist studies of science but also, on some accounts, for the practice of science itself. Harding makes the case that, if we are to produce knowledge claims that are, at least, 'less partial and distorted' than they otherwise might be, the appraisal of these claims should include a consideration not only of the evidence and arguments presented in their support but also of the social, historical conditions under which they have been produced and authorized.[58] This requirement for 'strong objectivity' illustrates how a rigorously developed feminist standpoint may substantially raise our epistemic standards rather than compromise them.

Conclusion

The philosophical challenge taken up by feminist philosophers of science is to make sense of the play of contextual factors in science. We are concerned to understand how the gendered dimensions of background beliefs, institutional structures, social relations and identities shape scientific practice both for better and for worse. This does not indicate a failure of epistemic nerve, a capitulation to 'coloniz[ing]' instincts, as Haack suggests.[59] Rather, it is a reasoned response to a number of lines of argument which by now are commonplace in post-positivist philosophy of science, and are exemplified by feminist critiques of science and feminist practice within the sciences. In principle, then, feminist projects fall well within the ambit of contemporary philosophical thinking about science. A commitment to ensure that gender is taken into account in the philosophical study of science is 'plausible and unremarkable'; crucially, it does not settle in advance the central and most controversial questions raised 'in and by' feminist inquiries.[60] Feminist philosophers of science have answered these questions in widely different ways but for all the epistemological differences among us, there is broad consensus that extreme relativism is precisely *not* what follows from the 'new fallibilism and anti-foundationalism' that we take as our point of departure. The exigencies of feminist political engagement counter any easy reduction of science either to the contingencies of social construction or to the constraints of 'evidence' and 'good reasons'.

NOTES

1 For example, S. Haack, 'Knowledge and Propaganda: Reflections of an Old Feminist', *Partisan Review* 60:4 (1993), 556–64; and P. R. Gross and N. Levitt, *Higher Superstition: The Academic Left and Its Quarrels with Science* (Baltimore: Johns Hopkins University Press, 1994), especially ch. 5, 'Auspicating Gender', pp. 107–48.

2 In an influential overview of these developments, Frederick Suppe describes these 'contextualist' critiques as both the impetus for and one response to growing crisis within 'received view' philosophy of science, broadly, logical positivist and logical empiricist theories of science. See Suppe's lengthy introduction to *The Structure of Scientific Theories*, 2nd edition (Urbana, IL: University of Illinois Press, 1979), pp. 119–220. Post-positivist analyses from an explicitly feminist point of view began to appear within a few years of Suppe's overview, e.g., in the collection edited by Sandra Harding and Merrill B. Hintikka, *Discovering Reality: Feminist Perspectives on Epistemology, Metaphysics, Methodology, and Philosophy of Science* (Boston: D. Reidel, 1983), and in a two special issues of the journal *Hypatia* on *Feminism and Science*, ed. Nancy Tuana: *Hypatia* 2:3 (1987) and 3:1 (1988). Sandra Harding published an influential overview of work in this area in *The Science Question in Feminism* (Ithaca, NY: Cornell University Press, 1986), and a few years later Linda Alcoff and Elizabeth Potter included a number of representative examples of feminist philosophy of science in their widely used collection, *Feminist Epistemologies* (New York: Routledge, 1993); see also *A Mind of One's Own*, ed. Louise Antony and Charlotte Witt (Boulder, CO: Westview Press, 1993). Feminist philosophy of science and epistemology has since been the theme of special issues published by at least three mainstream philosophical journals: *Feminist Epistemology: For and Against*, ed. Susan Haack, *The Monist* 77:4 (1994); *Feminist Perspectives on Language, Knowledge, and Reality*, ed. Sally Haslanger, *Philosophical Topics* 23:2 (1995); and *Feminism and Science*, ed. Lynn Hankinson Nelson, *Synthèse* 104:3 (1995).

3 The commitment to ground philosophy of science in the sciences takes two forms. On one hand it reflects a growing concern that philosophical analyses of science should embody a sophisticated understanding of the sciences under study. The legacy of this commitment can be seen in two developments typical of post-positivist philosophy of science: the uneasy but highly productive rapprochement between history and philosophy of science and the growth of interest in foundational studies of science that focus on the content, not just the logic, of scientific theories. On the other hand, however, a number of philosophers of science have made the case for 'naturalizing' their field, inspired by Quine's insistence that philosophers (generally) must make use of the tools of science if they are to be effective in addressing their central questions. Contemporary advocates of naturalistic approaches to philosophy of science draw on the resources of a much wider range of disciplines than Quine had

considered, including a number of social and historical sciences; some are intent on 'socializing' as well as naturalizing philosophy of science. A useful review of these positions is provided by James Maffie, 'Recent Work on Naturalized Epistemology', *American Philosophical Quarterly* 27:4 (1990), 281–93. See also contributions to *Naturalizing Epistemology*, 2nd edition, ed. Hilary Kornblith (Cambridge, MA: MIT Press, 1993), and to *Socializing Epistemology: The Social Dimensions of Knowledge*, ed. F. F. Schmitt (London: Rowman & Littlefield, 1994); as well as W. Callebaut, *Taking the Naturalistic Turn or, How Real Philosophy of Science Is Done* (Chicago: University of Chicago Press, 1993).

4 L. Schiebinger, *The Mind Has No Sex?: Women in the Origins of Modern Science* (Cambridge, MA: Harvard University Press, 1989). See also M. W. Rossiter, *Women Scientists in America: Struggles and Strategies to 1940* (Baltimore: Johns Hopkins University Press, 1982).

5 For a more detailed account of these equity critiques, see A. Wylie, 'The Contexts of Activism on "Climate" Issues', in The Chilly Collective, *Breaking Anonymity: The Chilly Climate for Women Faculty* (Waterloo, Ont.: Wilfrid Laurier Press, 1995), pp. 29–60; and 'Good Science, Bad Science, or Science as Usual?: Feminist Critiques of Science', in L. Hager, ed., *Women in Human Evolution* (New York: Routledge, 1997), pp. 29–55.

6 The various forms of content bias that arise in these fields have been categorized in a number of ways; one of the most detailed analyses is due to Margrit Eichler and Jeanne Lapointe, *On the Treatment of the Sexes in Research* (Ottawa, Ont.: Social Sciences and Humanities Research Council of Canada, 1985). This section is adapted from Wylie, 'Good Science, Bad Science'.

7 C. Gilligan, *In a Different Voice: Psychological Theory and Women's Development* (Cambridge, MA: Harvard University Press, 1982). Gilligan's studies of girls' moral reasoning suggest that what had been treated as puzzling immaturity in girls at some stages of development actually reflects a distinct pattern of moral maturation that had gone unnoticed so long as the experience of boys was treated as a gender-neutral norm applicable to all children.

8 J. Kelly-Gadol, 'Did Women Have a Renaissance?', in R. Bridenthal and C. Koony, eds., *Becoming Visible: Women in European History* (Boston: Houghton Mifflin Co., 1977), pp. 137–64.

9 S. Slocum, 'Woman the Gatherer: Male Bias in Anthropology', in R. Reiter, ed., *Toward an Anthropology of Women* (New York: Monthly Review Press, 1975), pp. 36–50; L. D. Hager, ed., *Women in Evolution* (New York: Routledge, 1997).

10 See, for example, A. Fausto-Sterling, *Myths of Gender: Biological Theories of Women and Men* (New York: Basic Books, 1985).

11 D. Gifford-Gonzalez, 'You Can Hide but You Can't Run: Representation of Women's Work in Illustrations of Paleolithic Life', *Visual Anthropology* 9 (1995), 3–21; and 'The Drudge-on-the-Hide', *Archaeology* 48:2 (1995), 84; S. Moser, *Ancestral Images* (Ithaca, NY: Cornell University Press, 1998).

12 Consider, for example, Michelle Z. Rosaldo's analysis of the legacy of Victorian assumptions about the segregation of male and female domains, 'The Use and Abuse of Anthropology: Reflections on Feminism and Cross-Cultural Understanding', *Signs* 5 (1980), 389–417; and J. Ringelheim, 'Women and the Holocaust: A Reconsideration of Research', *Signs* 10:4(1985), 741–61.

13 For a general discussion, see V. Morrell, 'Seeing Nature Through the Lens of Gender', *Science* 260 (1993), 428–9.

14 See, for example, E. Martin, 'The Egg and the Sperm: How Science has Constructed a Romance Based on Stereotypical Male-Female Roles', in E. F. Keller and H. E. Longino, eds., *Feminism and Science* (Oxford: Oxford University Press, 1996), pp. 103–17. See also E. F. Keller's discussion of research on embryo development in 'Developmental Biology as a Feminist Cause', *Osiris* 12 (1997), 16–28; and her account of the reconceptualization of 'gene action' in *Refiguring Life: Metaphors of 20th Century Biology* (New York: Columbia University Press, 1995); as well as A. Fausto-Sterling on models of sexual development: 'Of Genes and Gender', in *Myths of Gender*, pp. 61–89.

15 S. Traweek, *Beamtimes and Lifetimes* (Cambridge, MA: Harvard University Press, 1988), p. 162.

16 See, for example, the title essay in E. F. Keller, *Reflections on Gender and Science* (New Haven: Yale University Press, 1985). Nancy Hartsock also appeals to object relations theory in her influential early essay, 'The Feminist Standpoint: Developing the Ground for a Specifically Feminist Historical Materialism', in Harding and Hintikka, eds., *Discovering Reality*, pp. 283–310.

17 For example, by 1986 Harding had made the case that the characteristics associated with women on these psychoanalytic accounts are strikingly similar to those which are routinely attributed to subordinate or colonized men and women. Rather than assuming a unique association with gender differences, it is more plausible that these attributes are simply the negation of dominant norms, projected on to any group whose marginality defines (by contrast) what counts as the identifying features of the relevant power elite. Harding, 'Other "Others" and Fractured Identities', in *The Science Question in Feminism*, ch. 7.

18 This response to such criticisms is outlined by Jane Roland Martin in 'Science in a Different Style', *American Philosophical Quarterly* 25 (1988), 129–40.

19 On the question of how far, to what disciplines, feminist analyses may be extended, see Sergio Sismundo, 'The Scientific Domains of Feminist Standpoints', *Perspectives on Science* 3:1 (1995), 49–65. For examples of recent feminist analyses in the physical sciences, see K. Barad, 'Meeting the Universe Halfway', in L. H. Nelson and J. Nelson, eds., *Feminism, Science, and the Philosophy of Science* (Dordrecht: Kluwer, 1997), pp. 161–94; Traweek, *Beamtimes*; B. B. Spanier, *Im/Partial Science: Gender Ideology in Molecular Biology* (Bloomington, IN: Indiana University Press, 1995); E. Potter, 'Making Gender/Making Science: Gender Ideology and Boyle's Experimental Philosophy', in B. B. Spanier, ed., *Making a Difference* (Bloomington, IN: Indiana University Press, forthcoming).

20 This is Harding's formulation in *The Science Question in Feminism*, pp. 19 and 102–5.

21 Fausto-Sterling, *Myths of Gender*, p. 11.

22 See H. Longino's distinction between contextual and constitutive values; *Science as Social Knowledge: Values and Objectivity in Scientific Inquiry* (Princeton, NJ: Princeton University Press, 1990).

23 As Helen Longino puts this point, 'constitutive values conceived as epistemological (i.e., truth-seeking) are not adequate to screen out the influence of

contextual values in the very structuring of scientific knowledge'; 'Can There Be a Feminist Science?' *Hypatia* 2 (1987), 51–64 (p. 56).

24 H. Longino, 'In Search of Feminist Epistemology', *The Monist* 77 (1994), 472–85. Longino characterizes this 'bottom line' as a 'community value' shared by feminist scientists; I propose a meta-philosophical counterpart in 'Doing Philosophy as a Feminist: Longino on the Search for a Feminist Epistemology', *Philosophical Topics* 23:2 (1995), 345–58.

25 'Knowledge and Propaganda', p. 564.

26 Ibid., p. 565.

27 Ibid., p. 560.

28 For detailed critiques of Haack's position see Elizabeth Anderson, 'Knowledge, Human Interests, and Objectivity in Feminist Epistemology', *Philosophical Topics* 23:2 (1995), 27–58; and L. H. Nelson, 'The Very Idea of Feminist Epistemology', *Hypatia* 10:3 (1995), 31–49.

29 I have developed this argument in more detail with reference to feminist research in archaeology: A. Wylie, 'Feminist Theories of Social Power', *Norwegian Archaeological Review* 25:1 (1992), 51–68; 'The Constitution of Archaeological Evidence: Gender Politics and Science', in P. Galison and D. J. Stump, eds., *The Disunity of Science: Boundaries, Contexts, and Power* (Stanford: Stanford University Press, 1996), pp. 311–43.

30 See, for example, M. Hesse, 'How to Be Postmodern Without Being a Feminist', *The Monist* 77:4 (1994), 445–61. Hesse's argument is discussed in Wylie, 'Doing Philosophy as a Feminist'.

31 E. Lloyd, 'Objectivity and the Double Standard for Feminist Epistemologies', *Synthèse* 104 (1996), 351–81.

32 Ibid., pp. 365–73.

33 Ibid., p. 368.

34 For a parallel argument, see L. H. Nelson, 'The Very Idea of Feminist Epistemology', *Hypatia* 10:3 (1995), 31–49 (pp. 33–42).

35 L. Code, *What Can She Know?* (Ithaca, NY: Cornell University Press, 1991), p. 314.

36 Ibid., p. 315.

37 L. Code, 'Taking Subjectivity into Account', in Alcoff and Potter, eds., *Feminist Epistemologies*, pp. 15–48 (p. 20).

38 See, for example, Nelson, 'The Very Idea of Feminist Epistemology'; J. Nelson and L. H. Nelson, 'No Rush to Judgement', *The Monist* 77:4 (1994), 486–508.

39 Harding, *The Science Question*, pp. 24–9.

40 Ibid., pp. 36–7.

41 Hartsock, 'The Feminist Standpoint', pp. 283–310. See also D. E. Smith's earlier discussion, 'Women's Perspective as a Radical Critique of Sociology', *Sociological Inquiry* 44 (1974), 7–14. For a useful chronology of contributions to the development of feminist standpoint theory, see Sandra Harding, 'Comment on Hekman's "Truth and Method: Feminist Standpoint Revisited": Whose Standpoint Needs the Regimes of Truth and Reality?', *Signs* 22:2 (1997), 382–91 (pp. 388–9).

42 Sismundo, 'Scientific Domains', p. 52.

43 D. Smith, *The Everyday World as Problematic: A Feminist Sociology* (Toronto:

University of Toronto Press, 1987); *The Conceptual Practices of Power: A Feminist Sociology of Knowledge* (Toronto: University of Toronto Press, 1990). As Hartsock puts this point, women are immersed in 'the world of use – in concrete, many-qualitied, changing material processes'; their work is typically repetitive, often collective and occurs outside the realm of commodity exchange, in ways that gender-appropriate work for men does not; 'The Feminist Standpoint', p. 292.

44 Harding, 'Other "Others"'.

45 S. Hekman, 'Truth and Method: Feminist Standpoint Revisited', *Signs* 22:2 (1997), 341–65 (p. 341).

46 Ibid., p. 342.

47 Sismundo, 'Scientific Domains', p. 50.

48 Harding, *The Science Question*, p. 196.

49 A. Wylie, 'The Philosophy of Ambivalence: Sandra Harding on *The Science Question in Feminism*', *Canadian Journal of Philosophy* supplementary volume 13 (1987), 59–73.

50 Harding, *Whose Science? Whose Knowledge?* (Ithaca, NY: Cornell University Press, 1991); 'Rethinking Standpoint Epistemology: "What Is Strong Objectivity?"', in Alcoff and Potter, eds., *Feminist Epistemologies*, pp. 49–82.

51 Barad, 'Meeting the Universe Halfway', p. 162.

52 L. H. Nelson, *Who Knows: From Quine to a Feminist Empiricism* (Philadelphia, PA: Temple University Press, 1990).

53 Longino, *Science As Social Knowledge*.

54 This argument is developed in greatest detail in Longino, *Science As Social Knowledge*, but see, as well, H. Longino and R. Doell, 'Body, Bias and Behaviour: A Comparative Analysis of Reasoning in Two Areas of Biological Science', *Signs* 9 (1983), 206–27.

55 U. Narayan, 'Working Together Across Difference', *Hypatia* 32 (1988), 31–48; P. H. Collins, *Black Feminist Thought* (New York: Routledge, 1990); P. H. Collins, 'Learning from the Outsider Within', in M. M. Fonow and J. A. Cook, eds., *Beyond Methodology: Feminist Scholarship as Lived Research* (Bloomington: Indiana University Press, 1991), pp. 35–59; Harding, *Whose Science?*.

56 Collins, 'The Outsider Within', pp. 52–3.

57 See, for example, Longino's discussion of how the values constitutive of science are reinforced, or compromised, by the various institutional structures through which scientific practice is funded and organized; *Science as Social Knowledge* (ch. 4).

58 Harding, *Whose Science?*.

59 Haack, 'Knowledge and Propaganda', p. 560.

60 Nelson and Nelson, 'No Rush to Judgement', pp. 488–9, 492.

10

DIEMUT BUBECK

Feminism in political philosophy
Women's difference

The question of difference has preoccupied feminists in one way or another for a decade and a half.[1] And even where difference is not in the foreground of feminist thinking and writing, it remains in the background as a point of contention that can be used against any empirical or theoretical generalizations that may be advanced. To focus on difference would thus seem a suitable approach not only to a discussion of feminist political theory, but to feminist theory and philosophy more generally.

Feminists have reflected on three kinds of difference: first, their own difference as women in relation to men, usually taken as a socially constructed gender difference; secondly, social differences between women; and thirdly, theoretical differences between feminists. The second and third types of difference have been seen as threatening the very possibility of feminist theory. My thesis will be that the reason why difference has become so divisive and threatening to feminists is that there has been a conflation of the second and third types of difference, i.e. of social and theoretical differences. This conflation can be seen as happening in second-wave feminist thought at the moment when the main divisions between the various feminist positions ceased to be conceived in political terms – as differences between liberal, radical, marxist, socialist and anarchist feminists with their respective analytical frameworks and political perspectives and commitments – and came to be reinterpreted in identity terms – as derived from differences between, for example, black and white, or lesbian and heterosexual women, leading to black and white, lesbian and heterosexual feminisms. In this conflation, social differences between women become the source of, and rationale for, different feminist theories, perspectives and political aims.

In this chapter, I address the problem of difference in a roundabout way by revisiting feminist standpoint theory and discussing the *aporias* it generates (sections 1 and 2). I then proceed to identify the antagonistic model of the epistemic process as the culprit which produces these *aporias*, and suggest an alternative dialogical model (section 3). I argue that the solution to the problems raised lies in the recognition of the importance of a will to cooperation and to finding commonality as a route out of the impasse that difference leads us into (section 4). This solution is equally applicable to theoretical and political processes (section 5), and it throws light on the role of feminist inquiry in philosophy more generally (section 6).

1 Feminist political theory and standpoint theory

Feminist political theory can be seen as comprising three distinct types of inquiry. The first type is the critical discussion of 'malestream' political thought, both historical and contemporary. The focus in such critique is typically on male-biased conceptions and false generalizations. Male-biased conceptions are interpretations of concepts – such as liberty, autonomy, equality, justice, democracy, rights – which derive from and capture men's experience in a gender-divided world, but not women's. False generalizations are claims made about human nature, behaviour or values that turn out to be true of men, but not of women. Given that women have been excluded from politics and political thought, it is not surprising that political theorists have thought only about men, mentioning women at most in discussions of the family, nor is it surprising that the focus of initial feminist interventions in political theory lay in the critique of such male bias. Classical critiques in this vein are Mary Wollstonecraft's *Vindication of the Rights of Woman* and John Stuart Mill's *The Subjection of Women*.[2] Prominent second-wave feminist critiques of the male bias in the history of political philosophy are Susan Moller Okin's *Women in Western Political Thought*, Jean Bethke Elshtain's *Public Man, Private Woman* and Diana Coole's *Women in Political Theory*.[3] Contemporary political philosophy is taken to task in, among many others, Susan Okin's discussion of theories of justice in *Justice, Gender and the Family*, Carol Pateman's critique of contractarian theories in *The Sexual Contract*, and Catharine MacKinnon's critique of the liberal conception of the state in *Toward a Feminist Theory of the State*.[4]

A second type of inquiry in feminist political theory is less negative: it consists in the constructive reinterpretation of traditional concepts and the reworking of claims and arguments. Its aim is to address gender relations and divisions explicitly, and to write truly gender-neutral theory. Most feminist theorizing – as in fact most theorizing more generally – proceeds from critique to more constructive suggestions. Thus most of the critiques mentioned above also engage in conceptual and theoretical reconstruction. The most prominent recent example of an explicitly two-pronged discussion containing both critique and reconstruction which has also influenced feminist political theory is the discussion of the merits of justice, as against care-based approaches: Sara Ruddick's *Maternal Thinking* is a classic in this field, using a theory of mothering to develop a new approach to peace politics, whilst Joan Tronto's *Moral Boundaries* is a more general argument for a care perspective in political theory.[5] A third type of inquiry arises from the reflection on the experience of feminist theorizing and political activism within the women's movement, with the aim of learning from that experience and drawing more general political philosophical conclusions from it. Anne Phillips's discussion of democracy in *Engendering Democracy* remains the outstanding example of this type of theorizing.[6]

One way in which these strands of feminist theory have been given epistemological interpretation and backing is through feminist standpoint theory.[7] Standpoint theory was originally developed in marxist epistemology. Two premises generate the idea of different standpoints. First, different material conditions, especially different kinds of work and work relations, generate not only different experiences but also different conceptualizations and perspectives, and thus ultimately different theories about the world. Secondly, there are systematic divisions between different groups in society with respect to the material conditions of their lives. Given these groups' different material locations, standpoint theorists conclude that their experience of the world is characteristically different, and therefore their beliefs and theories are also different: they have different standpoints. A further claim is central to standpoint theory, *viz.* that the standpoint of an oppressed social group has epistemic privilege. Its privilege is owed to an experience, and therefore ultimately knowledge, of social reality which is less distorted and more immediately a reflection of social conditions and even human nature than the experience and knowledge of the oppressors. The rationale supporting this third claim is as follows: if there are antagonistic relations of oppression and exploitation between two social groups,[8] the oppressors benefit from, and have an interest in, belief systems which distort reality, since such distortions will allow the oppressive system to maintain itself; the oppressed, by contrast, have an interest in revealing social relations for the oppressive relations they are and struggling against them. In the course of doing so, the oppressed also reveal oppressive belief systems or ideologies as oppressive and false.[9] Marxist theorists traditionally pointed to class as the social division which generates different standpoints. Feminist standpoint theorists, by contrast, have focused on gender, but they continue to endorse the materialist conception of knowledge underlying the idea of a standpoint and expressed in the first premise of standpoint theory discussed above.

In the light of standpoint theory, then, feminist political theory can be understood as the development and usage of a feminist standpoint, based on women's gendered experience (including their attempt to struggle out of their social position and condition). Its purpose is to throw new light on what comes to be seen as a partial and distorted perspective of men. Feminist standpoint theory in particular, then, aims to provide an explanation of the necessity and validity of the feminist critique of male bias in political theory. So far so good. However, as we shall see, standpoint theory can be turned against feminist theory understood as the product of a feminist standpoint, much as it can be turned against the malestream canon. I shall discuss the *aporias* this leads feminist standpoint theory into in the next section.

2 The *aporias* of feminist standpoint theory

If standpoints are defined by social divisions, any social division ought to be taken seriously as a source of a standpoint. Consider divisions of race/ethnicity, sexual orientation, physical ability, or age, for example. Women are divided against each other on the basis of these further social divisions, and these divisions in their turn determine the experiences of what in this new light come to be seen as different kinds of women, and hence as different standpoints. Thus there may be a black women's standpoint or a lesbian standpoint, or, to reintroduce that old division, a working-class women's standpoint, from any of which a predominantly white, middle-class and heterosexist feminist theory can be criticized regarding its inclusiveness and the truth of its generalizations over 'all women'. As will be obvious, however, there is no reason why such critical usage of standpoints should stop there. Since social divisions crosscut each other, presumably there would have to be a black working-class feminist standpoint, or even a lesbian black working-class feminist standpoint, from which to examine the claims of black feminist theorists, let alone feminist theorists. The logic of standpoint theory, therefore, seems unavoidably to undercut any asserted standpoint with yet further possible differences in social and material condition. This process of proliferating standpoints can be continued until one reaches one of two possible endpoints: *either* each person's unique social condition warrants her or his own unique standpoint; *or* the group oppressed by all possible systems of oppression must be identified as having the epistemically most privileged standpoint, and hence the most cutting edge critique of everybody else's theory.

Joyce Trebilcot, whose first principle of 'dyke methods' is that she 'speak only for [herself]', endorses the first of these positions:

> I speak 'only for myself' . . . in the sense that I intend my words to express only my understanding of the world. I expect that some wimmin will find that what I say is more or less true for them and that some will find that it is false, distorted, or irrelevant. The latter sort of case may hurt because I often want what I say to be accepted by wimmin I respect and love. But it is more important to me to acknowledge plenty of spaces for differences.[10]

Trebilcot's explicitly stated reasons for proposing this principle reflect the more general feminist rationale for theorizing from a feminist standpoint. She rejects (and expresses anger about) being controlled in two ways: by 'erasure' through false inclusion in general claims, and by 'false naming', that is, the naming by others of her experience in ways that do not reflect that experience.[11] Moreover, a further motivation for her position clearly is the acknowledgment of differences between women and the determined attempt to make theoretical and practical space for such differences.[12]

Three objections can be made to such a particularist position.[13] First, its very proposition is arguably a *reductio* of standpoint theory, especially as it is not even obvious why one should stop at one individual's standpoint, rather than at an individual's various standpoints (defined either by different points in time in her life, or by various different strands of her personality, or both). Secondly, individual, let alone sub-individual, standpoints can only generate stories rather than theories, since no general claims beyond one's own particular experience can be made:[14] social and political theory seem impossible without the possibility of such general claims. Thirdly, and most importantly, the complete individualization of standpoints fails to conform to the characteristic rationale of standpoint theory as a theory taking account of the material and social circumstances, particularly of antagonistic divisions, under which knowledge comes about: the proliferation of standpoints, if it is to be true to its materialist roots, has to find its endpoint not in individuals, but in the most oppressed social group.

The last objection, then, leads us to the second of the two alternatives, and the claim to epistemic privilege by the most oppressed social group. This endpoint, however, is equally problematic in that it leads to an epistemic impasse. The problem derives from the fact that different standpoints do not have equal epistemic validity. Standpoint theory is not a relativist theory, but realist in that the standpoint of the oppressed is posited as the only standpoint which will lead to a valid conceptualization and theorization of social reality. Thus Nancy Hartsock claims that a feminist standpoint can reveal the partiality and perversity of malestream theory because of its privileged access to social reality via a theorization of women's experience, much as marxist theorists claimed the epistemic privilege of the standpoint of the proletariat.[15] It is according to the very same rationale that bell hooks takes epistemic privilege to apply to black women as a social group oppressed by both sexism and racism and in a position to oppress no other social group:[16]

> It is essential for continued feminist struggle that black women recognize the special vantage point our marginality gives us and make use of this perspective to criticize the dominant racist, classist, sexist hegemony as well as to envision and create a counter-hegemony. I am suggesting that we have a central role to play in the making of feminist theory and a contribution to offer that is unique and valuable.[17]

Black women's contribution to feminist theory is unique and valuable, according to hooks, precisely because they have a less distorted access to reality and truth in virtue of their social location. Her assertion of epistemic privilege for black women, however, will be questioned and 'trumped' by black lesbians on the basis of the very same logic of epistemic privilege, who in their turn may be dismissed by black disabled lesbians, and so forth. Is this, then, the ultimate, because more germane, *reductio* of standpoint theory?

Note that a solution open to marxist theorists will not be acceptable to most feminists. One way of resisting the proliferation of standpoints is by giving one social division greater or even exclusive ontological and historical weight. For marxists, the phenomenon of various actual social divisions was not a problem because the main social division and antagonism was coming to be – if it was not already – the division between capitalists and wage workers. Hence epistemically the proletariat and its intellectuals had no competitors to fear. Most feminists, however, do not have access to this solution, since they are committed to taking into account whatever oppressive social divisions there may be. Given that there are a number of such divisions, this feminist commitment seems to generate the problem of proliferating standpoints and thus ultimately the *reductio*.[18]

This, then, is the epistemic impasse to which standpoint theory will lead in any society that has several kinds of social division. Only the most oppressed group can develop a standpoint from which to criticize all other standpoints and theories. Two problems arise from this idea. First, how are members of this group to tell which aspects of their experience are due to which form of oppression, as all forms of oppression are confounded in the social conditions and experience of the most oppressed? The only way they could tell is by comparing their experience with that of others who are less oppressed. The less oppressed, however, will be oppressors towards some other group. Their conceptualizations and claims are likely to be partial and distorted in some way, therefore, and reference to their standpoint will not necessarily help to distinguish distortions from truth either. Secondly, the more oppressed a group, the more and more varied are the mystifications and distortions its members will have to struggle through to formulate their standpoint: the very condition that accords them the highest epistemic privilege is also the condition, according to standpoint theory, that necessitates the most struggle. But why should those who are most oppressed shoulder most if not all of the burden of theorizing? And what is the position and responsibility of all those potential knowers who, because of their social status as oppressors, have less epistemic privilege, or even no epistemic privilege whatsoever? Are they to stop theorizing altogether, given that they can only produce varying degrees of distortion and mystification?

Instead of trying to respond to these points in detail, I'd like to suggest that the picture of the process of knowledge production in standpoint theory is wrong.[19] It does not allow us to think about theorizing in a way that is helpful to an understanding of feminist theory (or even of any kind of social or political theory). I shall elaborate this point in the next section.

3 Coming to know: antagonistic and dialogical models

In order to see what has gone wrong with the picture of knowledge production in standpoint theory, it is worth tracing our steps back to the original marxist theory. Marxism is a theory about class antagonism. Class antagonism takes various forms in history, and the last form is the antagonism between capitalists and workers which will be overcome through revolution at the economic, and social and political levels. Standpoints exist because of the existence of classes which are locked into antagonistic, oppressive class relations. Thus under capitalism, the bourgeoisie has an interest in perpetuating the system of capitalist production and exploitation whilst at the same time mystifying it in its ideology (including the social sciences); the proletariat by contrast has an interest in revealing the system for what it is and changing it. The reason why truth will out, then, is that the proletariat is involved in a struggle against the capitalists, and part of this struggle is the de-mystification of its own position and role in society. Epistemic privilege, in this picture, is grounded in antagonistic social relations: coming to know is part of class struggle, where there can only be victors and vanquished, knowers of truth and ideologues perpetuating falsehoods. Much as the proletariat wrests political and economic power from the capitalists in its revolution, it wrests the power of knowledge from them as well by shaping a society in which knowledge, like the means of production, is accessible to all. The proletariat is the universal class, as the early Marx says, and by universalizing the means of production and thus abolishing class antagonism, the proletariat also universalizes the possibility of knowledge: the class antagonism was what introduced the distortion and mystification in the first place.

Much can be drawn from this picture. What interests me about it are two points in particular: the systematic connection between social conditions and knowledge, and the antagonism that pervades the representation of both. The idea that there is a connection between social conditions and knowledge – that different social positions yield different perspectives – is what is attractive to standpoint theorists, including feminist standpoint theorists of different kinds. This idea is both fundamental to and distinctive of the materialist conception of knowledge endorsed by standpoint theorists. It is important, however, to distinguish this idea from the idea of antagonistic relations, and I shall argue that it is the failure to do so that leads to the *aporias* of standpoint theory that I presented in the first section.

The social antagonism of class struggle seems to pervade not just economic, social and political relations, but also those between knowers. Theories and claims are characteristically classified either as mystifying, false and in the interest of the oppressors, or as de-mystifying, true, and in the interest of the oppressed. But the very fact that false claims are characterized in such terms as 'mystifying', or even 'oppressive', indicates that the social antagonism is seen as played out between and through people when conceived as knowers. And this seems plausible: indeed it is part of the materialist conception of knowledge that the relations under which we come to know reflect social relations more generally. Hence if there are antagonistic social relations, there must be antagonistic relations between knowers, as well as between theories.

The adequacy of the antagonistic model may be questioned both regarding social relations generally and, more specifically, regarding relations between knowers, theories and standpoints. In what follows, I shall focus on the epistemic realm and leave aside the question of the model's adequacy as a picture of oppressive social relations.[20] Are relations between knowers antagonistic, then? An important example from the feminist community would suggest that they are not necessarily, even if the social identities of knowers may be. In the wake of criticisms from lesbian and black feminists, women in the women's movement and the feminist academic community attempted to think critically about the effects on their thought of their own social positioning as oppressors. Such critical thinking was based on familiarity with the claims and criticisms of those claiming to have been silenced and overlooked by feminist theory and activism, and it was often conducted in conversation with those making the claims. Indeed, in this discussion the model of antagonistic relations is replaced very early on with a dialogical model, and with the language of speaking in one's own voice and of listening to other voices.[21]

Witness María Lugones, a latina, and Elizabeth Spelman, a white american, in an early path-breaking paper entitled 'Have We Got a Theory For You!':

> Our suggestion in this paper . . . is that only when genuine and reciprocal dialogue takes place between 'outsiders' and 'insiders' can we trust the outsider's account. At first sight it may appear that the insider/outsider distinction disappears in the dialogue, but it is important to notice that all that happens is that we are now both outsider and insider with respect to each other. The dialogue puts us both in a position to give a better account of each other's and our own experience.[22]

Oppressors and oppressed, in a situation of dialogue, become potential knowers who *both* know some things and are ignorant of others, and are both insiders and outsiders in relation to their own and other social groups, respectively. While using the seemingly symmetrical model of dialogue, however, Lugones and Spelman stress that there is a crucial 'asymmetry' between black/latina and white women's 'working knowledge of each other' – an asymmetry stemming from the fact that the former tend to know more about the latter than vice versa because of the oppressive relations between them:[23]

> Here we should . . . note that white/Anglo women are much less prepared for this dialogue with women of color than women of color are for dialogue with them in that women of color have had to learn white/Anglo ways, self-conceptions, and conceptions of them.[24]

However, even if oppressive relations skew the positions in the dialogue, they do not render it impossible, according to Lugones and Spelman.

Several points are worth noting in this call for dialogue between potential knowers. First, knowledge is 'produced' jointly, through mutual listening and talking (although the oppressors will have to do a lot more listening than the oppressed). Secondly, therefore, the relations within which knowledge arises are cooperative rather than antagonistic. Thirdly, knowledge, far from being a private good fought over in an antagonistic zero-sum game, is seen as a public good which is accessible both to oppressors and oppressed.[25] Fourthly, the process by which knowledge is gained is at least as important as the final product, knowledge itself. More specifically, it is the characteristics and quality of the interaction between potential knowers divided by oppressive relations that will legitimate the knowledge produced by the dialogue. These characteristics of the dialogical model draw attention to where standpoint theory goes wrong: in its endorsement of the antagonistic model. The 'epistemic impasse' I pointed to, of the standpoint of the most oppressed versus all others, can be understood as generated by the postulation of antagonistic rather than cooperative relations between potential knowers from different standpoints. It would seem, then, that the antagonistic model has to be given up if standpoint theory is to be useful for reflecting about the possibility and characteristics of any feminist theory, and for the making of such theory in the feminist community.

Now it might be objected that the impasse of standpoint theory, as I described it earlier, seemed to derive from the fact that there were too many social divisions which, in their turn, generated implausibly many standpoints, and not from the antagonistic relations that they may be based on. However, I think it is a more plausible representation of the problem to see the variety of social divisions as highlighting something which has always been a problem in standpoint theory: its endorsement of the antagonistic model. If this has not been obviously problematic in marxist standpoint theory, that is because of the latter's postulation of class relations as primary. The basic problem of the epistemic impasse was that knowledge without distortion and mystification seemed inaccessible to almost everybody, either in virtue of their position as oppressors of some kind, or, in the case of the most oppressed, in virtue of the fact that many different kinds of oppression were confounded into one social position and experience and were thus difficult to disentangle. The solution, it seems to me, is to acknowledge that this situation is represented in too antagonistic and too static a fashion. Why should it not be possible for potential knowers of various social positions to try to disentangle truth from distortion *in discussion with each other*?

Three reasons might be given for thinking this solution impossible. First, it might be said that oppressors are too caught up in their own ideology to be capable of participating in such cooperative discussion. But it is clearly not in the realm of the impossible – as the ironic case of Marx and Engels shows[26] – that oppressors can critically engage with the mystifications caused by their own social position and standpoint: such critical reflection and engagement may be unlikely, but it is not impossible. Secondly, it might be suggested that oppressors cannot be motivated by anything other than their interests *qua* oppressors, hence could not want to disengage from the benefits and mystifications of their own privileged position. As with the first reason, this may be true as a rough sociological generalization, but it does not exclude the possibility of oppressors being morally or politically motivated by considerations and interests other than those they would be expected to have in virtue of their own social position. Thirdly, it might be objected that, even if we accept the replies to the first two reasons, cooperative dialogue is still practically impossible because it would be too riddled with the power differentials and antagonisms, and the various consequences thereof, between oppressors and oppressed. In other words, there can be no oasis of epistemic cooperation in an antagonistic social desert. I shall respond to this last challenge by looking at the experience of the feminist community with 'difference'.

4 Difference, cooperation and commonalities

It is interesting to realize that feminists have, as a matter of fact, often overridden doubts concerning the possibility of cooperative and mutually supportive relations in their own community despite social divisions within it. Thus even feminists who criticized others for their racism, classism or heterosexism gave these others enough credit to assume that their commitment to the end of all forms of oppression would make them want to shed their racist or heterosexist prejudices and privileges if given a chance to do so. Such commitment is presumed in the dialogue Lugones and Spelman call for, as well as in hooks's argument for a common and solidaric 'liberatory ideology' and political practice. Common theory and practice, however, can only come about

> if the experiences of people on the margin who suffer sexist oppression and other forms of group oppression are understood, addressed, and incorporated. They must participate in feminist movement as makers of theory and as leaders of action.[27]

Thus hooks, despite her usage of the antagonistic model in describing oppressive relations and the standpoints arising from them, recognizes that feminist theory and politics depend for their possibility on epistemic and political processes which presuppose relations very different from the social antagonisms which divide women. The reason, then, why feminists could disregard the third objection in the context of their own community and movement was that they assumed that feminists had the political or moral commitment to transcend their own position of power – a commitment usually termed '(political) 'solidarity',[28] or, less often, 'friendship'.[29] Given such a commitment, it would be possible to transform antagonistic relations into cooperative, dialogical ones.

It is instructive at this point to take a closer look at the struggle of the feminist community with identity divisions, and at the corresponding development of feminist theory. To begin with, feminists assumed enthusiastically that a common politics could be grounded in a theory of women's oppression valid for all women – a common theory which in its turn was grounded in the existence of gender oppression. This assumption could be maintained initially because disagreements between feminists seemed to arise from different political orientations, leading them to characteristically different theories of women's oppression and of the feminist politics required to overcome it.[30] Once divisions between feminists came to be seen as based in different social locations and identities, however, the possibility of a theory of women's oppression common to all women seemed irretrievably lost. The differences between women had been there all along, of course, but their theoretically divisive potential on the whole went unnoticed at the beginning of second-wave feminism.[31] The crucial change, then, was not so much the 'discovery' of difference, but the grounding of feminist theory in such differences: many feminists proceeded to theorize their 'difference' in various forms of identity-based theory and politics. At this point the *aporias* of standpoint theory are relevant: standpoint theory is a perfect illustration of how and why a retreat into difference cannot but be self-defeating, since it can only generate yet further waves of retreat into difference, and so on right into the antagonistic epistemic impasse.[32] The theoretical retreat into difference is an undesirable and self-defeating response to the problem of difference.

There is a possible alternative response: a commitment to epistemic cooperation and the search for commonality *in the face of acknowledged differences and divisions*. This commitment cannot now be grounded innocently, as before it had been, in the assumption of women's common oppression or experience. Postmodernist feminists are right to point out that this assumption is unwarranted, and can be oppressive in as much as it obfuscates and silences the diverse experiences of women.[33] In any case, given a world riven with social divisions, commonality could not possibly be guaranteed ontologically, that is, in reference to a world 'out there'. Postmodernists are wrong, however, to abandon the search for a common theory and politics. Cooperation and commonality can be grounded instead in the moral and/or political will to overcome and transcend the antagonistic relations and divisions that we face. The crucial point in this alternative response to difference is the claim that there can be a practical ground for commonality which allows us to avoid getting stuck in antagonistic divisions of difference.

The lesson from the feminist movement, then, is the following: while the recognition of difference is theoretically and politically essential, such recognition will be divisive and self-defeating if it is constructed in terms of antagonistic standpoints and theories. The only way these terms can be resisted – and have in fact been resisted to some extent in the feminist community – is through a moral and/or political will or commitment to cooperative dialogue. Given such a will, commonality may well reappear, both theoretically and politically, although this may take a long process of mutual recognition of differences and negotiation about common conceptualizations, formulations and claims, common values, interests and strategies.[34]

In conclusion, the more general answer to the challenge that there can be no cooperative oasis in an antagonistic desert is that, while a lot is stacked against their existence, cooperative oases can be willed into existence. Their creation is a collective (and individual) act of will, and an act of faith in their very possibility. Some feminists or humanists may want to insist that if there is any hope for the success of such acts of will, it can only lie in women's shared condition, or in a shared human condition, respectively. In their understanding, it is our shared gender or humanity that guarantees the possibility of cooperation. The existence of such a shared condition, however, can neither be presumed, nor be denied *a priori*. I take it that this is the lesson to be learnt from the 'problem of difference' the feminist community encountered. It is thus worth insisting that the question whether there are any commonalities has to remain open. But we will find out only if we dare to commit ourselves to looking for them, discussing the question with each other as we go. Furthermore, it may well be that such commitment allows not only the discovery of commonality that is there, but also ultimately the creation of commonality through individual and social interaction and change.[35] It may be a ground for hope that the act of will, by its very nature, creates commonality between those who engage in it, in the worst case even *ex nihilo*.[36]

5 Epistemic and political dialogue

If the argument of the previous section is right, the lesson to be learnt from the feminist encounter with difference is that the moral and/or political commitment to cooperative dialogue provides the only possible ground for a common feminist theory. Although this lesson is shown to arise in the sphere of knowledge, my claim in this section is that the problem raised by difference in the political sphere is usefully understood as similar to that in the epistemic sphere. Moreover, I think that the answer to both problems lies in similar procedural solutions – cooperation and dialogue. The parallel between the two cases is established by the fact that both problems arise from collective processes which are systematically distorted by the oppressive social conditions under which they take place. As standpoint theorists point out correctly, under such oppressive conditions the epistemic process produces results (theories, arguments) which reflect the interests, views and understandings of the oppressors. Similarly, the political process will produce results (policies, laws, institutions) which are biased in favour of the interests of the oppressors. Given this structural parallel, we can speculate that it takes similar conditions to remedy these distortions and to ensure that these processes generate the 'right' results.

If we use the dialogical model to reflect on both sorts of processes, epistemic and political, we can consider them as extended, collective conversations or discussions between various kinds of people, with different kinds of social backgrounds and differing views about the world and about politics; as conversations in which differences and disagreements can be expressed, and in which agreements and common conclusions may be found. They are processes where different voices are listened to, where meanings, claims and arguments are negotiated and possibly agreed on by those whose backgrounds, views, aims and interests may initially differ. They are open and dynamic processes, not necessarily predictable in their outcomes.

What might the conditions producing the 'right' results in the epistemic and political process be? Such conditions would work to counteract the distorting effects that an oppressive context has. Three types of conditions are relevant, relating to three different elements of these processes: (i) the structures and institutional settings in which the processes take place (ii) the participants and those of their activities that constitute the processes (iii) the different phases or aspects of these processes viewed as taking place in time and over time.

The most important structural condition is *non-exclusion*, i.e. that nobody should be excluded from participating in either process. This condition is pivotal because exclusion tends to be a crucial dimension of oppression. Hence ending exclusion will end one of the main ways in which these processes are distorted. More positively, however, it may be necessary to counteract the lingering effects of past exclusion and current disadvantage by establishing and guaranteeing spaces for those hitherto excluded. In the epistemic sphere, women's, ethnic minority, or gay and lesbian studies departments, chairs or programmes may provide such spaces, as well as earmarked research funds for the study of oppressed groups; in the political sphere, separate organization and group representation may do so.[37]

In tandem with this structural condition, certain moral commitments and skills are required in the participants in the process. The most important of these is the *commitment and ability to listen to everybody's claims*. Listening is crucial in overcoming the structural asymmetry that characterizes social situations in an oppressive social context. As Lugones and Spelman point out – and as standpoint theorists claim, too – oppressors have less knowledge of the oppressed than vice versa. Indeed, oppressive structures can often only be perpetuated if oppressors are able to silence the oppressed and their knowledge and interests. Thus oppressors have to do a lot of listening if the epistemic or political process is to produce the right results.[38]

Listening is not only a condition of right results, however. It is equally important because it provides the context in which antagonistic difference can be overcome. Difference cannot be transcended unless it is heard and taken seriously. So long as difference is denied (implicitly or explicitly), it has to be insisted on, protested, flung in the face of those who deny it. As difference is recognized, however, it can be given a different role: rather than dividing one from others, it can be acknowledged as simply a way of being, a fact of life. Some differences, moreover, may on consideration turn out to be socially constructed divisions that both sides may want to overcome so as to claim the full range of human possibilities for themselves. For example, once care is recognized as a different but possible and even desirable mode of moral and practical life, it becomes possible for men to reclaim it as an alternative for themselves and possible for women to transcend it as that which uniquely defines them. The very act of listening and recognizing, then, may resolve some of the antagonism that difference is caught up in as long as it is part of oppressive relations.[39]

The commitment to listen and to develop their listening skills is required not only in oppressors. The oppressed, too, have to overcome tendencies which prevent them from listening. Most of all righteous anger at the oppressors, which undermines any desire to listen to them, has to be critically examined; but also the conviction that their social position gives them a superior purchase on the truth (formulated as epistemic privilege in standpoint theory), which produces a tendency to discount oppressors' claims as distorted or ideological. Lugones and Spelman are surely right in holding that full knowledge of oppressive relations can be gained only by taking seriously the perspective of both oppressors and oppressed.[40] With critical scrutiny of their own experience, oppressors can come to understand how they participate in, reproduce, and create oppressive structures and situations, and this knowledge is certainly crucial in arriving at a complete picture that can be embraced by both sides.

A further important requirement is that the participants have an *ability to stand back from and reflect critically on their own experience, views and values*. This ability is crucial in all participants in the dialogue, although it may be required to a larger extent in the oppressors, given that their lives depend more on distorted perception than those of the oppressed. The abilities to listen and critically to reflect are interdependent. The ability critically to reflect on one's own experience is, to some extent, dependent on having come to realize what aspects may be criticized by others, and this realization can only come from listening to those others. Conversely, the ability truly to listen to and understand others is, to some extent, dependent on the ability to stand apart from one's own experience and to suspend the judgment or evaluation suggested by one's own framework of thought and perspective, and this ability is certainly fostered and developed by critical reflection.

A last set of conditions concerns the dynamic of the process by which decisions are made or knowledge is arrived at. In both cases, theoretical and political, this process has two necessary aspects or phases:[41] separation and negotiation. The need for negotiation has been discussed at length, but the need for the phase of separation may need some explanation. Given a history in which difference has not only been oppressively reinforced but also silenced, separation is necessary so that those who share a similar social location and experience can formulate their experience and interests together. Separation, in other words, is necessitated by the effects of oppression, and indispensable if oppression is to be overcome. Hence as long as oppression exists, there will be a need for separation: for separate spaces, separate groups, separate activities. However, separation is just one of the aspects or phases of the dynamic. Coming together in negotiation is the necessary other phase.

Negotiation itself has two parts: first, the voicing of and listening to difference, and secondly, the negotiating about commonalities in the light of the differences that have been aired. This two-part process can be transformative in at least two ways. First, once the 'figure' of difference has received enough attention, a 'background' of commonality may well come into view. Secondly, assuming that much 'difference' is socially constructed through oppressive processes, a possible outcome of dialogue is the understanding of difference as an artificial division which, though 'frozen' into place, can be overcome through social change. Commonality, even if not much of it is present yet, can thus become an aim agreed upon by those participating in the negotiation. Thus commonality, far from being either 'the case' or 'not the case', can emerge and be socially created if there is the political will for such emergence or creation. Once the divisive antagonistic model is abandoned there is no good reason for thinking that there could not be such a will to commonality.

In conclusion, the dialogical model allows us to see how commonality can become a possibility in the face of acknowledged difference. Given dialogical processes, the biases and distortions produced by oppressive conditions can be counteracted and overcome: difference does not have to be eternally divisive, nor do oppressive conditions have to be perpetuated forever.

6 Conclusion

I have tried to rescue the possibility of feminist theory and politics from the clutches of a counterproductive picture of difference suggested by the antagonistic model that is implicit in standpoint theory. If we see the processes both of reaching decisions and of acquiring knowledge in the feminist community as a form of extended dialogue with the characteristics specified in the last section, feminist theory and politics are not rendered impossible by differences between women.

An interesting corollary of accepting the dialogical model is that feminist theory and politics themselves have to be seen as the separation phase of a more general, universal dialogue. Feminist generalizations and decisions, in other words, are born out of a separation from a universal dialogue that is necessitated by gender oppression. As such, feminist thought itself has to be committed to its own transcendence, since the very conception that guarantees its possibility (seeing it as a process of dialogue created by the will to find commonalities between women) also reveals it as the separatist phase in a larger dialogue. In standpoint theory, a parallel thought is expressed in the idea that the feminist standpoint is *transitional*, in that once gender oppression is abolished there is no social division left to generate it. As and when political philosophers listen to feminist critiques of false generalizations and conceptualizations and take on board feminist reconceptualizations and theories and the lessons from the women's movement, the idea of specifically feminist interventions will have become obsolete. Ultimately, there is only one large dialogue, but feminist and other types of separation and negotiation may remain necessary phases for yet some time to come.

NOTES

1 I would like to thank Miranda Fricker, Norman Geras, Jennifer Hornsby, Alison Jaggar, Martha Nussbaum, Karen Wright and the participants of seminars at the London School of Economics and the University of Cambridge for helpful comments and discussion of earlier versions of this paper. I am also grateful to Anna Maresso for her research assistance.
2 M. Wollstonecraft, *A Vindication of the Rights of Woman*, ed. M. Brody (London: Penguin, 1992); J. S. Mill, *The Subjection of Women*, ed. S. M. Okin (Indianapolis: Hackett, 1988).

3 Susan Moller Okin, *Women in Western Political Thought* (Princeton, NJ: Princeton University Press); Jean Bethke Elshtain, *Public Man, Private Woman* (Princeton NJ: Princeton University Press, 1981); Diana Coole, *Women in Political Theory*, 2nd edition (Brighton: Harvester Press, 1993). See also the following useful anthologies: M. G. L. Clark and L. Lange, eds., *The Sexism of Social and Political Theory* (Toronto: University of Toronto Press, 1979); E. Kennedy and S. Mendus, eds., *Women in Western Political Philosophy* (Brighton: Wheatsheaf, 1987); M. L. Shanley and C. Pateman, eds., *Feminist Interpretations and Political Theory* (Cambridge: Polity Press, 1990).

4 Susan Okin, *Justice, Gender and the Family* (New York: Basic Books, 1989); Carol Pateman, *The Sexual Contract* (Cambridge: Polity Press, 1988); Catherine MacKinnon, *Toward a Feminist Theory of the State* (Cambridge, MA: Harvard University Press, 1989). See also the following useful anthologies, addressing various concepts such as the public/private dichotomy, liberty, equality, justice and the self: N. J. Hirschmann and C. Di Stefano, eds., *Revisioning the Political: Feminist Reconstructions of Traditional Concepts in Western Political Theory* (Boulder, CO: Westview Press, 1996); M. L. Shanley and U. Narayan, eds., *Reconstructing Political Theory: Feminist Perspectives* (Cambridge: Polity Press, 1997).

5 S. Ruddick, *Maternal Thinking: Toward a Politics of Peace* (London: Women's Press, 1989); J. Tronto, *Moral Boundaries: A Political Argument for an Ethic of Care* (London: Routledge, 1993). See also D. Bubeck, *Care, Gender, and Justice* (Oxford: Clarendon Press, 1995), G. Clement, *Care, Autonomy, and Justice* (Boulder, CO: Westview Press, 1996), the very useful anthology edited by Virginia Held, *Justice and Care: Essential Readings in Feminist Ethics* (Boulder, CO: Westview Press, 1995), and my recent review of the ethic of care literature over the last fifteen years, 'Ethic of Care and Feminist Ethics', *Women's Philosophy Review* 18 (Spring 1998).

6 A. Phillips, *Engendering Democracy* (Cambridge: Polity Press, 1991), *Democracy and Difference* (Cambridge: Polity Press, 1993) and *The Politics of Presence* (Oxford: Clarendon Press, 1995).

7 For a classical exposition of feminist standpoint theory see Nancy Hartsock, 'The Feminist Standpoint: Developing the Ground for a Specifically Feminist Historical Materialism', in S. Harding, ed., *Feminism and Methodology* (Bloomington: Indiana University Press and Milton Keynes: Open University Press, 1987), originally published in 1983. See also S. Harding, *The Science Question in Feminism* (Milton Keynes: Open University Press, 1986) and *Whose Science? Whose Knowledge?* (Buckingham: Open University Press, 1991).

8 I use 'oppression' in this chapter as a shorthand for unequal and unjust social relations which disadvantage and disempower members of one group to the benefit of members of another. For a more systematic discussion of the notion of oppression see I. M. Young, *Justice and the Politics of Difference* (Princeton, NJ: Princeton University Press, 1990), ch. 2.

9 I can only sketch the bare essentials of standpoint theory here. It might be objected to the assertion of epistemic privilege that distortions may also be found in the experiences and views of the oppressed: won't the oppressed take over the ideology that helps oppress them, or form adaptive preferences to help them make the best of their situation? Standpoint theorists would reply to these

questions by saying that they point up the reason why a standpoint has to be struggled for: it is not necessarily obvious or directly accessible (see Hartsock, 'Feminist Standpoint'). For a more critical assessment of the epistemic privilege claim see Uma Narayan, 'The Project of Feminist Epistemology: Perspectives from a Nonwestern Feminist', in A. M. Jaggar and S. R. Bordo, eds., *Gender/Body/Knowledge* (New Brunswick: Rutgers University Press, 1992). See also my discussion of the epistemic impasse in section 2.

10 Joyce Trebilcot, 'Dyke Methods', in Jeffner Allen, ed., *Lesbian Philosophies and Cultures* (New York: State University of New York Press, 1990), p. 18.

11 Ibid., pp. 15–16. In the light of this principle, it seems inconsistent that Trebilcot calls her principles 'dyke methods' rather than 'Joyce Trebilcot's methods', given that any definition of 'dykism' can be rejected as a form of 'false naming' by those women who identify as dykes but who disagree with her definition of 'dykism' (cf. p. 28).

12 Ibid., pp. 25–7.

13 It is also worth noting that it is not the only option available to feminists who want to take differences between women seriously: see my argument in sections 4 and 5.

14 Cf. J. Trebilcot, 'Ethics of Method: Greasing the Machine and Telling Stories', in C. Card, ed., *Feminist Ethics* (Lawrence: University Press of Kansas, 1991).

15 N. Hartsock, 'Feminist Standpoint'.

16 bell hooks, *Feminist Theory*, p. 14.

17 Ibid., p. 15.

18 Early radical feminists might be said to have followed the marxist 'solution' by claiming that it was gender oppression rather than class that was historically and ontologically primary: see e.g. Shulamith Firestone, *The Dialectic of Sex* (London: Women's Press, 1979), originally published in 1970.

19 An alternative conclusion would be to reject the notion of epistemic privilege: see Bat-Ami Bar On, 'Marginality and Epistemic Privilege', in L. Alcoff and E. Potter, eds., *Feminist Epistemologies* (London: Routledge, 1993).

20 I do not think that it depicts social relations adequately either, since it mistakenly suggests that oppressors only gain and never lose from oppressive relations, in other words, that oppressive relations are always zero-sum situations, never lose-lose ones.

21 For a more general discussion of the conception of moral discourse implicit in second-wave feminist literature see A. Jaggar, 'Toward a Feminist Conception of Moral Reasoning', in J. P. Sterba et al., eds., *Morality and Social Justice* (Lanham, MD: Rowman & Littlefield, 1995).

22 María Lugones and Elizabeth Spelman, 'Have We Got a Theory for You! Feminist Theory, Cultural Imperialism and the Demand for "The Woman's Voice"', *Women's Studies International Forum* 6:2 (1983), 573–81 (p. 577).

23 Ibid., p. 580.

24 Ibid., p. 577.

25 One of the characteristics of private goods is that their possession or consumption is exclusive, while the consumption of public goods is 'non-rival': my knowing, for example, doesn't exclude anybody else from also knowing.

26 Their case is ironic in that they were critically aware of class oppression but woefully unaware of the nature of gender oppression, which they saw as

existing only in the bourgeoisie. John Stuart Mill and William Thompson, as well as various white critics of slavery, are examples regarding the oppression of women and slaves, respectively.

27 hooks, *Feminist Theory*, p. 161.
28 Cf. hooks, *Feminist Theory*, p. 17 and ch. 4.
29 Cf. Lugones and Spelman, 'Have We Got a Theory', pp. 576 and 581.
30 A. Jaggar, *Feminist Politics and Human Nature* (Brighton: Harvester Press, 1983), remains the best and most detailed introduction to the main political divisions between feminists.
31 Some theorists, notably socialist feminists, acknowledged (some) differences fairly early on: see Lynne Segal, 'Generations of Feminism', *Radical Philosophy* 83 (1997). It is also worth remembering that the initial project of second-wave feminism was to 'establish . . . that *all* women were oppressed in similar ways, that women shared something in common across the lines of class, race, culture, etc.' (Alison Jaggar, personal communication).
32 I do not address the possibility of an alternative, relativist reading of a plurality of standpoints. I think relativism is not an attractive position for feminists, but I cannot provide an argument here.
33 E.g. J. Butler, *Gender Trouble* (London: Routledge, 1990).
34 By 'commonality' I mean something like the list I give in this sentence, i.e.: common conceptualizations, formulations and claims, common values, interests and strategies. Which commonalities are relevant will depend on the discussion at hand. Note also that commonalities are not necessarily fixed and stable (see section 5 and note 39 below).
35 For a more detailed discussion of this point see section 5.
36 The recent 'discovery' and success of mediation in various arenas of seemingly irresolvable conflict attests to this, I think.
37 For a discussion of group representation see Young, *Justice and the Politics of Difference*, ch. 6, and Anne Phillips, *The Politics of Presence* (Oxford: Clarendon Press, 1995).
38 See also Jaggar, 'Feminist Conception', pp. 127–8 and 133.
39 It is interesting to note how conceptions of difference as mainly socially constructed can lead to much less pessimistic conclusions than conceptions of difference modelled on cultural or religious differences: the latter, typically found in liberal political theories, seem irresolvable and therefore have to be relegated to the private sphere so as to not be too politically explosive; the former, derived from (marxist, feminist, anti-racist) theories of social oppression and liberation, leave hope for a political resolution of these differences via social and political change.
40 Lugones and Spelman, 'Have We Got a Theory', p. 577; see also P. Hill Collins, *Black Feminist Thought* (Cambridge, MA, and London: Unwin Hyman, 1990), pp. 36–7.
41 I use 'aspects or phases' since I want to avoid the implication that they cannot both occur simultaneously.

11

MARILYN FRIEDMAN

Feminism in ethics
Conceptions of autonomy

Feminist ethics

Ethics, or moral philosophy, as a field of intellectual inquiry developed in the west for well over two thousand years with minimal input from women. Women's voices have been virtually absent from western ethics until this century, as they have been from every field of intellectual endeavour. The absence of female voices has meant that the moral concerns of men have preoccupied traditional western ethics, the moral perspectives of men have shaped its methods and concepts, and male biases against women have gone virtually unchallenged within it. Feminist ethics explores the substantive effect of this imbalance on moral philosophy and seeks to rectify it.

Like other areas of feminist thought, feminist ethics is grounded in a commitment to ending the oppression, subordination, abuse and exploitation of women and girls, wherever these may arise. In the late 1960s, when feminist ethics began, it consisted mainly of applying the resources of traditional moral philosophy to the array of moral issues that were being brought to public attention by the women's movements then arising in many western societies. Those issues, such as economic discrimination against women, restrictive sex roles, domestic violence, rape, inegalitarian marriage and ideals of self-sacrificing motherhood, were of special concern to women and had been largely neglected by traditional philosophical ethics. Feminist ethics, from the start, thus sought to shift philosophical attention to topics that philosophers, almost exclusively male, had previously ignored.

To be sure, some of the issues of special concern to women, such as prostitution and pornography, had already received attention from the predominantly male philosophical profession. In addition, abortion, though not much discussed professionally prior to 1970, became a hot topic for philosophers in general soon after 1970 as a result of the growing trend toward decriminalization of abortion in western countries. The feminist innovation has been not so much to introduce such topics to philosophical audiences as to emphasize dimensions that had otherwise been neglected, such as the perspectives of the women involved, the relevant gender relationships, and the cultural context of women's subordination. On the subject of pornography, for example, the mostly male, non-feminist philosophers had debated whether the mere *use* of sexually explicit and arousing materials was itself immoral. Feminists, by contrast, turned their attention to the impact of pornography on *women*, particularly whether its production and use promoted women's subordination, objectification, or vulnerability to sexual assault.[1]

By the early 1980s, the concepts and strategies of feminist ethics had grown in complexity, and feminist ethics emerged as a self-consciously distinct area of feminist theory. Instead of merely applying traditional ethical tools to women's issues, as had been the trend in the 1970s, feminist ethics now turned its attention also to the tools themselves. Careful analysis exposed what seemed to be male biases in the very concepts and methods of traditional philosophical ethics. Not only had male philosophers neglected women-centred issues; they had also developed tools of articulation, interpretation, and analysis that appeared to reflect their male standpoints, despite a presumption of abstract universality. Feminist philosophers accordingly sought to introduce specifically female moral perspectives into philosophical ethics and to forge conceptual and methodological tools that reflected women's standpoints.

A major catalyst for this development came from feminist research in the field of moral psychology, particularly that of Carol Gilligan.[2] Based on empirical studies, Gilligan reported a significant degree of correlation between gender and moral orientation. According to her early writings, males are characteristically concerned with substantive moral matters of justice, rights, autonomy and individuation. In their moral reasonings, they tend to rely on abstract principles and to seek universality of scope. Women, by contrast, are more often concerned with substantive moral matters of care, personal relationships and avoiding hurt to others. They tend to avoid abstract principles and universalist pretensions and to focus instead on contextual detail and interpersonal emotional responsiveness.

Gilligan's ideas were not entirely new to feminist thought. By the early 1980s, some feminist theorists had already begun to theorize that caring relationships entered significantly into women's conceptions of selfhood and personal identity.[3] Gilligan gave this trend great impetus, by articulating those concerns in the form of a detailed moral perspective, one that contrasted starkly with male-generated traditions of thought in moral psychology and philosophy. She also provided empirical evidence for regarding the care perspective as a distinctively female moral orientation.

Perhaps most importantly, Gilligan *honoured* what she presented as women's moral reasoning; she presented care ethics as a moral equal to traditional justice-oriented moral theories. Her work thus epitomized a feminist approach already emerging at the time that some would later call 'cultural feminism'.[4] According to this approach, women have distinctive traits as women, but these traits are not necessarily inferior to those of men; they are sometimes as valuable as, or even superior to, those of men. The real social problem for women is not so much that they have been denied opportunities to attain the experiences or character traits of men, but rather that society has failed to appreciate or reward what is distinctively valuable in *women's* character traits. 'Man' had indeed been 'the measure of all things', and women had been mismeasured and unfairly found wanting by that standard. Instead of seeking opportunities for women to emulate men's traditional lives or viewpoints, cultural feminists wanted to elevate social esteem for the equal, and sometimes superior, merits of women's distinctive perspectives and concerns.

While there is certainly more to feminist ethics than Gilligan's account of care ethics, the influence of this account on moral philosophy is significant in a number of ways. First, it stimulated many philosophers to consider whether moral concepts and methodologies are, in some substantive sense, gender-based or gender-biased. The idea that different genders tend to adopt different moral perspectives resonated then, and still does today, with the experiences of many people. Indeed, it has widespread non-academic appeal, as shown, for example, by popular bestsellers that tell us that women are 'from Venus' while men are 'from Mars'.[5] Gilligan grounded those gender stereotypes in specific moral traits and attitudes. She thereby provided resources for feminists to use in arguing that certain moral concepts and methods were not universal after all but were instead mere reflections of a characteristically male moral standpoint.

Second, Gilligan's care/justice dichotomy contributed to a movement that was already under way in the field of ethics generally – the search for alternative moral orientations to the utilitarian and Kantian frameworks which had dominated ethical theory through the 1970s and which still loom large over the field. On Gilligan's interpretation, the two competing mainstays of modern ethical theory, utilitarianism and Kantian ethics, appear rather more like allies than opponents. Defenders of both of those traditions tend to regard the moral point of view as impartial, impersonal, universal and principle-based, and to give great importance to matters of justice. The recent revival of Aristotelian ethics, with its emphasis on virtue and community, has been a product of the mainstream search for alternatives to utilitarianism and Kantian ethics. Gilligan's care ethic offers yet another seeming alternative to those ethical traditions.

To be sure, Gilligan wavers in her treatment of the relationship between care and justice orientations. Sometimes Gilligan suggests that care and justice perspectives are distinct and mutually exclusive moral outlooks which, like the alternative aspects under which different patterns are found in ambiguous gestalt images, cannot be utilized simultaneously. At other times, however, she suggests that care and justice perspectives are each incomplete, and that they can and should be integrated to form a truly adequate, more 'mature' moral orientation. On this latter approach, care could be reinterpreted as a part of justice toward loved ones, or justice could be reinterpreted as a special mode of caring for others. There is as yet no general agreement on the relationship between care ethics and moral theories that emphasize justice. A wise working strategy for the present time is to regard care ethics as at the very least an account of a distinctive style or approach to ethical problems and concerns.

Thus, third, Gilligan's conception of a moral perspective centred specifically on caring and personal relationships moves those concerns to moral centre stage. In addition to promoting the search for alternative moral theories, a care ethic highlights the moral importance of caring practices, moral attentiveness to other persons in their unique particularity, and the sheer maintenance of the social fabric of close personal relationships. As they had developed by the early 1980s, neither utilitarianism nor Kantian ethics had devoted much attention to these matters. Even Aristotelian ethics pays little attention to caring and to the efforts required to maintain relationships.

In modern moral theory, concerns pertaining to close personal relationships and private domains of life, such as sexuality, family and friendship have tended to be ignored. Although the canonical figures of philosophical ethics all had something to say about these domains of life, the written works which have dominated ethical discourse in recent centuries focus on matters of public morality, that is, matters that presuppose no close or special connection between persons. Gilligan's writings belong to a growing counter-current in ethics toward regarding the *personal* point of view as an appropriate, and perhaps the only possible, standpoint for justified moral reasoning. Many mainstream moral philosophers had previously held that justification in moral reasoning requires such features as impartiality and universalizability. The personal point of view reflects someone's distinctive history, embodiment and network of social relationships, not to mention her desires and emotions. It seems to be irreducibly partial and particular. The notion that the personal point of view is unavoidable in moral reasoning thus requires a reconceptualization of what it means for moral reasoning, or, more broadly, moral understanding, to be justified. Particularly for sympathizers of care ethics, a moral perspective that is self-reflectively aware of its own relational-embeddedness is superior as a standpoint for moral reasoning to any would-be detached, disinterested, impartial, universalistic point of view.

In virtue of this focus on the personal, a fourth influence of Gilligan's work was to add a feminist perspective to another trend in philosophy – the defence of the role of emotion in moral life. Mainstream moral philosophy had previously tended to view the moral point of view as based on reason. Emotion was regarded not merely as irrelevant but as a cause of bias and distortion in moral understanding. Some mainstream philosophers had already begun to argue on various grounds that emotion was morally important.[6] Feminists added to this challenge the idea that the denigration of emotion was part and parcel of the cultural devaluation of women. Defending emotion, including its role in moral understanding, has become for feminists part of the project of elevating cultural esteem for women.

Fifth, Gilligan's work contributed to the growing conviction that women are more relationally oriented than men, and that men are more individualistic than women. This conviction is widespread among feminists despite their reluctance to generalize about the moral perspectives of all women. Many feminists believe that women are more likely than men to realize and acknowledge the interdependencies between people, and that people's identities depend upon those interdependencies. Men, on this view, are more likely than women to ignore the importance of relationships. As a result, men are more likely than women to retain an implausibly individualistic outlook and to seek an impersonal, impartial, universalistic stance for moral reasoning.

Gilligan's work was followed by a torrent of feminist-inspired writings about personal relationships, caring and nurturing, the differences between care and justice, relational self-identity and the importance of emotional responsiveness to others. Contributors to this development include: Annette Baier, Seyla Benhabib, Lawrence Blum, Claudia Card, Owen Flanagan, Marilyn Friedman, Jean Grimshaw, Virginia Held, Kathryn Jackson, Alison Jaggar, Nel Noddings, Bill Puka, Sara Ruddick, Joan C. Tronto and Margaret Walker.[7]

Despite the widespread, interdisciplinary influence of Gilligan's work, some feminists began by the mid 1980s to raise criticisms of care ethics and of Gilligan's arguments for a distinctively female moral orientation. Several objections are noteworthy here. First, the empirical correlation between gender and moral perspective was not uniform and the data themselves were open to various interpretations. Some feminists suggested detaching Gilligan's (apparent) claim of a gender difference from her claim about the distinction between justice and care perspectives, and evaluating each claim separately.

Second, women's orientation toward care and personal relationships seemed mainly to reflect the social role of the traditional, full-time heterosexual wife and mother. (Certain female-oriented professions, such as nursing, exhibit a caring focus, but Gilligan's discussion of it did not draw on specifically professional details.) This role, however, is morally problematic. Although it has brought satisfaction to many women, it limits women's lives in important ways. It requires female heterosexuality, promotes women's dependence on men and consequent economic and social vulnerability, and submerges women's own desires and aspirations in the moral project of caring endlessly for others. Few would disagree with Gilligan that a care orientation reflects women's traditional role experiences. The dispute is over how to evaluate the resulting orientation. The fact that a moral orientation reflects women's experiences and standpoints is not in itself a reason to think that it is superior to all others or even sound in its own right. A relational care perspective might well be limited and flawed by the oppressive aspects of the role experiences that produced it.[8]

A third objection is that the empirical research underlying Gilligan's discussion of care ethics was based only on white, middle-class, heterosexual women, and her writings did not acknowledge that differences *among* women might make a difference to their moral perspectives. It is an open question whether a care ethics would emerge in the perspectives of lesbians, black women, poor women, or any others who diverge in important ways from Gilligan's research sample.[9] In the 1980s, many feminists grew resistant to generalizations that purported to represent 'women' without qualification. Concern to articulate differences among women due to such factors as sexual orientation, race, class, religion, ethnicity, nationality, age and ableness became a major feminist theme. If moral orientation is linked to significant life experiences and if life experiences vary in tandem with these other factors, then we might well need lesbian ethics, black womanist ethics and so on.[10] Thus, where Gilligan initially referred to only two moral orientations, care and justice, some feminists now began to talk about a multiplicity of perspectives among women.

To summarize: feminist ethics shares the general feminist goal of eliminating the subordination and oppression of women and enhancing societal respect for women's viewpoints and capacities. Toward this end, feminist ethics adopts a number of diverse methodological strategies, including the defence of theories and concepts that seem more compatible with women's modes of reflection and understanding than do those of mainstream ethics. Some of these strategies were developing simultaneously for non-feminist reasons in mainstream philosophical ethics. These coincident strategies include: a search for alternatives to Kantian and utilitarian ethics, legitimation of the personal point of view, defence of the role of emotion in moral judgment and development of a relationally oriented moral psychology.

Other strategies of feminist ethics are distinctive to it. One such strategy is broadly critical: to expose and to challenge male-oriented biases in traditional and contemporary mainstream work, especially attitudes that would justify or excuse the subordination of women. Such attitudes include derogatory assumptions about women,[11] a preoccupation with moral problems arising in typically male experiences,[12] and (in the view of many feminist theorists) individualistic approaches to moral theory.[13] Many feminists also see male bias in claims to universality and impartiality that are frequently made by mainstream ethical theorists on behalf of their favoured theories. The feminists' objection is that merely parochial notions – in particular, male moral notions – masquerade as unbiased moral universals.

A second distinctive strategy of feminist ethics is to emphasize the interconnections between the political and the personal, or the public and the private – or to reject these distinctions entirely. A third distinctive strategy is to develop moral concepts, theories and methodologies that incorporate the moral perspectives and understandings of (diverse) women. Without claiming to 'universalize' over all women, feminists nevertheless tend to treat a relational orientation and a defence of emotion as epitomes of female moral concern, regardless of differences among women. Feminists tend in general to seek relational reconceptions of major moral ideals and concepts. Fourth, feminist ethics aims to incorporate into our moral understandings, where appropriate, a recognition of diversities among women grounded in such differences as sexual orientation, race, class, religion, ethnicity, nationality, age and ableness.

Some of these strategies are exemplified in feminist discussions of autonomy. To that topic I now turn.

Moral autonomy

The word 'autonomy' has etymological roots in the idea of self-government or self-determination, an idea that philosophers have explicated in a variety of ways. Roughly and generally speaking, an autonomous person behaves and lives her life in accordance with values and commitments that are, in some important sense, her own. Many philosophers take moral autonomy, that is, self-determination in moral understanding and decision-making, to be a precondition of moral agency and responsibility.

The concept of moral autonomy was a cornerstone of Kant's (1724–1804) moral philosophy and is most often associated today with Kantian ethical traditions.[14] On Kant's view, moral autonomy is the foundation of moral agency. The morally autonomous person does not merely follow either the teachings of moral traditions or his own desires or inclinations. Instead, he (and for Kant, 'he' is always a *he*[15]) uses his capacity for rationality to apprehend the moral law, and he obeys it from no cause except his rational respect for the moral law as such. He becomes, in so doing, morally self-legislative or morally autonomous.

On the Kantian view, generalized maxims are not matters of morality unless they have the form of universal and categorically necessary laws. The morally autonomous person is one who grasps the categorical necessity of universal moral law, and who attempts to act accordingly. Categorically necessary universal laws are only comprehensible through reason. Emotion, desire, and inclination in general are not capable of generating insight into moral law because they are contingent, and lack universality. The morally self-determining person gives himself the moral law by apprehending it as universal and as categorically necessary. The rational standpoint he adopts is impartial inasmuch as it is not governed by any of the contingencies that define the moral reasoner (or any other person) as a particular empirical being in the world.

The reasons, stated earlier, which have led feminists to embrace care ethics have served for them also as reasons for rejecting the Kantian approach to moral autonomy. Feminists have argued that the Kantian approach must be rejected if ethical theory is to recognize the moral importance of emotions, close personal relationships, social relationships generally, and the non-impartial nature of any actual ethical standpoint.

Impartialist normative theories have often preoccupied themselves with the public realm and the moral concerns of citizens who meet each other as mutually disinterested but co-equal strangers. Focusing as they have on matters of justice and rights, Kantian theories of moral autonomy have tended to neglect matters of care and close personal relationships. Construing reason as the route to moral autonomy, Kantian accounts allow no place for emotion as a legitimate ingredient of moral understanding. Yet a moral agent surely understands herself and her situation in part by grasping the significance of her own emotional reactions. Also she may come to understand how it is with others by first empathizing with them in reaction to their plights. If we lacked the resources for emotional sensitivity to the feelings and attitudes of other persons, it would be difficult, if not impossible, for us to develop deep concern for their moral situations.[16]

Kant's account neglects also the interpersonal nature of moral reasoning. Moral understanding, like any sort of human understanding, is an enterprise undertaken jointly by communities of individuals who communicate with each other and share social practices. Rather than being the isolated achievement suggested by Kant's original account, moral reasoning is thus grounded in social life.[17] And the reasoning in which it is based is not the impartial reasoning of Kantian moral autonomy. Reasoning is situated in the lives of embodied and socially located persons. One's reasoning habits and capacities are shaped by one's experiences. Since there is no 'view from nowhere'[18] that persons can adopt, it is quite implausible that any moral agent should reason in detachment from the empirical contingencies that make her the particular person she is.[19]

It may now have come to seem that feminists, who defend women's moral perspectives, must reject the notion of moral autonomy wholesale. A different reaction to these criticisms of the Kantian account is possible, however. Philosophers considering moral autonomy have focused almost exclusively on Kant's specific conception of it, an understandable emphasis given that the Kantian ethical tradition has given the ideal its fullest formulation.[20] But there seems to be a valuable core idea of moral self-determination that feminist criticisms leave untouched. If we wish to retain this core meaning of the ideal of self-determination, then we must find a different account, one which is both more plausible than Kant's theory and more congenial to feminist concerns. This is the project to which I now turn.

Toward a feminist conception of autonomy

The core idea of moral autonomy is simply the notion of *behaving according to norms or ideals that, given one's social nature, one has determined for oneself to be justified as moral guidelines.* This conception acknowledges, though it does not specify the nature of, human interconnection and its relevance to autonomy. Furthermore, it does not construe reason as the exclusive source of moral autonomy; emotional understanding may contribute to a moral agent's choice of moral guidelines. The core idea, in addition, does not require impartiality in the form of reasoning detached from the empirical contingencies of a particular person's identity or life.[21] It is also not limited in application to the public realm; close personal relationships may belong in the realm of life in which a moral agent exercises her understanding about how to live.

There are good reasons for thinking that this core notion of moral self-determination should appeal to feminists. The oppression of women has often denied them the opportunities to shape morally significant features of their lives in accordance with their own reflective considerations about how best to live – considerations grounded in an understanding of their own needs and values. As subordinates in nearly all social institutions, women's own points of view about important cultural matters have been historically disregarded and systematically suppressed. Even in the domestic realm, which has traditionally been the domain of women, women have been subordinated to male authority and expected to centre their lives around the needs and concerns of particular others to whom they were related. Sandra Bartky argues that the emotional nurturance and ego support that women have traditionally been expected to provide for men promotes in women a tendency to identify with the standpoint of their beloveds and to suspend their own independent moral evaluation.[22]

According to Jerome Schneewind, Kant's conception of autonomy was the revolutionary culmination of modern moral philosophy's developing conception of morality as self-governance, an idea which replaced the earlier western conception of morality as obedience.[23] Moralities of obedience hold, among other things, that people are not equal to each other in the capacity to grasp what morality requires. In order to lead moral lives, therefore, most people need to obey those few other persons who do understand the requirements of morality. Modern moral philosophy, in direct repudiation of this idea, developed the abstract notion that all persons are equally capable of understanding what morality calls for and of being motivated to act accordingly. This idea depended in turn on the development of a moral psychology that treated persons as individually competent in capacities of moral discernment and motivation. Kantian moral philosophy was a revolutionary culmination to this historical trend toward according substantially more abstract moral respect to individual persons.[24]

For most of the modern period, however, only men benefited from this development – and only some men, at that. While more and more men were coming to be recognized as competent moral agents, women tended to remain morally subordinated in practice to the authority and control of their fathers, husbands, priests and governors. It was not until the twentieth century that women in substantial numbers across a wide social spectrum were allowed to exercise their moral agency in a variety of social contexts. Even so, major religions and most human societies fall short to some degree or other in acknowledging women's full moral equality with men as moral agents who are competent to participate in the whole range of human activities and social institutions.[25] Thus the conception of morality as self-governance has never been applied as fully to women as it has been to men.

Many feminists have argued that the problem with modern moral philosophies such as that of Kant goes beyond the mere fact that men were the main beneficiaries of the theories. Those philosophies are alleged to be deeply masculinist in their very conceptions and values, as evidenced, for example, by their neglect of the social nature of moral understanding.[26] This view of modern moral philosophies, however, is not the only critical line open to feminists. It is crucial for feminist thinking in general to challenge the cultural remnants of the conception of morality as obedience, as applied to women. This requires challenging the idea that women *as individuals* are less capable than men as individuals of grasping what morality requires and being motivated to act accordingly. Toward this end, it seems necessary to insist that women harbour, as individuals, the ability to attain competence as moral agents without having to be dominated or controlled by others. A focus on individual moral capacity, as in the Kantian tradition, seems required by any ethical perspective that aims to challenge the conception of morality as obedience or the application of such a conception to women.

The social conception of moral understanding, however plausible it may be from a feminist standpoint, by itself provides no reason to reject the dangerous conception of morality as obedience. It provides no reason to think that persons should contribute *equally* to the moral enterprise. Hierarchies of knowledge and authority characterize most social under-takings; some individuals acquire a greater share than others of the knowledge generated by the group's endeavours. Most people think that greater knowledge justifies the exercise of greater authority and command in joint endeavours. Thus social conceptions of moral understanding do not preclude the idea that some persons should be ruled morally by others, in particular, those others whose moral knowledge is greater. Nor do they rule out the idea that greater moral knowledge will reside in men, who should, therefore, control women in various moral matters. For this reason, a social conception of moral understanding that neglects (women's) individual moral competence cannot by itself serve the feminist goal of ending women's moral subordination to men.

Too much attention to the social nature of the moral enterprise, especially when conjoined with the idea that women are much more relationally oriented than men within this enterprise, can make it seem as if women were especially incapable *as individuals* of grasping what morality requires and acting accordingly. This social emphasis can cast doubt on women's ability to make moral decisions when alone or to resist the sway of morally misguided communities. In order to challenge the formidable structures of male domination that remain in this world, it is crucial for feminism to insist that mature women are as capable as men of being full moral agents in their own rights and should no more be dominated or controlled over the course of their adult lives than men are.

Towards this end, a feminist ethics should stress more than merely the social nature of moral autonomy. It should stress in addition that the moral capacities of women *as individuals* are at least equal to those of men as individuals. This approach does not rule out the thesis that individual moral competence is a social product. Moral competence emerges from prior socialization and depends for its manifestation on ongoing shared cultural resources for moral meaning and communication. Within the context of a moral enterprise that is necessarily a social project, however, women are at least as capable as men of determining *individually* what morality requires and of being *individually* self-governing.

Personal autonomy

Having seen the importance for feminism of reconceptualizing moral autonomy, we should explore a more general notion of autonomy to which feminists have attended. Here the special requirements of the moral realm need not be in question. Whereas we defined moral autonomy as self-determination in moral understanding and choice, *personal*, or individual, autonomy may be defined as self-determination in the quite general sense of choosing how to act and to live one's own life.

Feminist attitudes toward personal autonomy have changed over the years. In the 1970s, the ideal of autonomy itself was not problematized. Feminists believed instead that personal autonomy was a desirable trait for women, one which could enable them to resist oppression and live fulfilling lives. The main feminist concern then was that processes of gender socialization and political suppression had unfairly denied autonomy to women. Larry Blum, et al., Sharon Bishop Hill and, more recently, Diana T. Meyers all made this case.[27]

In the 1980s, however, feminists began objecting to the very ideal of autonomy as it was understood in the philosophical mainstream. One criticism is that mainstream philosophical conceptions of autonomy rely on an unrealistic psychology of the person. Most mainstream theories of autonomy make some mode of accurate self-reflection and self-endorsement crucial to the realization of autonomy, thereby assuming that veridical self-awareness is an easy achievement and that self-deception is not a serious problem. Feminists argue in contrast that veridical self-understanding is a rare achievement that should not be taken for granted. As Jean Grimshaw suggests, accounts of autonomy that do not acknowledge the difficulties of knowing one's own desires and that give no suggestions about overcoming these difficulties are seriously incomplete and misleading.[28]

Perhaps the single most important feminist objection to mainstream accounts is their overly individualistic character. The ideal of autonomy is closely allied with liberal traditions of moral and political thought. According to the feminist critique, such traditions conceive of individuals as social atoms who realize autonomy through independent self-sufficiency and self-creation in selfish detachment from human connection. Feminists have charged these theories with treating social relationships and interdependencies simply as threats to autonomy.[29]

An atomistic account of persons and personal autonomy is indeed implausible. Individuals do not create themselves; there are no literal 'self-made men'. All human beings must be raised and socialized by other human beings in order to survive and lead distinctively human lives. Most human beings remain dependent on others in at least some ways over the whole course of their lives. Even the rare individuals who can survive for long periods of time without any human companionship nevertheless had to have previously learned skills of survival from other persons. Furthermore, the process of socialization incorporates cultural resources such as language, modes of thinking and practical habits into the very identity and consciousness of persons. In addition, awareness of oneself as a self and the related capacity for self-reflection require a context of other selves from whom one learns to differentiate oneself both numerically and qualitatively. Finally, shared social concepts and norms inform and make meaningful the choices and commitments by way of which individual autonomy is realized. Thus, rather than threatening autonomy, social relationships and human interdependencies are necessary for its realization.

In place of atomistic accounts of autonomy, feminists recommend either abandoning the ideal of autonomy altogether or modifying the account to acknowledge the social nature of persons and their modes of self-determination.[30] The standard current feminist account of autonomy may be called a social or relational account. Variants have been developed by many feminist philosophers, including Evelyn Fox Keller, Jennifer Nedelsky, Seyla Benhabib, Lorraine Code, Morwenna Griffiths, Alison Weir and Susan Brison.[31] The accounts put forward by these theorists make two crucial relational claims. First, the sort of self who could realize personal autonomy is an inherently social being who becomes a distinct self with a particular identity only through interpersonal relationships with other persons. Second, autonomy requires capacities that must either be *learned* from others, such as self-understanding, questioning, doubting, or imagining alternatives, or that must be exercised in *interaction* with others, for example, the telling of narratives about oneself. These capacities are all additionally social in requiring meaningful systems of representation for understanding self and circumstances, systems that must be embedded in social practices.

Relational accounts of autonomy have a great deal of plausibility. Indeed, for some time now, many mainstream philosophers of autonomy have acknowledged both that only socialized beings can realize autonomy and that they must do so in virtue of processes that are grounded in social relationships and practices.[32] In addition, no mainstream conception requires a person to choose detachment from others or self-sufficient independence in order to realize autonomy. A person can realize autonomy while remaining dependent on others, caring for them intensely, taking ample account of the needs and desires of loved ones, cooperating with others in collective endeavours, or, on some accounts, even subordinating herself to others. Someone can do these things autonomously, according to various mainstream accounts, so long as her choices to do so have been based on the right sort of self-reflection.[33]

Since current mainstream philosophical accounts of autonomy acknowledge that social relationships ground personal autonomy, have feminist theorists of autonomy been wrong to criticize them? Perhaps. I suggest, however, that the appropriate target of feminist autonomy critiques is not mainstream philosophy but rather an ideal of *masculine* autonomy that pervades the popular cultures of many societies. In the western societies that idealize autonomy, men are idealized for being self-sufficient, substantively independent, and avoiding financial or emotional dependence on others. Ordinary norms of masculinity laud traits and behaviours that amount to an ideal of substantive independence, an ideal that is not procedurally neutral at all. This model of (male) autonomy manifests the atomistic individualism that feminists have criticized.

Mainstream philosophical accounts of autonomy have little to say about what is wrong with those popular masculine ideals. They simply ignore the ideals that shape the popular understanding of autonomy. Unfortunately, to disregard those ideals is to ignore how conceptions of gender bear on, and distort, that popular understanding. By neglecting these cultural gender ideals, mainstream philosophical approaches to autonomy thus overlook the practices that shape how real women and men understand and strive for personal autonomy. They disregard the ways in which the actual pursuit of autonomy falls short of philosophical ideals due to the influence of gender practices. Feminist approaches to autonomy are precisely aimed at remedying this deficit. Feminist theories of autonomy thus embody a dimension of social awareness and commentary that is lacking in most mainstream philosophical approaches.

At least two challenges now face feminist relational accounts of autonomy. First, social relationships are not always benign in their effects on women. In intimate, sexual and familial relationships, for example, women have historically been subjected to economic control, hierarchical subordination, rape and domestic violence with the indifference, if not the blessing, of churches and states. As a result, women have suffered in many ways from social relationships, including the denial of whatever degree of personal autonomy might otherwise have been theirs.

Consider the abuse of women by their husbands or other intimate partners. Such abuse threatens the victim's security in her own home. Instead of being able to focus autonomously on living a life that accords with her deepest values and commitments, she is forced to concentrate all her attention on survival and safety. These survival needs, in turn, direct her attention to the desires and demands of her abuser. An abused woman tends to develop a heightened awareness of what her partner wants and needs in order to accommodate his wishes and whims, all in the attempt to minimize his violent reactions.[34] Having to let the needs and desires of another person determine the course of one's behaviour in order to survive is a tragically heteronomous mode of existence.

Feminist research into the violence and the violations that social relationships sometimes inflict on women is thus strikingly relevant to feminist accounts of autonomy. Feminist writings on autonomy from the 1980s onward already acknowledge that social relationships are both necessary for yet sometimes barriers to autonomy.[35] The theoretical problem now is to give each of these contrasting theses their due and to make them cohere.

A second challenge for feminist relational accounts of autonomy is to reconceptualize the nature of selfhood and individuality[36] in a coherent manner. In particular this calls for eliminating the possible tensions between two views, first, that personhood is inherently social and, second, that autonomy requires a significant degree of separate personhood. To *determine* its self, a being must, at the very least, *be* a self. Selves must, for example, be numerically distinct from other beings and separately identifiable as actors, agents, or authors of choice and behaviour in the world. A self must have some degree of coherent unity as a separate self and be capable of some degree of reliable self-reflection. These seem to be the minimal conditions necessary for the sort of selfhood that enables a being to be capable of realizing autonomy, however much that autonomy cannot be realized except in a context of social relationships.

Postmodernism, deconstructionism, psychoanalysis and other movements in contemporary philosophy have challenged in various ways the concept of the unified, coherent, self-conscious self. Substantial segments of feminist philosophy have been influenced by these intellectual movements. Some feminist philosophers have accordingly rejected the view that human beings are unified, coherent, or reliably self-aware.[37] Needless to say, feminists of this persuasion will have little interest in the concept of autonomy.

Unity, coherence and self-consciousness, however, are matters of degree. A subject need not be absolutely unified, coherent, or transparently and incorrigibly self-aware in order to exercise autonomy; she need merely have those traits to a sufficient degree. Nothing about feminism in itself necessitates rejection of the idea that selves have some minimal degree of unity, coherence, reliable self-awareness, or differentiation from others. Feminist explorations of the concept of autonomy can help to articulate the nature of this minimally distinct and coherent self – and to determine the complex ways in which social relationships bear on its prospects for autonomy.[38]

NOTES

1 A representative collection of sources from the late 1970s is Laura Lederer, ed., *Take Back the Night: Women on Pornography* (New York: William Morrow and Company, 1980). See also Catharine MacKinnon, *Feminism Unmodified: Discourses on Life and Law* (Cambridge, MA: Harvard University Press, 1987).

2 See especially Carol Gilligan, *In a Different Voice: Psychological Theory and Women's Development* (Cambridge, MA: Harvard University Press, 1982); and Carol Gilligan, 'Moral Orientation and Moral Development', in Eva Feder Kittay and Diana T. Meyers, eds., *Women and Moral Theory* (Totowa, NJ: Rowman & Littlefield, 1987), pp. 19–33.

3 A book that had wide interdisciplinary influence is Nancy Chodorow's *The Reproduction of Mothering: Psychoanalysis and the Sociology of Gender* (Berkeley: University of California Press, 1978); see also Jean Baker Miller, *Toward a New Psychology of Women* (Boston: Beacon Press, 1976).

4 See, for example, Linda Alcoff, 'Cultural Feminism Versus Post-Structuralism: The Identity Crisis in Feminist Theory', *Signs: Journal of Women in Culture and Society*, 13:3 (1988), 405–36.

5 J. Gray, *Men Are from Mars; Women Are from Venus* (New York: Harper Collins, 1993).

6 Cf. Bernard Williams, 'Morality and the Emotions', in *Problems of the Self* (Cambridge: Cambridge University Press, 1973).

7 Papers on care ethics by Annette Baier, Seyla Benhabib, Lawrence Blum, Claudia Card, Owen Flanagan, Marilyn Friedman, Virginia Held, Kathryn Jackson, Alison Jaggar, Bill Puka, Joan Tronto, Margaret Walker and others can be found in the following excellent collections on care ethics: Eva F. Kittay and Diana T. Meyers, eds., *Women and Moral Theory*; Mary Jeanne Larrabee, ed., *An Ethic of Care: Feminist and Interdisciplinary Perspectives* (New York: Routledge, 1993); and Virginia Held, ed., *Justice and Care: Essential Readings in Feminist Ethics* (Boulder, CO: Westview Press, 1995).

Authored books devoted entirely or in substantial part to discussing care ethics include: Nel Noddings, *Caring: A Feminine Approach to Ethics and Moral Education* (Berkeley: University of California Press, 1984); Jean Grimshaw, *Philosophy and Feminist Thinking* (Minneapolis: University of Minnesota Press, 1986); Seyla Benhabib, *Situating the Self: Gender, Community and Postmodernism in Contemporary Ethics* (New York: Routledge, 1992); Marilyn Friedman, *What Are Friends For? Feminist Perspectives on Personal Relationships and Moral Theory* (Ithaca: Cornell University Press, 1993); Joan C. Tronto, *Moral Boundaries: A Political Argument for an Ethic of Care* (New York: Routledge, 1993); Susan Hekman, *Moral Voices, Moral Selves: Carol Gilligan and Feminist Moral Theory* (University Park, PA: Pennsylvania State University Press, 1995).

8 See, for example, Card, 'Gender and Moral Luck', in Held, ed., *Justice and Care*, pp. 79–98; and Barbara Houston, 'Rescuing Womanly Virtues: Some Dangers of Moral Reclamation', in Marsha Hanen and Kai Nielsen, eds., *Science, Morality and Feminist Theory*, *Canadian Journal of Philosophy*, supplementary volume 13 (1987), 237–62.

9 Michele M. Moody-Adams, 'Gender and the Complexity of Moral Voices', in Claudia Card, ed., *Feminist Ethics* (Lawrence, KS: University Press of Kansas, 1991), pp. 195–212.

10 On lesbian ethics, see Sarah Lucia Hoagland, *Lesbian Ethics: Toward New Value* (Palo Alto, CA: Institute of Lesbian Studies, 1988); and Claudia Card, *Lesbian Choices* (New York: Columbia University Press, 1995). The term 'womanist' is Alice Walker's alternative to 'feminist'; see Alice Walker, *In Search of Our Mothers' Gardens* (New York: Harcourt Brace Jovanovich, 1983). On ethical perspectives reflecting black women's experiences, see also Patricia Hill Collins, *Black Feminist Thought: Knowledge, Consciousness, and the Politics of Empowerment* (New York: Routledge, 1991); bell hooks, *Ain't I a Woman: Black Women and Feminism* (Boston: South End Press, 1981); and bell hooks, *Talking Back: Thinking Feminist, Thinking Black* (Boston: South End Press, 1989).

11 Aristotle, for example, believed that women lacked the authority of reason that men could attain; Kant believed that women were incapable of the kind of principled thinking that is the mark of rational autonomy. For excerpts from the classics of the western philosophical tradition that express these and other derogatory views of women, see Martha Lee Osborne, ed., *Woman in Western Thought* (New York: Random House, 1979).

12 J. O. Urmson, for example, counts soldiers who fall on live grenades to save their comrades as paradigm examples of heroes while dismissing 'the sacrifice made by a mother for her child' as merely an instance of 'natural affection' that

does not 'fall under the concept of morality' at all; see his 'Saints and Heroes', in Joel Feinberg, ed., *Moral Concepts* (Oxford: Oxford University Press, 1969), pp. 62–3. In general, most philosophers until recently had neglected the morality of family life and intimate relationships in favour of the public morality of the workplace and polis.

13 Concepts of autonomy, impartiality, rights, liberty and social contract can be interpreted in ways that presuppose highly separate individual selves who lack mutual concern and deep interpersonal attachment. These charges have been levelled, for example, against John Rawls, *A Theory of Justice* (Cambridge, MA: Harvard University Press, 1971), both from a non-feminist perspective (Michael J. Sandel, *Liberalism and the Limits of Justice* (Cambridge: Cambridge University Press, 1982)) and from a feminist perspective (Seyla Benhabib, 'The Generalized and the Concrete Other: The Kohlberg–Gilligan Controversy and Moral Theory', *Situating the Self*, pp. 148–77).

14 See, for example, Immanuel Kant, *Grounding for the Metaphysics of Morals*, trans. James W. Ellington (Indianapolis: Hackett, 1981).

15 See, for example, the excerpt from Kant's 'Observations on the Feeling of the Beautiful and the Sublime', in Osborne, ed., *Women in Western Thought*, pp. 154–61.

16 See, however, John Christman, 'Feminism and Autonomy', in Dana E. Bushnell, ed., *Nagging Questions: Feminist Ethics in Everyday Life* (Lanham, MD: Rowman & Littlefield, 1995), pp. 24–7, who argues that the Kantian conception of moral autonomy can accommodate emotionality.

17 Barbara Herman argues that before one can apply the Categorical Imperative to a situation, one must regard that situation as having morally significant features. On Herman's view, one attains such a grasp in virtue of 'rules of moral salience' which 'structure an agent's perception of his situation so that what he perceives is a world with moral features'. Most importantly, these rules are 'elements in a moral education'; they are, on Herman's view, *acquired from others*. Herman's moral theory thus takes account of the social context underlying human moral understanding while remaining decidedly Kantian. See Barbara Herman, *The Practice of Moral Judgment* (Cambridge, MA: Harvard University Press, 1993), p. 77.

18 The phrase comes from Thomas Nagel's *The View from Nowhere* (New York: Oxford University Press, 1986).

19 See, for example, Friedman, *What Are Friends For?*, ch. 1; and Iris Marion Young, *Justice and the Politics of Difference* (Princeton, NJ: Princeton University Press, 1990), ch. 4.

20 A few feminists have discussed concepts of moral autonomy that were developed outside the Kantian tradition. See, for example, Lynne Arnault, 'The Radical Future of a Classic Moral Theory', in Alison M. Jaggar and Susan R. Bordo, eds., *Gender/Body/Knowledge: Feminist Reconstructions of Being and Knowing* (New Brunswick, NJ: Rutgers University Press, 1989), pp. 188–206.

21 Feminists do not need to give up the ideal of impartiality altogether. Impartiality is a crucial feature of the justification of moral norms. Moral norms are justifiable for a community only if they are acceptable from a standpoint which does not privilege the interests of certain individuals or groups over those of other individuals or groups. The problem is that due to the finite and partial

nature of individual human psychology, there is no guarantee that any one individual's reasoning can embody this sort of personal detachment.

The interactive dialogue of a group, however, can help to overcome individual biases. If each party is equally capable of representing her own standpoint, then the group's dialogue as a whole embodies consideration for the interests of each party. Those who might be the victims of the biases of some participants can reject the moral reasoning that disadvantages them for another's benefit. On this view, impartiality is construed specifically as the absence of bias, and a social process, namely dialogue, becomes the method for best ensuring its realization in human moral reasoning. This approach to impartiality indirectly reinforces the feminist call for a social or interpersonal approach to autonomy. For a greater elaboration of this argument, see my *What Are Friends For?*, ch. 1.

22 Sandra Bartky, *Femininity and Domination: Studies in the Phenomenology of Oppression* (New York: Routledge, 1990), ch. 7.

23 Jerome Schneewind, *The Invention of Autonomy* (Cambridge: Cambridge University Press, 1998).

24 In practice, of course, some groups of men – and all women – were long denied their due in the growing trend toward allowing individuals the liberty to live their moral lives as they saw fit.

25 The Southern Baptist Church, the largest Protestant denomination in the United States, recently altered its key confessional document, 'The Baptist Faith and Message', to assert the principle that women should 'submit graciously' to their husbands, justifying this dictum on biblical grounds; 'Southern Baptists Call for Wives to Be Submissive', *St. Louis Post-Dispatch*, 10 June 1998, pp. A1, 9.

26 See, for example, Susan J. Hekman, *Moral Voices, Moral Selves: Carol Gilligan and Feminist Moral Theory* (University Park, PA: Pennsylvania State University Press, 1995), esp. ch. 2 and pp. 72–6.

27 Larry Blum, Marcia Homiak, Judy Housman and Naomi Scheman, 'Altruism and Women's Oppression', *The Philosophical Forum* 5:1–2 (Fall–Winter 1973–74), 196–221; Sharon Bishop Hill, 'Self-Determination and Autonomy', in Richard Wasserstrom, ed., *Today's Moral Problems*, 2nd edition (New York: Macmillan, 1979), pp. 118–33; and Diana T. Meyers, *Self, Society, and Personal Choice* (New York: Columbia University Press, 1989).

28 Jean Grimshaw, 'Autonomy and Identity in Feminist Thinking', in Morwenna Griffiths and Margaret Whitford, eds., *Feminist Perspectives in Philosophy* (Bloomington: Indiana University Press, 1988), pp. 90–108.

29 See, for example, Evelyn Fox Keller, *Reflections of Gender and Science* (New Haven: Yale University Press, 1985); Jennifer Nedelsky, 'Reconceiving Autonomy: Sources, Thoughts and Possibilities', *Yale Journal of Law and Feminism* 1:1 (Spring 1989), 7–36; Lorraine Code, *What Can She Know? Feminist Theory and the Construction of Knowledge* (Ithaca: Cornell University Press, 1991); and Morwenna Griffiths, *Feminisms and the Self: The Web of Identity* (London: Routledge, 1995).

30 Defenders of the liberal tradition deny that it holds such atomistic or individualistic conceptions; see for example Will Kymlicka, *Liberalism, Community and Culture* (Oxford: Clarendon Press, 1989), ch. 1. More in the text below on how mainstream conceptions of autonomy in general have converged with those of feminism on this point.

31 See, for example, Keller, *Reflections of Gender and Science*; Nedelsky, 'Reconceiving Autonomy'; Benhabib, *Situating the Self*; Code, *What Can She Know?*; Griffiths, *Feminisms and the Self*; Alison Weir, *Sacrificial Logics: Feminist Theory and the Critique of Identity* (New York: Routledge, 1996); and Susan Brison, 'Outliving Oneself: Trauma, Memory, and Personal Identity', in Meyers, ed., *Feminists Rethink the Self*, pp. 12–39.

32 For a discussion of how mainstream conceptions of autonomy acknowledge the social nature of autonomy, thus concurring with feminist accounts, see my 'Autonomy and Social Relationships: Rethinking the Feminist Critique', in Meyers, ed., *Feminists Rethink the Self*, pp. 40–61.

33 One mainstream account that exemplifies this approach is that of Gerald Dworkin, *The Theory and Practice of Autonomy* (Cambridge: Cambridge University Press, 1988). For a discussion of how contemporary accounts of autonomy are consistent with feminist concerns, see Christman, 'Feminism and Autonomy'.

34 See, for example, Kathleen J. Ferraro, 'Battered Women: Strategies for Survival', in Albert P. Cardarelli, ed., *Violence Between Intimate Partners: Patterns, Causes, and Effects* (Boston: Allyn and Bacon, 1997), pp. 124–40, esp. pp. 128–9.

35 See, for example, Keller, *Reflections on Gender and Science*, pp. 112–13; Nedelsky, 'Reconceiving Autonomy', pp. 21, 33–4; and Code, 'Second Persons', pp. 87–94, 108. See also my 'Autonomy, Social Disruption, and Women', in Natalie Stoljar and Catriona Mackenzie, eds., *Relational Autonomy: Feminist Perspectives on Autonomy, Agency and the Social Self* (Oxford: Oxford University Press, forthcoming).

36 See, for example, Meyers, ed., *Feminists Rethink the Self*.

37 Judith Butler makes this case specifically in regard to gender identity; cf. *Gender Trouble: Feminism and the Subversion of Identity* (New York: Routledge, 1990).

38 See, for example, Stoljar and Mackenzie, eds., *Relational Autonomy*.

12

ALISON JAGGAR

Feminism in ethics
Moral justification

The philosophical question of moral justification inquires how substantive moral assertions – claims that particular actions or practices are right or wrong, permissible or impermissible – may be confirmed or disconfirmed. This question has always been central in western moral philosophy and it holds special significance for feminism, which is defined by its moral opposition to male dominance. Feminists need some means of establishing that their critiques of those actions, practices and institutions that rationalize or maintain male dominance are not merely personal opinions but instead are objectively justified.

This chapter discusses some recent feminist contributions to the philosophical debate about moral justification. Part 1 traces feminist engagements with four major moral theorists of the twentieth century, and part 2 makes explicit several common themes running through those feminist critiques. Part 3 outlines some elements of an alternative feminist approach to moral justification, informed by the earlier critiques. Part 4 offers some feminist reflections on the project of providing a philosophical account of moral justification, suggesting that philosophers' claims to authority in defining moral justification may themselves constitute practice of dominance.

1 Feminist challenges to the analytic canon

Intuitionism: Elizabeth Anderson on G. E. Moore

Analytic ethics is often said to begin in 1903 with the publication of G. E. Moore's *Principia Ethica*. Moore is credited with being the father of the linguistic turn in moral philosophy, directing philosophical attention away from explicit consideration of normative issues and refocusing it on the analysis of moral language. Moore's best-known contribution to ethics is his analysis of what he took to be its central concept, namely, the concept 'good'. Moore wanted to determine the intrinsic, as opposed to instrumental, meaning of 'good', and, in his attempt to ascertain this, he sought to discover what was good in isolation from everything else. In order to avoid what he termed the naturalistic fallacy of identifying the meaning of 'good' with empirical property, he assumed that the word referred instead to some non-natural property which, he thought, must be simple and indefinable. Being non-natural, this property could not be identified through empirical observation, and so Moore concluded that internal contemplation or moral intuition must discover it.

Moore's intuitionist method has received much criticism. Here I shall focus on the critique offered by Elizabeth Anderson, whose larger project is to refute Moore's account of value. Anderson begins by observing that Moore's conclusion, that only personal relations, beauty and knowledge are intrinsically good, is incompatible with the intuitions of many people, who value such things as meaningful work, athletic achievement, justice and freedom. Anderson initially attributes Moore's surprising conclusion to the extremely narrow range of intuitions he consulted. She remarks:

> Moore and his followers removed themselves from active engagements in the larger world, withdrew to private spaces in the company of intimate friends, and introspectively contemplated the isolated objects of their imaginations. It is not surprising that many goods were not salient to people in such a privileged, exclusive aristocratic setting, insulated from the experiences of work and practical activity with strangers.[1]

Anderson observes that Moore, in addition to consulting an unrepresentative sample of intuitions, gave little credence to any that conflicted with his own. She quotes John Maynard Keynes's description of the manipulation and bullying through which Moore produced consensus among his friends in the Bloomsbury group.

> Victory was with those who could speak with the greatest appearance of clear, undoubting conviction and could best use the accents of infallibility. Moore . . . was a great master of this method – greeting one's remarks with a gasp of incredulity – Do you *really* think *that*, an expression of face as if to hear such a thing said reduced him to a state of wonder verging on imbecility, with his mouth wide open and wagging his head in the negative so violently that his hair shook. '*Oh!*' he would say, goggling at you as if either you or he must be mad; and no reply was possible . . . In practice it was a kind of combat in which strength of character was really much more valuable than subtlety of mind.[2]

Anderson shows that Moore's conclusions concerning 'our' moral intuitions in fact reflected the beliefs of those with the most social power even within his own narrow and elite circle; she suggests that such a biased outcome was not accidental but reflected a tendency endemic in individualist intuitionism. If individuals' value judgements are construed as unmediated and ineffable perceptions, unsusceptible to rational argument, then intuitionism is incapable of grounding a publicly accessible distinction between objective judgements and subjective preferences. In these circumstances, either moral claims are undecidable or, if treated as decidable, then the intuitions of those with the greatest social authority are the most likely to be accepted. Thus, individualist intuitionism not only has a tendency to rationalize conventional moral beliefs but, in a hierarchical social context, lends itself to justifying the moral beliefs of the powerful. In Moore's case, and notwithstanding Virginia Woolf's presence in the Bloomsbury group, these were the beliefs of people privileged by class, race, gender and empire.

Universal prescriptivism: Lynne S. Arnault on Richard M. Hare

Like Moore, Richard Hare aims to derive substantive moral claims from supposedly neutral investigations of the logical properties of moral concepts; his first book is aptly entitled, *The Language of Morals*. Hare also analyses concepts of moral evaluation, including 'good', but he reaches different conclusions from Moore's. He contends that moral terms do not refer to anything, natural or non-natural, but instead are characterized by their action-guiding function. To fulfil this function, moral claims require reasons and these, Hare argues, must take the form of arguments that a particular course of action could be prescribed universally. Hare considers universalizability to be the criterion of moral rationality; if a course of action can be prescribed universally, then it is objectively justified. In order to determine whether a proposed course of action is universalizable, Hare recommends that a moral deliberator should identify sympathetically with each of the parties who will be affected if the proposal is implemented, imaginatively representing to herself each party's desires and aversions in turn.

> When I have been the round of all the affected parties, and come back, in my own person, to make an impartial moral judgment giving equal weight to the interests of all parties, what can I possibly do except advocate that course which will, taken all in all, least frustrate the desires which I have imagined myself having? But this (it is plausible to go on) is to maximize satisfactions.[3]

Hare concludes that asking the classic Kantian question will produce the classic utilitarian answer.

Hare observes that reasoning with universalizability requires humans to think like 'ideal observers' or 'archangels', beings that are fully rational and impartial and possess perfect knowledge. Hare acknowledges that no one can really think like an archangel, since human reason is imperfect and human knowledge, including self-knowledge, is finite, but he finds here an empirical rather than a logical impossibility, a difficulty of practice rather than principle. Hare acknowledges that there are 'practical difficulties in getting to know the states of mind of other sentient beings, which increase with the remoteness of their experiences from ours', but he believes that these difficulties can 'be overcome by getting as closely acquainted as we can with their circumstances, verbal and other behaviour, anatomies, etc., and comparing them with our own'.[4] When a moral deliberator follows Hare's methodological recommendations, *inter*personal conflicts of preferences or prescriptions move 'inside' that individual to become *intra*personal ones.[5]

Hare is explicit about the assumptions underlying his method of moral justification. One is that people are fundamentally alike: 'people's inclinations about most of the important matters in life tend to be the same (very few people, for example, like being starved or run over by motor cars)'.[6] In addition to assuming that people are basically similar, Hare also supposes a particular conception of what they are like: in his view, individuals' primary inclination or desire is to have their own interests satisfied and he explains away apparent counter-examples. For example, as Lynne Arnault notes, Hare interprets people's 'particular loyalties and affections' in socio-biological terms that reduce them to strategies for preserving an individual's genes; this move enables him to deny that they are genuine manifestations of non-instrumental care about others.[7] Arnault concludes that Hare's universal prescriptivist method relies on the classically liberal conception of the person as an instrumentally rational, self-interested, fundamentally isolated individual who cooperates with others only in order to promote his own interests.

Arnault contends that both of Hare's assumptions about human motivation are empirically unwarranted: not only are people's conceptions of their own interests quite diverse, but many people also care about others for non-instrumental reasons. In Arnault's view, differences among individuals tend to be linked systematically with their differing social identities; she sees these identities as having profound epistemic significance, shaping not only people's needs and values but also their perceptions and interpretations of situations.

> Individuals define what the situation is, and their constructions depend on their life-history, social experience and social situatedness. Thus, for example, a male manager may define the situation as simple flirtation, but a female secretary may construct it as sexual harassment.[8]

If the epistemological consequences of differences among individuals were taken seriously, Arnault contends, Hare's method of moral justification would be revealed as evidently unworkable: his recommendation to adopt the standpoint of the other would be exposed as incoherent, impossible not only in practice but in principle.[9] Arnault's point may be elaborated by considering how the issue of sexual harassment might be addressed by Hare's method. The male manager might attempt to stand imaginatively in the shoes of his secretary but the individual wearing those shoes would be the manager, with his distinctive perceptions and values, rather than the secretary, with her different perceptions and values. That many men have expressed the wish that someone would sexually harass them illustrates the unreliability of the method of sympathetic identification; one cannot imaginatively identify with a different person and still remain oneself. If Hare is mistaken in believing that people's social identities are irrelevant to their moral thinking, his theory of moral justification encounters fatal difficulties.

Arnault adds that Hare's model of the moral agent is ill-suited to represent experiences involving ongoing dependence, such as occur within families, or 'to give voice to the forms of connectedness and solidarity that members of a subordinated group experience'.[10] If the 'possessive individualist' is taken as the paradigm of individual rationality, then anyone who attempts to express experiences of connectedness and interdependence risks having her words dismissed as confused or irrational. Because Hare's theory of moral justification does not provide for women or members of disadvantaged or marginalized groups representing their experiences in undistorted, non-repressed ways, Arnault concludes that it is biased against them.

Hypothetical contractarianism: Susan Okin on John Rawls; Alison Jaggar on Susan Okin

In the latter half of the twentieth century, John Rawls revived normative ethics from the near-death state induced in it by the neo-positivist assumption that philosophical ethics must be restricted to the analysis of concepts. Rawls not only propounds a substantive normative theory of justice as fairness but also defends his theory with an original account of moral justification. To overcome the problems he perceives in both intuitionism and ideal utilitarianism, Rawls's account draws on the contractarian tradition in political philosophy.[11]

Rawls's account of moral justification postulates an imaginary original position, corresponding to the state of nature in political contract theories, in which parties meet to conclude a permanently binding agreement on the principles for regulating the 'basic structure' or 'major social institutions' of the society they are to inhabit.[12] The parties in the original position are conceived as free, equal and rational 'in the narrow sense, standard in economic theory, of taking the most effective means to given ends'.[13] They are located behind a 'veil of ignorance' which ensures that 'no one knows his place in society, his class position or social status, nor does any one know his fortune in the distribution of natural assets and abilities, his intelligence, strength and the like'. The parties do not even know 'their conceptions of the good or their special psychological propensities'.[14] Despite their purportedly generic nature, the parties do retain two markers of social identity: they are heads of households, a stipulation that Rawls makes in order to ensure justice for the next generation, and each may be viewed as 'the least advantaged representative man', a condition intended to guarantee that the interests of the worst off receive due weight in the deliberations that occur behind the veil of ignorance.

The various features of the original position are designed to ensure that the principles of justice generated in it are fair, impartial and reached autonomously; this design encourages Rawls to assert that the point of view embedded in the principles provides 'an Archimedean point from which the basic structure (of society) itself can be judged'.[15] However, the original position is not a moral foundation from which the principles of justice are deduced; on the contrary, Rawls's account of moral justification is ultimately coherentist, 'a matter of the mutual support of many considerations, of everything fitting together into one coherent view'.[16] Our accounts of the original position are to be revised in conjunction with making modifications to various formulations of the principles of justice and to what Rawls calls 'our considered (moral) judgments', with a view to making all three mutually consistent. The goal is to produce the state of affairs that Rawls calls 'reflective equilibrium'.[17] Reflective equilibrium is a state of mind that responsible moral individuals should aspire to achieve.

Several feminists have argued that Rawls's method, as he describes it, is biased against women.[18] One obvious problem is that Rawls's supposedly generic party in the original position, 'the representative man', is described as the head of a household; assigning 'him' this social identity has the effect of excluding from the domain of justice issues concerning relations among family members. Susan Okin argues forcefully that marriage and family life must be subjected to the scrutiny of justice in order to address the unjust burdens that traditional family roles assign to women. These burdens include: a disproportionate share of housework and child-care; less decision-making power, leisure and nurture; and vulnerability to domestic violence. In addition, when women bear the main responsibility for domestic work, they are deprived of equal opportunities for economic or political power and prestige in the public world outside the home.[19]

Okin proposes to remedy the male bias inherent in Rawls's method of moral justification by modifying his characterization of the original position in two ways. First, sex should be identified explicitly as a characteristic that is hidden behind the veil of ignorance; second, the social organization of gender, especially the family, should be recognized explicitly and consistently as falling within the domain of justice.[20] Okin believes that these modifications would ensure that the interests of 'the least advantaged representative woman' would be considered equally with those of the least advantaged representative man[21] and would enable the revised original position to serve as a theoretical device facilitating thinking from the standpoint of women.[22] Like Hare, Okin recognizes that thinking from the standpoint of less advantaged others involves some practical difficulties; she also acknowledges that it assumes considerable knowledge of the social world, knowledge requiring empathy and concern for others. Again like Hare, however, Okin does not view the problem of limited knowledge as an insuperable obstacle to moral justification via reflective equilibrium.

In opposition to both Rawls and Okin, I have argued elsewhere that hypothetical contractarianism is inadequate in principle as a method of moral justification.[23] Using this method requires formulating conceptions of human needs and interests and principles of rational choice that are at once sufficiently abstract to be universal and sufficiently determinate that they will not invite endless disputes over their interpretation. Because the natures of human needs and interests, as well as of the principles of reason, are essentially contested, I contend that it is impossible to substitute private reflection for public discussion about principles of morality and justice. I go on to argue that the method of justifying moral claims by appeal to a postulated but hypothetical agreement is covertly elitist because it requires the construction of elaborate philosophical arguments for which most people have no inclination, time or training. (The early Rawls even says it requires complex mathematics.) A method of justification that ordinary people cannot use necessarily assigns final moral authority to those few philosophical experts who are able to use it. In western societies, such people are generally white, male and middle class.

Because the deliberation attributed to parties in the original position is hypothetical, Rawls's method remains essentially monological, reflecting only the views of the individual theorist – as illustrated by the male bias we have observed in Rawls's account of justice as fairness. The hypothetical contractarian method is unreliable, no matter how well-meaning the individual who uses it. However, its elaborate theoretical machinery obscures its monological character and gives the impression of generating a theory of justice that is objective in the sense of transcending the subjective views of any given individual. These unjustified pretensions to objectivity give the method an authoritarian potential, encouraging those who use it to dismiss the expressed views of real people (of sex workers, perhaps, or of welfare recipients) by alleging that their opinions are incompatible with the conclusions that would be reached by parties in the original position.

Domination-free discourse: Seyla Benhabib on Jürgen Habermas; Iris Young and others on Seyla Benhabib

The communicative or discourse ethics of Karl-Otto Apel and Jürgen Habermas offers a contrast with the Anglo-American theories of moral justification considered above. Habermas accepts the Kantian intuition that the moral validity of any norm is to be defined in terms of what could be agreed in free and equal discussion among all those affected; however, he insists that the substantive content of moral agreements cannot be inferred through philosophical thought experiments but instead requires real-world discourse.

Its insistence on the need for actual public discussion reveals the recognition by discourse ethics that moral subjects are diverse; at the same time, its requirement that such discussion should be domination-free moves discourse ethics beyond the conventionalism often thought to threaten both communitarianism and postmodernism, the main contemporary challengers of neo-Enlightenment moral philosophy. Seyla Benhabib regards discourse ethics as offering the most promising model of moral justification available to feminism but suggests some modifications to Habermas's account, in order that this promise may be fulfilled.[24] Of the several revisions she recommends, I mention here only two.

First, Benhabib challenges Habermas's acceptance of the standard liberal distinction between a public 'moral' domain, regulated by objective principles of justice or right, and a private 'ethical' domain, in which people may pursue their various subjective conceptions of value or goodness. She notes that this distinction has served to exclude from moral scrutiny many questions of special concern to women, such as questions about abortion, pornography and domestic violence. Benhabib disputes the assumption that the distinction between moral issues of justice and ethical issues of goodness is unproblematic; she asserts that the distinction itself must be questioned in moral discourse. Second, Benhabib revises Habermas's account of moral judgement, denying the pre-eminence he assigns to the culturally masculine ability to formulate general norms through abstraction from concrete situations; she asserts that it is equally important to be able to perceive sensitively the specificities of particular contexts, an ability requiring the culturally feminine capacities for moral imagination, interpretation and sympathy. Benhabib argues that moral judgement involves enlarged thinking or reciprocal recognition, the ability to reverse perspectives with others in order to see the world as they see it.

Some feminist philosophers welcome Benhabib's revisions to discourse ethics but contend that they do not go far enough. Nancy Fraser notes that language is not a neutral means of communication, but reflects culturally specific ways of interpreting the world. She criticizes Benhabib for neglecting to address the problem that dominant discourses may well be incapable of expressing the interests and concerns of subordinated groups.[25] Iris Young argues that Benhabib's conception of enlarged thinking is ultimately incoherent, because the idea of reversing perspectives with someone else is unintelligible.

> The reciprocal recognition by which I know that I am other for you just as you are other for me cannot entail a reversibility of perspectives, precisely because our positions are partly constituted by the perspectives each of us has on the other.[26]

Young further contends that the belief that we can adopt other people's standpoints is disrespectful and presumptuous: in assuming that other people are similar to us, it obscures their differences from us. This belief is problematic politically as well as morally, because privileged people who try to put themselves in the position of those who are less privileged are likely to rely on projections and fantasies and so to misrepresent the situations of the disadvantaged. Moreover, 'asking the oppressed to reverse perspectives with the privileged in adjudicating a conflict may itself be an injustice and an insult'.[27] Benhabib's proposals, like Habermas's, surely remain overly idealized in failing to address the inevitable problems of systematic inequality among participants in practical discourses.

2 'The master's tools will never dismantle the master's house' – Audre Lorde

The parallels among these various critiques of the most eminent theorists of analytic ethics suggest that feminists have identified several male-biased assumptions that are not held idiosyncratically by a few isolated philosophers but that instead infect a whole tradition of thinking about moral justification. This is the liberal tradition descending from the European Enlightenment.

1. First, 'the' moral subject of this tradition appears to be generic but in fact reflects a specific social type: he is a western male head of household, upper or middle class and therefore probably white. The motivations and style of reasoning characteristic of this social type are ascribed to all rational moral subjects, despite the overwhelming empirical evidence that many people have different motivations and employ alternative styles of reasoning.[28]

2. When this social type is taken as the moral norm, people whose thinking deviates from his are presented as deficient in moral rationality. Idealizing his mode of thinking is thus covertly authoritarian because it invalidates the moral thinking of many women as well as of male members of subordinated groups.

3. The sphere of moral reason is arbitrarily limited so as to exclude matters of intimate and family relations.

4. In consequence, numerous issues that have special importance for women's lives become morally undecidable; there is no conceptual space for criticizing many practices oppressive to women.

5. The foregoing points together entail that mainstream conceptions of moral justification deny the conceptual resources that would permit women and male members of subordinated groups to express their own moral perspectives in their own terms.

6. Despite the impartiality and universality claimed by these conceptions of moral justification, they are in fact self-serving and circular because they rationalize the views of the philosopher who invokes them while silencing dissenting voices.

For these reasons, the very conceptual tools that purport to guarantee moral objectivity are biased in favour of the privileged.

Implicit in feminists' criticisms of mainstream ethics is an expectation that any adequate account of moral justification must not only be able to distinguish justified moral claims from both subjective desires and established conventions; it must also fulfil the following conditions:

1. Its conception of the moral subject must be carefully scrutinized to eliminate covert bias on the basis of race, class, gender or any other axis of domination.

2. Therefore, it must take care not to discredit or disregard the moral narratives, vocabularies and styles of thinking characteristic of women, lower-class and marginalized persons.

3. It must be practically available for use by all moral subjects, including those with little formal education; thus, it should not be highly technical nor rely on overly idealized, counter-factual assumptions.

4. It must not exclude from moral scrutiny aspects of life that are of special concern to women or to male members of disadvantaged and marginalized groups.

In short, a feminist account of moral justification must be non-elitist and truly unbiased; it must not privilege the perspectives of the powerful nor assign disproportionate moral authority to their voices. The next section sketches some feminist work that moves in the direction of meeting these conditions.

3 Towards a feminist conception of moral justification

Positioning the moral subject

Liberal moral theory has typically discussed moral subjects at a high level of abstraction, presenting them as generic rational agents who are essentially – though not empirically – solitary. The classic liberal theorists were certainly aware that empirical subjects are embodied members of specific communities, but they dismissed people's bodies and community memberships as 'accidental' properties, inessential to their moral subjectivity. Some may have supposed that treating moral subjects as indistinguishable was required by the Enlightenment commitment to the equal moral value of every human individual. By focusing on people's commonalities and ignoring their differences, liberalism implies that moral subjects are indiscernible in all theoretical respects. In Seyla Benhabib's words, it treats them as 'generalized' rather than 'concrete'.

Over the past twenty-five years, the liberal conception of the moral subject has been challenged from many directions. Communitarian critics have been particularly vocal in insisting that moral subjects are essentially embodied, thereby entailing that they are 'embedded' in communities and 'encumbered' by particular loyalties and obligations that constitute essential aspects of their identities. Many feminist accounts of moral subjects resemble communitarianism in emphasizing bodies, communities and relationships, but feminist work is distinguished by its attention to inequality. Feminist discussions of embodiment, for instance, typically treat the body neither merely as an individuator of persons nor merely as a universal condition of human life but as a bearer of contingent and varying social meanings which locate bodies and their persons not only in particular communities but also in specific structures of privilege and power.[29] Similarly, feminists not only present moral subjects as constituted by particular relations but also assert that these relations invariably involve dimensions of systematic dominance and inequality. Finally, feminists typically focus on those aspects of moral subjects' identities that are constituted by their membership in distinct – though overlapping – social collectivities defined not only by history and geography but also by categories such as gender, class and race, in which power inequalities are inherent.

Feminists do not deny that moral subjects are alike on some level of abstraction, but their consciousness of the many false humanisms that have purveyed generalizations about specific populations as universal truths of human nature motivates them to highlight human differences over human commonalities. Nor do feminists dispute the equal moral worth of each individual but, when individuals are so differently situated, they insist that a genuine commitment to moral equality requires sensitivity to actual inequalities. Feminists further contend that the differences and inequalities that are most important for moral theory are systematic rather than idiosyncratic, and that they separate groups or collectivities rather than particular individuals.

Those features of moral subjectivity emphasized by feminists have implications for moral justification. For relationally constituted subjects, possessive individualism is not a natural – let alone rational – human motivation. For embodied subjects, the only knowledge they can hope to attain is finite and situated. Subjects who are socially constituted by their membership in different collectivities, especially collectivities that stand to each other in relations of dominance and subordination, are likely to have disparate moral viewpoints and styles of reasoning. Such disparities and inequalities create obstacles to projects of imaginative identification and even to productive discussion. To recognize these obstacles is to challenge mainstream assumptions that there is a single correct model of moral reason, and that moral subjects are interchangeable. Abandoning these assumptions requires rejecting monological conceptions of moral justification.

Socializing moral rationality

Most contemporary feminist philosophers repudiate the possibility of moral justification through solitary reflection, whether this takes the form of consulting one's intuition, staging a hypothetical discourse or pretending to be someone else. Monological thought experiments may sometimes have heuristic value but they are equally likely to mislead. Many feminists argue that recommendations that moral agents think from the standpoint of others, reverse perspectives with them, and so on, are not only disrespectful of others but epistemically incoherent. There exists no substitute for listening to real people explain their moral perspectives in their own terms.

Engaging in actual discussion not only permits the collective assessment of what Hare calls proposed courses of action, alternative resolutions of a given moral problem; it also permits 'the' problem itself to be problematized. Empirical discourse allows people to raise questions such as: For whom is this situation problematic and what criteria are used to identify 'those affected'? In whose terms is the situation described, and what is highlighted and what obscured by those terms? What are the interests and values at stake and how do these change if the problem is redescribed? Who is responsible for addressing the situation and according to what account of responsibility? A monological method might be plausible if moral reasoning involved no more than consulting a moral calculus, but in fact every identification of a moral problem presupposes an interpretive point of view that should be made explicit and examined. It is because moral reasoning is inevitably hermeneutic that it must be pluralist and interactive.[30]

A full theory of moral rationality must include an account of individual rationality but, because of their scepticism about monological approaches, feminists' positive work on moral rationality has focused more on social processes than on individual capacities. Some feminist work has been done on the topic of individual rationality but there is no space to consider it here. One theme running throughout this work is that dominant philosophical accounts of individual moral rationality are biased by gender, class, race and ethnicity insofar as they reflect and rationalize the culturally specific values held by modern, western, bourgeois, men. However, few feminists believe that the remedy for existing bias is to replace one singular model that covertly represents moral rationality as bourgeois and masculine with another singular model that has more features considered characteristically feminine; there no more exists a representative or generic woman than a generic human or a representative man. Instead, many feminists argue that the remedy is to reconstrue moral rationality as a characteristic primarily of social processes and only secondarily as a property of individuals. On this view, individual rationality is no longer defined by the possession of specific motivations or values or by the utilization of a particular style of moral thinking; instead, it consists in proficiency in those interactive skills and virtues necessary to participate as an equal in productive moral discourse.

A considerable number of feminists, including myself, broadly concur with the long western philosophical tradition, stretching from Plato through Locke and Kant, to Rawls and Habermas, that holds moral conclusions to be rationally justified when they are reached by rational people through discursive processes that are open, inclusive and egalitarian. But even though philosophers in this tradition are aware that real people are not all alike, they have ignored the practical and theoretical problems posed for egalitarian discourse by systematic difference and inequality. Feminists, by contrast, have been deeply troubled by those problems; in response, they have developed an extensive literature on discursive communication, including its ethical and political aspects. In what follows, I indicate a few of the avenues feminists have explored in considering how open and egalitarian discourse might be possible among moral subjects who are inevitably diverse and unequal.

Mainstream accounts of domination-free discourse require that each participant equally have an opportunity to speak and be heard; however, they neglect to examine the conditions necessary for such opportunities to be real rather than merely formal. Speaking requires a language but dominant vocabularies may lack the resources necessary to express the perspectives of subordinated groups; as a young woman, for instance, I was unable to articulate many vague and confused feelings and perceptions because the language necessary to do so had not yet been invented. The vocabulary I needed included such terms as: 'gender' (applied beyond grammar to social norms and identities); 'sex role'; 'sexism'; 'sexual harassment'; 'the double day'; 'sexual objectification'; 'heterosexism'; 'the male gaze'; 'marital, acquaintance and date rape'; 'emotional work'; 'stalking'; 'hostile environment'; 'displaced homemaker'; and 'double standard of aging'. Because language is essentially public, creating new vocabularies is necessarily a collective rather than an individual project. In order that alternatives to dominant moral vocabularies may be developed, I have recently argued that, if discourses are to be open and inclusive for some, they may have to be closed to and exclusive of others.[31]

Feminist models of moral discourse are unusual in giving considerable attention to hearing as well as speaking; they have explained that hearing, especially hearing across diversity, is a complex and difficult activity in which people may fail for many reasons.[32] Laurence Thomas contends that, in an unjust society, there is no 'vantage point from which any and every person can rationally grasp whatever morally significant experiences a person might have'.[33] For instance, he asserts, African Americans who have endured the pains and humiliations of racism experience an emotional vulnerability, anger and hostility, even a bitterness and rancour, that most white Americans cannot imagine. '[J]ust as a person does not know what it is like to be a bat by hanging upside down with closed eyes, [so] a person does not know what it is like to be a member of a diminished social category merely on account of having been affronted and insulted by a diminished social category person.'[34] In order that members of subordinated or stigmatized groups may be heard, Thomas recommends that more privileged persons should respond to their descriptions of their experiences with 'moral deference'.

> The idea behind moral deference is not that a diminished social category person can never be wrong about the character of his own experiences. Surely he can, since anyone can . . . Rather, the idea is that there should be a presumption in favor of that person's account of her experiences. This presumption is warranted because the individual is speaking from a vantage point to which someone not belonging to her diminished social category group does not have access.[35]

Thomas did not develop his idea of moral deference in the specific context of feminist discourse but his concept captures the spirit of many feminist discussions of listening. As a defeasible presumption of a speaker's authority, moral deference may be viewed as a kind of discursive affirmative action necessary to achieving substantive rather than merely formal equality among participants in discourse.

Feminist models of moral discourse include a number of other characteristic features, in addition to their reinterpretations of equality, openness and inclusiveness. Among those features are a commitment to the collective moral evaluation of participants' emotions[36] and a conception of moral discourse as a nurturing rather than an adversarial practice.[37] For feminists, moral discourses are not neutral procedures in which people withdraw from the real world to debate moral concerns; instead, they are activities within the world and themselves are liable to moral and political evaluation.[38] Done well, moral discourse has a value that is intrinsic and not merely instrumental.

Situating moral objectivity

Western philosophers have often construed moral justification as the attainment of 'the moral point of view', a grandiose expression that hints heavily at a transcendent moral reality. In the twentieth century, they have interpreted the expression through such metaphors as a god's eye view, the perspective of an ideal observer or an archangel, an Archimedean point, a view from nowhere or a view from everywhere. The aim of these metaphors is to designate an imagined perspective that is precisely not a specific point of view, what might be called the father of all points of view, and contemporary feminists typically regard such metaphors as misleading. For most feminists, moral justification cannot be achieved by an individual appeal to transcendent ideals or absolute principles; instead, it consists in the on-going evaluation of individual actions and social practices by people in actual communities of discourse who collectively construct historically specific ideals, norms and values. On this understanding, moral justifications are socially developed and contingently situated; 'the' moral point of view loses its transcendent status and becomes not single but multiple, rooted in the social world rather than floating above or outside it.

Rejecting moral realism, construed as the postulation of a mind-independent moral reality, does not commit feminists to embracing relativism, interpreted as the claim that all moral points of view are equally valid. Indeed, relativism is inconsistent with feminism's non-negotiable moral commitment to opposing male dominance. The work surveyed here directs us to understand moral justification in terms of discursive processes that are open, inclusive and egalitarian. Since openness, inclusivity and equality are moral and epistemic ideals that are only ever met imperfectly, to a greater or lesser extent, the warrant for accepting particular moral assertions will be stronger or weaker according to the degree to which the ideals are realized. The conclusions of moral dialogues thus are always provisional and fallible rather than final or absolute and always dependent on a discursive social context that determines what count as good reasons.[39]

4 Who is authorized to define and interpret moral justification?

Feminist work on moral justification has revealed male and other biases lurking in common philosophical interpretations of ideals such as rationality, universality, impersonality, detachment, dispassion, neutrality and transcendence. It has not only challenged particular interpretations of those ideals but also suggested that they should be abandoned as guides to moral justification. Feminism is not alone in its challenges to these ideals: as Margaret Walker notes, scepticism about them has been expressed by 'Aristotelians, Humeans, communitarians, contemporary casuists, pragmatists, historicists, Wittgensteinians, and others in the last several decades'.[40] Faced with such opposition, even Rawls has now abandoned his aspiration to achieve an 'Archimedean point' and substituted the notion of a specific community's 'overlapping consensus' about justice. However, whereas non-feminist critics argue that Archimedean models of moral justification are simply mistaken, some feminists criticize them in terms that are explicitly moral and political.

Margaret Walker contends that the ideal of point-of-viewlessness fulfils an ideological function by concealing the specific, partial and situated character of views and positions that are put forward *'authoritatively* as truths about "human" interest, "our" intuitions, "rational" behavior, or "the" moral agent'.[41] By discounting the effects of people's social identities on their moral thinking, the ideal of point-of-viewlessness insulates itself from any critical examination of its own social origins or functions. It denies that any philosophical significance attaches to the facts that few are authorized to define moral knowledge and that 'To have the social, intellectual, or moral authority to perform this feat, one must already be on the advantaged side of some practices of privilege and uneven distributions of power and responsibilities in the community in which one does it'.[42] That 'Western Anglo-European philosophical ethics as a cultural tradition and product has been until just recently almost entirely a product of some men's – and almost no women's – thinking' is, from 'the' moral point of view, dismissed as a matter of only historical, not philosophical, interest. Thus, traditional understandings of moral justification operate as a mystifying moral ideology that shields from view 'the historical, cultural, and social location of the moral philosopher, and of moral philosophy itself, as a practice of authority sustained by particular institutions and arrangements'.[43]

Some feminist critics thus charge that traditional conceptions of moral justification are more than simply expressions of a moral perspective characteristic of bureaucratic societies divided by class and gender. They are more than a deceptive rhetorical device that adds a ring of magisterial authority to philosophers' rationalizations of practices oppressive to women and members of other subordinated groups. They even have a function beyond invalidating criticism of such practices. Philosophical accounts of moral justification have been, finally, a means by which philosophers have promoted their own claims to define moral validity and to determine when its criteria have been met. Perhaps uncomfortable in this authoritarian framework, some feminist philosophers have abandoned the traditional project of moral justification. Joyce Trebilcot insists that she speaks only for herself.[44] Care theorist Nel Noddings writes, 'An ethic of caring does not emphasize justification. As one-caring, I am not seeking justification for my action; I am not standing alone before some tribunal. What I seek is completion in the other . . . Thus, I am not justified but somehow fulfilled and completed . . .'[45] Postmodernist feminists insist on the multiplicity of possible narratives. Some feminists, however, are still concerned that feminism be able to justify its moral claims. Rather than abandoning the project of moral justification, we are working to reinterpret it in terms that are less covertly elitist and authoritarian and more transparent and democratic. Our accounts of moral justification operate at a lower level of abstraction than most philosophical accounts, and are in that sense less idealized and more naturalistic, but they are still explicitly normative. They link increased moral objectivity with the development of methods of justification that are increasingly open, egalitarian and inclusive.

Feminist challenges to canonical accounts of moral justification have pursued transparency by making visible what Walker calls 'the gendered structures of authority that produce and circulate existing moral under-standings'. But even as it challenges the dominant tradition of western ethics, feminism simultaneously contributes to that tradition. Its demand for transparency 'is embarrassing precisely because it exploits a tradition – its own – in which values of representation, consent, self-determination, respect, equality, and freedom are common currency'. The values it invokes 'are of specifically democratic, participatory, and emancipatory kinds, squarely founded on moral and political ideals of modern Western social thought'.[46] Rather than scrapping the master's tools, many feminist philo-sophers are working to transform them so that we may build a moral household that has no head nor master.

NOTES

1 Elizabeth Anderson, *Value in Ethics and Economics* (Cambridge, MA, and London: Harvard University Press, 1993) p. 120.
2 John Maynard Keynes, 'My Early Beliefs,' in *Two Memoirs* (New York: Augustus M. Kelley, 1949), pp. 85–8, quoted in Anderson, p. 121.
3 Richard M. Hare, *Freedom and Reason* (Oxford: Clarendon Press, 1963), p. 123. Quoted by Lynne S. Arnault, 'The Radical Future of a Classic Moral Theory', in Alison M. Jaggar and Susan R. Bordo, eds., *Gender/Body/Knowledge: Feminist Reconstructions of Being and Knowing* (New Brunswick and London: Rutgers University Press, 1989), p. 191.
4 Richard M. Hare, *Moral Thinking: Its Levels, Method and Point* (Oxford: Clarendon Press, 1981), pp. 126–7.
5 Ibid., p. 110.
6 Richard M. Hare, *Freedom and Reason* (Oxford: Clarendon Press, 1963), p. 97.
7 Hare, *Moral Thinking*, p. 137.
8 Arnault, 'Radical Future', p. 197.
9 Ibid., p. 196.
10 Ibid., p. 192.
11 Some version of Rawls's method of moral justification was adopted by many major philosophers in the 1970s and 1980s, including: Bruce Ackerman, Charles Beitz, Gerald Dworkin, David Gauthier, Alan Gewirth, Robert Nozick, Jeffrey Reiman and Thomas Scanlon.
12 John Rawls, *A Theory of Justice* (Cambridge, MA: Harvard University Press, 1971), p. 7.
13 Ibid., p. 14.

14 Ibid., p.12.

15 Ibid., p. 260.

16 Ibid., p. 21.

17 Ibid., p. 20.

18 Objectors include Jane English, 'Justice Between Generations', *Philosophical Studies* 31:2 (1977), 91–104 and Sybil Schwartzenbach, 'Rawls and Ownership: The Forgotten Category of Reproductive Labour', in Marsha Hanen and Kai Nielsen, eds., *Science, Morality and Feminist Theory* (Calgary, Canada: University of Calgary Press, 1987), pp. 139–67.

19 Susan Moller Okin, *Justice, Gender and the Family* (New York: Basic Books, 1989).

20 Okin notes that Rawls occasionally includes both these conditions in various descriptions of the original position. At the very outset of his theory, he includes the family among the major social institutions determining the basic structure of a society, though he goes on to assume rather than establish its justice, and he fails to mention it in a later article. In another paper subsequent to *A Theory of Justice*, Rawls includes sex among the contingencies hidden by the veil of ignorance. These occasional concessions appear to have no impact on Rawls's overall theory.

21 Susan Moller Okin, 'Reason and Feeling in Thinking about Justice', *Ethics: An International Journal of Social, Political, and Legal Philosophy* 99:2 (1989), 229–49.

22 Okin, *Justice, Gender and the Family*, pp. 106–9.

23 Alison M. Jaggar, 'Taking Consent Seriously: Feminist Practical Ethics and Actual Moral Dialogue', in Earl R. Winkler and Jerrold R. Coombs, eds., *Applied Ethics: A Reader* (Oxford: Blackwell, 1993), pp. 67–86.

24 Seyla Benhabib, *Situating the Self: Gender, Community and Postmodernism in Contemporary Ethics* (New York: Routledge, 1992).

25 Nancy Fraser, 'Toward a Discourse Ethic of Solidarity', *Praxis International* 5:4 (1986), 425–9.

26 Iris Marion Young, *Intersecting Voices: Dilemmas of Gender, Political Philosophy and Policy* (Princeton, NJ: Princeton University Press, 1997).

27 Ibid., p. 48.

28 For instance, empirical research shows that many women value care over justice, as do many African American, Native American and working-class men, not to mention persons from non-western cultures.

29 Excellent discussions of some of the gendered power dimensions of embodiment are offered by Susan Bordo, *Unbearable Weight: Feminism, Western Culture, and the Body* (Berkeley, Los Angeles and London: University of California Press, 1993) and Susan Wendell, *The Rejected Body: Feminist Philosophical Reflections on Disability* (New York: Routledge, 1996).

30 María C. Lugones, 'On the Logic of Pluralist Feminism', in Claudia Card, ed., *Feminist Ethics* (Lawrence, KS: University of Kansas Press, 1991), pp. 35–44.

31 Alison M. Jaggar, 'Globalizing Feminist Ethics', *Hypatia* 13:2 (1998), 7–31.

32 María C. Lugones and Elizabeth V. Spelman, 'Have We Got a Theory for You! Feminist Theory, Cultural Imperialism and the Demand for "the Woman's Voice"', *Hypatia* 1:1, special issue of *Women's Studies International Forum* 6:6 (1983), 573–81; Marsha Houston, 'Why the Dialogues are Difficult or 15 Ways

a Black Woman Knows When a White Woman's Not Listening', in Linda A. Bell and David Blumenfeld, eds., *Overcoming Racism and Sexism* (Lanham, MD: Rowman & Littlefield, 1995), pp. 52–5.

33 Laurence Thomas, 'Moral Deference', *Philosophical Forum* 14:1–3 (1992–3), 233.

34 Ibid., p. 240.

35 Ibid., p. 244.

36 Alison M. Jaggar, 'Love and Knowledge: Emotion in Feminist Epistemology', *Inquiry* 32 (1989), 151–76.

37 Patrocinio Schweickart, 'Engendering Critical Discourse', in Clayton Koelb and Virgil Lokke, eds., *The Current in Criticism* (West Lafayette: Purdue University Press, 1987), pp. 295–317.

38 Linda Alcoff, 'The Problem of Speaking for Others', *Cultural Critique* 20 (1991–92), 5–32.

39 On such a view, it is possible that autonomy should be thought of less as the first-order ability to weigh impartially the interests of all those affected and more as the second-order ability to accurately gauge the reliability of particular processes of justification.

40 Margaret Walker, *Moral Understandings: A Feminist Study in Ethics* (New York: Routledge, 1998), pp. 53–4.

41 Ibid., p. 54.

42 Ibid., p. 54.

43 Ibid., p. 56.

44 Joyce Trebilcot, *Dyke Ideas: Process, Politics, Daily Life* (Albany, NY: State University of New York Press, 1991).

45 Nel Noddings, *Caring: A Feminine Approach to Ethics and Moral Education* (Berkeley: University of California Press, 1984).

46 Walker, *Moral Understandings*, p. 73.

13

GENEVIEVE LLOYD

Feminism in history of philosophy
Appropriating the past

Introduction

The articulation of feminist perspectives on the history of western philosophy has been a significant development in feminist philosophy. Critique
of the alleged 'maleness' of the philosophical tradition has been a central
theme in this development. It has reflected more general divisions within
feminist theory between approaches centred on the affirmation of 'sameness' and approaches emphasizing 'difference'. Where some have defended
female character and capacities in relation to traditional ideals, others have
challenged the supposed gender-neutrality of the ideals themselves.

Despite the contrasts between these approaches, a common tone was
evident in the early stages of feminist history of philosophy: the history of
philosophy was seen as a repository of misogynist ideas and ideals,
towards which feminism took up a defensive posture. In more recent
work inspired by feminism, a more positive mood is evident. Rather than
defining itself through opposition to a 'male' tradition, feminist history of
philosophy has emerged as a shifting set of strategies which bring sexual
difference to bear on the reading of philosophical texts. Often those
strategies are directed to highlighting tensions within the texts, but their
upshot is not always negative; readings inspired by feminism are also
opening up traditional texts to enrich cultural self-understanding in the
present.

Scholarly work on the history of philosophy tends to be less methodologically self-reflective, and hence less well charted, than other areas where
feminist philosophy has made a distinctive contribution. There are both
difficulties and advantages in this comparative lack of definition. By trying
to map the place of feminism in an area which itself has no firm contours,
we gain insight into what is involved in reading past texts from present
perspectives. Here the contribution of feminist philosophy has been not so
much to challenge methodological practices and assumptions that were

already clear as to help develop a range of strategies through which the history of philosophy might become more self-reflective.

The work of Luce Irigaray has been influential in the development of strategies directed to the identification within philosophical texts of 'speaking positions' which, while supposedly gender-neutral, incorporate assumptions of maleness.[1] And the work of Michèle Le Dœuff has made it possible to see the philosophical import of the operations of metaphor and imagery.[2] Other approaches have focused on the oppositions which interact with the male–female distinction in philosophical texts – on dichotomies between reason and nature, intellect and emotion or imagination, public and private. This chapter will examine a range of such strategies, through which philosophers – not all of them self-avowedly 'feminist' – have attempted to read past texts from present perspectives. It aims to locate feminist history of philosophy in the broader context of the methodology of history of philosophy. I will argue that there is – and need be – no firm identity to 'feminist' history of philosophy. We can nonetheless see patterns in which feminist philosophy has provided some threads – patterns which enrich the practices through which philosophy attempts to understand its past and engage more closely with its present.

Women and the 'conversation' of philosophy

In an early mapping of the methodological divisions within modern history of philosophy, Richard Rorty drew the crucial distinctions in terms of the notion of 'conversation'.[3] The most important divide, in Rorty's map, is between 'past-centred' and 'present-centred' approaches to the history of philosophy. On the one side, we have those analytic philosophers who have attempted 'rational reconstructions' of the arguments of past philosophers – an exercise guided by the hope of treating the mighty dead as colleagues with whom they can engage in philosophical debate. On the 'past-centred' approach, in contrast, the aim is to understand past philosophers in their own terms, in relation to their own agenda.

The two alternatives, Rorty argues, do not really pose a dilemma: we should do both of these things, but do them separately. There is nothing wrong with self-consciously letting our own philosophical views dictate terms in which to describe the dead. But there are also reasons to describe them in other terms. Good history of philosophy needs to try both to reconstruct the conversations past philosophers might have had with their peers, and to bring them into our own contemporary philosophical debates. We have here, he argues, two different kinds of imaginary conversation; and we can engage in both provided we are clear about what we are doing and why it matters to us. Rorty's model of conversation helps unite two concerns which might initially seem at odds: the desire to know ourselves as different from the past, and the desire for continuity. We want to be able to see the history of our race as 'a long, conversational interchange', and this exercise of the imagination really involves both 'past-centred' and 'present-centred' orientations. We want to understand ourselves as different from our philosophical ancestors. But we want also to assure ourselves that there has been rational progress in the course of recorded history – that we differ from our ancestors on grounds which our ancestors could be led to accept.

The distinction – and ultimate unity – of the 'past-centred' and 'present-centred' approaches, articulated through the idea of imaginary conversation, is a useful starting point for understanding what goes on in feminist strategies for the reading of philosophical texts. But to understand these strategies we must go beyond the rationale of Rorty's distinction. Rorty's account of the two approaches draws on a precept enunciated in an early paper on the methodology of history of ideas by Quentin Skinner.[4] On Skinner's precept, 'No agent can eventually be said to have meant or done something which he could never be brought to accept as a correct description of what he had meant or done.' The rationale of the precept is to allow a clear distinction between what is true of ourselves, the interpreters, and what is true of the past subjects of interpretation. By avoiding anachronism as much as possible, Skinner says, we can attain what is of indispensable value in the history of ideas: to understand the distinction between 'what is necessary' and 'what is the product merely of our own contingent arrangements' is 'the key to self-awareness itself'.

Rorty's ironic addition to Skinner's precept is the claim that there is another need which is as great as the need for self-awareness: the need for assurance that we differ from our ancestors on grounds which our ancestors could be led to accept. 'We need to think that, in philosophy as in science, the mighty mistaken dead look down from heaven at our recent successes, and are happy to find that their mistakes have been corrected.'[5] So we are interested not only in what the Aristotle who walked the streets of Athens could be brought to accept as a correct description of what he had meant or done, but also in what 'an ideally reasonable and educated Aristotle' could be brought to accept as such a description. An 'ideal Aristotle' can be brought to describe himself, for example, as having mistaken the preparatory taxonomic stages of biological research for the essence of all scientific inquiry. This imaginary Aristotle, who accepts our description of what he meant or did, then becomes our contemporary, 'one of us'. There need, Rorty argues, be no conflict here between 'historical reconstructions', which satisfy Skinner's precept, and 'rational reconstructions' that do not satisfy it. We can move between giving an account of past thinkers in their own terms and giving an account in our terms. If we want 'self-awareness', we need, as Skinner says, to avoid anachronism as much as possible. If we want self-justification through conversation with the dead thinkers about our current problems, then we are free to indulge in as much anachronism as we like, as long as we realize that we are doing so.

The boundaries between authorial agents and their reading subjects have become less clear-cut under the impact of 'postmodern' textual theory. Deconstructive techniques derived from Derrida have had more direct influence on literary studies than on the interpretation of philosophical texts. But they have been incorporated back into feminist history of philosophy through more general developments in feminist theorization of sexual difference. In this context, the metaphor of conversation has rather different connotations from the timeless debates evoked in Rorty's account of 'rational reconstruction'. The idea of history of philosophy as engaging in conversation with 'the mighty dead' takes on special difficulties – and perhaps a special poignancy – from a female speaking position. The assumption that there is a neutral speaking position that can be occupied by a contemporary gender-neutral philosophical reader, intent on either self-knowledge or a reassuring put-down of the mighty dead, becomes less clear-cut when we think it through in relation to female readers. The work of Irigaray especially has been an important influence on feminist reading strategies which centre on the idea of the feminine as occupying the position of the excluded other of philosophy – a speaking position which, ironically, is located outside discourse. Irigaray describes the strategy in terms of mimicry – an appropriation of the speaking position of the excluded feminine, in order to effect a jamming of the theoretical machinery.[6]

Despite scepticism about the gender neutrality of the speaking positions involved in the 'conversation' of western philosophy, imaginary conversations with the 'mighty dead' can seem more congenial to female philosophers than the challenge of inserting a female voice into the conversation of the living. Many female philosophers, uneasy in the structures of male-dominated professional philosophy, have sought in the history of philosophy a different philosophical agenda – a lost closeness between philosophy and literature, a closer integration of philosophical writing with its cultural context, a more practical orientation towards the social. The balance between past and present is different here. The interest in history of philosophy, for female philosophers, is often motivated not by a desire to legitimate the philosophical problems of 'us' contemporary professional philosophers but, on the contrary, by the desire to establish an alternative conversation.

The point of course is not that things were better in the past for female philosophical thinkers. What is at stake here is not an idealization of the past. Feminist history of philosophy has indeed been largely concerned with critique of the 'male' assumptions of past philosophy. But nor is the point to legitimate philosophy's present. There is a different balance between past and present, reflecting different kinds of operation of the philosophical imagination. Female experience of unease in the modes of conversation prevailing in living philosophy finds expression in a desire to return to the past precisely as a means of engaging with the present. 'Present-centredness' is here not so much a matter of taking back to the past the philosophical agenda of the present as it is a way of opening up present philosophy to a wider agenda.

Martha Nussbaum: the education of Nikidion

To read the history of philosophy as a woman is to confront a succession of ways in which sexual difference has conditioned the accessibility of philosophical ideals, the forms of philosophical education. Thus Martha Nussbaum, in *The Therapy of Desire*, explores the philosophical treatment of emotion in Hellenistic philosophy.[7] Nussbaum's study is sensitive to the relations between philosophical texts and their cultural context. To come up with an adequate account of Hellenistic teachings on the emotions, she stresses, we must 'situate the philosophical doctrines in their historical and cultural contexts, Greek and Roman, attending carefully to the relationships between the pupil's diseases and her society, and between the philosophical cure and existing rhetorical and literary forms'.[8] It is an approach attuned to the character of the philosophical doctrines under discussion – to their rich 'responsiveness to the concrete', which can be obscured if their enterprise is characterized too timelessly and abstractly.

Nussbaum's response to the challenge of situating the texts in their social contexts is a complex exercise which is itself literary as well as philosophical. Throughout the book she imagines the career of a female pupil, a young woman 'perhaps historical and probably fictitious', named in Diogenes Laertius as a pupil of Epicurus. 'Nikidion – for that is the pupil's name – will not retain a fixed historical or social identity across the schools. She will have to be of a social class whose members can be included in philosophizing; and this changes. She will need to move from Greece to Rome, and to change her background beliefs and social status accordingly. In one case at least, she will have to pretend to be a male.'[9]

Nussbaum takes Nikidion through a 'polymorphous search for the good life' in a succession of philosophical schools. She has her disguise herself as a male in order to study ethics with Aristotle, simulating the characteristics and privileges – free time, relative prosperity, competence in poetry and rhetoric, first-hand experience of civic institutions – requisite for that period of Athenian ethical and political instruction. The exercise clarifies the limitations of an Aristotelian philosophical education in its cultural context. What becomes, Nussbaum asks, of those whom Aristotle does not and cannot teach?

> Such as Nikidion, if she takes off her elaborate and impossible disguise? Isn't he so busy perfecting the already blooming ethical and psychological health of privileged young gentlemen that he has nothing to offer to her diseases, to her lack of citizen experience, and the suffering of her excluded state? Looked at this way, isn't this apostle of fine-tuned perception a politically and ethically smug and self-satisfied character?[10]

The answer is not straightforward. The exclusion of an undisguised Nikidion, Nussbaum points out, does not of itself render Aristotle's educational practices irretrievably elitist. But there are limitations in the capacity of an Aristotelian philosophical education to address the needs of those who are not already 'refined and lucky young gentlemen'. To transcend its limitations Nikidion must move on to be instructed in later Hellenistic schools, which are, in their turn, found wanting. Reflecting on her love of transient beauty, she comes to see the limitations of Epicurean attempts to remove the longing for immortality. Nussbaum brings her to Stoic teachers who show her how to confront her lassitudes and confusions with the toughness and energetic activity of good reasoning; and introduces her to the study of Modes and Tropes in the search for equipoise with the Skeptics.

Like Samuel Johnson's Rasselas, Nussbaum's Nikidion conducts a succession of trials, seeking her preferred way of living. But, like Virginia Woolf's Orlando, Nikidion also leaps through history – her consciousness finding embodiment in a succession of cultural contexts. Nikidion enters each school as an as yet uneducated pupil. But the reader, unlike the imaginary Nikidion, must retain on her behalf, to the point of educational overload, the lessons of each educational experiment. Nussbaum's literary device serves to illuminate points of connection between the philosophical schools and the cultural assumptions that frame the education they offer. But, despite its contextualizing role, the fiction of Nikidion has in its very temporal mobility its own peculiar timelessness. In thinking the fiction through we come up against something as yet unresolved – perhaps as yet not even fully articulated as an issue for the rhetorical strategies of history of philosophy. Nikidion is not anchored in any present; and in her lack of a present she serves to highlight a methodological problem with which history of philosophy must come to terms: how are we to bring into manageable and fruitful relationship the present-ness of the reader and the pastness of the text? What models might we invoke for anchoring the critique of past philosophy in a firm sense of the changing present?

Engagement with the present

To understand the motivation of feminist history of philosophy, and its potential to enrich the study of philosophical texts, we must look to different configurations of past-centred and present-centred approaches from those highlighted in Rorty's analysis of the prevailing genres of history of philosophy. We need to articulate here a different kind of preoccupation with the present from that involved in the current 'problems' of modern professional philosophy. Here there are useful insights to be found in the readings offered by Michel Foucault and Jürgen Habermas of Kant's political essays.[11] Although Foucault and Habermas, in their debate on Kant's 'What is Enlightenment?', position themselves differently with regard to the continuation of the ideals of enlightenment reason, both take from Kant's essay a model of philosophy as involving political engagement with a unique present.

Foucault finds in Kant's 'What is Enlightenment?' a model for 'critique' as critical response to the historical moment. The present, as object of philosophical reflection, is here something more than the enactment of a distinguishable era of the world, or the heralding signs of a future event. The present is not just the point of transition, to be judged in relation to a future achievement. The question is rather: 'what difference does today introduce with respect to yesterday?'.[12] For Kant this 'philosophical question of the present day' involves movement into the process of enlightenment, the coming to maturity of autonomous reason. It amounts to the same thing as the emergence of a 'public' use of reason – the space of critique. By reflecting on enlightenment, Kant instigates a 'critical interrogation on the present and on ourselves'.[13]

The knowing, reflecting subject takes on a new significance in this philosophical engagement with the present. Kant, on Foucault's reading, poses 'the question of the present as a philosophical event incorporating within it the philosopher who speaks of it'.[14] The problematizing of the present as a 'philosophical event' incorporates a problematization of philosophers themselves. Adherence to the present is here no longer a question of adherence to a doctrine or tradition: 'It will no longer even simply be the question of his belonging to a human community in general, but rather that of his membership of a certain "we", a we corresponding to a cultural ensemble characteristic of his own contemporaneity.'[15] Foucault finds here a model for 'a critical ontology of ourselves' – not as an accumulating body of knowledge, but as 'an attitude, an ethos, a philosophical life in which the critique of what we are is at one and the same time the historical analysis of the limits that are imposed on us and an experiment with the possibility of going beyond them'.[16]

> The philosopher's own singular state of adherence to this 'we' now begins to become an indispensable theme of reflection for the philosopher himself. Philosophy as the problematization of a present-ness, the interrogation by philosophy of this present-ness of which it is part and relative to which it is obliged to locate itself: this may well be the characteristic trait of philosophy as a discourse of and upon modernity.[17]

The substance of this new interrogation of modernity is in the questions: What is my present? What is the meaning of this present? And what am I doing when I speak of the present?[18] The philosopher, rather than aligning himself timelessly with all other philosophical minds, is challenged to self-consciously position himself at his own historical moment – bringing to his philosophizing the distinctive concerns of his time.

As Habermas sums up Foucault's reading of Kant, 'Foucault discovers Kant as the first philosopher, an archer who aims his arrow at the heart of the most actual features of the present and so opens the discourse of modernity.'[19] The resistance to a universal nature, in favour of a multiplicity of 'we's is one of the issues that divides Foucault and Habermas. And Foucault's insistence on multiplicity is one of the themes which makes his appropriation of Kant's sense of 'the present' relevant to feminist repudiation of 'universal' and hence gender-neutral subjects and speaking positions. But what is more important here is the relevance for feminist history of philosophy of Foucault's stress on present contingencies as a proper focus of philosophical concern. What Foucault takes from Kant is an engagement with the present which is seen as itself philosophical – a form of reflection on ourselves as part of a unique present. For the content of 'the present' here is not confined to whatever happens to make the current agenda of professional philosophy; it encompasses the pressing social and political issues which distinguish this time from others. It is this broader, more politically oriented, way of thinking of the present that gives content to the idea of feminist history of philosophy as interrogating philosophical texts from the perspective of the present.

To clarify this convergence of the philosophical and the political in history of philosophy I want now to turn to another modern reading of Kant – one which shares some common themes with the Foucault–Habermas debate on 'What is Enlightenment?' – Hannah Arendt's *Lectures on Kant's Political Philosophy*. Foucault and Habermas take from Kant's political writings a model of philosophy as engagement with the present. Although they take that idea of philosophy from Kant, it is not for them particularly connected with the scholarly activity of history of philosophy. In Arendt's reading of Kant we find a strategy more directly related to the activity of history of philosophy. Her reconstruction of a Kantian political philosophy brings together close textual reading and a philosophical engagement with the present. Arendt reads Kant from a perspective of concern with her own present. In the process, both the past text and the present issues are mutually illuminated.

Hannah Arendt: Kant on judgement

Arendt's Lectures reflect a concern with issues of judgement arising from the political realities of her own present – issues of responsibility which she addresses also in other writings. She insists on the importance of passing judgement – on the importance of not suspending that crucial prerogative of the human mind, even under conditions of uncertainty and incomprehension. Particular themes in Kant's philosophy take on salience from this perspective. But it is not as if there was a pre-existing Kantian political philosophy waiting to be summoned from the past to answer to present needs. Arendt reconstructs the basis for a political philosophy which Kant did not himself produce. The lectures construct, as she puts it, 'a Kantian topic that, literally speaking, is non-existent – his non-written political philosophy'.

Why bother? Why, we might ask, should Arendt make this detour through Kant when she might simply respond philosophically to her own present? We can see in these lectures some affinities with Habermas's desire to continue the narrative of the enlightenment – a desire to make reassuring connection with old ideals that are not manifestly operative in the troubled present. But there is also something else going on. Arendt engages with the present by thinking with Kant. This is an exercise in collaborative thinking. Arendt is continuing a process of thought whose beginnings she finds in Kant. Her Lectures are an exercise in remembering philosophical resources and extending them by putting them to new uses, in response to circumstances which call them forth. Arendt interrogates the present with concepts formulated by Kant. It is in this middle zone between past and present that historically informed philosophical thinking goes on. By thinking with Kant, Arendt both responds to her present and gives determinate content to what is not fully expressed in the texts themselves. By thinking with Kant, she does not simply repeat something already done. In responding to her own present, she brings to our attention things in the texts that might not otherwise be visible – things that might not otherwise be fully thought. Let us look more closely at the reading.

Like Foucault and Habermas, Arendt stresses the nexus in Kant's essays between the philosophical and the political. The nexus, here again, centres on a new way of thinking of the relations between past, present and future. 'Kant', she says, 'is never interested in the past; what interests him is the future of the species'.[20] The sociability of mind is paramount here. It finds its expression in the unfolding of human powers of reason in the species over time as well as in the incorporation of the individual into wider collectivities. This is Arendt's version of Kant's talk of the 'public' use of reason. The sociable dimensions of the mind find expression in judgement, here construed as a fundamentally political mode of thinking. On Arendt's reading, Kant's third *Critique* is concerned with the political aspects of judgement no less than with its aesthetic aspects. Judgement is the faculty through which the mind deals with the particular; and particularity, whether in relation to a fact of nature or an event in history, is crucial to the political. Human sociability is the condition of the functioning of this faculty of judgement: human beings are dependent on one another, 'not only because of their having a body and physical needs but precisely for their mental faculties'.

Arendt's reading highlights the political dimensions of philosophy and the philosophical dimensions of politics. Judgement is the point of connection between the aesthetic and the political; and the force of imagination is crucial to her reconstruction of Kantian judgement. Imagination makes other minds present, 'enlarging' the thought of the solitary thinker. The link is through the idea of the spectator: this form of judgement belongs not with 'practical reason' but with contemplation. It is associated with 'contemplative pleasure', or 'inactive delight'. Kant's insights into aesthetic and reflective judgement, Arendt points out, have no practical consequences for action. They are concerned rather with the judge as spectator, as contemplative observer. The 'disinterested concern' of the onlooker allows him or her to read the significance of events. The 'pure onlooker – who does not act and relies entirely on what he sees' can discover in the course taken by events a meaning which the actors ignored.[21]

Kant articulates the discovery of meaning in terms of providence. The spectator, because he is not involved, can perceive the design of providence or nature, which is hidden from the actor. But this idea does not have to take a teleological form. The idea that it is 'only the spectator but never the actor' that 'knows what it is all about' is, Arendt reminds us, among the oldest, most decisive notions of philosophy. 'The whole idea of the superiority of the contemplative way of life comes from this early insight that meaning (or truth) is revealed only to those who restrain themselves from acting.' Arendt expresses the point through the parable ascribed to Pythagoras: 'Life . . . is like a festival; just as some come to the festival to compete, some to ply their trade, but the best people come as spectators, so in life the slavish men go hunting for fame or gain, the philosophers for truth.'[22] The notion of 'judgement' is here brought together with the ancient ideal of philosophical contemplation. In Arendt's reading of Kant, the emerging public realm of reason is the realm of the 'critics' and the 'spectators', not the 'actors' and 'makers'.[23]

Arendt looks to Kant then for a concept of imagination which will bring together the contemplative and the political.[24] The role of imagination for our cognitive faculties, she suggests, is perhaps the greatest discovery Kant made in the *Critique of Pure Reason*. Imagination, the faculty of making present to the mind what is absent from sense perception, is here not merely a passive capacity for remembering the traces of former perception but an active faculty, talked of from the beginnings of philosophy – 'that faculty through which you look steadfastly at things which are present though they are absent'. In the *Critique of Pure Reason*, Arendt notes, this faculty is at the service of intellect; in the *Critique of Judgement*, in contrast, the intellect is at the service of the imagination. The role of imagination, however, is similar in both works – bringing the particular and the general together, whether by allowing the general concept to acquire determinate content, as in the 'schemata' of the first *Critique*, or by finding examples to lead and guide judgement, as in the third *Critique*.

Arendt's reading of Kant's versions of imagination and judgement stresses the importance of 'examples'. The right choice of examples gives judgement 'exemplary validity'. So, in evaluating an act as courageous, if one were a Greek, one would have in the depths of one's mind the example of Achilles. Imagination is crucial here: one must have Achilles present even though he certainly is absent. But the exercise of imagination is crucial also in another way. The judgement has exemplary validity to the extent that the example is rightly chosen. In the context of French history, we can talk about Napoleon Bonaparte as a particular man: but when we speak about Bonapartism we have made an example of him. The validity of this example will be restricted to those who possess the particular experience of Napoleon, either as his contemporaries or as the heirs to this particular historical tradition. The example has its origin in some particular historical incident, and we then proceed to make it 'exemplary' – to see in the particular what is valid for more than one case.

I have gone into some detail in expounding Arendt's reading of Kant, even though Arendt does not present it as 'feminist' history of philosophy. For both in their content and in their approach to past texts, these lectures open up space within which it is possible to locate the kinds of critique of the philosophical tradition in which self-avowedly 'feminist' scholars have engaged. Feminist history of philosophy has often been taken as a repudiation of traditional ideals of reason. But much of it in fact operates as critique of past operations of the philosophical imagination. The point is not to repudiate intellectual ideals of reason but to make visible the operations of imagination which have sought in the feminine 'examples' of the non-rational. The role of the Kantian 'onlooker' and the role of imagination come together in the 'gaze' of Arendt's judging spectator. Feminist history of philosophy can be seen as directing such a gaze on the philosophical tradition itself – a gaze focused on the interface between philosophical inquiry and its cultural context, where the philosophical imagination chooses its 'validating examples'.

Many of the images and metaphors philosophers have used to articulate philosophical positions are not superficial illustrations which can be readily shed. They have been constitutive of discourses of the normalizing masculine and of the excluded feminine. Feminist critique may appear to be predominantly negative in its concern with disrupting the continuities, unsettling the reassuring narrative unities of the heritage of the ideals of enlightenment reason. But the deconstructive critique of the operations of the philosophical imagination are constructive as well as destructive – exercises in continuing more constructively the work of past philosophers as well as in castigating them. Some of the most illuminating insights here into what is involved in seeing history of philosophy as continuation of the 'work' of past philosophers have come from the work of Michèle Le Dœuff.

Michèle Le Dœuff: critique of the philosophical imaginary

In a brief but illuminating discussion of the methodological dimensions of history of philosophy, in *Hipparchia's Choice*,[25] Le Dœuff distinguishes between two ways of thinking of the relations between philosophy and history of philosophy. On the first, the guiding assumption is that authors know what they are saying, and the task of the historian of philosophy is to uncover that transparent connection between the text and the originary thought it expresses. On the second – which corresponds to some aspects of Le Dœuff's own earlier work – there is 'an immense unthought element' in philosophy; and the task of history of philosophy as a discipline is seen as reconnecting texts to what lies outside them. The exegete, unlike the author, is able to link the work to its 'outside'. In Le Dœuff's earlier work, *The Philosophical Imaginary*, this challenge is met through attention to the imagery and metaphors operating in the text – the more literary aspects of philosophical writing which are often dismissed as irrelevant to philo-sophical content. The imagery points to difficulties internal to the philo-sophical enterprise; its critique involves a serious philosophical engagement – uncovering the sensitive points of tension in the text where a meaning is sustained that is inconsistent with the work's explicit possibilities.

Le Dœuff's explorations of the 'philosophical imaginary' have been a strong influence on the emerging patterns of feminist history of philosophy. But Le Dœuff, in her most recent work, has shifted her emphasis to something else which is equally important. In *Hipparchia's Choice* she talks of an approach to the reading of texts in which neither author nor reader is construed as in a superior position. Here the ideal is that of a 'dynamic' in which philosophy and history of philosophy – construed as intellectual activity, rather than the repository of past thought – lead to and from each other. Philosophy is construed as the effort to 'shift thinking' – to move our patterns of thought from one configuration to another.

In Le Dœuff's earlier work the reader's present takes on a privileged position as the perspective from which it is possible to make the connec-tions between the 'inside' and the 'outside' of the text – the position from which it is possible to perceive tensions not accessible to the author. In the later approach, the shift to the present takes a different form: history of philosophy becomes an active continuation of the thought of past philosophers. There are similarities between Le Dœuff's rather elusive remarks here about continuing the 'work' of philosophy and some comments on history of philosophy in Deleuze's and Guattari's *What is Philosophy?*: 'If one can still be a Platonist, Cartesian, or Kantian today it is because one is justified in thinking that their concepts can be reactivated in our problems and inspire those concepts that need to be created. What is the best way to follow the great philosophers? Is it to repeat what they said or *to do what they did*, that is, create concepts for problems that necessarily change?'[26]

The activity of history of philosophy, as it is presented in Le Dœuff's later work, involves a collaborative positioning of the commentator in relation to the author. The kind of reading of texts envisaged here, like the earlier focus on imagery, opens philosophy out to concerns that cannot be circumscribed by what authors think they are about. But the text is now opened out not just to its own cultural context but to the independent concerns of the contemporary reader herself. The difference between the two approaches is one of emphasis. What becomes salient in the exploration of textual imagery, in the first approach, will reflect the operations of the reader's imagination in its present context. But the shift is an important one. History of philosophy becomes a collaborative effort – re-thinking past philosophical thought in a new context.

Le Dœuff's work has helped open up space in which philosophy can participate in the broader critique of the prevailing 'social imaginary' – critique of the guiding fictions of a living culture, reshaping, re-figuring the concepts through which we make sense of ourselves. The focus on metaphor and imagery has proved a very fruitful way of opening up texts to their cultural contexts, forging new unities between the past of texts and the present of their modern readers. History of philosophy becomes a positive continuation of philosophy as the ongoing constructive development of concepts in response to a changing social world. Issues of sexual difference have been prominent in this re-thinking of the relations between philosophy and its past. Feminist philosophers have looked to the past of philosophy to gain insight into the symbolism of the organization of sexual difference.

What restraints are there on this 'continuation' of past philosophy into a present not its own – on examining the upshot of a text in a context differing from its original setting? Feminist history of philosophy has been criticized as producing 'parodies' of the history of philosophy. Such criticism can rest on a mistaken view of the nature of the exercise. But if the criticism is to be avoided, it is crucial to give as clear articulation as possible to what the legitimate forms of the exercise are and what counts as doing it well. I want now to address some of the difficulties that arise in feminist philosophers' attempts to read texts of the past from the perspective of the present.

Doxography and demonizing

The challenge of articulating the insights of feminist critique of traditional philosophy arises partly from the general lack of methodological awareness in the practices of history of philosophy. In the space I have mapped out for feminist history of philosophy, concern with situating texts in their cultural context comes together with construing history of philosophy as a way of engaging with one's own present. There is nothing in principle impossible about this conjunction. Attention to authorial context and engagement with the present reinforce one another. But it is not surprising that the conjunction should prove an obstacle in the reception of feminist history of philosophy. For it belongs on neither side of the distinction between 'past-centred' and 'present-centred' approaches around which history of philosophy – to the extent that it has been self-reflective – has tended to articulate its methodological possibilities.

The emerging practices of feminist history of philosophy have been readily perceived as over-simplified demonizing of past philosophy.[27] But, as Susan Bordo comments in the Introduction to her edited collection *Feminist Interpretations of Descartes*,[28] it is often the upshot of a philosophy in its social context that is the real target of feminist critique – the dominant cultural and historical renderings, for example, of 'Cartesianism', rather than Descartes himself. Among the important ways in which feminist criticism has altered philosophy, she says, 'is by exposing the lifelessness of that mode of doing philosophy which abstracts arguments from philosophical texts and reads them as a timeless conversation among talking heads'. The point here coincides partly with Rorty's characterization of the assumptions of 'timelessness' implicit in present-centred 'rational constructions'. But what gives rise to most misunderstanding is the concern of feminist history of philosophy with what Bordo calls 'the upshot' of philosophical systems – their meaning and impact in these culturally situated contexts; and this concern with 'upshot' is easily misunderstood. As Bordo says, the point of feminist criticism has often been to reveal what dominant models have *excluded* rather than to attack what they have *offered*. But because of the lack of understanding of textual reading strategies which attempted to bring into focus the operations of imagination in philosophical texts, feminist discussions of the 'maleness' of reason have been taken as 'demonizations' of past philosophers and even as a repudiation of reason itself.[29]

Where its practitioners see a diverse range of reading strategies, converging on an interrogation of the supposed gender neutrality of philosophical writing, the critics of feminist history of philosophy frequently see a uniformly hostile repudiation of an allegedly misogynist tradition. Feminist history of philosophy, when it is pursued without self-reflection, can indeed fall into the category which Rorty calls 'doxography'. 'Doxography', in Rorty's classification, is the most familiar and dubious genre of history of philosophy, exemplified by books which 'start from Thales or Descartes and wind up with some figure roughly contemporary with the author, ticking off what various figures traditionally called "philosophers" had to say about problems called "philosophical"'. Such history of philosophy, he complains, induces boredom and despair; it should be allowed to wither away. The analogue of 'doxography' for feminist history of philosophy is the catalogue of misogynist views reaching from ancient philosophy to contemporary sexism – the histories of successive male denigrations and suppressions of the feminine.

What appears to be feminist 'demonizing' may, at least sometimes, be better seen as an engagement in the exercise of imagination which Arendt highlights in her reading of Kant – the identification of validating 'examples'. The 'examples' – of dichotomous mind–body oppositions, of oppressive models of domination of nature, of the distrust of emotion – may be not always well chosen. And even where they are well chosen, there may be some over-simplification, just as taking Achilles as an 'example' of courage may involve a simplification of a complex story. The validating force of the 'example' resides in its power of resonance in the consciousness of those for whom the example works. Philosophers' examples of the feminine have had that resonating validation. And feminist critique of 'Cartesianism' may sometimes be better seen as an opposed exercise of the philosophical imagination than as a scholarly analysis of explicit intellectual content. Feminist critique makes visible both the operation of the philosophical imagination in past choices of 'validating examples' of the non-rational associated with the feminine and the cultural effects of those choices.

There must, however, be some restraints on reading philosophical texts as illustrative of male imaginaries. 'Exemplary validity' depends on the exercise of philosophically informed judgement. Feminist history of philosophy must be prepared to balance imaginative interpretation of cultural meanings with painstaking close reading of texts in the context of their own philosophical concerns. Constructive criticism of feminist history of philosophy may also need to acknowledge that it is not always possible to do all things at once.

The wide range of reading strategies now available to feminist philosophers makes it easier to avoid the 'boredom and despair' of 'doxographic' or 'demonizing' varieties of feminist critique. It also demands of feminist history of philosophy an increased responsibility to be methodologically self-reflective about its own practices. The demands of feminist critique can be in tension with other legitimate demands for philosophically informed commentary. But these tensions can be fruitful; they reflect a growing complexity of identity which is part of the unique present of feminist history of philosophy.

Conclusion: 'we' feminists

Some of the most useful models for 'thinking with' past philosophers as a scholarly activity come from work which has not been produced in the name of feminist history of philosophy. Arendt's reconstruction of a

Kantian political philosophy does not present itself as 'feminist'. Nor does Amélie Rorty's imaginative exploration of the bearing of Spinoza's account of love on understanding the poignant twists and reversals in the familiar patterns of contemporary relationships.[30] In Annette Baier's fine work on Hume, explicit consideration of feminist issues shades subtly into a direct engagement with, and continuation of Hume's work, which resists any clear-cut classification as feminist.[31] So does the current explosion of first-rate readings of Kantian ethics by female philosophers.[32]

Concern with issues of sexual difference interweave with other political concerns in current writing by women on history of philosophy; and political engagement with the present interweaves also with more narrowly defined philosophical interests. Baier is as much concerned with articulating an enriched Humean version of reason as she is with explicitly appropriating Hume as a proto-feminist. And the new readings of Kantian ethics are as much concerned with formulating viable approaches to moral reasoning, taking emotion seriously, as with either attacking or defending Kant from feminist perspectives. Insights drawn from feminist theory and from practical feminism can be discerned in much of this philosophical commentary produced by women. The feminism is here more diffused than it was in earlier feminist critique. But perhaps this should be seen not as a dilution but rather as a coming to maturity. What is most needed now is not the demarcation of a distinctive feminist methodology but rather a continuing contribution to developing imaginative forms of history of philosophy as modes of serious engagement with the present. The motivation may come from feminism; but that need not mean that the outcome is distinctively feminist.

The lack of fixed identity of feminist history of philosophy is, I suggest, to be welcomed rather than bemoaned. For in its very fluidity it reflects one of the most challenging features of 'our' present – an ever-increasing diversity which is experienced as an inner multiplicity of identity.[33] The early challenge faced by feminist history of philosophy was to give visibility to the excluded feminine. The new challenge is to keep that visibility without being limited – perhaps diminished – by too insistent an identification with feminist perspectives. 'We feminist philosophers' are not the bearers of clearly bordered identities occupying stable 'speaking positions'. We are shifting subjects, taking on multiple identities.

Feminist philosophy is not insulated from the multiplicity of identity that is a feature of our present. If we are serious about engagement with that present, we cannot afford to let the identity of 'feminist philosopher' settle into a defensive posture of opposition to the undoubtedly 'male' past of philosophy. The challenge is to define and refine the strategies for thinking our way into that past – understanding better its processes of exclusion and constitution; appropriating and conciliating its intellectual possibilities, in the hope that by making ourselves more at home in it we can carry philosophical thought on into a more inclusive future.

NOTES

1 See especially Luce Irigaray, *Speculum of the Other Woman*, trans. Gillian T. Gill (Ithaca, NY: Cornell University Press, 1985) and *This Sex Which Is Not One*, trans. C. Porter with C. Burke (Ithaca, NY: Cornell University Press, 1985). For a useful discussion of Irigaray's work in relation to the critique of ideals of reason, see Margaret Whitford, 'Luce Irigaray's Critique of Rationality', in M. Griffiths and M. Whitford, eds., *Feminist Perspectives in Philosophy* (London: Macmillan, 1988), pp. 109–30.

2 See, especially, Michèle Le Dœuff, *The Philosophical Imaginary*, trans. Colin Gordon (Oxford: Blackwell, 1989).

3 Richard Rorty, 'The Historiography of Philosophy: Four Genres', in Richard Rorty, J. B. Schneewind and Quentin Skinner, eds., *Philosophy in History* (Cambridge: Cambridge University Press, 1984), pp. 49–76.

4 Quentin Skinner, 'Meaning and Understanding in the History of Ideas', *History and Theory* 8 (1969), 3–53.

5 Rorty, 'The Historiography', p. 51.

6 For a fuller discussion of this aspect of Irigaray's reading strategies, see Genevieve Lloyd, 'Maleness, Metaphor and the "Crisis" of Reason', in Louise M. Antony and Charlotte Witt, eds., *A Mind of One's Own: Feminist Essays on Reason and Objectivity* (Boulder, CO: Westview Press, 1993), pp. 69–83.

7 Martha C. Nussbaum, *The Therapy of Desire: Theory and Practice in Hellenistic Ethics* (Princeton, NJ: Princeton University Press, 1994).

8 Ibid., p. 44.

9 Ibid., p. 45.

10 Ibid., p. 77.

11 See especially Michel Foucault, 'What is Enlightenment?', in P. Rabinow, ed., *Foucault Reader* (New York: Pantheon Books, 1984), pp. 32–50; 'Kant on Enlightenment and Revolution', trans. C. Gordon, *Economy and Society* 15:1 (1986), 88–96; 'What is Critique?', in James Schmidt, ed., *What Is Enlightenment?* (Berkeley: University of California Press, 1996), pp. 382–98; and Jürgen Habermas, 'Taking Aim at the Heart of the Present', in D. Hoy, ed., *Foucault: A Critical Reader* (Oxford: Blackwell, 1986), pp. 103–8. For a useful discussion of the issues at stake in the Foucault–Habermas debate, see H. L. Dreyfus and P. Rabinow, 'What is Maturity?: Habermas and Foucault on "What is Enlightenment?"', in D. Hoy, ed., *Foucault: A Critical Reader* (Oxford: Blackwell, 1986), pp. 109–21.

12 Foucault, 'What Is Enlightenment?', p. 34.

13 Ibid., pp. 49–50.

14 Foucault, 'Kant on Enlightenment and Revolution', p. 89.

15 Ibid., p.89.

16 Foucault, 'What Is Enlightenment?', p. 50.

17 Foucault, 'Kant on Enlightenment and Revolution', p. 89.

18 Ibid., p. 90.
19 Habermas, 'Taking Aim at the Heart of the Present', p. 105.
20 Hannah Arendt, *Lectures on Kant's Political Philosophy*, ed. Ronald Beiner (Chicago: University of Chicago Press, 1982), p. 8.
21 Ibid., pp. 52–4.
22 Ibid., p. 55.
23 Ibid., p. 63.
24 'Imagination', Seminar on Kant's *Critique of Judgment*, in R. Beiner, ed., *Hannah Arendt: Lectures on Kant's Political Philosophy* (Chicago: University of Chicago Press, 1982), pp. 79–85.
25 Michèle Le Dœuff, *Hipparchia's Choice: An Essay Concerning Women, Philosophy, etc.* (Oxford: Blackwell, 1991), pp. 166–70.
26 Gilles Deleuze and Felix Guattari, *What is Philosophy?* (New York: Columbia University Press, 1991), p. 28.
27 For a useful discussion of this kind of criticism of feminist history of philosophy see the introduction to Susan James, *Passion and Action: The Emotions in Seventeenth-Century Philosophy* (Oxford: Clarendon Press, 1997), pp. 17–20.
28 Susan Bordo, ed., *Feminist Interpretations of Descartes* (Pennsylvania State University Press, forthcoming).
29 For some reflections on the reception of my own early attempts to articulate the maleness of reason in the history of philosophy, see the Introduction to the second edition of my *The Man of Reason* (London: Routledge, 1993) and 'Maleness, Metaphor and the "Crisis" of Reason', in Louise M. Antony and Charlotte Witt, eds., *A Mind of One's Own: Feminist Essays on Reason and Objectivity* (Boulder, CO: Westview Press, 1993), pp. 69–84.
30 Amélie Oksenberg Rorty, 'Spinoza on the Pathos of Idolatrous Love and the Hilarity of True Love', in R. C. Solomon and K. M. Higgins, eds., *The Philosophy of (Erotic) Love* (Lawrence: University Press of Kansas, 1991).
31 Annette Baier, 'Hume, the Women's Moral Theorist', in Eva Feder Kittay and Diana T. Meyers, eds., *Women and Moral Theory* (Totowa, NJ: Rowman & Littlefield, 1987); 'Hume: The Reflective Women's Epistemologist?', in Antony and Witt, eds., *A Mind of One's Own*, pp. 35–48; *A Progress of Sentiments* (Cambridge, MA: Harvard University Press, 1991).
32 Among others, Onora O'Neill, *Constructions of Reason* (Cambridge: Cambridge University Press, 1989); Barbara Herman, *The Practice of Moral Judgment* (Cambridge, MA: Harvard University Press, 1993); Nancy Sherman, *Making A Necessity of Virtue: Aristotle and Kant on Virtue* (Cambridge: Cambridge University Press, 1997).
33 For an illuminating discussion of multiplicity of identity under conditions of cultural diversity, see James Tully, *Strange Multiplicity: Constitutionalism in an Age of Diversity* (Cambridge: Cambridge University Press, 1995).

FURTHER READING

FEMINISM IN ANCIENT PHILOSOPHY

Bar On, B., ed. *Engendering Origins: Critical Feminist Readings in Plato and Aristotle*. Albany: SUNY Press, 1994.

Bluestone, N. H. *Women and the Ideal Society: Plato's Republic and Modern Myths of Gender*. Amherst: University of Massachusetts Press, 1987.

Cavarero, A. *In Spite of Plato: A Feminist Rewriting of Ancient Philosophy*, trans. S. Anderlini-D'Onofrio and Á. O'Healy. Cambridge: Polity Press, 1995.

DuBois, P. *Sowing the Body: Psychoanalysis and Ancient Representations of Women*. Chicago: University of Chicago Press, 1988.

Freeland, C. A., ed. *Feminist Interpretations of Aristotle*. University Park, PA: Pennsylvania State University Press, 1998.

Lloyd, G. *The Man of Reason: 'Male' and 'Female' in Western Philosophy*. London: Methuen, 1984.

Okin, S. M. *Women in Western Political Thought*. Princeton: Princeton University Press, 1979.

Saxonhouse, A. *Fear of Diversity: The Birth of Political Science in Ancient Greek Thought*. Chicago: University of Chicago Press, 1992.

Tuana, N., ed. *Feminist Interpretations of Plato'*. University Park, PA: Pennsylvania State University Press, 1994.

Waithe, M. E., ed. *A History of Women Philosophers*, Vol. 1: *Ancient Women Philosophers 600 BC–500 AD*. Dordrecht: Kluwer, 1987.

Ward, J. K., ed. *Feminism and Ancient Philosophy*. London: Routledge, 1996.

FEMINISM IN PHILOSOPHY OF MIND

Baier, Annette. *Postures of the Mind*. London: Methuen, 1985.

Bartky, Sandra Lee. 'Shame and Gender', in *Femininity and Domination: Studies in the Phenomenology of Oppression*. London: Routledge, 1990, pp. 83–98.

Battersby, Christine. *The Phenomenal Woman*. Cambridge: Polity Press, 1998.

Beauvoir, Simone de. *The Second Sex*, trans. and ed. H. M. Parshley. Harmondsworth: Penguin Books, 1972.

Braidotti, Rosi. *Patterns of Dissonance*. Cambridge: Polity Press, 1991.
  Nomadic Subjects. New York: Columbia University Press, 1994.

Brennan, Teresa. *The Interpretation of the Flesh: Freud and Femininity*. London: Routledge, 1992.

Brison, Susan J. 'Outliving Oneself: Trauma, Memory and Personal Identity', in Meyers, ed. *Feminists Rethink the Self*, pp. 12–39.

Butler, Judith. 'Sexual Ideology and Phenomenological Description: A Feminist Critique of Merleau-Ponty's *Phenomenology of Perception*', in Jeffner Allen and Iris Marion Young, eds. *The Thinking Muse: Feminism and Modern French Philosophy*. Bloomington: Indiana University Press, 1989, pp. 85–100.

Bodies that Matter: On the Discursive Limits of Sex. London: Routledge, 1993.

Gender Trouble: Feminism and the Subversion of Identity. London: Routledge, 1990.

Campbell, Sue. 'Women, "False Memory" and Personal Identity', *Hypatia* 12:2 (1997), 51–62.

Interpreting the Personal: Expression and the Formation of Feelings. Ithaca: Cornell University Press, 1997.

Chanter, Tina. *Ethics of Eros: Irigaray's Rewriting of the Philosophers*. London: Routledge, 1995.

Deutscher, Penelope. *Yielding Gender: Feminism, Deconstruction and the History of Philosophy*. London: Routledge, 1997.

Fox Keller, Evelyn. 'Gender and Science: An Update', in *Secrets of Life, Secrets of Death: Essays on Language, Gender and Science*. London: Routledge, 1992, pp. 15–36.

Reflections on Gender and Science. New Haven: Yale University Press, 1985.

Gatens, Moira. *Imaginary Bodies*. London: Routledge, 1996.

Grosz, Elizabeth. *Volatile Bodies*. Bloomington: Indiana University Press, 1994.

Irigaray, Luce. *An Ethics of Sexual Difference*, trans. Carolyn Burke and Gillian C. Gill. Ithaca: Cornell University Press, 1985.

Jaggar, Alison. 'Love and Knowledge: Emotion in Feminist Epistemology', in A. Garry and M. Pearsall, eds. *Women, Knowledge and Reality: Explorations in Feminist Philosophy*, 2nd edition. London: Routledge, 1996, pp. 166–90.

Le Dœuff, Michèle. *The Philosophical Imaginary*. London: Athlone, 1980.

Lloyd, Genevieve. *The Man of Reason: 'Male' and 'Female' in Western Philosophy*. London: Methuen, 1984.

'Maleness, Metaphor and the "Crisis" of Reason', in Louise M. Antony and Charlotte Witt, eds. *A Mind of One's Own. Feminist Essays on Reason and Objectivity*. Boulder, CO: Westview Press, 1993, pp. 69–83.

Lugones, M. 'Playfulness, "World"-Travelling, and Loving Perception', *Hypatia* 2 (1987), 3–19.

'Hard-to-Handle Anger', in L. A. Bell and D. Blumenfeld, eds. *Overcoming Racism and Sexism*. Lanham, MD: Rowman & Littlefield, 1995, pp. 203–17.

Merchant, Carolyn. *The Death of Nature: Women, Ecology and the Scientific Revolution*. San Francisco: Harper & Row, 1980; London: Wildwood House, 1980.

Meyers, D. Tietjens, ed. *Feminists Rethink the Self*. Boulder, CO: Westview Press, 1996.

Moi, Toril. *Simone de Beauvoir: The Making of an Intellectual Woman*. Oxford: Blackwell, 1994.

Oakley, Ann. *Sex, Gender and Society*. London: Temple Smith, 1972.

Scheman, Naomi. *Engenderings: Constructions of Knowledge, Authority and Privilege*. London and New York: Routledge, 1993.

'Feeling Our Way Toward Moral Objectivity', in A. Clark, M. Friedman and L. May, eds. *Mind and Morals*. Cambridge, MA: MIT Press, 1995, pp. 222–36.

Spelman, Elizabeth. 'Woman as Body: Ancient and Contemporary Views', *Feminist Studies* 8:1 (1982), 109–31.

'Anger and Insubordination', in A. Garry and M. Pearsall, eds. *Women, Knowledge and Reality: Explorations in Feminist Philosophy*, 1st edition, London: Routledge, 1996, pp. 263–73.

Sullivan, Sharon. 'Domination and Dialogue in Merleau-Ponty's *Phenomenology of Perception*', *Hypatia* 12:1 (1997), 1–19.

Young, Iris Marion. 'Throwing like a Girl: A Phenomenology of Feminine Body Comportment, Motility, and Spatiality', in *Throwing Like a Girl and Other Essays in Feminist Philosophy and Social Theory*. Bloomington: Indiana University Press, 1990, pp. 141–59.

FEMINISM AND PSYCHOANALYSIS

Psychoanalysis and feminist theory

Benjamin, J. *The Bonds of Love*. London: Virago Press, 1990.

Brennan, T. *Between Feminism and Psychoanalysis*. London: Routledge, 1989.

Chodorow, N. *The Reproduction of Mothering*. Berkeley: University of California Press, 1978.

Dinnerstein, D. *The Mermaid and the Minotaur*. New York: Harper and Row, 1976.

Mitchell, J. *Psychoanalysis and Feminism*. Harmondsworth: Penguin, 1974.

Sayers, J. *Mothering Psychoanalysis. Helene Deutsch, Karen Horney, Anna Freud and Melanie Klein*. London: Hamish Hamilton, 1992.

Lacanian feminism

Gallop, J. *Feminism and Psychoanalysis*. London: Macmillan, 1982.

Grosz, E. *Jacques Lacan: A Feminist Introduction*. London: Routledge, 1990.

Mitchell J. and J. Rose, eds. *Feminine Sexuality. Jacques Lacan and L'Ecole Freudienne*. London: Macmillan, 1982.

'French' psychoanalytical feminism: Irigaray and Kristeva

Irigaray, L. *The Irigaray Reader*, ed. M. Whitford. Oxford: Blackwell, 1991.

Kristeva, J. *The Kristeva Reader*, ed. T. Moi. Oxford: Blackwell, 1986.

The Portable Kristeva, ed. K. Oliver. New York: Columbia University Press, 1997.

Whitford, M. *Luce Irigaray. Philosophy in the Feminine*. London: Routledge, 1991.

FEMINISM IN PHILOSOPHY OF LANGUAGE

Collections

The following have parts containing relevant readings:

Feminism and Philosophy, eds. Mary Vetterling-Braggin, Frederick A. Elliston and Jane English (Totowa, NJ: Rowman & Allanhead, 1977). Part 3 'Sexism and

Ordinary Language' has an 'Introduction' and articles by Grim, Beardsley, Moulton, Korsmeyer and Valian.

Women's Studies: A Reader, eds. Stevi Jackson et al. (Hertfordshire: Harvester Wheatsheaf, 1993). Part 12 'Language and Gender', edited and introduced by Karen Anderson, contains feminist articles relating to 'female deficit theory'.

The Problem of Pornography, ed. Susan Dwyer (Montreal: Wadsworth, 1995). Part 4 'Pornography and Speech Acts' contains an 'Introduction' and articles by Langton (reprinted from *Philosophy and Public Affairs* 22:4 (1993), 293–330), and Hornsby (reprinted from *Women's Philosophy Review* [issue 10] Nov. 1993, 38–45).

The following special issue is devoted to feminist philosophy of language:

Hypatia: A Journal of Feminist Philosophy 7:2 (Spring 1997): *Philosophy and Language*, ed. Dale M. Bauer and Kelly Oliver.

Books

Butler, Judith. *Excitable Speech: A Politics of the Performative*. London: Routledge, 1997.

Cameron, Deborah. *Feminism and Linguistic Theory*. Andover: Macmillan, 1985.

Doyle, Margaret. *The A–Z of Non-Sexist Language*. London: Women's Press, 1995.

Spender, Dale. *Man Made Language*. London: Routledge & Kegan Paul, 1980.

Articles

Cameron, Deborah. '"Words, Words, Words": the Power of Language', in Sarah Dunant, ed. *The War of the Words: The Political Correctness Debate*. London: Virago, 1994, pp. 15–34.

Cohn, Carol. 'Nuclear Language and How We Learned to Pat the Bomb', reprinted in Evelyn Fox Keller and Helen Longino, eds. *Feminism and Science*. Oxford: Oxford University Press, 1996, pp. 173–84.

Henderson, Mae Gwendolyn. 'Speaking in Tongues: Dialogics, Dialectics, and the Black Woman Writer's Literary Tradition', in Cheryl A. Wall, ed. *Changing Our Own Words*. New Brunswick: Rutgers University Press, 1991. Reprinted in Judith Butler and Joan W. Scott, eds. *Feminists Theorize the Political*. London and New York: Routledge, 1992, pp. 144–66.

Hornsby, Jennifer. 'Disempowered Speech', in Sally Haslanger, ed. *Feminist Perspectives on Language, Knowledge and Reality*, special issue of *Philosophical Topics* 23:2 (1995), 127–47.

Lloyd, Genevieve. 'Maleness, Metaphor, and the "Crisis" of Reason', in Louise M. Antony and Charlotte Witt, eds. *A Mind of One's Own: Feminist Essays on Reason and Objectivity*. Boulder, CO: Westview Press, 1993, pp. 69–83.

Mercier, Adèle. 'A Perverse Case of the Contingent A Priori: On the Logic of Emasculating Language (A Reply to Dawkins and Dummett)', in Sally Haslanger, ed. *Feminist Perspectives on Language, Knowledge and Reality*, special issue of *Philosophical Topics* 23:2 (1995), 221–59.

Nye, Andrea. 'The Voice of the Serpent: French Feminism and the Philosophy of Language', in Ann Garry and Marilyn Pearsall, eds. *Women, Knowledge, and Reality: Explorations in Feminist Philosophy*. London: Unwin Hyman, 1989, pp. 233–49.

'Semantics in a New Key', in Janet A. Kourany, ed. *Philosophy in a Feminist Voice: Critiques and Reconstructions*. Princeton, NJ: Princeton University Press, 1998, pp. 263–95.

Tanesini, Alessandra. 'Whose Language?', in Kathleen Lennon and Margaret Whitford, eds. *Knowing the Difference: Feminist Perspectives in Epistemology*. London: Routledge, 1994, pp. 203–16.

FEMINISM IN METAPHYSICS

Anderson, Elizabeth. 'Knowledge, Human Interests, and Objectivity in Feminist Epistemology', in Sally Haslanger, ed. *Feminist Perspectives on Language, Knowledge and Reality*, special issue of *Philosophical Topics* 23:2 (1995), 27–58.

Beauvoir, Simone de. *The Second Sex*, trans. H. M. Parshley. New York: Vintage Books, 1989.

Butler, Judith. *Gender Trouble: Feminism and the Subversion of Identity*. New York: Routledge, 1990.

'Contingent Foundations', in J. Butler and J. Scott, eds. *Feminists Theorize the Political*. New York: Routledge, 1992, pp. 3–21.

Bodies That Matter: On the Discursive Limits of 'Sex'. New York: Routledge, 1993.

Frye, Marilyn. *The Politics of Reality: Essays in Feminist Theory*. New York: The Crossing Press, 1983.

'The Necessity of Differences: Constructing a Positive Category of Women', *Signs* 21:4 (Summer 1996), 991–1010.

Fuss, Diana. *Essentially Speaking: Feminism, Nature, and Difference*. New York: Routledge, 1989.

Gatens, Moira. *Imaginary Bodies*. New York: Routledge, 1996.

Haraway, Donna. 'A Cyborg Manifesto: Science, Technology and Socialist Feminism in the Late Twentieth Century', in her *Simians, Cyborgs and Women: The Reinvention of Nature*. New York: Routledge, 1991, pp. 149–81.

'Introduction', in her *Primate Visions*. New York: Routledge, 1989, pp. 1–15.

Haslanger, Sally. 'Ontology and Social Construction', in Sally Haslanger, ed. *Feminist Perspectives on Language, Knowledge and Reality*, special issue of *Philosophical Topics* 23:2 (1995), 95–125.

'On Being Objective and Being Objectified', in L. Antony and C. Witt, eds. *A Mind of One's Own*. Boulder, CO: Westview Press, 1993, pp. 85–125.

Longino, Helen and Evelynn Hammonds. 'Conflicts and Tensions in the Feminist Study of Gender and Science', in Marianne Hirsch and Evelyn Fox Keller, eds. *Conflicts in Feminism*. New York: Routledge, 1990, pp. 164–83.

Lugones, María. 'Purity, Impurity and Separation', *Signs* 19:2 (1994), 458–79.

MacKinnon, Catharine. *Toward a Feminist Theory of the State*. Cambridge, MA: Harvard University Press, 1989.

Schor, Naomi and Elizabeth Weed, eds. *The Essential Difference*. Bloomington: Indiana University Press, 1994.

Scott, Joan. 'Gender: A Useful Category of Historical Analysis', *American Historical Review* 9 (1986), 1053–75.

'Experience', in J. Butler and J. Scott, eds. *Feminists Theorize the Political*. New York: Routledge, 1992, pp. 22–40.

Spelman, Elizabeth V. *Inessential Woman: Problems of Exclusion in Feminist Thought*. Boston: Beacon Press, 1988.

Stoljar, Natalie. 'Essence, Identity, and the Concept of Woman', in Sally Haslanger, ed. *Feminist Perspectives on Language, Knowledge and Reality*, special issue of *Philosophical Topics* 23:2 (1995), 261–93.

Williams, Patricia. *The Alchemy of Race and Rights*. Cambridge, MA: Harvard University Press, 1991.

Witt, Charlotte. 'Feminist Metaphysics', in L. Antony and C. Witt, eds. *A Mind of One's Own*. Boulder, CO: Westview Press, 1993, pp. 273–88.

'Anti-Essentialism in Feminist Theory', in Sally Haslanger, ed. *Feminist Perspectives on Language, Knowledge and Reality*, special issue of *Philosophical Topics* 23:2 (1995), 321–44.

Wittig, Monique. *The Straight Mind*. Boston: Beacon Press, 1992.

Young, Iris. 'Gender as Seriality: Thinking about Women as a Social Collective', *Signs* 19:3 (Spring 1994), 733–4.

Throwing Like a Girl and Other Essays in Feminist Philosophy and Social Theory. Indianapolis: Indiana University Press, 1990.

FEMINISM IN EPISTEMOLOGY

Edited collections

Alcoff, Linda and Elizabeth Potter, eds. *Feminist Epistemologies*. London and New York: Routledge, 1993.

Antony, Louise and Charlotte Witt, eds. *A Mind of One's Own: Feminist Essays on Reason and Objectivity*. Boulder, CO: Westview Press, 1993.

Garry, Ann and Marilyn Pearsall, eds. *Women, Knowledge, and Reality*. 2nd edition. London and New York: Routledge, 1996.

Haack, Susan, ed. *Feminist Epistemology: For and Against* (special issue of *The Monist* 77:4 (1994)).

Harding, Sandra and Merrill B. Hintikka, eds. *Discovering Reality: Feminist Perspectives on Epistemology, Metaphysics, Methodology, and Philosophy of Science*. Dordrecht: Reidel, 1983.

Haslanger, Sally, ed. *Feminist Perspectives on Language, Knowledge, and Reality*, special issue of *Philosophical Topics* 23:2 (1995).

Lennon, Kathleen and Margaret Whitford, eds. *Knowing the Difference: Feminist Perspectives in Epistemology*. London and New York: Routledge, 1994.

Nicholson, Linda, ed. *Feminism/Postmodernism*. London and New York: Routledge, 1990.

Feminist standpoint theory

Fricker, Miranda. 'Epistemic Oppression and Epistemic Privilege', in Catherine Wilson, ed. *Civilization and Oppression*. *Canadian Journal of Philosophy*, supplementary volume (1999), 191–210.

Harding, Sandra. *Whose Science? Whose Knowledge?*. Milton Keynes: Open University Press, 1991.

'Rethinking Standpoint Epistemology: "What Is Strong Objectivity"?', in Alcoff and Potter, eds. *Feminist Epistemologies*, pp. 49–82.

Hartsock, Nancy. 'The Feminist Standpoint: Developing the Ground for a Specifically Feminist Historical Materialism', in Harding and Hintikka, eds. *Discovering Reality*, pp. 283–310.
  The Feminist Standpoint Revisited and Other Essays. Boulder, CO: Westview Press, 1998, chapter 11.
Hekman, Susan. 'Truth and Method: Feminist Standpoint Revisited', *Signs* 22:2 (1977), 341–65.
Jaggar, Alison. *Feminist Politics and Human Nature*. Sussex: Harvester Press, 1983, chapter 11.
Longino, Helen. 'Subjects, Power and Knowledge: Description and Prescription in Feminist Philosophies of Science', in Alcoff and Potter, eds. *Feminist Epistemologies*, pp. 101–20.

Conceptions of reason, and gender

Alcoff, Linda. 'Is the Feminist Critique of Reason Rational?', in Haslanger, ed. *Feminist Perspectives*, pp. 1–26.
Atherton, Margaret. 'Cartesian Reason and Gendered Reason', in Antony and Witt, eds. *A Mind of One's Own*, pp. 69–83.
Grosz, Elizabeth. 'Bodies and Knowledges: Feminism and the Crisis of Reason', in Alcoff and Potter, eds. *Feminist Epistemologies*, pp. 187–215.
Lloyd, Genevieve. *The Man of Reason: 'Male' and 'Female' in Western Philosophy*. London: Methuen, 1984.
  'Maleness, Metaphor, and the "Crisis" of Reason', in Antony and Witt, eds. *A Mind of One's Own*, pp. 69–83.
Lovibond, Sabina. 'Feminism and the "Crisis of Rationality"', *New Left Review* 207 (Sept/Oct 1994), 72–86.

Feminist postmodernism and epistemology

Benhabib, Seyla, Judith Butler, Drucilla Cornell and Nancy Fraser. *Feminist Contentions: A Philosophical Exchange*. London and New York: Routledge, 1995.
Braidotti, Rosi. *Patterns of Dissonance: A Study of Women in Contemporary Philosophy*. Cambridge: Polity Press, 1991.
Haraway, Donna. 'Situated Knowledges: The Science Question in Feminism and the Privilege of Partial Perspective', *Feminist Studies* 14:3 (Fall 1988), 575–600.
Lovibond, Sabina. 'Feminism and Postmodernism', *New Left Review* 178 (1989), 5–28.
Nicholson, Linda, ed. *Feminism/Postmodernism*, 'Introduction' and essays in Part I: 'Feminism as Against Epistemology?'.
Strickland, Susan. 'Feminism, Postmodernism and Difference', in Lennon and Whitford, eds. *Knowing the Difference*, pp. 265–74.

FEMINISM IN PHILOSOPHY OF SCIENCE

Alcoff, L. and E. Potter, eds. *Feminist Epistemologies*. New York: Routledge, 1993.
Antony, L. and C. Witt, eds. *A Mind of One's Own: Feminist Essays on Reason and Objectivity*. Boulder, CO: Westview Press, 1993.

Fausto-Sterling, A. *Myths of Gender: Biological Theories of Women and Men*. New York: Basic Books, 1985.

Harding, S. *The Science Question in Feminism*. Ithaca, NY: Cornell University Press, 1986.

Whose Science? Whose Knowledge? Thinking From Women's Lives. Ithaca, NY: Cornell University Press, 1991.

Harding, S. and Hintikka, M. B., eds. *Discovering Reality: Feminist Perspectives on Epistemology, Metaphysics, Methodology, and Philosophy of Science*. Boston: D. Reidel, 1983.

Haslanger, S., ed. *Feminist Perspectives on Language, Knowledge, and Reality*, special issue of *Philosophical Topics* 23:2 (1995).

Hekman, S. 'Truth and Method: Feminist Standpoint Revisited', *Signs* 22:2 (1997), 341–65. (See also responses by N. C. M. Hartsock, P. H. Collins, S. Harding, D. E. Smith, pp. 367–99.)

Keller, E. F. *Reflections on Gender and Science*. New Haven: Yale University Press, 1985.

Secrets of Life, Secrets of Death. New York: Routledge, 1992.

Kohlstedt, S. G. and H. E. Longino, eds. *Women, Gender, and Science*, special issue of *Osiris* 12 (1997).

Longino, Helen. 'In Search of Feminist Philosophy', *The Monist* 77:4 (1994), 472–86.

Longino, H. *Science as Social Knowledge: Values and Objectivity in Scientific Inquiry*. Princeton, NJ: Princeton University Press, 1990.

Nelson, L. H., ed. *Feminism and Science*, special issue of *Synthèse* 104:3 (1995).

Nelson, J. and L. H. Nelson. 'No Rush to Judgement', *The Monist* 77:4 (1994), 486–508.

Nelson, L. H. and J. Nelson, eds. *Feminism, Science and the Philosophy of Science*. Dordrecht: Kluwer, 1997.

Rosser, S. V., ed. *Feminism and Science*, special issue of *Women's Studies International Forum* 12:3 (1989).

Schiebinger, L. *The Mind Has No Sex?: Women in the Origins of Modern Science*. Cambridge, MA: Harvard University Press, 1989.

Tuana, N., ed. *Feminism and Science*, two-part special issue, *Hypatia* 2:3 (1987); *Hypatia* 3:1 (1988).

Wylie, A. 'Good Science, Bad Science, or Science as Usual?: Feminist Critiques of Science', in L. Hager, ed. *Women in Human Evolution*. New York: Routledge, 1997, pp. 29–55.

FEMINISM IN POLITICAL PHILOSOPHY

Bubeck, D. *Care, Gender, and Justice*. Oxford: Clarendon Press, 1995.

Butler, J. and J. W. Scott, eds. *Feminists Theorize the Political*. London: Routledge, 1992.

Coole, D. *Women in Political Theory*, 2nd edition. Brighton: Harvester Press, 1993.

Frye, M. *The Politics of Reality*. Trumansburg, NY: Crossing Press, 1983.

Hirschmann, N. J. and C. Di Stefano, eds. *Revisioning the Political: Feminist Reconstructions of Traditional Concepts in Western Political Theory*. Boulder, CO: Westview Press, 1996.

Jaggar, A. *Feminist Politics and Human Nature*. Brighton: Harvester Press, 1983.

MacKinnon, C. A. *Toward a Feminist Theory of the State*. Cambridge, MA: Harvard University Press, 1989.

Meyers, D. T., ed. *Feminists Rethink the Self*. Boulder, CO: Westview Press, 1996.

Nicholson, L., ed. *Feminism/Postmodernism*. London: Routledge, 1990.

Okin, S. M. *Women in Western Political Thought*. Princeton, NJ: Princeton University Press, 1979.

Justice, Gender and the Family. New York: Basic Books, 1989.

Pateman, C. *The Sexual Contract*. Cambridge: Polity Press, 1988.

Phillips, A. *Engendering Democracy*. Cambridge: Polity Press, 1991.

Ruddick, S. *Maternal Thinking: Toward a Politics of Peace*. London: Women's Press, 1989.

Shanley, M. L. and U. Narayan, eds. *Reconstructing Political Theory: Feminist Perspectives*. Cambridge: Polity Press, 1997.

Shanley, M. L. and C. Pateman. *Feminist Interpretations and Political Theory*. Cambridge: Polity Press, 1990.

Spelman, E. V. *Inessential Woman: Problems of Exclusion in Feminist Thought*. London: Women's Press, 1988.

Tong, R. *Feminist Thought: A Comprehensive Introduction*. London: Routledge, 1992.

Young, I. M. *Justice and the Politics of Difference*. Princeton, NJ: Princeton University Press, 1990.

FEMINISM IN ETHICS

Alcoff, Linda. 'Cultural Feminism Versus Post-Structuralism: The Identity Crisis in Feminist Theory', *Signs: Journal of Women in Culture and Society* 13:3 (1988), 405-36.

Anderson, Elizabeth. *Value in Ethics and Economics*. Cambridge, MA, and London: Harvard University Press, 1993.

Arnault, Lynne S. 'The Radical Future of a Classic Moral Theory', in Alison M. Jaggar and Susan R. Bordo, eds. *Gender/Body/Knowledge: Feminist Reconstructions of Being and Knowing*. New Brunswick, NJ: Rutgers University Press, 1989, pp. 188-206.

Benhabib, Seyla. *Situating the Self: Gender, Community and Postmodernism in Contemporary Ethics*. New York: Routledge, 1992.

Blum, Larry, Marcia Homiak, Judy Housman and Naomi Scheman. 'Altruism and Women's Oppression', *The Philosophical Forum* 5:1-2 (Fall-Winter 1973-74), 196-221.

Card, Claudia. *Lesbian Choices*. New York: Columbia University Press, 1995.

Christman, John. 'Feminism and Autonomy', in Dana E. Bushnell, ed. *Nagging Questions: Feminist Ethics in Everyday Life*. Lanham, MD: Rowman & Littlefield, 1995, pp. 17-39.

Code, Lorraine. *What Can She Know? Feminist Theory and the Construction of Knowledge*. Ithaca: Cornell University Press, 1991.

Collins, Patricia Hill. *Black Feminist Thought: Knowledge, Consciousness, and the Politics of Empowerment*. New York: Routledge, 1991.

Friedman, Marilyn. *What Are Friends For? Feminist Perspectives on Personal Relationships and Moral Theory*. Ithaca: Cornell University Press, 1993.

Gilligan, Carol. *In a Different Voice: Psychological Theory and Women's Development*. Cambridge, MA: Harvard University Press, 1982.

Griffiths, Morwenna. *Feminisms and the Self: The Web of Identity*. London: Routledge, 1995.

Grimshaw, Jean. 'Autonomy and Identity in Feminist Thinking', in Morwenna Griffiths and Margaret Whitford, eds. *Feminist Perspectives in Philosophy*. Bloomington: Indiana University Press, 1988, pp. 90–108.

Philosophy and Feminist Thinking. Minneapolis: University of Minnesota Press, 1986.

Hanen, Marsha and Kai Nielsen, eds. *Science, Morality and Feminist Theory. Canadian Journal of Philosophy*, supplementary volume 13 (1987).

Hekman, Susan. *Moral Voices, Moral Selves: Carol Gilligan and Feminist Moral Theory*. University Park, PA: Pennsylvania State University Press, 1995.

Held, Virginia. *Feminist Morality: Transforming Culture, Society, and Politics*. Chicago: University of Chicago Press, 1993.

Held, Virginia, ed. *Justice and Care: Essential Readings in Feminist Ethics*. Boulder, CO: Westview Press, 1995.

Hill, Sharon Bishop. 'Self-Determination and Autonomy', in Richard Wasserstrom, ed. *Today's Moral Problems*, 2nd edition. New York: Macmillan, 1979, pp. 118–33.

Hoagland, Sarah Lucia. *Lesbian Ethics: Toward New Value*. Palo Alto, CA: Institute of Lesbian Studies, 1988.

hooks, bell. *Ain't I A Woman: Black Women and Feminism*. Boston: South End Press, 1981.

Talking Back: Thinking Feminist, Thinking Black. Boston: South End Press, 1989.

Keller, Evelyn Fox. *Reflections of Gender and Science*. New Haven: Yale University Press, 1985.

Kittay, Eva Feder and Diana T. Meyers, eds. *Women and Moral Theory*. Totowa, NJ: Rowman & Littlefield, 1987.

Larrabee, Mary Jeanne, ed. *An Ethic of Care: Feminist and Interdisciplinary Perspectives*. New York: Routledge, 1993.

Meyers, Diana T. *Self, Society, and Personal Choice*. New York: Columbia University Press, 1989.

Meyers, Diana Tietjens, ed. *Feminists Rethink the Self*. Boulder, CO: Westview Press, 1997.

Moody-Adams, Michele M. 'Gender and the Complexity of Moral Voices', in Claudia Card, ed. *Feminist Ethics*. Lawrence, KS: University Press of Kansas, 1991, pp. 195–212.

Nedelsky, Jennifer. 'Reconceiving Autonomy: Sources, Thoughts and Possibilities', *Yale Journal of Law and Feminism* 1:1 (Spring 1989), 7–36.

Noddings, Nel. *Caring: A Feminine Approach to Ethics and Moral Education*. Berkeley: University of California Press, 1984.

Okin, Susan Moller. *Justice, Gender and the Family*. New York: Basic Books, 1989.

Stoljar, Natalie and Catriona Mackenzie, eds. *Relational Autonomy: Feminist Perspectives on Autonomy, Agency and the Social Self*. Oxford: Oxford University Press, forthcoming.

Tronto, Joan C. *Moral Boundaries: A Political Argument for an Ethic of Care*. New York: Routledge, 1993.

Walker, Margaret. *Moral Understandings: A Feminist Study in Ethics*. New York: Routledge, 1998.

Weir, Alison. *Sacrificial Logics: Feminist Theory and the Critique of Identity*. New York: Routledge, 1996.

FEMINISM IN HISTORY OF PHILOSOPHY

Baier, Annette. 'Hume: The Women's Moral Theorist?', in Eva Feder Kittay and Diana T. Meyers, eds. *Women and Moral Theory*. Totowa, NJ: Rowman & Littlefield, 1987.

'Hume, The Reflective Women's Epistemologist?', in Louise M. Antony and Charlotte Witt, eds. *A Mind of One's Own: Feminist Essays on Reason and Objectivity*. Boulder, CO: Westview Press, 1993, pp. 35–48.

Benhabib, Seyla. 'On Hegel, Women and Irony', in Mary Lyndon Shanley and Carole Pateman, eds. *Feminist Interpretations and Political Theory*. Cambridge: Polity Press, 1991, pp. 129–45.

Bordo, Susan. *The Flight to Objectivity: Essays on Cartesianism and Culture*. Albany: State University of New York Press, 1987.

ed. *Feminist Interpretations of Descartes*. Pennsylvania State University Press, forthcoming.

Deutscher, Penelope. '"Is it not remarkable that Nietzsche ... should have hated Rousseau?": Woman, Femininity: Distancing Nietzsche from Rousseau', in Paul Patton, ed. *Nietzsche: Feminism and Political Theory*. Sydney: Allen & Unwin, 1993, pp. 162–88.

Gatens, Moira. 'Spinoza, Law and Responsibility', in *Imaginary Bodies: Ethics, Power and Corporeality*. London: Routledge, 1996, pp. 108–24.

Herman, Barbara. 'Could it be Worth Thinking About Kant on Sex and Marriage?', in Louise M. Antony and Charlotte Witt, eds. *A Mind of One's Own: Feminist Essays on Reason and Objectivity*. Boulder, CO: Westview Press, 1993, pp. 49–68.

Irigaray, Luce. *Speculum of the Other Woman*, trans. Gillian C. Gill. Ithaca, NY: Cornell University Press, 1985.

This Sex Which Is Not One, trans. C. Porter with C. Burke. Ithaca, NY: Cornell University Press, 1985.

'Sorcerer Love: A Reading of Plato's *Symposium*', *Hypatia* 3 (1989), 32–44.

Le Dœuff, Michèle. *The Philosophical Imaginary*, trans. Colin Gordon. Oxford: Blackwell, 1989.

Hipparchia's Choice: An Essay Concerning Women, Philosophy, etc., trans. Trista Selous. Oxford: Blackwell, 1991.

Lloyd, Genevieve. *The Man of Reason: 'Male' and 'Female' in Western Philosophy*, 2nd edition. London: Routledge, 1993.

'Maleness, Metaphor, and the "Crisis" of Reason', in Louise M. Antony and Charlotte Witt, eds. *A Mind of One's Own: Feminist Essays on Reason and Objectivity*. Boulder, CO: Westview Press, 1993, pp. 69–83.

Nye, Andrea. 'The Hidden Host: Irigaray and Diotima at Plato's Symposium', *Hypatia* 3 (1989), 45–61.

Rooney, Phyllis. 'Sex, Metaphor and Conceptions of Reason', *Hypatia* 6:2 (1991), 77–103.

'Recent Work in Feminist Discussions of Reason', *American Philosophical Quarterly* 31:1 (1994), 1–21.

Sedgwick, Sally. 'Can Kant's Ethics Survive the Feminist Critique?', *Pacific Philosophical Quarterly* 7 (1990), 60–79.

Tuana, Nancy. *Woman and the History of Philosophy.* New York: Paragon House, 1992.

Whitford, Margaret. 'Luce Irigaray's Critique of Rationality', in Morwenna Griffiths and Margaret Whitford, eds. *Feminist Perspectives in Philosophy.* London: Macmillan, 1988, pp. 109–30.

Luce Irigaray: Philosophy in the Feminine. London: Routledge, 1991.

INDEX

Index